Betty Tyl

W9-BQU-554

Ralph Earl

George & Betty Tyler
Collection

RALPH EARL

The Face of the Young Republic

Elizabeth Mankin Kornhauser

with

Richard L. Bushman

Stephen H. Kornhauser

Aileen Ribeiro

Yale University Press   *New Haven and London*

Wadsworth Atheneum   *Hartford*

THIS CATALOGUE is published in conjunction with the exhibition Ralph Earl: The Face of the Young Republic, organized by the Wadsworth Atheneum in celebration of the 150th anniversary of its founding. The exhibition and the catalogue were made possible by generous grants from the following sources:

NATIONAL ENDOWMENT FOR THE HUMANITIES

NATIONAL ENDOWMENT FOR THE ARTS

THE HENRY LUCE FOUNDATION, INC.

HARTFORD STEAM BOILER INSPECTION AND INSURANCE COMPANY, which supported this exhibition to commemorate the 125th anniversary of its founding

Exhibition dates

NATIONAL PORTRAIT GALLERY, Washington, D.C.
November 1, 1991–January 1, 1992

WADSWORTH ATHENEUM, Hartford, Connecticut
February 2–April 5, 1992

AMON CARTER MUSEUM, Fort Worth, Texas
May 16–July 12, 1992

Library of Congress Cataloging-in-Publication Data
Kornhauser, Elizabeth Mankin, 1950–
    Ralph Earl : the face of the young Republic / Elizabeth Mankin Kornhauser with Richard L. Bushman, Stephen H. Kornhauser, Aileen Ribeiro.
        p. cm.
    Catalog of an exhibition organized by the Wadsworth Atheneum. Exhibition dates: National Portrait Gallery, Washington, D.C., Nov. 1, 1991–Jan. 1, 1992; Wadsworth Atheneum, Hartford, Conn., Feb. 2–Apr. 5, 1992; Amon Carter Museum, Fort Worth, Tex., May 16–July 12, 1992.
    Includes bibliographical references (p.   ) and index.
    ISBN 0-300-05041-0 (cloth). — ISBN 0-918333-09-1 (paper).
    1. Earl, Ralph, 1751–1801—Exhibitions.   2. Portrait painting—18th century—New England—Exhibitions.
I. Earl, Ralph, 1751–1801.   II. Wadsworth Atheneum.
III. National Portrait Gallery (Smithsonian Institution).
IV. Amon Carter Museum of Western Art.   V. Title.
ND1329.E23A4   1991
759.13—dc20   91-6397
                                                 CIP

The paper in this book meets the guidelines for permanence and durability of the Committee on Production Guidelines for Book Longevity of the Council on Library Resources.

10 9 8 7 6 5 4 3 2 1

Published with the assistance of the F. B. Adams, Jr., Publication Fund.

Designed by Kenneth Botnick.
Set in Garamond #3 type by Tseng Information Systems.
Printed in Hong Kong by Everbest Printing Company.

Frontispiece: Ralph Earl, detail of *Reclining Hunter* (cat. 14)

Photographic Credits
Peter Accettola: cat. 30
Robert Houser: cats. 27, 37, 38, and 54; fig. 1.25 and figs. on p. 209
David Stansbury: cats. 60, 61, and 62
Joseph Szaszfai: cats. 4, 25, 41, 42, 48, 56, 57, 63, 72, and 73; figs. 1.2, 1.7, 1.30, and 1.32
Claire White-Peterson: fig. 1.33
Graydon Wood: cat. 52; fig. 1.17

Contents

VII   Lenders

IX   Foreword
Patrick McCaughey

XI   Acknowledgments

1   Introduction
Elizabeth Mankin Kornhauser

I

5   Ralph Earl: The Face of the Young Republic
Elizabeth Mankin Kornhauser

II

69   Portraiture and Society in Late Eighteenth-Century Connecticut
Richard L. Bushman

III

85   Ralph Earl's Working Methods and Materials
Stephen H. Kornhauser

92   Notes

101   Catalogue
Elizabeth Mankin Kornhauser with Aileen Ribeiro

253   Select Bibliography

255   Index

Lenders

ABBY ALDRICH ROCKEFELLER FOLK ART CENTER
Williamsburg, Va.
THE ADDISON GALLERY OF AMERICAN ART,
PHILLIPS ACADEMY
Andover, Massachusetts
ALBRIGHT-KNOX ART GALLERY
Buffalo, N.Y.
ANDERSON HOUSE
Washington, D.C.
ARGOSY GALLERY
New York
THE BENNINGTON MUSEUM
Bennington, Vermont
THE BROOKLYN MUSEUM
New York
THE CONNECTICUT HISTORICAL SOCIETY
Hartford
CORPORATE ART COLLECTION
Reader's Digest Association, Inc.
DALLAS MUSEUM OF ART
Texas
COUNT CHARLES DE SALIS
Switzerland
THE DETROIT INSTITUTE OF ARTS
Detroit, Michigan
THE HENRY E. HUNTINGTON LIBRARY AND ART GALLERY
San Marino, California
HISTORIC DEERFIELD, INC.
Deerfield, Massachusetts
HOOD MUSEUM OF ART, DARTMOUTH COLLEGE
Hanover, New Hampshire
INDEPENDENCE NATIONAL HISTORICAL PARK
Philadelphia
KENNEDY GALLERIES, INC.
New York
DRS. CAROLINE AND PETER KOBLENZER
THE LITCHFIELD HISTORICAL SOCIETY
Litchfield, Connecticut
LYMAN ALLYN MUSEUM
New London, Connecticut

MEAD ART MUSEUM, AMHERST COLLEGE
Amherst, Massachusetts
THE METROPOLITAN MUSEUM OF ART
New York
MUSEUM OF CONNECTICUT HISTORY
Hartford
MUSEUM OF FINE ARTS
Boston, Massachusetts
THE MUSEUM OF FINE ARTS
Houston
MUSEUM OF FINE ARTS
Springfield, Massachusetts
MUSEUM OF THE CITY OF NEW YORK
NATIONAL GALLERY OF ART
Washington, D.C.
NATIONAL MUSEUM OF AMERICAN ART,
SMITHSONIAN INSTITUTION
Washington, D.C.
NATIONAL PORTRAIT GALLERY
London
THE NEWARK MUSEUM
Newark, New Jersey
THE NEW MILFORD HISTORICAL SOCIETY
New Milford, Connecticut
THE NEW-YORK HISTORICAL SOCIETY
New York
NEW YORK STATE HISTORICAL ASSOCIATION
Cooperstown
EDITH AND HENRY NOSS
PALMER MUSEUM OF ART, THE PENNSYLVANIA
STATE UNIVERSITY
University Park
PRIVATE COLLECTION
G. W. SAMAHA
Milan, Ohio
SMITH COLLEGE MUSEUM OF ART
Northampton, Massachusetts
STOWE-DAY FOUNDATION
Hartford, Connecticut
VIRGINIA MUSEUM OF FINE ARTS
Richmond
WADSWORTH ATHENEUM
Hartford, Connecticut
WORCESTER ART MUSEUM
Worcester, Massachusetts
YALE UNIVERSITY ART GALLERY
New Haven, Connecticut

Foreword

ART MUSEUMS and their curators have played an important role in furthering fundamental art-historical research. Exhibition catalogues have grown from relatively ephemeral publications to permanent contributions to the literature of art, embracing the highest standards of scholarship. Such catalogues have the added excitement of bringing scattered works together so that a wider public can enjoy, and be stimulated to learn more about, the artist, period, or theme surveyed in the exhibition.

Elizabeth Mankin Kornhauser has worked for over a decade on Ralph Earl, moving from primary research to the completion of the first modern monograph on this exemplary figure of colonial and early republican America. She has brought to the work the intense scrutiny of the connoisseur-curator, as well as a scrupulous documentary and art-historical concern, and gives a lively portrayal of a remarkable artist and the rich cultural context in which he painted. The intricate world of Anglo-American painting at the close of the eighteenth century provides a full background for the vagaries of Earl's life, which is touched at times with pathos and at other times with comedy. We also find here an authoritative artistic account of the American landscape long before the visionary work of the Hudson River School.

Ralph Earl stands preeminent as a portraitist of the early republic – of the men and women who forged a distinctive American society in the last two decades of the eighteenth century; he provides some of the most memorable documents of the era. His figures possess a vivid modern presence and are ineluctably imbedded in their own turbulent times. All this and more has been brilliantly captured by Dr. Kornhauser, and the Wadsworth Atheneum takes pride in her research and in the exhibition that has happily arisen from it.

During the extended period of researching, writing, and formulating both the exhibition and the catalogue, the Wadsworth Atheneum has been grateful to the Henry Luce Foundation, which has been a major contributor to many other American art projects at the Atheneum; the National Endowment for the Arts; and the National Endowment for the Humanities – all of which have given substantive and continuing support for this project. The Hartford Steam Boiler Inspection and Insurance Company, a great Hartford-based corporation, has generously contributed to this exhibition and publication to commemorate its own 125th anniversary and to celebrate the 150th anniversary of the Wadsworth Atheneum. Without their support and without the ceaseless labors of Dr. Kornhauser, Ralph Earl would have remained a vital but elusive figure. The Wadsworth Atheneum is proud and pleased to present the foremost artist of Connecticut in the eighteenth century, who now stands in vigorous relief for all to see and know.

PATRICK MCCAUGHEY
Director

Acknowledgments

THIS CATALOGUE reflects the assistance of a great many people offered over a number of years whose contributions call for recognition and thanks. Some have helped in the exploration of Ralph Earl's life and career, and others have contributed information on individual works by the artist. Still others have provided additional intellectual, moral, financial, and technical support.

In May 1987 a team of scholars assembled at the Wadsworth Atheneum to discuss the conceptual and logistical development of an exhibition and book on Ralph Earl. This team included Richard L. Bushman, Professor, Department of History, Columbia University; Ellen Miles, Curator, National Portrait Gallery, Washington, D.C.; Jules D. Prown, Paul Mellon Professor of the History of Art, Yale University; and Robert Blair St. George, Professor of History and American Studies, University of Pennsylvania. A second meeting, in February 1988, was followed by continual input and support from the team members, culminating in their critical reading of the final manuscript in 1990. Their contributions over a four-year period proved invaluable.

I am equally indebted to the contributors to the catalogue, Richard Bushman; Stephen H. Kornhauser, Chief Conservator, Wadsworth Atheneum; and Aileen Ribeiro, Head, History of Dress Department, Courtauld Institute of Art, whose essays and notes have broadened our understanding of Earl, his art, and his patrons. Not only were these three individuals a joy to work with, but each added an invaluable dimension to the catalogue. My colleague at the Atheneum, Elizabeth R. McClintock, Curatorial Assistant, American Paintings, Sculpture, and Drawings, did extensive research on Earl's sitters for the catalogue entries, as well as oversaw many organizational aspects of the preparation of the manuscript with great loyalty and efficiency. She was ably assisted by Marcia Hinckley, a graduate student in American Studies at Trinity College. Several interns in the American Paintings, Sculpture, and Drawings Department have also assisted in catalogue research over the years, including David Brigham, Laura Robinson, and Martha Willoughby.

A number of people lent their expertise toward the investigation of individual works by Earl. I am particularly grateful to Carl Boardman Cobb; Abbott Cummings, Charles Montgomery Professor of Art History, Yale University; David W. Dangremond; Count Charles de Salis; Nancy Goyne Evans, Registrar, The Henry Francis du Pont Winterthur Museum; Elizabeth R. Fairman, Assistant Curator of Rare Books, Yale Center for British Art; Christopher Gilbert, Director of Art Galleries,

Temple Newsam House; Morrison Heckscher, Curator of American Decorative Arts, The Metropolitan Museum of Art; Joyce Hill; Nina Fletcher Little; Kathleen Luhrs, Editor, The Pierpont Morgan Library; Mark Mankin; Andrew Moore, Curator, and Charlotte Crawly, Assistant Curator, Norwich Castle Museum; Robert Trent, Curator of Collections, The Henry Francis du Pont Winterthur Museum; Gilbert T. Vincent; and John Wright. Many others, too numerous to mention, deserve thanks as well and are cited individually in the notes.

Countless museum colleagues who provided information on works in their collections and assisted in the negotiation of loans deserve my thanks. I am particularly grateful to Rose-Marie Ballard, Curator, Ellsworth Homestead; Annette Blaugrund, Chief Curator, The New-York Historical Society; Nicolai Cikovsky, Jr., Curator of American Art, National Gallery of Art, Washington, D.C.; Catherine Keene Fields, Director, The Litchfield Historical Society; Elizabeth Pratt Fox, Curator, The Connecticut Historical Society; Anthony Hirschel, Assistant to the Director, and Paula Friedman, Assistant Curator, American Art, Yale University Art Gallery; John K. Howat, The Lawrence A. Fleischman Chairman of the Departments of American Art, and Carrie Rebora, Assistant Curator, The Metropolitan Museum of Art; John D. Kilbourne, Director, The Anderson House Museum, The Society of the Cincinnati; Barbara Luck, Curator, Abby Aldrich Rockefeller Folk Art Collection, Colonial Williamsburg; Barbara J. MacAdam, Curator, Hood Museum of Art, Dartmouth College; Gary Reynolds, Curator of American Art, Newark Museum; Jacob Simon, Senior Curator, National Portrait Gallery, London; and Susan Strickler, Director of Curatorial Affairs, Worcester Art Museum.

I wish to thank those who authorized the reprinting of selected material in this volume: Material reprinted from the Wyllys Family Papers; George Colton Diary, August 16, 1801, MS; Oliver Wolcott Papers; Oliver Ellsworth Papers; Rev. James Cogswell Papers, Rev. James Cogswell Diary, December 13, 1790; and the Mason Fitch Cogswell Papers, Physician Ledgers, Account Book, by permission of The Connecticut Historical Society, Hartford. Material reprinted from the Capt. John Pratt Collection, 2 vols., by permission of the Connecticut State Library, Hartford. Material reprinted from the Gage Family Papers; Ralph E. W. Earl Papers, 1810–38; and Trumbull Family Papers, 1773–1896, by permission of the American Antiquarian Society, Worcester, Mass. Material reprinted from James Duane, Daybook F, Duane Papers, MS; and the Beekman Papers by permission of The New-York Historical Society, New York. Material reprinted from Moses Seymour, Account Book, courtesy of The Litchfield Historical Society, Litchfield, Conn. Material reprinted from the letters of Nehemiah Strong to Ezra Stiles, August 30 and September 8, 1790, Ezra Stiles Papers; the letter of Dr. James Cogswell to Mason Fitch Cogswell, October 23, 1791, Cogswell Family Papers, by permission of The Beinecke Rare Book and Manuscript Library, Yale University, New Haven, Conn. Material reprinted from the Charles Henry Hart Papers, 1868–1918, by permission of the Archives of American Art, Smithsonian Institution, Washington, D.C. Material reprinted from *A Sketch of the Origin and Progress of the Humane Society of the City of New-York. Together with the Act of Incorporation and By-laws, Inc.*, pamphlet (New York: Van Winkle and Wiley, 1814), N.Y.C.-Subject Boxes-Societies, by permission of the Rare Books and Manuscripts Division, The New York Public Library, Astor, Lenox and Tilden Foundations.

The work of many conservators allowed the paintings to be shown to their best advantage. In addition, many conservators provided their expertise in assessing Earl's paintings and helped facilitate loans. I am especially grateful to Sarah L. Fisher, Senior

Painting Conservator, National Gallery of Art, Washington, D.C.; Gisela Helm-kampf, Senior Painting Conservator, and Dorothy Mahon, Painting Conservator, The Metropolitan Museum of Art; Kristin Hoermann, Chief Conservator, Yale University Art Gallery; Lance Mayer, Conservator, and Gay Meyers, Conservator, Lyman Allyn Museum; Jennifer Spohn, Conservator, Worcester Art Museum; F. Christopher Tahk, Director, Dan Kushel, Associate Professor, and James Hamm, Associate Professor and Painting Conservator, Art Conservation Department, Buffalo State College; and Frank Zuccari, Painting Conservator, The Art Institute of Chicago.

Even though the numerous funding sources have been acknowledged elsewhere, I would particularly like to thank Andrea Anderson, Programs Officer, National Endowment for the Humanities; David Bancroft, Programs Officer, National Endowment for the Arts; Mary Jane Crook, Programs Officer, The Henry Luce Foundation; and Wilson Wilde, President and Chief Executive Officer, and Judith Lefebvre, Vice President and Curator, The Hartford Steam Boiler Inspection and Insurance Company.

A great debt of gratitude is owed my colleagues on the museum staff, who, under the directorship of Patrick McCaughey, have supplied unstinting support, encouragement, and advice. Patrick McCaughey wholeheartedly promoted this project, providing guidance and insight at every stage along the way. Linda Ayres, Deputy Director, has assisted in various organizational matters, as well as provided input on the manuscript. Among my curatorial colleagues I am particularly indebted to Jean Cadogan, Eugene Gaddis, William H. Hosley, Andrea Miller-Keller, and Linda Roth. Stephen Kornhauser, Chief Conservator, and Patricia S. Garland, Painting Conservator, treated numerous works for the exhibition. I would also like to thank Hugh Crowley, Muriel Fleischmann, and Patricia Sprague in the Development Office and Mary Ellen Goeke and Mary Schroeder in the Office of the Registrar. Cecil Adams and Edward Russo in the Design Department made essential contributions, and Raymond Petke, Head of Photographic Services, gave invaluable assistance and advice, far beyond the call of duty, in obtaining photographs for the catalogue. I would like to thank them, too.

It has been a pleasure to work with the staffs of the two institutions that will be sharing the exhibition with the Wadsworth Atheneum. I am particularly grateful to Doreen Bolger, Curator of Paintings and Sculpture, Amon Carter Museum, and Ellen Miles, at the National Portrait Gallery, for their enthusiastic participation.

I have found the association with Yale University Press to be a pleasure from start to finish. Judy Metro, senior editor, was initially receptive to the idea of the book and has expertly overseen its production. Mary Pasti, manuscript editor, demonstrated her exceptional skills, patience, and good humor in handling a very dense manuscript by multiple authors. The book has also benefited from the creativity of its designer, Kenneth Botnick. I am also grateful to Anita Karl and James Kemp, Compass Projections, for the two maps.

On the domestic front, I am indebted to my parents, Guy and Elizabeth Mankin, for my own early roots in Litchfield County, Connecticut, accounting for my initial interest in Earl and his sitters. My husband, Stephen Kornhauser, must be thanked, along with our children, Robert and Sara, for their behind-the-scenes patience and moral support.

Since the project has taken a number of years to complete and has profited from the contributions of so many individuals, there are bound to be omissions here; let me thank those people as well.

EMK

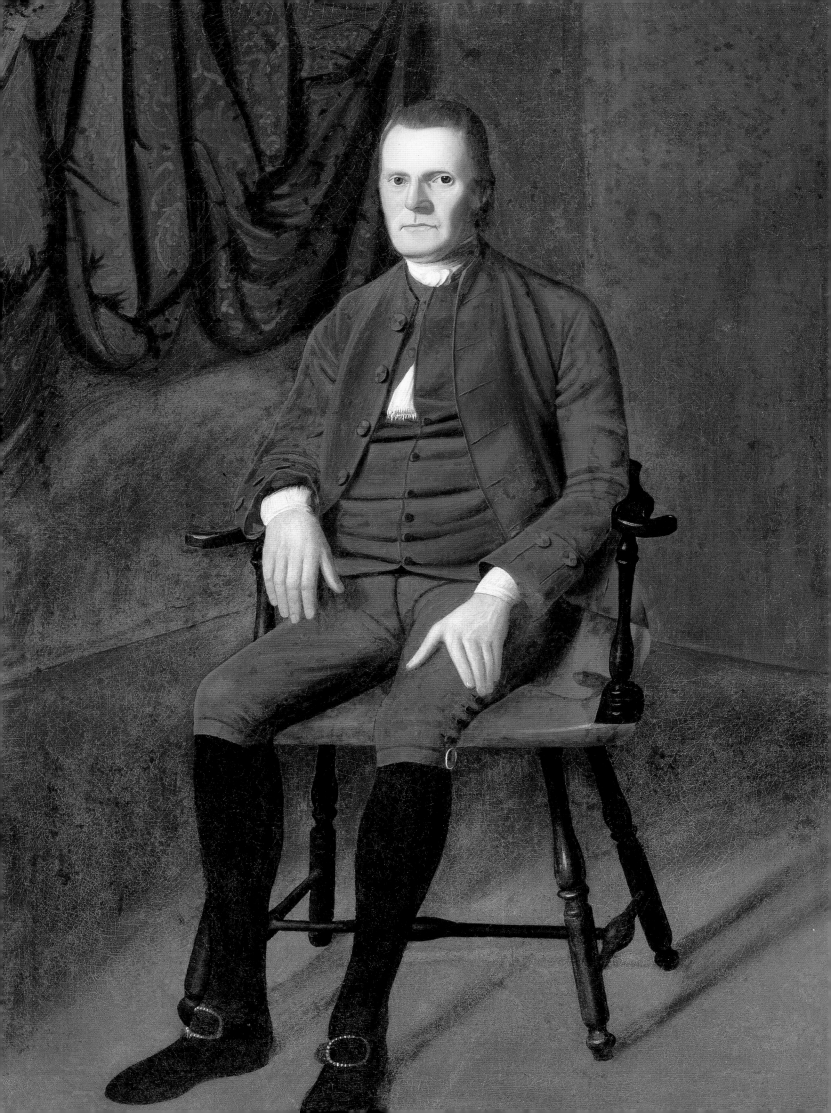

Introduction

Elizabeth Mankin Kornhauser

WHEN RALPH EARL died in the small town of Bolton, Connecticut, in 1801, he left behind an artistic legacy that embodied many of the most enduring images of American people and places painted during the last quarter of the eighteenth century. The power of his imagery appealed to a broad segment of New England society and inspired a school of followers during his lifetime. His works influenced the look of New England portraiture in his lifetime and for decades beyond.

Earl focused his artistic skills on a sector of rural America that had never before benefited from the attentions of a highly gifted artist. Because for the most part he stayed away from urban centers and out of the limelight, his substantial contribution to American art has largely gone unrecognized. The purpose here is to examine the life and art of Ralph Earl, with the knowledge that his portraits and landscapes expressed the beliefs and values of his patrons and the era in which they lived.

One reason for the lack of sustained scholarly interest in Ralph Earl is that he left virtually no contemporary papers, with the exception of his Loyalist Claim of 1778 and one letter to his friend Dr. Joseph Trumbull written in 1784. The only nineteenth-century account of his life is contained in William Dunlap's *History of the Rise and Progress of the Arts of Design in the United States* (1834). In spite of its brevity and occasional errors and in the absence of a contemporary life history, present-day biographical references continue to rely on this source. The sole attempt at a biography in this century is Laurence B. Goodrich's *Ralph Earl: Recorder for an Era* (1967), a slender volume that does not undertake a comprehensive study.

The lack of biographical information on the artist notwithstanding, Earl's portraits and landscapes drew the attention of several major museums in the first decade of the twentieth century, when the Metropolitan Museum of Art and the Worcester Art Museum, among others, actively acquired his paintings, even though little was known about the artist. It was not until the 1930s that Earl's works first attracted the notice of scholars as part of a general interest in indigenous American art. In a series of six articles that appeared in *Art in America*, Frederick F. Sherman celebrated the "American qualities" he perceived in Earl's portraits.

Detail of
Roger Sherman
(cat. 5).

1

In the same decade, William Sawitzky devoted more serious attention to Earl's life and career. His work culminated in two exhibitions: a show of thirty-five of Earl's Connecticut portraits for the Connecticut Tercentenary Celebration of 1935, held at the Yale University Art Gallery, and a more comprehensive exhibition, held in 1945 at the Whitney Museum of American Art and the Worcester Art Museum. Although William Sawitzky provided only brief essays for the catalogues that accompanied these exhibitions, his widow, Susan Sawitzky, published a substantial article summarizing the couple's joint research and focusing on Earl's English career; it appeared in the *Worcester Art Museum Annual* (1960). The William Sawitzky and Susan Sawitzky Papers, held by the New-York Historical Society, remain a valuable resource on the artist.

More recently, recognition has been given to the Earl family of artists, who, in addition to Ralph Earl, include his brother James Earl and his son Ralph E. W. Earl. An exhibition organized by Harold Spencer and presented in 1972 at the William Benton Museum of Art in Storrs, Connecticut, brought together works by all three members of the family for the first time.

Most students of American art in this century have dutifully mentioned the name of Ralph Earl; but their comments often suffer from insufficient knowledge about the most basic details of the artist's life and career, as well as incomplete familiarity with his works. In an influential survey of American painting, Edgar P. Richardson assessed Earl as "the most notable of 'untrained professionals' or the most unskilled of the professional painters," relegating the artist to a position in limbo: he failed to recognize that Earl deliberately altered his style to suit the aesthetic sensibilities of his patrons in the various regions in which he worked. The misconceptions about and clouded understanding of this artist exist to the present.

In presenting the verifiable facts of Earl's life, analyzing his style for the first time based on the full body of his known works, and assessing the substantial contribution he made to the development of American art, I have drawn in part on the information contained in my doctoral dissertation, "Ralph Earl: Artist-Entrepreneur" (1988), which includes a complete biography and a catalogue raisonné of over two hundred of the artist's works. In addition to relying on the physical evidence of Earl's paintings, I have conducted an exhaustive investigation of his patrons, particularly in Connecticut, where he produced many of his greatest paintings. The findings of this study not only help to explain the stylistic and technical changes in his portraits from one region to the next but also enhance our knowledge of the era in which they were created.

The exhibition and this catalogue bring together for the first time all of Earl's major paintings, representing over a quarter of his known oeuvre. I am deeply indebted to the generosity of the lenders for making this possible. With few exceptions, I have chosen portraits and landscapes that are firmly identified as to sitter or location and that are either signed and dated by the artist or solidly documented. I present a number of works by Earl's contemporaries to illuminate the various influences on the artist's development, in particular his direct emulation of the portraits of John Singleton Copley, and representative works by Earl's followers, including his son Ralph E. W. Earl, to demonstrate the influence Earl had on New England portraiture during his lifetime and beyond. Finally, I have made an effort to select only works that have remained in good condition, allowing viewers to appreciate fully the artists' skills.

The need to explore the works of Ralph Earl within an expanded context is apparent in the breadth of subject matter covered here. Chapter 1 and the catalogue entries provide the first comprehensive assessment of Earl's life and works, as well as detailed discussions of the artist's patrons. In chapter 2, Richard L. Bushman has brought his proficiency as a social historian to bear on the political and social issues of the era in which Earl worked, analyzing these issues in light of Earl's extraordinary success in remote regions of Connecticut. With a definition of who Earl's local patrons were, we can better understand why they wished to appear as they do in their portraits. In chapter 3, Stephen H. Kornhauser examines the artist's working methods and materials, considering the training Earl received in England and the unusual conditions he encountered as an itinerant artist in New England, thereby illuminating some of the unorthodox characteristics of his paintings. Finally, within the catalogue entries, Aileen Ribeiro's comments on the costume of Earl's sitters substantiate the accuracy of his renditions of clothing and the broad basis of his patronage. By concentrating on the artist, his works, his patrons, and the era in which he flourished, we can hope to gain a new understanding of Ralph Earl and a new way of looking at his paintings and their significance in the history of American art.

I

Ralph Earl
The Face of the Young Republic

Elizabeth Mankin Kornhauser

LIKE MANY of the finest early American artists, Ralph Earl emerged from a simple background, impelled by aspirations beyond his station in life. Driven by a strong ambition to succeed and possessing the skills of an entrepreneur, he overcame the hurdles placed in his path by the events of the Revolution, becoming one of a few American artists to achieve success in both England and America in the last quarter of the eighteenth century. Earl distinguished himself by returning to paint the society he had abandoned as a youth; he drew on his rural New England roots for inspiration, achieving his greatest works by capturing the many faces of the people who helped to forge the new nation.

Ralph Earl was born on May 11, 1751, in Worcester County, Massachusetts. His ancestors were English Quakers who had immigrated to Rhode Island from Exeter, England, around 1634. By 1717 members of the family, including Earl's great-grandfather, Ralph Earle (d. 1757), had moved to Worcester County. There, by midcentury, the Earl family had established sizable farms, settling the towns of Leicester and, later, Paxton (fig. 1.19).[1]

Earl was the eldest of four sons (one of whom died in infancy) born to Ralph Earll (1726–1808) and Phebe Wittemore Earll (1727–c. 1770).[2] Earl's surviving brothers were Clark, born in 1753, and James, born in 1761. The Earlls raised their sons in Paxton, which had about five hundred inhabitants in the 1770s; its green rolling hills and fertile land inspired one of the artist's last and most beautiful works, *Looking East from Denny Hill* (cat. 66).

Ralph Earll, Sr., a member of the third generation of the family to operate a farm in Worcester County, inherited a substantial amount of acreage. As a leading landowner, he was elected to represent the town at the many meetings held in Paxton and Leicester during the years leading up to the American Revolution. As a prominent patriot, he later gained the rank of captain in the local militia company.[3]

The Earlls reared their children in a simple, Protestant household. They were members of the Leicester Congregational Church, which, as was customary in New England towns in the eighteenth century, seated its constituents by rank; the Earlls held pew

Detail of
*Oliver Ellsworth and
Abigail Wolcott Ellsworth*
(cat. 41).

fourteen, suggesting their prominent status. The artist and his brothers attended the school in Leicester in the 1760s.[4]

Of the three sons, only Clark followed in his father's footsteps. He remained in Paxton, where he married a local woman, Hepsebah Howard, and helped his father manage the family farm. A patriot during the Revolution, he joined his father's militia regiment and fought at the Battle of Lexington and Concord.[5] Ralph, who stood to inherit the farm and lands, instead chose to pursue a life-style and career that deviated sharply from the simple traditions of his family. Liberating himself from the pattern of his ancestors, Earl sought a career as a professional artist. His ambition led to conflict with his family's moral principles.

It is possible to speculate on the distress of the Earll family upon learning of their eldest son's wish to become an artist. His father's response undoubtedly mirrored that of Gov. Jonathan Trumbull of Connecticut, who, at about the same time, learned of his son's similar desire. "I am sensible of his natural genius and inclination for limning; an art I have frequently told him, will be of no use to him." Governor Trumbull intended that his son John Trumbull should follow a learned career in law or the ministry. Although Earl's family held more modest goals for their son, intending that he earn his living from the soil, they surely viewed art as a useless and unsuitable career.[6]

As if to confirm his parents' misgivings, Earl's ambition to become an artist led to his refusal to serve in his father's militia company, which elicited public accusations of his loyalty to Britain in the early years of the war. Earl's example influenced his youngest brother to follow a similar career. Unlike Ralph, however, James came of age after the Revolution. Sharing his brother's Loyalist inclinations, he followed him to England, arriving in London in 1787. Surprisingly, no evidence has come to light indicating that the two brothers encountered one another in either England or America. James arrived in England after Ralph's departure for America, and he died an untimely death in 1796 in Charleston, South Carolina, during a brief stay in that city.[7]

Earl's desire to become an artist is all the more exceptional because of the lack of inspiration, instruction, or role models available to him in the rural farming community in which he was raised. Boston was the nearest artistic center at this time. The only artist known to have been painting anywhere near Worcester County in the 1770s was Winthrop Chandler (1747–90). Only four years older than Ralph Earl, Chandler spent most of his life in Woodstock, Connecticut, about twenty-five miles southwest of Paxton. Chandler's career as a painter provides an illuminating contrast with Earl's, for the many hardships he faced represented the norm for a rural artist – Earl's extraordinary success was an exception.[8]

The careers of Earl and Chandler diverged from the outset, with Earl demonstrating artistic aspirations far greater than those of Chandler. In spite of the close proximity of their native towns, no direct exposure to each other's works is known. They both, however, responded to the entrenched regional aesthetic, which informed their portraits. It is perhaps their shared patronage that has caused scholars to link their careers.[9]

Around 1770, Chandler, a self-taught painter, began his lifework. He executed approximately fifty known portraits in the course of his career, his patrons being limited to a tightly knit network of family and friends in eastern Connecticut and, by 1785, in Worcester, Massachusetts. Earl and Chandler shared a similar upbringing, as did Chandler's sitters. The people of this region had a pietistic attitude toward their lives, which influenced the way they wished to appear in their portraits. Many of Chandler's subjects (as well as Earl's later Connecticut subjects), for example, were related to Gov. Samuel Huntington (fig. 2.3) of Norwich, who typified the values of this community;

I . I
William Johnston
Mary Ledyard
(Mrs. Thomas Seymour, Jr.), c. 1764
oil on canvas
50 1/4 x 40 1/4 in. (127.6 x 102.2 cm.)
The Connecticut Historical Society,
Hartford.

a descendant described him thus. "A man of great simplicity and plainness of manners, he was averse to all pageantry and parade, and strictly economical in all expendi-
tures. . . . His principal aim in his domestic arrangements was comfort and convenience
without splendor; although not hostile to good living, he was simple, sparing and tem-
perate in his diet." [10] To make a living in this frugal society, Chandler pursued several
branches of his trade, painting ornaments, houses, and landscapes for overmantles, as
well as carving and gilding. [11]

Chandler's earliest known works indicate his familiarity with the works of such
Boston painters as John Singleton Copley (1738–1815), Joseph Badger (1708–65), and
William Johnston (1732–72). Chandler could have seen portraits by these painters in
houses in Connecticut and the upper Connecticut River Valley and may have traveled
to Boston to view others. [12]

William Johnston, in particular, may have influenced Chandler, for he was the first
professional artist to paint in the state. From 1762 to 1764, Johnston worked in New
London, New Haven, Middletown (where his sister, Sarah Hobby, lived), and Hartford. Johnston's portrait *Mary Ledyard (Mrs. Thomas Seymour, Jr.)* (fig. 1 . 1), painted in
Hartford in 1764, reflects the rococo style that became popular in New England in the
1750s, at the same time showing restraint in the flat and simple coloring and modeling. Johnston borrowed from English mezzotint prints to provide background details
and furnishings for his portraits, a common practice for artists in the eighteenth cen-

1.2
John Durand
Reverend Abraham Jarvis, c. 1765
oil on canvas
48½ x 39⅓ in. (122.2 x 99.8 cm.)
Wadsworth Atheneum, Hart-
ford, Conn. William B. and Mary
Arabella Goodwin Collection.

tury. Borrowing is also evident in the Connecticut portraits of John Durand (active 1765–82), who painted in New Haven and Norwich in 1768 and 1772; his treatment, like Johnston's, is flat and simple. In his portrait of the Middletown minister, *Reverend Abraham Jarvis* (fig. 1.2), Durand includes an upholstered high-backed chair and ornate pier table, both borrowed from an English print.[13]

The conservative manner of portraiture practiced by Chandler and other artists working in colonial Connecticut, can be characterized by the restrained treatment of the subject, tight, linear brushwork, and subdued lighting effects. Unlike the itinerant artists Johnston and Durand, however, Chandler did not borrow from English print sources, but instead favored the inclusion of intensely observed details of the sitter's environment. For example, his portraits *Judge Ebenezer Devotion* and *Mrs. Ebenezer Devotion* (cats. 1, 2), like his portraits of other members of the Devotion family, including the judge's parents, Ebenezer and Martha Devotion (figs. 1.3, 1.4) feature accurate depictions of the sitters' locally made furnishings, clothing, and accoutrements. Chandler's straightforward manner became characteristic of portraiture in Connecticut in the years leading up to the American Revolution, since it was suited to the modest pretensions of his conservative sitters, who valued a faithful representation of themselves. In addition, some Americans began consciously to reject references to aristocratic British imagery, frequently drawn from British print sources.

In 1790, at the age of forty-three, after a short and tragic career, Chandler died penniless, his five children having been distributed to relatives after the death of his wife the previous year. A passage in Chandler's obituary alludes to the lack of support and patronage he received. "The world was not his enemy, but as is too common, his genius was not matured on the bosom of encouragement. Embarrassment, like strong weeds in a garden of delicate flowers, checked his enthusiasm and disheartened the man."[14] In 1790, Earl, aged thirty-nine, was at the height of his career in northwestern Connecticut.

Unlike his own father, who was a man of strong moral convictions, Earl was a pragmatist. His artistic aspirations guided his actions, setting him apart from his rural colleagues and causing tension within his immediate family. Whereas Chandler's obituary indicated his compromise with necessity – "by profession he was a house painter"[15] – Earl pursued his vocation singlemindedly, leaving the security of his rural surroundings for a more urban setting in order to succeed as an artist.

Political tension over the events that led to the outbreak of the revolutionary war signaled Earl's departure from Worcester County. In 1774, Earl's father was elected a representative from Paxton at a series of local meetings held in July and August to consider such matters as "the state of public affairs concerning suspension of all commerce with Great Britain" and the formation of a Committee of Correspondence and Inspection to "watch the conduct of Torys," of which there were many in the region.[16] Earl avoided the inevitable call to enlist in his father's militia company. Instead, he left his father's house that summer and established himself as a painter in New Haven, Connecticut.

New Haven was the largest town in the state, with a population of over eight thousand people.[17] Unlike Boston, which had a comparatively active artistic community – Henry Pelham (1749–1806) was there; Copley left for Europe on June 10, 1774 – New Haven supported no established artists in the colonial period.[18] The region had attracted a few traveling painters: William Johnston in 1763, John Durand in 1768 and 1772, and Henry Pelham in 1774. The young artist John Trumbull (1756–1843) began his career at his parents' home in nearby Lebanon in the early 1770s, where he painted

1.3
Winthrop Chandler
Reverend Ebenezer Devotion, 1770
oil on canvas
55 x 43¾ in. (139.7 x 111.1 cm.)
Collection Brookline Historical
Society, Brookline, Mass.

1.4
Winthrop Chandler
Martha Lathrop Devotion, 1770
oil on canvas
55 x 43¾ in. (139.7 x 111.1 cm.)
Collection Brookline Historical
Society, Brookline, Mass.

portraits of family members, including his father, the governor, as well as historical subjects, but soon left for Boston to attend Harvard College. Earl found little competition in New Haven and sought inspiration from the portraits that hung in the local houses.

When he arrived, an announcement appeared in the New Haven newspaper, undoubtedly placed by Earl despite the error in his first name (perhaps a mistake made by the newspaper): "John Earll, Portrait Painter hereby informs the public that on suitable encouragement he intends to carry on his business in this town. He may be spoke with at Medad Lyman's where examples of his performance may be seen. He paints Landscapes, coats of arms, etc. on the lowest terms."[19] Medad Lyman (1722–76) ran a tavern in New Haven, near Yale College, and may have boarded Earl at this time.[20]

The following fall, Earl left New Haven, returning to Leicester to marry his second cousin Sarah Gates (1755–1831), who, at the time of the wedding, was five months pregnant. The ceremony took place at the home of Daniel Henshaw, a justice of the peace, in the presence of Clark Earll. Immediately after the wedding, Earl left his bride with her parents in Worcester and returned to New Haven. Sarah gave birth to a daughter, Phebe Earl, on January 25, 1775, at her parents' home. Earl did not actually live with his wife until two years after the marriage, from November 1776 to May 1777, when they resided in New Haven. Sarah gave birth to a son, John Earl, in Worcester on May 13, 1777, shortly after Earl's departure for England.[21] The Gates family history does not speak well of Ralph Earl, asserting that he "was a Tory and skedaddled, leaving [Sarah] behind."[22] No record of a divorce between Ralph and Sarah Earl has been found. Both the lack of a shared life together and Earl's eventual desertion of his family indicate that he viewed this marriage as an impediment to his career.

Early Career in New Haven   "In the manner of Copley" – William Dunlap, *History of Design*

The first and ultimately the most important artistic influence on Earl was John Singleton Copley. Although Copley had departed for Europe just as Earl was establishing himself as a painter in New Haven, it was the American works of Copley that Earl directly imitated in his first portraits and that continued to inspire his later works. Earl's emulation of Copley, the greatest American artist of the period, is further evidence of the seriousness of his ambition.

Copley's half brother, Henry Pelham, provided Earl with direct access to the works of Copley. Pelham may have first encountered Earl in New Haven during his own visit to that town in November and December 1774, where he used his relationship to Copley to secure commissions. Pelham wrote to Copley from Philadelphia on November 2 that he intended to "sett out for home, stoping for about a fortnight at New Haven, where Mr. Babcock has engaged me to do two or three miniature Pictures." Following his arrival in New Haven, Pelham wrote to his mother on November 18: "I have begun 20 Guines worth of Buisness here, the Heads and hands of which only I shall finish here, and send the Pictu[r]es home to finish the other Parts. I have found it extremely difficult to procure meterials here for oil Paint'g but have after some time got them."[23] This letter provides some indication of the meager state of the fine arts in New Haven: even artists' materials were difficult to procure.

Following this trip, Pelham wrote to his New Haven client, the merchant Adam Babcock, for whom he had painted several watercolor miniatures of Babcock family members, including Babcock's mother-in-law, Mrs. Smith. Copley had also recently painted *Adam Babcock* and *Mrs. Adam Babcock* (cat. 3). Earl's familiarity with these portraits is made clear by his association with Pelham, whom he visited at his Boston studio on at least one occasion.

> *The post just setting out I have only time briefly to express my disappointment at not having received Mrs. Smith's Picture which by your favor of the 24th December I understood was to be sent in a short time. Mr. Earl who called upon me 2 or 3 weeks ago told me he believed it was sent I think he said three weeks before he left New Haven if so there must be a material neglect somewhere as I have seen nothing of it.*[24]

Given Earl's lack of opportunity for artistic instruction or example, Pelham's influence must be considered of some importance. Pelham worked as a painter of life-size and miniature portraits and as an engraver and a mapmaker. Two years older than Earl, he had been trained by Copley and eventually attained a sufficient degree of proficiency to assist with the background of Copley's portraits (on at least one occasion).[25] Although few works have been assigned to him with assurance, a small number of documented watercolor miniature portraits by Pelham attest to his skill. His miniature of Adam Babcock (fig. 1.5), most likely executed during his visit to New Haven in 1774, indicates that he confidently employed a stippled technique in the face and unpowdered hair.[26] As a result of his Loyalist sympathies, Pelham left Boston on May 17, 1776, embarking at Halifax for London, where he joined the Copley family. Pelham exhibited at the Royal Academy in 1777 and 1778 and later went as an engineer and cartographer to Ireland, where he died in 1806.

During the visit to Pelham's studio in March 1775, Earl had the opportunity to view his work in progress. In addition, Pelham may have provided Earl with an introduction to other Boston painters, such as the brother of William Johnston, John Johnston (c. 1753–1818), who with his cousin Daniel Rea ran an artisan-painter shop in Cambridge.[27] Earl later painted a portrait of John Johnston's wife, Martha Spear Johnston (cat. 20). While in Boston, Earl also undoubtedly viewed the many works of Copley that hung there. Such noted portraits of the early 1770s as Copley's *Samuel Adams* (fig. 1.6), demonstrate the simple, straightforward poses, dramatic lighting effects, forceful characterizations, and politically charged symbolism that so impressed Earl.

In his own early works, executed in New Haven, Earl emulated Copley's muted colors, strong sidelighting, careful attention to detail, and strong characterizations. Beginning around 1774, Earl painted a series of portraits of prominent patriots, most of whom had some association with Yale College. Earl's earliest known portraits in this group are directly based on Copley's portraits of Adam and Abigail Babcock (cat. 3), which hung in their New Haven home. For his portraits of the New Haven merchant Henry Daggett and his wife, Elizabeth Prescott Daggett (cat. 4), Earl took the pose and costume almost directly from the Babcock portraits.

In spite of the crudeness of the Daggett portraits, Earl received commissions from other prominent New Haven patriots, all of whom were closely acquainted with each other. Earl's most important commission at this time came from a leading patriot of the Revolution. A self-educated surveyor, lawyer, and mathematician, Roger Sherman (1721–93) was a man of impressive intellectual powers but simple tastes. He was married to Elizabeth Daggett's sister, Rebecca Prescott Sherman. When his portrait was painted, he was treasurer of Yale College. He became the only one of his contemporaries to sign the Declaration of Independence, the Articles of Association, the Articles of Confederation, and the Constitution of the United States.[28]

Unlike his portraits of the Daggetts, Earl's depiction of Roger Sherman (cat. 5) represents a masterly and promising early effort. The nearly life-size portrait imparts both the strength of Sherman's character and the awkwardness of his manner. John

1.5
Henry Pelham
Adam Babcock, c. 1774
miniature watercolor on ivory
1 ½ x 1 ³⁄₁₆ in. (3.8 x 3.0 cm.)
On loan to the Diplomatic
Reception Rooms,
U.S. Department of State.
Collection of Louisa B. Parker.

1.6
John Singleton Copley
Samuel Adams, 1770–72
oil on canvas
50 x 40¼ in. (127.0 x 102.2 cm.)
Deposited by the City of Boston.
Courtesy, Museum of Fine Arts,
Boston.

Adams observed these contrary traits after hearing Sherman debate in the Congress in 1775. "Sherman is one of the soundest and strongest pillars of the Revolution [even if his] air is the reverse of grace; there cannot be a more striking contrast to beautiful action, than the motion of his hands. . . . Hogarth's genius could not have invented a motion more opposite of grace – it is stiffness and awkwardness itself." [29] In a powerful characterization of his sitter, Earl placed his subject in a plain setting, the only furnishing being a carefully depicted Philadelphia low-backed Windsor armchair, symbolizing Sherman's recent role at the Constitutional Convention in that city. Dressed in a well-worn, somber suit of clothes, Sherman gazes out at the viewer directly, his arms dropping stiffly in front of him. Light strikes the carefully delineated face and the rough hands. The scale of the portrait, the subdued palette, and strong contrasts of light and shade are reminiscent of Copley.

Earl painted a similar portrait of Sherman's friend and political colleague Eliphalet Dyer (fig. 1.7) of Windham, Connecticut. Like Sherman, Dyer (1721–1807) was a noted lawyer, and with Sherman and Silas Deane, he served as a delegate at the Philadelphia Continental Congress in 1774. [30] Although the portrait has suffered consider-

1.7
Ralph Earl
Eliphalet Dyer, c. 1774–75
oil on canvas
40⅓ x 36 in. (102.4 x 91.4 cm.)
Private collection.

able damage, the remaining portion suggests that it may originally have been full-length, identical in size and composition to the Sherman portrait.[31] Dyer is seated in a Philadelphia Windsor chair similar to the one in the Sherman portrait, suggesting that the portraits were painted to commemorate the men's recent service in Philadelphia.

Earl painted at least three more portraits during his years in New Haven, again of individuals associated with Yale College (all remain unlocated). In connection with two of these portraits, the historical biographer and artist William Dunlap (1766–1839) was the first to note Earl's strong debt to Copley. After seeing Earl's *Reverend Timothy Dwight* and *Mrs. Timothy (Mary Woolsey) Dwight*, he wrote: "In the year 1775 Mr. Earl painted portraits in Connecticut. I remember seeing two full-lengths of the Rev. Timothy Dwight and his wife, painted in 1777, as Earl thought, in the manner of Copley. They showed some talent, but the shadows were black as charcoal or ink."[32] Mary Woolsey married Timothy Dwight in New Haven on March 3, 1777, when Dwight was serving as the pastor of Yale College. Their portraits commemorate their wedding.

The third portrait is Earl's likeness of the Rev. Nehemiah Strong (unlocated), who was a professor of mathematics and natural philosophy at Yale College. The portrait hung in the college library. After Earl's return from England, he painted a second portrait of Strong (cat. 36), also for the college library, as a "Fairer Specimen of his Skill."[33]

After his death, Earl gained considerable notoriety for his role in producing sketches for four engravings of the Battle of Lexington and Concord while he was in New Haven. Dunlap noted that Earl's sketches were "the first historical pictures, perhaps ever attempted in America."[34] They were engraved by his associate Amos Doolittle (1754–1832) of New Haven.

The inspiration for this entrepreneurial venture may have come from Henry Pelham, who had tried his hand at similar endeavors. Pelham had produced several prints in Boston, beginning in 1770, when he published a print of the Boston Massacre.[35] He later complained to an uncle, John Singleton, regarding the effect of the battle at Lexington and Concord on his profession. "This last Maneuvour had entirely stopp'd all my business, and annialated all my Property, the fruits of 4 or 5 years Labor. I find it impossible to collect any Monies that are due me, so that I am forced to find some other place where I may at least make a living, my present proposed plan is to remove to Great Britain."[36] For the next two years Pelham found employment in drawing and producing a map of Boston, which was later published in London on June 2, 1777, as *A Plan of Boston*.[37]

Earl visited Pelham in mid-March 1775, just weeks before the Battle of Lexington and Concord, which occurred on April 19. Hopeful of financial gain, Earl may have taken his example from Pelham's current activities in printmaking and his inspiration from Doolittle, who had been present at the battlefield shortly after the skirmish as a member of Capt. Benedict Arnold's New Haven militia company. According to Doolittle's own account of his collaboration with Earl as related later by his friend John W. Barber, he "acted as a kind of model for Mr. Earl to make his drawings, so that when he wished to represent one of the Provincials as loading his gun, crouching behind a stone wall when firing on the enemy, he would require Mr. D. to put himself in such a position."[38]

Doolittle advertised the prints, his first known effort as an engraver, in the *Connecticut Journal and New Haven Post Boy*, on December 13, 1775 (cat. 9). Although crude in technique, the engravings (cats. 6–9) provide an honest depiction of this critical battle in a reportorial style that lacks the heroic conventions of history painting. The prints were not intended to commemorate the battle, but rather to inform the citizens of Connecticut of this momentous advance toward war with Britain by capturing the events of several hours in four scenes. At the very end of his career, Earl once again collaborated with Doolittle on an entrepreneurial venture when he exhibited his panorama of Niagara Falls at Doolittle's house in New Haven.

Earl had managed to secure commissions for portraits of leading patriots and had collaborated on the production of four historical prints at a time when most artists in America had difficulty pursuing their profession. But his determination to avoid military service and continue to develop his artistic career forced him to take a political stance. While many artists managed to maintain a neutral position during the war years, Earl was publicly pronounced a Loyalist on the eve of the Revolution, and barely escaped imprisonment.

Earl's troubles first come to light when his name appeared on the Grand Tax List of January 1776 for New Haven, which cited him for "absconding out of state" without paying his taxes for the year.[39] Earl returned to Connecticut only to be singled out in the press again, this time for a more serious offense. The following complaint appeared in print on April 2, 1777. "About six weeks ago an impeachment was signed by about fifty inhabitants and presented to the authority, charging . . . [four men, including] Ralph Earle, with having positively declared, that they were friends to George the third, and would not take up arms against him or his troops."[40] Even though this signaled the end of his career in New Haven, Earl had managed to avoid military enlistment, which could have ended his career altogether.

The major source of information concerning Earl's activities as a Loyalist is his own petition to the British government, submitted on January 28, 1779, less than a year after his arrival in England. Much of the claim proves to be accurate, though he probably embellished certain points to put himself in a better position to receive compensation. In the claim Earl stated that his father was a "Colonel in the Rebel Service" (in reality, he held the rank of captain).[41] Because of his refusal to take up arms, Earl asserted, he was "turned out and obliged to seek support among the friends of Government and was thereby not only deprived of a very genteel Maintenance which he enjoyed under his Father, but at the same Time forfeited all hopes of enjoying a very good Estate which he is entitled to on the Death of his Father."[42]

The petition went on to relate Earl's activities as a spy for the British army. "With Five others in the Month of March 1777 getting private intelligence of the Rebel Armies Intention of making a Descent on Long Island the following Night, [I] immediately dispatched a person (on whom they could depend) in a Boat to that Place being Thirty Miles who apprised the British Soldiers of the intended Visit by the Rebels the same Night. Whereupon they were immediately put in such a Posture of Defence as to preserve themselves, repulse the Enemy, and prevent Bloodshed and Plunder."[43] No other account verifies Earl's role in warning the British on Long Island, but the Americans apparently planned such an attack. On March 5, 1777, Gen. George Washington wrote to Brig. Gen. Samuel Parsons describing "a Long Island Plan" and asking of the "practicability . . . to effect an attempt on Long Island, to destroy, forage, etc."[44]

Earl then faced an untenable position. "Your petitioner and Six others in April following were apprehended and taken into Custody by virtue of a warrant issued from the above Committee [of Safety, or Correspondence and Inspection]"—a claim verified by the newspaper complaint of April 2, 1777. Earl and the others were again requested to take up arms

> but still refused And your petitioner verily believes (had it not been through the respect which they paid his Father as an officer of high Rank in their Army) he should certainly have received sentence of Death as they were suspicious of his correspondence with the British Officers. However, they again insisted of his being confined in prison or immediately quitting the Province which he did. . . . He found it impossible much longer to escape punishment and therefore was determined . . . to embark for England.

Forced to leave the state and "having very fortunately met with Captn Money, Qr Master Genl. of the [British] Northern Army and having given him every Information of the State of that Country he could desire, He [Money] had the goodness to disguise him [Earl] as a Servant and bring him from Providence to Newport in a Flag of Truce and from thence to England where they arrived in April last."[45] By refusing to take up arms, Earl thus managed to continue his career in England.

English Years

"Great improvements in the Business of his profession"
— Rev. Nehemiah Strong, *Letter to Ezra Stiles*

Earl reached London in April 1778, disguised as the servant of Capt. John Money (1752–1817), the quartermaster general of Burgoyne's army. Money returned to England, presumably as a result of the Saratoga Convention, in an exchange of prisoners. His military rank rose to general during a successful career. One year younger than Earl, Money probably served as Earl's guide to London, a city fifty times the size of Boston and unlike anything the young artist from rural Massachusetts had ever seen.

Earl's presence in London followed a pattern established by many other American painters. The first generation of American-born artists to travel to England in the 1760s and 1770s included Matthew Pratt (1734–1805), Abraham Delanoy, Jr. (1742–95), Charles Willson Peale (1741–1827), Joseph Wright (1756–93), Gilbert Stuart (1755–1828), John Singleton Copley, and Earl's acquaintance Henry Pelham.[46] Most had come, on their own initiative or in response to the threat of war, to improve their artistic skills in the studio of Benjamin West or, as in the case of Copley, to compete with the leading artists of the day. Benjamin West (1738–1820), the first American painter to achieve international fame, had established himself as England's foremost history painter, renowned for his scenes from classical mythology and ancient history. As a teacher, his kind and generous nature attracted a succession of promising young painters to his studio.

Unlike his predecessors, however, Earl apparently did not go immediately to West's studio. London was the portrait capital of the world, with more than one hundred active portrait painters in the 1780s. An artist seeking entrance to this artistic community confronted a highly complex and established system of patronage networks. In addition to demonstrating skill at capturing a likeness, an aspiring artist had to possess "business acumen, a disposition capable of constant public performance, a sensitivity to rank and hierarchy, verbal ingenuity, personal charm, and management skills."[47] Earl exhibited many of these qualities as his career matured, but he apparently chose not to compete with the London artists, instead taking advantage of his friendship with Captain Money. He left London, following Money to his country house in Norwich, in the English coastal province of East Anglia (fig. 1.8). In dire need of financial assistance, Earl was at least assured of a place to reside. Earl's ability to gain the support of prominent individuals, first witnessed in his relationship with Money and made evident by successive friendships, proved invaluable as his career progressed.

Earl's friendship with Money allowed the young artist to gain a footing in this unfamiliar country. Both young men shared a spirit of adventure. When not engaged in military ventures, Money resided at his country house, Trowse Hall, two miles southeast of the town center. One of England's earliest aeronauts, he made a balloon ascension on July 22, 1785, which ended in the sea off Norwich.[48] His rescue was recorded by the local painter Philip Reinagle (fig. 1.9). Money never married but had two illegitimate children, a son, Frederick, and a daughter, Elizabeth. Money later befriended Earl's son, Ralph E. W. Earl (c. 1785 or 1788–1837), who also became a painter; he allowed Earl, Jr., to paint his portrait in 1810.[49]

Nine months after his arrival in England, and likely at Money's urging, Earl submitted his petition to the lord commissioners of the treasury for Loyalist compensation. Earl claimed to have been "reduced to the utmost Distress"; "by the assistance of a well disposed Friend or Two [he has] ever since been supported." Money, who must have assisted Earl in composing this document, verified the claims Earl had made regarding his activities as a spy for the British government, and concluded, "I believe Mr. Earl to be now in great Distress."[50] There is no record of a response by the commission.

Facing page 1.8
Ralph Earl's Travels in England, 1778–1785.

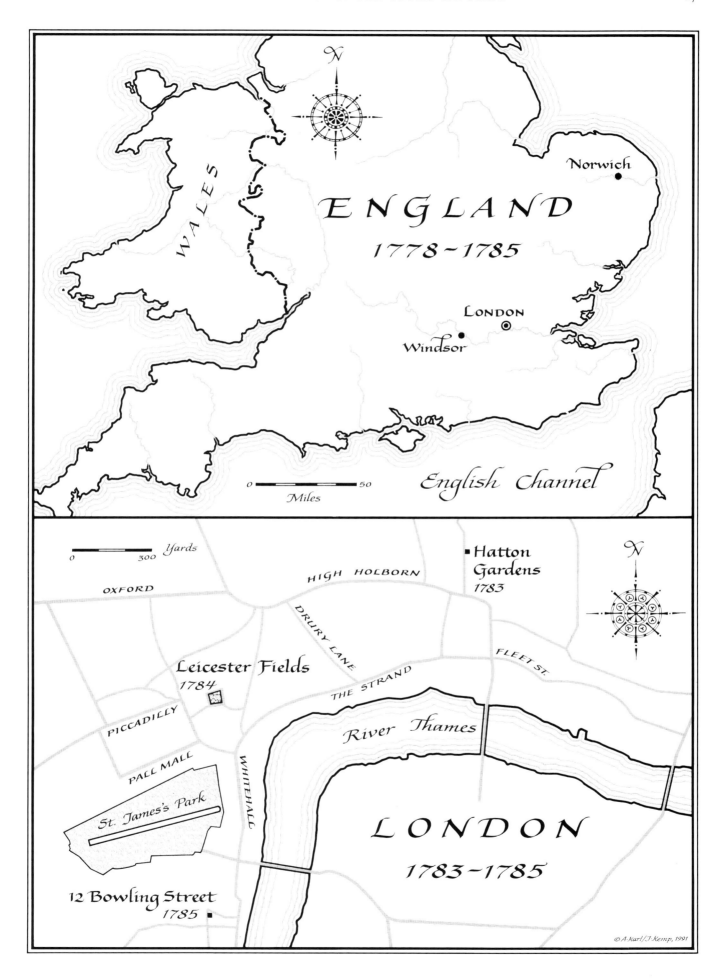

N

Norwich

WALES

ENGLAND
1778~1785

London

Windsor

0 ____ 50
Miles

English Channel

0 ____ 300 *Yards*

OXFORD

HIGH HOLBORN

■ Hatton
Gardens
1783

N

DRURY LANE

Leicester Fields
1784

FLEET ST.

THE STRAND

PICCADILLY

River Thames

PALL MALL

WHITEHALL

St. James's Park

LONDON
1783~1785

12 Bowling Street
1785 ■

© A. Karl/J. Kemp, 1991

1.9
John Murphy after Philip Reinagle
The Perilous Situation of Major Money and His Balloon at Sea, published in 1789
mezzotint
17 ^{11}/$_{16}$ x 23 ^{5}/$_{8}$ in. (45.0 x 60.0 cm.)
Library of Congress,
Washington, D.C.

Earl's early years in England, from 1778 to 1782, virtually escape historical record. No known mention of the artist exists in written accounts of the day. This absence of contemporary comment suggests that Earl remained, for the most part, in Norwich, where his presence went unnoticed by the artistic community in London. Indeed, the only known signed and dated portraits from this period place the artist in Norwich.[51]

Earl had received little formal artistic training beyond his acquaintance with Henry Pelham and his admiration for and emulation of the American works of Copley. By gravitating to the English countryside, he could hope to establish himself in an environment closely resembling the one he had left in America. The ancient city of Norwich, largely settled by Dutch Protestants, had become a major port for Flemish trade, as well as the center of a thriving textile industry.[52] As the city's cultural institutions improved, so too did the visual arts, which flourished in a diverse social setting, "one in which patronage might depend as much on individual pretensions to civility and polish as on aesthetic enlightenment or the availability of surplus wealth."[53] Here, with the help of his friend, Earl could hope to gain local commissions. Earl's exposure to the art patrons in this region prepared him well for his later career in New England, where he encountered a similarly diverse, provincial clientele who also exhibited "individual pretensions."

Norwich attracted artists with a wide range of skills in the eighteenth century, as evidenced by the advertisements placed in the local paper. The painter Henry Mumford, for example, claimed to execute portraits "to the Life in Young or Old for a Guinea a Head, and if not like the Person when done, he takes the Picture and no Damage."[54] The more successful artists working in Norwich trained in London, which was considered a desirable asset. The artist John Sanders, who arrived in Norwich in 1777, made a point of noting that he had come from "the London Royal Academy" and stated further that since he came with "an intention of residing constantly here as a Portrait Painter . . . [he] hopes this City will not consider him as an itinerant Painter, being desirous of gaining the Esteem and Respect of those on whom he will be happy to rely."[55] Evidently itinerancy was not looked upon with favor in England. Earl would find that with the proper sanctions, this manner of pursuing one's artistic career was more acceptable in America.

Money was acquainted with many of the prominent local artists who were working in Norwich while Earl was there. Philip Reinagle (1749–1833), who painted *The Perilous Situation of Major Money* (fig. 1.9), worked as a portrait painter in his native Norwich in the early 1780s.[56] A leading artist in the region, Sir William Beechey (1753–1839), who painted portraits and provided artistic instruction in Norwich from about 1782 to 1787, also knew Money.[57] He painted the East Anglian gentry in a style described as "sound, provincial, [and] unfashionable," as evidenced by his many civic portrait commissions that still hang in St. Andrew's Hall, Norwich, including *Robert Partridge, Mayor of Norwich, 1784* (fig. 1.10). Beechey painted conversation pieces while working in Norwich in the 1780s; it had gone out of fashion in London in the previous decade, but Earl was to show his familiarity with the format later in America.[58]

Even though there is a great deal more to be learned about provincial British portraiture, it is nevertheless clear that Earl's years in Norwich, combined with his time in London, taught him that the dictates of fashion varied in each region because of differing tastes and social rank. Earl successfully applied this knowledge on his return to America, developing highly contrasting styles to suit his cosmopolitan New York City clients and his provincial New England ones.[59]

Earl's first English portraits were of the two children of Money's neighbors William and Mary Carpenter of Aldeby Priory, near Norwich. *William Carpenter* and *Mary Ann Carpenter* (cats. 10, 11), painted in 1779, retain many of the elements found in his earlier New Haven works; his continuing emulation of Copley is seen in the heavy shadows, strong lighting effects, and attention to detail. Some improvement in technical ability and the more complex compositional setting suggest, however, the impact of English portraiture.

Earl demonstrates a finer use of color and a sense of texture, seen in the brilliant red coat worn by William and the white floral-trimmed dress worn by Mary Ann. In addition, the artist achieves more relaxed and graceful poses for his subjects. The compositional format seen in Mary Ann's portrait, including red drapery, a green-cloth-covered table, and a geometrically patterned carpet, is used frequently in Earl's later Connecticut portraits, becoming a signature of sorts, perhaps indicative of a commonality of taste between these two groups of patrons. The decorative carpet, in particular, is evident in many portraits painted by English artists in Norwich and, later, in many Connecticut portraits by Earl and his followers.[60]

The Carpenter portraits are the only documented works by Earl in his early years in England. By 1783 he had established a residence in London, where he remained, at different addresses, until 1785.[61] In contrast to the seemingly unremarkable beginnings of his English career, Earl painted an impressive number of grand-scale portraits of prominent English subjects while in London, to wit, the sixteen signed and dated or

I. IO
William Beechey
Robert Partridge, Mayor of Norwich,
1784, c. 1784
oil on canvas
94¼ x 60¾ in. (239.4 x 154.3 cm.)
St. Andrew's Hall, Norwich,
England. Courtesy, Norfolk Museums Service.

documented works from these years, as well as the eight attributed portraits. He exhibited four of these works at the Royal Academy exhibitions of 1783, 1784, and 1785.[62] The seemingly abrupt shift from virtual obscurity to a relatively high level of artistic activity appears to coincide with Earl's acceptance into the studio of Benjamin West.

The precise nature and timing of Earl's first encounter with West may never be known. Several contemporary sources substantiate their relationship, however. The painter William Dunlap, Earl's contemporary, was himself a student in West's studio by 1784. He later wrote that he believed Earl studied "under the direction of Mr. West, immediately after the independence of his country was established," which would have placed Earl in West's studio by the fall of 1783.[63] Dunlap was better acquainted with Earl than his writings suggest. Not only did he doubtless encounter Earl in West's studio, but he also later shared with Earl the patronage of Dunlap's brother-in-law, the Rev. Timothy Dwight.[64] His account of Earl's career was based on personal knowledge and appears to be, for the most part, accurate.

A letter written by Earl in 1784 to his friend Dr. Joseph Trumbull (1756–1824) is the most tangible source linking Earl with West. Earl addressed the letter to Trumbull at his London residence.

Windsor Thursday 23 Sept
Dear Sir
 I have received both your lettors
the reason why I did not anser the first
is because I was coming to London this day
had I not received your lettor earley this
Morning finding You was likely to Stay
five or six days longer, I have put it off till
Saturday, which evening I will call on You
on Sunday You must appear with me earley
in the morning to proceed to business and to
dine with me if you posebley can—
 I was much alarmed at Your first lettor
by Your starting off to America in such a hurey
I was or I am under constant feeris and apprehentions
that your lookes may some day or other prove
fatiol to You) I have applyed Your love to the
Misses Duttons and they have returned theirs
to you in ballonce) I made Your Com{pliments} to Mr West
I have finished the large picture, and lately
finished another and half done a thirde the picture
which I have begun and finished scince you was
heir is the best that eaver I painted, I intend to
offer it to Copley to coppey for his improvement
    I am Sir Your most &c
    R Earl

I shall either call on you at two o'clock
or at Seaven O'Clock on Saturday) day after tomorrow
both the Mr. Wests desires to be remembered to you
and wish you a plesont and a safe passaj[65]

1.11
John Singleton Copley
*The Three Youngest Daughters of
King George III (Mary, Sophia, and
Amelia)*, 1785
oil on canvas
104½ x 73 in. (265.4 x 185.4 cm.)
Her Majesty Queen Elizabeth II,
Buckingham Palace, London.

1.12
Ralph Earl
Portrait of Two Sisters, c. 1783–84
oil on canvas
50 x 40 in. (127.0 x 101.6 cm.)
Norton Gallery of Art, West Palm
Beach, Fla.

Dr. Trumbull of Worcester, Massachusetts, Earl's friend and a frequent traveler to London, had recently visited the artist at Windsor and had made arrangements to sit for his portrait in London. Earl's portrait of Trumbull (cat. 18) captures the handsome features of his young friend, who sits in a relaxed and graceful pose in an accomplished landscape setting.

Earl's mention of West provides evidence of his presence in the entourage of pupils and admirers who followed the great artist to Windsor, the site of the royal residence, where West spent a large part of the summer and autumn during the years that he enjoyed the patronage of the king. There West had the use of an official castle studio and a large house nearby, in the town. In 1784, West was accompanied by his wife, Elizabeth, and their two sons, Raphael (1766–1850) and Benjamin, Jr. (1772–1848), one of whom (most likely Raphael) is referred to in Earl's letter. The Misses Duttons in the letter ran a fashionable school for young ladies in Windsor; from them Earl procured a number of commissions to paint portraits of their students.

Besides indicating a high level of productivity (the letter says that Earl had several portraits in hand), Earl displays a certain irreverence when he remarks in jest to his friend that the painting he had recently completed, "the best that eaver I painted," would be "offered to Copley to coppey for his improvement." In the guise of humor, Copley is offered as the standard against which to measure quality, reflecting Earl's continued admiration for the artist. Yet his suggestion appears all the more ridiculous when one considers that Copley was at the height of his English career, having exhibited his celebrated history painting *The Death of Major Pierson* in the summer of 1784 and received acclaim for it from King George III.[66] As a result of his success, Copley gained permission from the king to paint a portrait of the king's three youngest daughters. Copley was painting this portrait (which he finished in 1785) when Earl wrote his letter. In fact, Earl may have been inspired by *The Three Youngest Daughters of King George III* (fig. 1.11) in painting *Portrait of Two Sisters* (fig. 1.12), which similarly incorporates grapevines as a background motif.

Earl appears to have remained on the periphery of West's circle of students, for no mention of the artist can be found in the correspondence and papers of West or his American students. Nor, according to the records of the Royal Academy, did Earl attend the drawing classes offered at the Royal Academy School. To be admitted as a student, one had to obtain permission to make chalk drawings from the plaster casts owned by the academy. An artist's admission or rejection depended upon the potential talent demonstrated in these drawings. The Boston painter Mather Brown (1761–1831) arrived in England in 1782, immediately entering West's studio. He obtained West's permission to draw from the casts and was admitted as a student on January 7, 1782.[67] Gilbert Stuart, in contrast, arrived at West's studio in 1777, remaining until about 1782, but was never formally a student at the Royal Academy. Drawings by most of West's students, including Stuart, have survived, but there are no known drawings by Earl.

Earl also chose not to pursue the elevated genre of history painting during his English years, then considered to be the highest form of art. Both West and Copley had attained great fame as the leading history painters of the day. Several of West's students, including Mather Brown and John Trumbull, followed their master's example, feeling that portrait painting continued to carry the stigma of a trade, whereas history painting could be seen as morally uplifting.[68] Unlike Brown and Trumbull, who had received a formal education, Earl, like most American artists of the era, was hindered by a lack of the classical and literary education essential for history painting.

1.13
Thomas Gainsborough
Sir Benjamin Truman, c. 1773–74
oil on canvas
93¾ x 59⁹⁄₁₆ in. (237.8 x 151.3 cm.)
Tate Gallery, London. Photo
courtesy Art Resource, New York.

Even though Earl chose not to compete with his contemporaries, his English experience did provide him with a new mode of artistic expression, landscape painting. His English portraits have many skillfully executed backgrounds of loosely executed foliage, pastoral scenery, and pink and blue skies reminiscent of the works of Thomas Gainsborough (d. 1788), for example, *Sir Benjamin Truman* (fig. 1.13). Having acquired expertise in this genre, Earl later helped to cultivate a taste for landscape art among his New England patrons.

1.15
Ralph Earl
Mr. John Hyndman, c. 1784
oil on canvas
50 x 40½ in. (127.0 x 102.9 cm.)
Collection of the Newark Museum,
Newark, N.J. Gift of Mr. and
Mrs. Orrin W. June, 1959.

During the third quarter of the eighteenth century, Sir Joshua Reynolds (1723–92), the first president of the Royal Academy, developed the heightened, formal style of English portraiture to its highest degree, creating an elevated style related to history painting.[69] Earl was undoubtedly exposed to the Grand Manner style as a student of Benjamin West, but he continued to adhere to a less flamboyant, somewhat heightened formal portraiture. He never attempted to present his subjects in the dramatic poses, classical costumes, or allegorical guises characteristic of the most fashionable English portraiture. Nor did he fully embrace Reynolds's dictum that "in portraits, the grace, and we may add, the likeness, consists more in taking the general air, than observing the exact similitude of every feature."[70] Earl, in fact, took care in capturing faithful likenesses of his English subjects, a predilection that became far more pronounced in his later Connecticut portraits. Additionally, his English (and, later, New York) subjects appear more idealized than his Connecticut sitters because of their conventional poses and backgrounds.

Earl's English compositions show the influence of such artists as Thomas Gainsborough and George Romney (1734–1802), seen in the elaborate landscape settings and intricate room interiors. His technical abilities improved markedly as he began to use more subtle modeling and glazing, freer brushwork, and more relaxed and imaginative poses. However, he persisted in painting forceful characterizations and honest depictions of his subjects, evident in the contemporary costumes and settings, and maintained an intense interest in capturing the reality of objects, frequently employing trompe l'oeil effects – all of which reveal the continuing influence of Copley's American works.

In particular, Earl's portraits of subjects placed in elaborate room settings, such as *Lady Williams and Child* (fig. 1.14), demonstrate the artist's concern for the depiction of fabrics, costume details, furnishings, and illusionary passages, such as the reflection of the inkstand in the tabletop. Similarly, his portraits of the Hyndmans (figs. 1.15,

Facing page 1.14
Ralph Earl
Lady Williams and Child, 1783
oil on canvas
50¼ x 39¾ in. (127.6 x 101.0 cm.)
The Metropolitan Museum of Art,
New York. Rogers Fund, 1906
(06.179).

1.16
Ralph Earl
Mrs. John Hyndman, c. 1784
oil on canvas
50 x 40½ in. (127.0 x 102.9 cm.)
Collection of the Newark Museum,
Newark, N.J. Gift of Mr. and
Mrs. Orrin W. June, 1959.

Facing page 1.17
Ralph Earl
Colonel George Onslow, 1782 or 1783
oil on canvas
52⅛ x 42½ in. (132.4 x 108.0 cm.)
Mrs. Ralph Earle.

1.16) provide meticulously detailed renditions of his subjects' environment, including red brocade drapery, ornate costumes, and a patterned carpet. The subjects are distinguished further by such elements as the card John Hyndman holds in his hand, which identifies him by name, and the shell-flower bouquet with which Mrs. Hyndman occupies herself. Her pastime, a favorite one of the day, is indicative of her gentry status.

The first evidence of Earl's presence in London is indicated by his establishment of a London residence in 1783, at Hatton Garden near Holborn (fig. 1.8), and his exhibition of two portraits at the Royal Academy the same year. One of the portraits has been identified as that of Col. George Onslow (fig. 1.17), a personage of some prominence.[71] Precisely how Earl obtained this important commission remains unclear. Onslow (1731–92), a member of Parliament from Guilford, was described by Horace Walpole as "a short, round man . . . one of those burlesque orators who are favored in all public assemblies."[72] The master of Desborough House at Ripley and an outranger of Windsor Forest, Onslow is depicted informally, in shooting dress with his dog by his side.[73]

Earl undoubtedly received assistance, perhaps from West, in obtaining an entrée to the Royal Academy exhibition, which was the major source of publicity for an artist and an important means of establishing a reputation in London. Of significance for his career was the favorable review his entry received in a London newspaper, praising the work as "a most excellent likeness. . . . There are parts of the drapery [clothing] remarkably well cast."[74]

In 1783, Earl also received several important commissions for portraits of prominent military and political figures. In general, his patrons were members of established British families; unlike his brother James, Ralph Earl is not known to have painted American Loyalists. Perhaps John Money assisted in obtaining some of these commissions. For example, Earl completed a portrait of the English naval hero Adm. Richard Kempenfelt (cat. 12) in 1782 or more likely, 1783. Kempenfelt (1718–82) drowned in

August 1782 with eight hundred others when his ship, the *Royal George*, suddenly sank at anchor off Spithead. Earl produced a highly accomplished portrait of Kempenfelt, inspired by the fashionable rococo style of Reynolds and Gainsborough. The lively likeness of the man may have been taken from life, the rest being completed after his untimely death. The background elements are borrowed from a variety of sources, including noted portraits by Gainsborough and Tilly Kettle (1740–86), demonstrating Earl's awareness and acceptance of the English portrait tradition. Earl later used this formal military portrait style upon his return to America, when he became one of the first artists to paint portraits of the recent heroes of the American Revolution.

Earl continued to demonstrate versatility in the types of portraits he painted during his English years. In 1783 he painted a formal portrait entitled *A Master in Chancery Entering the House of Lords* (cat. 13), which he entered in the Royal Academy exhibition of the following year. The artist depicted the master in Chancery standing in the parliamentary chamber, dressed in the robes of the high court. Under his left arm is a meticulously lettered scroll that refers to two bills written by Lord North in 1775 to restrain trade with the American colonies. Ironically, Earl would employ this same device of the lettered scroll in a series of portraits he later painted of prominent supporters of the American Constitution, most notably *Oliver Ellsworth and Abigail Wolcott Ellsworth* (cat. 41).

In addition to formal portraits celebrating eminent military and civilian careers, Earl painted numerous sporting pictures, like his first Royal Academy entry, *Colonel George Onslow* (fig. 1.17). British sporting art appealed to Earl for several reasons, for one, because English country gentlemen and landowners, rather than their urban counterparts, desired it. City dwellers did not, after all, partake in "the rustick and illiberal sports of gun, dog, and horse."[75] The genre also satisfied Earl's interest in landscape painting, for landscape was essential to the composition of the sporting scene. Furthermore, the desired effect was documentary, which suited Earl's inclinations as an artist. Finally, the pleasure of rural sport often received pictorial expression with a specifically humorous emphasis, as in the work of British satirists such as Thomas Rowlandson (1756–1827).[76] Earl probably relished the opportunity to display his own wit, evident in his letter to Trumbull and in some of his paintings.

Reclining Hunter (cat. 14) represents a monumental but somewhat enigmatic spoof on the sporting ideal. Originally attributed to Gainsborough, the painting has in more recent years been assigned to Ralph Earl.[77] The unfortunate subject of this work reclines on a bank, grinning superciliously, having just shot everything in sight, none of which—birds, donkey, or cow—is legitimate game. As if that were not enough, he has filled his tricorn hat with mushrooms, probably poisonous. Earl has used an advanced scumbling technique that adds a sheen to the blue silk waistcoat, which is hardly sporting attire, and created a landscape of sketchy foliage and a pink sky.

In contrast to *Reclining Hunter*, Earl's more conventional sporting picture, *A Gentleman with a Gun and Two Dogs* (cat. 15) painted in 1784, provides an accurate portrayal of an English sportsman. Earl achieves a relaxed and elegant air in his depiction of the hunter but continues to devote meticulous attention to such details as the sheen on the hunter's leather boots and the fowling piece. The landscape is beautifully rendered as well, in subtle hues and adept brush strokes.

Many of Earl's commissions, in his later English years, were for portraits of young girls, several of whom were students at the school run by the Dutton sisters in Windsor, mentioned in his letter to Joseph Trumbull. Sophia Isham (fig. 1.18), a student at the school in 1783, was painted by Earl when she was twelve years old. Delicately por-

1.18
Ralph Earl
Sophia Isham, 1783
oil on canvas
38½ x 28 in. (97.8 x 71.1 cm.)
Lamport Hall, Northampton,
England. Courtesy, Lamport Hall
Preservation Trust.

trayed in a soft green summer dress, the girl leans on the back of a Windsor chair, set against a background of foliage and river scenery with a church steeple in the distance. Earl received the substantial amount of five pounds five shillings for this portrait.[78]

In addition, Earl received a commission from Adm. Francis William Drake to paint Drake's two daughters in 1783 and 1784, either one or both of whom attended the school run by the Dutton sisters. Earl's portraits of Marianne Drake (cat. 16) and Sophia Drake (cat. 17) beautifully complement one another. Marianne is placed in a cleverly constructed composition that alludes to her accomplishments as a properly educated young lady of fashion. Earl puts an elaborately inlaid baroque harpsichord at the right, yet turns the sitter away from the instrument so she can display a second achievement: an amateur watercolor. Again Earl delights in capturing the trompe l'oeil effect of the glass of water reflected in the tabletop. In contrast, Earl places Sophia Drake in a summer landscape, seated on an embankment with foliage and an expansive view in the distance. The artist uses fresh colors and a freer technique, loosening his brushwork and working in a less precise manner than in his previous works. He alludes to the young woman's educational accomplishments, placing a book entitled "History" in her hand. The landscape seen through the window and beyond the sitter in this and other English portraits inspired similar backgrounds in Earl's numerous portraits of young women painted later in Litchfield County, Connecticut.

In 1784, Earl was living in Leicester Fields, where a number of the most prominent artists of the day lived (fig. 1.8). Sir Joshua Reynolds, then president of the Royal Academy, lived at 47 Leicester Square until his death in 1792; Copley settled with his family across the street at 12 Leicester Square from 1776 to 1783; several lesser-known artists and engravers, as well as the auctioneer James Christie and the antiquarian James Tassie, also lived on the square.[79] By 1785, Earl listed his address as 12 Bowling Street (near St. John's Church and Tothill Fields). Since the expense of maintaining living quarters in London was substantial, it seems likely that Earl shared his quarters or was employed by a London artist as a studio assistant. Reynolds, in particular, had a large number of assistants and students, some of whom lived with the artist. Joseph Farrington commented in his *Memoirs of the Life of Sir Joshua Reynolds* (1819) that Reynolds's "school . . . resembled a manufactory, in which the young men who were sent to him for tuition were chiefly occupied in copying portraits, or assisting in draperies, and preparing backgrounds."[80] Upon his return to America, Earl customarily cited Reynolds (in his numerous newspaper advertisements) as one of three artists he received inspiration from during his English years, the others being West and Copley. Unfortunately, the details of Earl's residence in London have remained elusive. He did not remain there for long, however; he became one of the first of West's students to return to America after the establishment of peace.

One of the last dated works of Earl's English career was that of Ann Whiteside (cat. 19), who became his second wife. In his final years in England, Earl evidently continued to spend time in Norwich, where he courted Ann Whiteside, the daughter of Eleazer Whiteside. The Whiteside family, friends and neighbors of John Money, owned a modest farm. In this highly sensitive portrayal of his bride, Earl included a globe showing a segment of North America in anticipation of the voyage the couple would take in the spring of 1785. There is no record of a ceremony, but a wedding probably took place in 1784 or 1785. There is no record of a divorce between Earl and his first wife, Sarah, suggesting that his relationship with Ann Whiteside was bigamous.

New York Prison Years

"A very capital Portrait Painter" – Advertisement, *Connecticut Courant*

Earl left London, setting sail for Boston during the last week of April 1785, accompanied by his wife Ann (the couple were presumably married by this time, for she was called Mr. Earl's "lady" upon their arrival). Paradoxically, Earl was drawn back to the very society he had abandoned seven years earlier. Still ambitious, he aspired to become the artist of the American people and anticipated new opportunities for employment, generated by the recent war. Confident that his English training would set him apart from his American colleagues, he sent an announcement to New York, which appeared in several newspapers, of his intention to establish himself in that city (fig. 1.19). "There is a very capital Portrait Painter, Mr. Earl, of Massachusetts, scholar of Copley, West and Sir Joshua Reynolds, and of great eminence in that branch, on the passage to the continent, where in all probability, he will soon take a very capital lead."[81]

Earl sailed with a number of Americans, including his friend Joseph Trumbull.[82]

Facing page 1.19
Ralph Earl's Travels in New York and New England, 1751–1801.

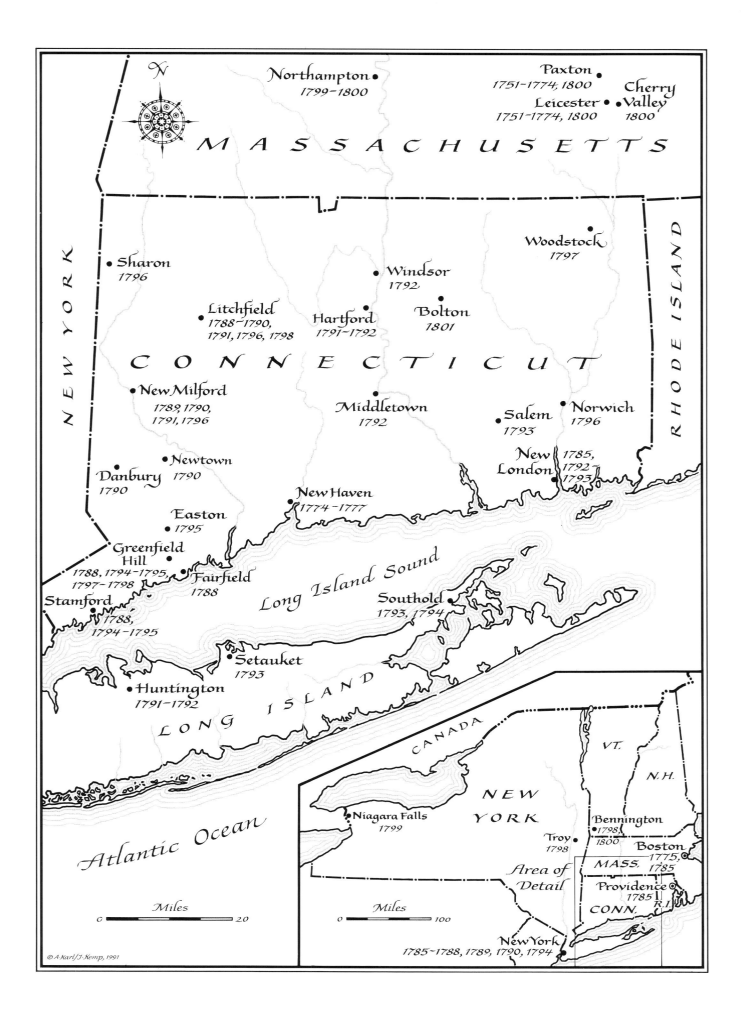

N

Northampton
1799–1800

Paxton
1751–1774, 1800

Cherry
Valley
1800

Leicester
1751–1774, 1800

MASSACHUSETTS

NEW YORK

Woodstock
1797

RHODE ISLAND

Sharon
1796

Windsor
1792

Litchfield
1788–1790,
1791, 1796, 1798

Hartford
1791–1792

Bolton
1801

CONNECTICUT

New Milford
1789, 1790,
1791, 1796

Middletown
1792

Salem
1793

Norwich
1796

New
London

1785,
1792–
1793

Newtown
1790

Danbury
1790

New Haven
1774–1777

Easton
1795

Greenfield
Hill
1788, 1794–1795,
1797–1798

Fairfield
1788

Long Island Sound

Southold
1793, 1794

Stamford
1788,
1794–1795

Setauket
1793

LONG ISLAND

Huntington
1791–1792

Atlantic Ocean

Miles
0   20

CANADA

NEW
YORK

Niagara Falls
1799

VT.

N.H.

Bennington
1798,
1800

Troy
1798

Boston
1775,
1785

Area of
Detail

MASS.

Providence
1785

CONN.

R.I.

Miles
0   100

New York
1785–1788, 1789, 1790, 1794

© A. Karl / J. Kemp, 1991

1.20
Ralph Earl
Portrait of Silas Talbot, 1785
oil on canvas
36½ x 28 in. (92.7 x 71.1 cm.)
Location presently unknown. Copy
photograph from the William
Sawitzky Papers. Courtesy, The
New-York Historical Society,
New York.

During the monthlong voyage, Earl had the opportunity to learn from Trumbull of the political climate of postwar America, as well as hear news of his family, who continued to manage their farm in Paxton. Trumbull, a resident of Worcester, may even have informed Earl of the circumstances of his first wife, Sarah, and their two children, who, after Earl's departure, had continued to reside with her parents in Worcester.

During the voyage, Earl borrowed an unspecified amount of money from a fellow passenger, Levi Williard, a resident of Worcester County whom Earl may have previously known. (Williard would later sue Earl for repayment of the loan.) Earl may have required the money to help cover the cost of the voyage, surely a considerable amount for him to pay.[83]

While on board the *Neptune*, Earl occupied himself by painting a lively group portrait of the ship's captain, John Callahan (1744–1806), a well-known Boston shipmaster, with his wife, Lucretia Greene Callahan (1748–1824), and their two daughters, Abigail and Lucretia.[84] Executed on bed ticking (perhaps used because of a lack of linen canvas), the spirited family portrait conveys familial affection. The Callahans gave it to Joseph Trumbull "as a token of friendship"[85] and, in paying for it, assisted Earl with some much-needed income.

Earl remained in Boston for four or five months after his May 23 arrival.[86] The Revolution had drastically curtailed artistic activity in America; Earl found little competition upon his return and took advantage of the pent-up desire for portraits, painting while in Boston an accomplished portrait of Martha Spear Johnston (cat. 20), the wife of the Boston portrait painter John Johnston. As one of the few artists then working in the city,[87] Johnston may have wished to view a work by a more experienced painter. Earl's portrait of Johnston's wife is reminiscent of the relaxed, graceful poses found in the works of such English artists as George Romney, clearly indicating the artist's intention of introducing this fashionable portrait style to America. The subtle palette of soft colors enhanced by glazes and the delicate brush strokes convey the lessons he had learned in England.[88]

As his newspaper announcements imply, Earl intended to establish himself in New York City, then the liveliest urban center in America. Leaving Boston in the late summer or early fall, he stopped in Providence, Rhode Island, where he painted a portrait of Capt. Silas Talbot (1751–1815; fig. 1.20) – the first of an impressive number of commissions Earl received to paint military portraits of the recent heroes of the American Revolution. In his stirring portrayals Earl successfully invoked patriotic feeling. To paint Talbot, Earl drew on his British experience, using a pose similar to that seen in his portrait of Adm. Richard Kempenfelt (cat. 12). He shows Talbot in the uniform of the Rhode Island regiment in which he had valiantly served, wearing the eagle badge of the Society of the Cincinnati prominently displayed on his left lapel. The spyglass he holds in his right hand symbolizes his dual service in the army and navy. A receipt of October 21, 1785, indicates that Talbot paid Earl three pounds for "one portraiture of himself." This amount may not reflect the full payment Earl received, since he and his wife were frequently boarded by his sitters for several weeks while he completed their portraits; the Earls' living expenses, as well as artists' materials, were often accounted for separately in his subjects' business ledgers.[89]

Leaving Providence in late October, Earl traveled along the coastline on his way to New York (fig. 1.19), stopping briefly in New London, Connecticut, to paint a portrait of Bishop Samuel Seabury (1785; National Portrait Gallery, Washington, D.C.), the first consecrated bishop of the American Episcopal Church. Earl painted Seabury (1729–96) in his clerical robes shortly after Seabury had arrived at his new parish.[90]

1.21
Plan of the City of New York from the
New-York Register, 1789
Courtesy, American Antiquarian
Society, Worcester, Mass.

Having earned additional money from this and another portrait commission or two, Earl and his wife continued on their journey to New York.

Two years earlier, the portraitist Abraham Delanoy, Jr., had attempted to lease a house in then British-occupied New York with the intention of turning it into a paint shop. "Such matters will be in demand," he thought, "if we are once more to be blest with Peace."[91] Although he was not present to benefit from the later revival of the city, Delanoy's prophecy proved accurate. The Earls' arrival in New York in November 1785 coincided with its postwar economic recovery.[92] With the establishment of the Bank of New York in 1784 and the commercial development of maritime trade, particularly with the Caribbean, the economy rapidly improved. Fortuitously, as Earl was aware, the city became at this time the central political meeting place in America. In 1785 the U.S. Congress met at the city hall (later called Federal Hall), which meant that for the next five years, New York became the seat of government of the United States, the state, and the municipality. The New York State Legislature met at the Exchange Building, down Broad Street from the city hall, between 1784 and 1796. (Fig. 1.21 is a contemporary map of lower Manhattan.) Earl chose an opportune moment to establish himself as a portrait painter in this burgeoning urban center.

As he had in the past, Earl fashioned a portrait style to suit his subjects' status and social position. As his American career progressed, he would perceptively alter his style and technique, responding to the tastes and values of his patrons in the various regions to which he traveled. For his New York clients, Earl drew on his English experience.

The artist took the opportunity to use the newspapers (as he continued to do throughout his American career) to advertise his arrival. In late November he placed the following announcement. "Last Sunday arrived in town from England by way of Boston, Mr. Ralph Earl, a native of Massachusetts; he passed a number of years in London under those distinguished and most celebrated Masters in Painting, Sir Joshua Reynolds, Mr. West, and Mr. Copley. The gentleman now proposes to enter upon his profession in this city, where a specimen of his abilities may be seen by calling at Mr. Rivington's No. 1 Queen Street." James Rivington (c. 1724–1802), a newspaper publisher and bookseller who had attracted many artists to his establishment in the past, was a once-notorious Loyalist. An Englishman, Rivington arrived in America in 1760 and from 1773 to 1775 published a pro-Loyalist newspaper, *Rivington's New-York Gazette*, in which he attacked the revolutionary movement. In his next paper, the *New York Loyal Gazette*, his editorial position gradually shifted toward the side of independence. After the war, he gave up the publishing business and continued as a bookseller.[93]

Upon his arrival in New York, which had been a stronghold of Loyalism during the Revolution, Earl not only associated himself with a Loyalist but immediately painted a second Englishman, Thomas Barrow (1735–1825), who had also held firm to a Loyalist stance during the war years. Earl completed this portrait, his first known New York portrait (fig. 1.22), in May 1786, six months after his arrival.[94]

Barrow, like the majority of Earl's New York patrons, was closely associated with Trinity Episcopal Church, a Loyalist stronghold during the war and a Federalist stronghold afterward.[95] A well-known print dealer in the city, Barrow offered a broad range of artists' materials for sale and advertised that he would do "coach, house and sign painting."[96] Earl's portrait of Barrow, identified by the card in his hand, is, again, a tribute to the artist's English experience.

Three months after completing Barrow's portrait, Earl's promising start in New York came to an abrupt halt when he was sued by Levi Williard for nonpayment of the loan he had made on board the *Neptune*.[97] His inability to repay the loan clearly suggests his straitened financial circumstances. The minutes of the Mayor's Court of New York give a detailed account of the complicated legal events that ensued, beginning on August 3 at the city hall. Mayor James Duane of New York presided. Also involved with the trial were Richard Varick, the trial recorder; six aldermen; and Marinus Willett, the sheriff of New York, for many of whom Earl later painted portraits, including James Duane, Robert Troup, Richard Varick, Alexander Hamilton, Joseph Winter, and Marinus Willett (cat. 39).[98]

Almost concurrently with his own trial, Earl sued a New York bookdealer, Samuel Campbell, whose shop was located at 41 Hanover Street. To further complicate matters, on the same day, September 6, John Lockwood, a New York merchant, brought suit against Earl. The court records do not specify the monetary amounts of the various litigations (it is known, however, that Earl's debt at the time of his release from prison was less than twenty-five dollars). Nor is there any indication of the nature of Earl's suit against Samuel Campbell or of the resolution of the case. It is clear that Earl was jailed in connection with Lockwood's suit. Having failed to appear at the hearing, he was ordered to pay forty shillings within seven days. Earl was in prison, evidently unable to pay the forty-shilling fine, by the time Williard's suit was brought to court for the second time, on October 26. An inventory of Earl's effects at the time of his imprisonment should have been made and submitted to the court; however, no such document has been found.[99]

Earl was imprisoned in the city hall, on the corner of Wall and Nassau streets, from

1.22
Ralph Earl
Portrait of Thomas Barrow, 1786
oil on canvas
30 x 25 in. (76.2 x 63.5 cm.)
Location presently unknown. Copy
photograph from the William
Sawitzky Papers. Courtesy, The
New-York Historical Society,
New York.

September 1786 to January 1788. The city hall functioned as the center of political
and judicial life in New York, housing the courtroom, hosting the U.S. Congress from
1785 to 1790, functioning as the capitol for the state, and housing a library.[100] Crimi-
nals were jailed in the basement, and debtors were jailed in the attic, from the dormer
windows of which prisoners "used to hang out old shoes and bags to solicit alms of the
passers by."[101]

During the unsettled years following the British evacuation of New York, an individual who was unable to repay a modest debt was commonly jailed. Most debtors
could not obtain their release from jail because they had no means of earning the money
to repay the debt. As a further encumbrance, jailed debtors were responsible for paying
their own living expenses and, if they were heads of household, those of their family.
Thus debtors could remain in prison indefinitely unless assisted by relatives or friends.

The untenable position of debtors inspired a group of New Yorkers to form the
Society for the Relief of Distressed Debtors. Most of the twenty-four members (later
including George Washington) were prominent political and judicial figures who fre-
quented the city hall. The society functioned as a voluntary, charitable organization
whose purpose was to improve the debtors' living conditions while in prison, minimize
the corrupting impact of the miserable conditions, and improve the debtors' chances
for release from jail. The society met monthly and formed a committee of three to visit
the jail and "administer to the comfort of prisoners, by providing food, fuel, clothing,

and the necessaries of life" and "procure the liberation of such as were confined for small sums, and were of meritorious conduct, by discharging their debts."[102]

Shocked by what they saw in the city hall jail, the committee made the following report.

> *The members . . . have observed a large number of persons confined within the walls of the Gaol, deprived of the comfort of their families, prevented from the opportunity of obtaining the means of subsistence by their own industry, subjected to the danger arising from putrid and contagious disorders occasioned by crowded rooms and corrupted air, and liable to become useless if not pernicious members of society from the great danger they are in of acquiring habits of intemperance and debauchery while attempting to drown the recollection of their present misfortunes and distresses by the excessive use of spiritous liquors. The memorialist{s} are persuaded that the existence of these evils will be fully conceived when it is considered that from the end of January, 1787, to the 3rd of December, 1788, there have been 1162 commitments to the jail . . . for debt.*

They were instrumental in liberalizing the debtor laws, largely through the passage of the Act for the Relief of Insolvent Debtors on April 13, 1786, which provided a humane system for prisoners of small debts to obtain their release.[103] Earl gained his freedom through this act. In 1791 the society managed to have a law passed forbidding alcohol in the prison.[104]

Ralph Earl was a perfect candidate for the attention of this illustrious group, for he and his family faced a desperate situation. Ann Earl had to fend for herself during his imprisonment. There is some indication that she stayed at the boardinghouse of John Clark at 33 Broad Street, near the city hall, and she apparently worked as a shopkeeper on Broadway. Ann gave birth to a son, Ralph E. W. Earl, in 1785 or 1788 and a daughter, Mary Ann Earl, on August 31, 1787.[105] Since Earl was not released from prison until the following January, he was evidently allowed visitation privileges with his wife.

The society devised an ingenious plan that allowed Earl to continue his profession as a portrait painter while in prison, sending their wives, children, and friends to the jail to sit for their portraits. Earl's earnings were held in trust until he had accumulated enough money to obtain his release. The society's battle against alcohol in the jail came too late for Earl, however. During his confinement, Earl suffered the "evils" described above, and he probably succumbed then to the intemperate habits of which he was accused by later biographers. His drinking not only hindered the advancement of his career but did little to enhance a reputation already tarnished by his disloyalty to his country, by his bigamy, and by his indebtedness. Alcoholism eventually caused his death.[106]

The attention Earl received from the members of the Society for the Relief of Distressed Debtors is not surprising, considering how rare his talent as an artist was in post-revolutionary America. Earl was the most gifted portrait painter in New York. The only other artist of note, Joseph Wright, arrived in 1786, hoping, like Earl, to take advantage of the presence of the U.S. Congress. He painted without great success until 1790 (after Earl's departure), when he received several important commissions, resulting in his portraits of Frederick Augustus Muhlenberg (1790; National Portrait Gallery, Washington, D.C.) and Benjamin Goodhue (1790; private collection).[107] William Dunlap, who returned from England to New York in 1787, found Wright to be his neighbor on Queen Street. "I was installed as a portrait-painter in my father's house, and had sitters; but I felt my own ignorance, and felt the superiority of Joseph Wright, who was my next door neighbor, and painting with but little success as to emolument.

By degrees my employers became fewer . . . and after a year or two [I] abandoned painting." [108] Of the three artists, Earl received by far the largest number of important commissions, in spite of his unsavory circumstances.

As the twenty known portraits from this period demonstrate, Earl's New York patrons were associated in their political, religious, and professional lives. Several had first encountered the artist through their respective roles in the Mayor's Court of New York. Most attended Trinity Episcopal Church where several served as vestrymen. Their families intermarried. The majority had held conservative political views during the Revolution, but most of the men had served as officers in the Continental Army and were instrumental in establishing a number of organizations after the war, including the military association called the Society of the Cincinnati, as well as the many humanitarian and beneficent societies that developed in the republican era. In fact, the most immediate bond linking Earl's patrons was their shared membership in the Society for the Relief of Distressed Debtors. [109] They naturally gravitated toward the Federalist party. Alexander Hamilton, who established the party, and James Duane, then mayor of New York, typify the group.

James Duane, who had presided over Earl's trial and who was an active member of the society to aid debtors, was one of the first to commission portraits from the imprisoned artist. He is said to have commissioned two portraits of Maj. Gen. Baron Friedrich von Steuben (cat. 21), one of which he kept in his possession, the other remaining with von Steuben. His wife, Mary Livingston Duane (fig. 1.23), also sat for Earl, wearing an elaborate purple dress with a white lace collar and a blue neck ribbon; she is seated in an elegant red upholstered chair with a generalized landscape in the distance. James Duane noted in his daybook on April 19, 1787, that he "pd. Ralph Earl for portrait of my wife, ten pounds," [110] an indication of Earl's income for his prison portraits.

Earl's portrait of Elizabeth Schuyler Hamilton (cat. 22) is nearly identical in composition to that of her close friend Mary Duane. Earl took particular care in the execution of this portrait of an influential patron and strikingly handsome woman, transcending his surroundings to produce a sensuous bust-length presentation. Once again he demonstrates the technical finesse and fashionable compositional elements he acquired while in London. Here, as with other portraits Earl painted of the wives and children of members of the Society for the Relief of Distressed Debtors, an assessment suggests the distinct possibility that Earl was given a studio room apart from the squalor of his prison surroundings, suitable for sittings for his distinguished patrons.

A great number of Earl's commissions for portraits while in prison came from members of the Society of the Cincinnati. Duane, for instance, was made an honorary member of the Society of the Cincinnati, which von Steuben had helped form. It is ironic, considering Earl's former Loyalist leanings, that a society made up of American war heroes provided Earl with an opportunity to tap a new market for portrait commissions in postwar America.

The society was first established in Newburgh, New York, on March 10, 1783, by a group of officers of the Continental Army led by von Steuben, Gen. Henry Knox and Col. Jedediah Huntington; George Washington was named the society's first president. Named for the Roman patriot Titus Quinctius Cincinnatus of the fifth century B.C., the society restricted its members to officers of the Continental Army and their eldest male offspring. An official medal, designed in the form of an eagle, was to be worn on the left lapel. The officers were concerned that with the disbanding of the army, they would be unable to protect their interests, for issues such as back pay and pensions

1.23
Ralph Earl
Mrs. James Duane, 1787
oil on canvas
36 x 26¾ in. (91.4 x 68.0 cm.)
Courtesy, The New-York Historical Society, New York. Purchased
by the Society, 1948.55.

had not yet been addressed by the newly formed government. Because of its exclusive nature and obvious self-interests, many Americans feared that the society would
come to represent an aristocratic military nobility. In fact, it did come to be associated
with the Federalist party, but the commonly held perception of an aristocratic destiny
proved unfounded.[111]

A national organization composed of politically prominent figures, the society welcomed the opportunity to have official portraits made; the portraits would add an important element of prestige to the group and document the members' historical significance. Earl painted portraits of six members during his prison years.[112] Drawing on his
previous English experience, he embodied in these portraits the sense of achievement
expected of military heroes, thereby enhancing their special status.

In general, Earl's New York portraits demonstrate an accomplished style, for which
the artist favored the fashionable bust-length and three-quarter-length formats, painting loosely executed, elegant images of his distinguished subjects. His conventional
compositions show little inspiration, given his presumable restriction to the vicinity of
the jail. Earl abandons landscape features in these portraits and, for most of his works,
uses a stock English chair, most likely created from memory.[113]

Through the efforts of the debt-relief society, Earl eventually earned enough money painting portraits to petition for his release. He was also aided by the passage of the law, drafted by society members and passed by the legislature in 1788, that allowed people with a debt of less than twenty-five dollars to be released after thirty days. In line with the Act for the Relief of Insolvent Debtors, a notice of the artist's impending release was published in the newspaper, requesting Earl's creditors to appear at the offices of the judge of the Mayor's Court if they wanted to raise any objections. Earl was released on January 29, 1788, into the custody of his court-appointed guardian, Dr. Mason Fitch Cogswell.[114]

The Cogswells—in particular Mason Fitch Cogswell (1768–1830), his brother James Cogswell (1746–92), and James's wife, Abigail Floyd Cogswell (1750–1831)—played an essential role in helping Earl reestablish his reputation and career. The Cogswell brothers, founding members of the society for debt relief, were physicians in New York when the artist came to their attention.

Mason and James were the sons of the Rev. James Cogswell (fig. 1.29) and Alice Fitch Cogswell of Scotland, Connecticut, both of whom were members of notable Connecticut families with important social connections. The brothers had been stationed in Stamford, Connecticut, during the war, where James was the examining surgeon of volunteers and Mason was his apprentice. After the war, they formed a partnership at 219 Queen Street, New York, advertising themselves in the city directory as "surgeon and apothecary."

It is ironic that the Cogswells, Earl's rescuers, epitomized the pietistic New England society from which he had fled as a young man. Adhering to the puritanical beliefs preached by their father, they led restrained and simple lives despite their wealth and social position. Although Earl remained in New York for a time after his release from prison, painting portraits of prominent New Yorkers,[115] he was drawn back to New England through his connections with the Cogswells. There he would spend the remainder of his career, painting profoundly perceptive images of this rural society. He had strayed far from the religious and cultural tenets of his youth, but his deep understanding of those values enabled him to communicate them in his Connecticut portraits, his masterpieces.

"His paintings seem to start them into life"
— Advertisement, *Litchfield Weekly Monitor*

**Connecticut Years:
Pattern of Patronage**

Earl's release from debtors' prison marked a turning point in his career. At the age of thirty-seven, he was, surprisingly, one of the most accomplished artists in America. Yet his ambition to succeed in his chosen profession had resulted in a downward spiral in his personal life. To salvage his reputation and regain financial stability for himself and his family, Earl modified his artistic ambitions, moving further away from his earlier English experience. He abandoned his plan to remain near the center of political life in America; unlike most of his colleagues, he did not follow the Congress when it moved from New York to Philadelphia in 1790. Instead, accepting the counsel and assistance of his guardian, he left New York to ply his trade as an itinerant artist in the agriculturally based society of Connecticut. He found his greatest success in this region, where he painted for the next ten years (fig. 1.19).

Earl's career, from this point on, diverged markedly from the careers of his American colleagues, particularly those who, like Earl, had the benefit of artistic instruction with Benjamin West in London. His distinctiveness is most clearly seen in a comparison with his more famous contemporaries, Charles Willson Peale, John Trumbull, and Gilbert Stuart. These artists courted an international audience, devoting themselves to portraits and history paintings of national import. To achieve their goal, they positioned themselves in major urban centers. Peale painted life portraits of George Washington, as well as portraits of many other heroes of the American Revolution, for his newly established museum in Philadelphia, which opened to the American public in 1786. At about the same time, Trumbull gathered life portraits for his series of large-scale canvases of the events of the Revolution, which were intended for mass distribution as engravings. Gilbert Stuart returned to America in 1793 with the intention of painting President Washington's portrait to further enhance his own international reputation. Stuart's "Vaughan," "Landsdowne," and "Atheneum" portraits of Washington, painted in a new style, became icons for the new nation. The works of these artists helped to forge a national identity for the new republic.[116]

Earl himself furthered the formation of a national imagery by portraying a segment of American society that had never before received the attention of a trained and highly gifted artist. His contribution to the development of American art functioned at a different level from that of Peale, Trumbull, and Stuart, for he did not seek a national audience. His works nonetheless hold an equal value in their ability to capture—for his New England audience and for future generations—the spirit of the age in which he worked. Earl chose to move away from the artistic centers of the day and abandon the formality of a studio setting, to follow an itinerant life-style and confront his conservative, rural patrons face to face in their own environment and on their own terms.

The catalyst for the shift in Earl's career and patronage was Mason Fitch Cogswell. The invaluable friendship between Earl and Cogswell was much like that of the artist's earlier relationship with John Money. In his role as Earl's financial and perhaps spiritual guardian, Cogswell managed to convince the artist to offer his talents in Connecticut, feeling perhaps that away from the city, Earl could overcome his previous failings and thereby gain some stability for his family.

Cogswell moved back to Connecticut from New York, assuring his pious father that "I feel more and more rejoiced that I am away from that noisy tumultuous City. I find even here temptations sufficient to invite one from the time of their duty. . . . I well know that I am always surrounded by temptations . . . and that I am constantly in need of . . . the influences of restraining Grace to preserve that temper of mind which is particularly necessary for my well being here and hereafter."[117] Cogswell settled in Hartford, a decision inspired by a journey he took in the fall of 1787 in search of a new place to establish himself. Hartford proved an attractive and flourishing town with numerous cultural amenities. Through his family connections, he could hope to build a sound medical practice.

By the late 1700s an intricate web of kinship relations had linked the leading families of Connecticut for two centuries, Cogswell's among them, as the visits he made, entered in his diary, illustrate. Cogswell was closely tied to these families and well known to them—the Dwights, Trumbulls, Huntingtons, Wadsworths, and Wolcotts who lived in various towns in Fairfield County, New Haven, Middletown, and Hartford.[118]

Earl took advantage of Cogswell's impressive connections in the state, anticipating the advantages of the entrée he would receive with Cogswell's sanction. Since Cogswell was the son of a prominent minister and the nephew of the then governor of the state, he could vouch for Earl's suitability as a portrait painter; he could assure Earl's conservative patrons that the artist was a "mighty plain, peaceable man." His own role as a trusted and respected physician also placed him in an ideal position to recommend Earl as a portrait painter, for he dealt with families at times of birth, illness, and death, occasions when portraits are frequently commissioned. As a careful study of his account books reveals, all of Earl's Connecticut patrons for the next ten years, with few exceptions, were Cogswell's patients. There is much additional evidence to suggest that Cogswell functioned as a tastemaker in Connecticut, recommending to his patients, relations, and friends appropriate artists besides Earl to paint their portraits.[119]

More than any other artist of the time, Earl was qualified to create an appropriate style to satisfy the aesthetic sensibilities of his Connecticut subjects. His English experience proved a valuable asset, allowing him to impress his patrons with his technical skills and stylish compositions. Yet it was the artist's roots in Worcester County that allowed him to comprehend fully the restrained tastes, republican virtues, and pious values of the Connecticut inhabitants. He achieved the desired effect in his portraits by a deliberate rejection of British aristocratic imagery, cleverly tempering his academic style to suit his subjects' modest pretensions.

The dramatic visual change that took place in Earl's portraits upon his move from New York to Connecticut is best understood by studying the distinctiveness of each society to which Earl catered so insightfully. Even though his New York and Connecticut sitters came from the upper and middle classes, they wished to be perceived in quite different ways in their portraits. In New York, Earl had served a worldly, well-born, Episcopalian community, the political and social leaders of a major urban center. Earl responded in his portraits to his subjects' genteel perception of themselves, creating images that convey worldliness, sensuality, affluence, and social position. Several decades later, the New York poet Fitz Hugh Halleck articulated to the artist Edward Hicks a sentiment similar to that of Earl's New York patrons. "I want you to paint me so that I shall look like a gentleman. Never mind the likeness. In fifty years nobody will be able to tell whether the portrait is a likeness or not; but I want to be handed down to posterity as a gentleman."[120]

Like their New York counterparts, many of Earl's Connecticut patrons descended from the founding families of the state and maintained tight control of the political, commercial, and religious leadership. In Connecticut, however, Earl also catered to members of a broader social spectrum, perceptively defined by Richard L. Bushman (chapter 2) as the second-rank leaders who became the new Standing Order, families with rural roots who replaced the River Gods, or the old Standing Order, of the colonial era. Most were well educated; an extraordinary number were graduates of Yale College. To a greater degree than in New York, they had espoused patriotic sentiments during the Revolution. Although many later became members of their state chapter of the Society of the Cincinnati, here the portraits present one visual contrast with those of the New York members of this society. Earl's numerous New York patrons chose to be depicted in full military regalia, wearing the eagle badge. In Connecticut, however, membership in the society was rarely indicated, probably because the society was highly unpopular among the populace. The only exception occurs in Earl's portrait of Capt. John Pratt (cat. 43), painted in Middletown in 1792.

Earl successfully created an appealing balance of traditional and fashionable elements. By blending some of the stylized components of English portraiture, such as the backdrop of red drapery to enhance a subject's importance, Earl's compositions retain certain emblems of social status. Still, his Connecticut portraits are more noteworthy for their departure from pure English convention.

To achieve the desired effect (and perhaps, to some degree, taking advantage of his less discriminating patrons), Earl employed a markedly simplified technique. He may also have been adapting to the lack of certain artists' materials in some of the rural towns he painted in (see chapter 3) as well as to the varied locations for sittings, many of which took place in his sitters' homes. Earl abandoned subtle modeling and the application of layers of warm glazing over a palette of pastel colors, used in his London and New York portraits; instead, he favored a palette of broadly applied primary colors, especially brilliant reds and greens, and the creation of patterned surfaces. His brushwork altered too: departing from the quick, short strokes evident in his English works, Earl employed long, linear strokes in his Connecticut portraits.

In representing objects, Earl returned to elements characteristic of Copley's American portraits: an emphasis on verisimilitude (particularly trompe l'oeil illusionism), linearity, strong coloring, and precise execution. For the most part, Earl forsook the stylish bust-length format of his New York portraits, choosing rather the now-antiquated, full-length format. Life-size images, which required lengthy sittings, continued to be preferred in Connecticut long after this scale had gone out of fashion in urban American centers. The desire for a life-size portrait may reflect the value placed on a literal translation of the sitter's appearance; Earl, comprehending this desire, created portraits so convincing in their realism that they seemed to "start them into life."

Earl honored the predilection for a lifelike appearance in his depictions of his Connecticut subjects, as is evident in the many stern, penetrating likenesses that avoid flattery. A young patient of Cogswell's, afraid of dying from consumption, expressed this desire for a lifelike portrait. "I wish very much to have my likeness taken. . . . My earnest request is that if you know a limner that would take a *likeness* (I do not want a picture without) that [you] would encourage him to come to Norwich."[121]

Earl encountered his subjects directly in their own surroundings, hence, perhaps, the startling realism. Throughout his Connecticut years, Earl and his family boarded at local taverns or, on occasion, stayed with clients.[122] Thus he lacked a formal studio, where he could retain control of the furnishings, backdrops, and scenery. The compositions were necessarily personalized, reflecting both the artist's talents and inclinations and the sitters' wishes.

Earl's Connecticut subjects were distinguished from those in New York by their religious affiliation: nearly all were Congregationalists. Whereas they aspired to a certain social standing, they adhered, for the most part, to a modest life-style.

Like Chandler before him, Earl continued the tradition of Connecticut portraiture that showed subjects in their own environment. Earl added specific regional details, most likely at the suggestion of his sitters. The pride his patrons felt in their regional identity, whether their home was Litchfield County, New London Harbor, or the Connecticut River Valley, is reinforced through the depiction of a subject's house and surrounding lands, rooms within the house, and personal possessions of local origin.[123]

Earl referred to his Connecticut subjects' newly won citizenship by including emblems of the new nation in his portraits, his response to the sitters' awareness of the historical significance of the period. He painted in copies of the recently ratified Constitution, sites signifying the founding of the state or nation, newly made furnishings incorporating Federal forms, and references to patriotic endeavors.

As an extension of their growing sense of nationhood, Earl's sitters felt a pride in the physical beauty of their state. Earl conveys this pride of place by putting elaborate regional landscapes in the backgrounds of his portraits. Similar sentiments were echoed by visitors to the state, including Jean Pierre Brissot de Warville, who, in 1790, commented on Connecticut's natural beauty and agricultural economy.

Nature and art have here displayed all their treasures; it is really the paradise of the United States. The state owes all its advantages to its situation. It is a fertile plain, enclosed between two mountains which render difficult its communications by land with the other states. It is watered by the superb Connecticut River, safe and easy to navigate, which flows into the sea. The riches of this state are here more equally divided, since they are based on agriculture. There is here more virtue, less misery, more of everything which constitutes republicanism.[124]

The Connecticut sitters, unlike the New York sitters, were tied to the land, and most continued to follow an agrarian way of life. Although they pursued political and other professional careers, they maintained large landholdings and working farms. The residents of Connecticut not only took pride in the beauty of the landscape but sought to acquire a portion of it, for landownership bespoke status. The "riches of this state" were not as equally divided as de Warville perceived them to be. Earl's patrons were large landowners, and for them, personal adornment, cultural affectation, and houses were not quite so important as well-groomed acres. One of the most distinctive features of Earl's Connecticut portraits is the landscape views, townscapes, and representations of houses that fill the backgrounds.

In 1788, the year of his release from prison, Earl began his Connecticut career. He undoubtedly arrived in Fairfield County with letters of introduction from Mason Fitch Cogswell, for he straightaway painted ten portraits of Cogswell's relations and friends there.[125] His portraits of the wealthy Fairfield County merchants, farmers, lawyers, doctors, and their families exemplify the stylistic changes that took place in his works after his departure from New York. The portrait of Cogswell's relative Judge Abraham Davenport (fig. 1.24) of Stamford is a fine example of the life-size scale, directness of approach, and verisimilitude that Earl now employed, reminiscent of his early portrait of Roger Sherman (cat. 5). Earl here does not attempt to soften the effects of age, allowing light to strike the face of his subject, who died the following year.[126]

In nearby Fairfield, Earl painted Cogswell's friend and professional associate Dr. David Rogers (cat. 23) and his wife, Martha Tennent Rogers, and their child (cat. 24). Using a bright palette of broadly applied primary colors, Earl captured lively likenesses of his handsome subjects. David Rogers is shown with his library of individually titled medical books behind him. In an attempt to professionalize the practice of medicine, the medical community organized as a formal group after the Revolution. Both Cogswell and Rogers helped found this organization of leading physicians, the Connecticut Medical Society. Martha Rogers, modestly attired, is depicted in an appropriate gender role for a woman at this time – as the image of maternal affection.[127]

In Greenfield Hill, Earl encountered Timothy and Mary Dwight (whom he had painted more than ten years earlier in New Haven). The Rev. Timothy Dwight currently served as the town minister. A prominent member of the literary coterie the Connecticut Wits, he became a spokesman for his era, traveling throughout his native state and beyond and writing of the regional consciousness he sensed among its inhabitants. His prose and such poems as *Greenfield Hill*, in which he praises the rural character and republican virtues of his hometown and its residents, provide a verbal counterpart to Earl's Connecticut portraits.

At the end of 1788 or early in 1789, Earl and his family traveled inland to the northwestern corner of the state, where he first painted in the Litchfield County towns of New Milford and Litchfield, as well as in the nearby Fairfield County towns of Newtown and Danbury. As the first artist to travel to this area, he was welcomed by the affluent local citizens, obtaining enough commissions to occupy himself there for at least two years.

Earl was drawn to Litchfield County through the connections of his guardian, Mason Fitch Cogswell, who had many friends and some patients in these towns.[128] Litchfield, in particular, as the leading town in the county, had many ties with Hartford, thirty miles to the east. Because of its inland location, Litchfield served as an important military storage center during the Revolution and suffered little from the war. By 1795, Litchfield had become the fourth largest town in the state. The first law school in the new nation was established there by Tapping Reeve in 1784, and one of the country's first schools of higher education for women was founded there by Sarah Pierce in 1792. The leading families of Litchfield had played important roles during the Revolution and later became state and national leaders in government and commerce.

One Litchfield resident, Oliver Wolcott, Sr., lieutenant governor of the state, was present on January 4, 1788, at the convention held in Hartford to debate the ratification of the new federal Constitution. As one of several men to deliver pleas in its favor,

Wolcott was instrumental in making Connecticut the fifth state to ratify it. Earl's presence in Litchfield in the following year undoubtedly inspired Wolcott to commission portraits of himself and his family at this important historic moment.

Earl depicted Oliver Wolcott (cat. 25) in a formal setting that clearly portrays his subject's role as an advocate of the new Constitution. Wolcott rests his hand on a copy of the Constitution, and he is seated next to a fluted column. Earl was careful to convey the social prominence of the Wolcott family in his portraits of Oliver's wife, Laura Collins Wolcott (cat. 26), and their daughter Mariann Wolcott (cat. 27), both women of beauty and intelligence. Here Earl returned to his interest in landscapes, painting the Wolcotts' house in the background of Laura Wolcott's portrait (a whimsical device – the subject is seated in the very same home – found in other Connecticut portraits by Earl) and placing Mariann Wolcott in a setting of cultivated fields, the Shepaug River that runs through the town behind her. In his English and American portraits alike, Earl favored landscapes as appropriate settings for women.

While in Litchfield, Earl painted the Congregational minister, the Rev. Judah Champion (fig. 1.25). A graduate of Yale College, Champion (1729–1810) is surrounded in his portrait by such references to his learned background as his impressive library of books and writing implements.[129] In a bit of illusionism Champion's left foot is shown stepping off the floorboards, seemingly out of the plane of the picture. In addition, Earl painted a simulated molded frame on which he insinuates areas of red bole (the priming layer of a frame) underneath a gilt surface.

Earl undoubtedly impressed his Litchfield patrons with his ability to capture a good likeness, with his skill in rendering fabrics and furnishings, with his ability as a landscape artist, and with his whimsical compositional elements that included startling trompe l'oeil details. It is also likely that he charmed his subjects with his amiable personality. His reputation spread to nearby New Milford, where he found a somewhat less affluent and less publicly prominent citizenry than in Litchfield. In this small agrarian community, Earl painted an extraordinary number of portraits during the decade he spent in Connecticut, many of which rank among his finest works.

New Milford was settled in the early decades of the eighteenth century by a handful of families; chief among them were the town's first minister, the Rev. Daniel Boardman, and the town's second minister, the Rev. Nathaniel Taylor.[130] Earl eventually painted nineteen descendants of the Boardman and Taylor families, providing a unique family and artistic record. Earl's portraits documented the prominent role the Boardmans and Taylors assumed in the post-revolutionary era, capturing their handsome visages, their intellectual pursuits, their personal possessions, their newly built mansion houses, their extensive landholdings, and their businesses.

Once again Earl demonstrated his virtuosity as a landscape painter, not just his obvious skill in portraiture, as well as amazed his viewers with convincing passages of illusionism. Because Earl was the first artist to travel to New Milford, local families overcame whatever reservations they might have had concerning the suitability of having their portraits painted. Instead, taking advantage of the unique opportunity, they encouraged Earl's best efforts.

Among Earl's initial portraits in New Milford were those of the four children and one daughter-in-law of Sherman and Sarah Boardman, painted in 1789 and 1790. The Boardmans had raised their children on a substantial farm they called Maryland, situated on the Housatonic River. Earl demonstrated the full range of his artistic skills in his series of portraits of the Boardman family. His remarkable full-length portraits of the two elder sons, Daniel and Elijah Boardman (cats. 28, 29) convey, among other

1.25
Ralph Earl
The Reverend Judah Champion, 1789
oil on canvas
73 x 52 ½ in. (185.4 x 133.4 cm.)
The Litchfield Historical Society,
Litchfield, Conn.

things, the prosperity of the brothers' business partnership. Elegantly attired, Daniel stands in a graceful pose, with an expansive view of New Milford filling the background. This view of the thriving town center may have symbolized the extensive landholdings the brothers had acquired by this time, making them, along with their father, among the highest taxpayers in the town.

Elijah Boardman is portrayed in the brothers' shop on Town Street. Here Earl ingeniously applied his virtuosity at trompe l'oeil effects, portraying the full-length figure of Elijah walking off the floorboards, seemingly out of the picture. This treatment, along with the illusionary space created by the two doors – one opening forward into the front room and the second opening backward to reveal the storage room beyond – suggests this work as an antecedent of Charles Willson Peale's more famous full-length trompe l'oeil *Staircase Group* (1795; Philadelphia Museum of Art). Both Peale and Earl wished to impress their respective viewers with their virtuosity in creating such old-fashioned but still-valued illusionary effects.

The portrait of Elijah Boardman is innovative in its literal depiction of a merchant at work in his drygoods store, displaying his merchandise. Merchants had more traditionally been painted as gentlemen, in domestic settings, occasionally at a desk handling receipts. The Boardman portrait is far less pretentious, serving in a way as an advertisement for the latest shipment of fabrics, some of which were imported, as is clearly indicated by the prominent British tax stamp. Furthermore, as Aileen Ribeiro observes in the Catalogue, "Elijah Boardman, dressed with formal elegance, is a visible sartorial testimony to the fine fabrics on sale in his shop."

Earl's additional portraits of the Boardman children are equally skillful in their rendering. Esther Boardman (cat. 30), painted at the age of twenty-seven, is portrayed in Earl's favored format for young women: seated on a hillside. In this instance, however, Earl includes a detailed view of the town center, similar to the one in the portrait of her brother Daniel, symbolizing the prominent role the Boardman family had played in the development of New Milford.

Not to be outdone by the Boardmans, the Taylor family commissioned Earl to paint a similar series of portraits beginning in 1789. In assessing the two groups of family portraits, one sees Earl's effort to create novel compositions for each work. In his highly personalized renditions of the Taylor family he successfully conveys their stature in the town.

Earl painted the patriarch of the family, the Rev. Nathaniel Taylor (cat. 31) at the time of his retirement as town minister, a position he had held for fifty-two years. In Earl's conservative rendition, Nathaniel is shown in his New Milford meetinghouse, standing at his pulpit and resting his hand on a Bible. His wife, Tamar Taylor (cat. 32), sixty-six at the time, is depicted without flattery. Just as her husband's portrait celebrates his life as a clergyman, Tamar's shows her in a domestic environment, conservatively attired. The view of the meetinghouse through the window symbolizes her role as the wife of the present minister and the daughter of the town's first minister. The house in the background is probably the Taylors' house, which was just north of the meetinghouse on Town Street.

Earl devised less formal, livelier compositions for the Taylors' grown children; his finest efforts for the family are seen in the portraits *Colonel William Taylor* and *Mrs. William Taylor and Son Daniel* (cats. 33, 34). A war hero and recent recipient of a master's degree from Yale College, William Taylor was a successful merchant in New Milford. He is shown engaged in his avocation as an amateur landscape painter. Landscape painting continued to be rare in America until the second quarter of the nineteenth century.[131] One certainly would not have expected to find an amateur practitioner in this remote region, but perhaps Earl himself provided instruction.

Earl employs an ingenious composition for his portrait of Tamar and Daniel Taylor to convey maternal affection. He relates the two figures on a parallel plane by placing the two-year-old boy in a Windsor high chair. The mother affectionately grasps the bare foot of her son, who is holding a pet cat.

In a sharp departure from his large-scale portraits of the leading New Milford families, Earl painted a conversation piece, *Angus Nickelson and Family* (cat. 35), in 1790. A Scottish immigrant who had also lived in England, Angus Nickelson was a new-comer to town and would have been familiar with this popular form of English family portraiture. Earl had also been exposed to this genre while in Norwich, where the conversation-piece format continued to be employed by local artists into the 1780s, after it had gone out of fashion in London.[132] In this portrait the stiffly posed figures and evident changes by the artist suggest Earl's discomfort with the conversation-piece format, which required working on a small scale with multiple figures. Earl stressed his patron's hard-earned affluence by carefully rendering the fashionably attired daughters of the family and the elaborate furnishings.

In this remarkably productive year Earl traveled to both Newtown and Danbury, where he painted a number of fine portraits, including one of the local merchant David Baldwin (fig. 1.26) and, most noteworthy, one of the Rev. Nehemiah Strong (cat. 36). Having previously painted Strong's portrait in New Haven, Earl offered to paint a second portrait, which, as Strong suggested to Ezra Stiles, then president of Yale College, would be "a Fairer Specimen of his Skill and improvement in his Art."[133] Earl produced a startlingly realistic portrayal of Strong that provides further evidence of the predilection for a true likeness. Here Earl has accentuated his subject's severe skin disease, seen in the bright red discoloration of the face and hands. Earl concentrated on conveying Strong's intellectual interests in astronomy and mathematics. This was an important commission for the artist, for he intended to present the portrait as a gift to Yale College on the condition that it hang in a prominent location in the library. It was accepted by the college and hung in the year of its completion, 1790.

Until this time, Earl had not felt the need to advertise his presence in the various towns to which he had traveled. His association with Mason Fitch Cogswell accounted for the ease with which he gained access to patrons, and as the first artist to appear in the region, he faced virtually no competition. Nonetheless, on a return visit to Litch-field in the summer of 1790, Earl placed the following announcement, likely an effort to encourage additional commissions.

> *To the Patrons of the Fine Arts, The Portrait Paintings by Mr. Earl, in this town, do him honor as an American and as an artist of great taste and ingenuity — Connoisseurs in this truly noble and refined art, pronounce several of his performances the most masterly ever exhibited in the U.S. Mr. Earl was pupil to the celebrated West; and acquired great reputation in London by his pencil; — and possessing a lively imagination, and pure talent in the principles of his profession, we cannot doubt, and hope, that in this age of refinement, the well-born and well-bred of his countrymen will patronize him in the road to Fame. Some of his paintings are admirably finished; and display that similarity and expression, as would seem to start them into life — though inanimate they speak.*[134]

Earl was careful to identify himself as an American before boasting of his reputation in London. He flattered his "well-born and well-bred" fellow citizens, urging them to patronize him "in this age of refinement." Appealing to their conservative aesthetic values, he stressed his ability to capture portrayals so convincing that they would seem to speak.

1.26
Ralph Earl
David Baldwin, 1790
oil on canvas
57 x 62 ¼ in. (144.8 x 158.1 cm.)
Collection High Museum of Art,
Atlanta. Purchase in honor of Lawrence L. Gellerstedt, Jr., President
of the Board of Directors of the
High Museum of Art with funds
given by Alfred Austell Thornton
in memory of Leila Austell Thornton and Albert Edward Thornton, Sr., and Sarah Miller Venable
and William Hoyt Venable.

In Litchfield, Earl painted *Colonel Benjamin Tallmadge and Son William Tallmadge* (cat. 37) and *Mrs. Benjamin Tallmadge and Son Henry Floyd and Daughter Maria Jones* (cat. 38), portraits of an affluent merchant and his wife, both of whom had been raised in prominent Long Island families and had only recently moved to Litchfield. Here, deviating somewhat from the style of his Connecticut portraits, Earl abandoned all sense of restraint, creating aristocratic images of his elegantly attired subjects and even including a reference to Benjamin Tallmadge's membership in the Society of the Cin-cinnati – the eagle badge on his left lapel. As mentioned earlier, few of Earl's Connecti-cut subjects who were members of the society chose to be depicted wearing the society badge, but the Tallmadges, who were relative newcomers to the state, evidently felt no constraint about appearing aristocratic in their portraits.

During this period, Earl demonstrated his extraordinary versatility, perceptively capturing the typically austere aesthetic of another Connecticut sitter in his portrait *Mrs. John Watson* (fig. 1.27). Painted a year before her death, Bethia Tyler Watson (1708–92) is attired in a sober black gown, signifying her status as a widow. After the death of her husband in 1781, Watson moved from Hartford to Litchfield, where she

spent her final years. In her portrait, she holds a pair of spectacles and rests her hand on a large family Bible, which is open to 1 Kings. The view through the window represents Great Pond (now Bantam Lake), with Litchfield and the church spire in the distance. Bethia Watson was buried the following year in the Old East Cemetery that borders the lake.[135]

Besides assuming the role of leading Connecticut artist, Earl frequently returned to New York City and also traveled to Long Island nearly every year between 1789 and 1794. His New York portraits, in particular, continue to show startling differences in composition and technique from those painted in Connecticut, stylistic changes best demonstrated in his grand-scale portrait *Marinus Willett* (cat. 39). Willet's graceful pose, inspired by British prototypes, conveys his status as a military hero. Here Earl employs flamboyant brushwork conveying a painterly treatment of the figure and the landscape.

Earl may have been responding to John Trumbull's presence in New York when he painted the Willett portrait. The scale and format of Earl's portrait relate to the full-length portraits of Washington and George Clinton (fig. 1.28) painted by Trumbull for the New York city hall in 1790 and 1791. Trumbull, who had arrived in New York in November 1789, may have received official commissions to paint these public portraits because he had gained fame as the leading history painter in America. Earl did not attempt to compete with Trumbull in this elevated genre.

After his trip to New York City and Long Island,[136] Earl spent two highly productive years in the Hartford area. Hartford had developed into the most important center of artistic activity in post-revolutionary Connecticut. Largely because of its inland location, it was one of the few New England cities that came out of the Revolution stronger than it had entered it. By the 1790s, the city had an established art museum and a literary circle, the Connecticut Wits. The presence of important patrons of the arts, especially Jeremiah Wadsworth and his son Daniel, provided an essential element for its development as an artistic center.[137]

Both Earl and John Trumbull painted in the Hartford area in 1791 and 1792. Earl again benefited from his close association with Cogswell, who reassured the local people of Earl's suitability as a portrait painter and helped him to obtain portrait commissions from many prominent Connecticut River Valley families. Trumbull, drawn to the city through his relationship with the Wadsworths, painted members of the family and gathered portraits for his history series. Whereas Trumbull clearly catered to the social and political leaders of the colonial era (the old Standing Order), represented by such families as the Wadsworths, Earl appealed to a broader social spectrum. His portraits, in particular, provided a model for the many local artists who began to establish careers at this time.

Earl painted an engaging portrait of Mason Fitch Cogswell (cat. 40) in his first year in Hartford, one that conveys Cogswell's kind nature, as well as his professional stature. In addition to assisting Earl in securing important commissions in the region, Cogswell attempted to persuade his own father, who lived in Scotland, Connecticut, to have Earl paint his portrait. At the suggestion of his brother James, who asked if he would "prevail on Mr. Earl to take my father's likeness," Mason wrote to his father in December. "Mr. Earl is now in Hartford. Should you be willing that he should come to Scotland and remain there a week or so until he would partly take your portrait and then finish it in Hartford? I wish you would let me know." Failing in his efforts, three months later, Mason tried again to arrange a sitting. "Our friends in Hartford anticipate much satisfaction from your visit in June or July. . . . Mr. Earl cannot complete the

1.28
John Trumbull
George Clinton, 1791
oil on canvas
108 x 71 ½ in. (274.3 x 181.6 cm.)
Collection of the City of New York, City Hall, Governor's Room. Courtesy, Art Commission of the City of New York.

Facing page 1.27
Ralph Earl
Mrs. John Watson, 1791
oil on canvas
68 ¼ x 54 ⅜ in. (173.4 x 138.1 cm.)
Munson-Williams-Proctor
Institute Museum of Art, Proctor
Collection, Utica, N.Y.

1.29
Joseph Steward
The Reverend James Cogswell, c. 1796
oil on canvas
44 x 38 in. (111.8 x 96.5 cm.)
Private collection.

1.30
John Trumbull
*Portrait of Jeremiah Wadsworth and
Son, Daniel Wadsworth*, 1784
oil on canvas
36¼ x 28½ in. (92.1 x 72.4 cm.)
Wadsworth Atheneum, Hart-
ford, Conn. Gift of Mr. Faneuil
Adams, 1970.

portrait in three or four days, which will be all you can spend if you do not tarry over
sabbath." The senior Cogswell, apparently loath to be away from his pulpit for even
one Sabbath, never made the trip. Mason then offered to take Earl out to Scotland himself, in the summer, but his father evidently refused. In a final plea, Mason offered once
again to take Earl to Scotland, this time in the fall, with an assurance of the artist's character. "I do not think it probable that I shall be able to leave home until sometime in
the fall. . . . Mr. Earl has lately been engaged at Windsor in taking Mr. and Mrs. Ellsworth. Possibly I may bring him with me. How should you like it? He is a mighty plain
peaceable man." [138] Earl never took the portrait. Instead, several years later, the Rev.
James Cogswell had his friend and colleague the Rev. Joseph Steward paint his portrait
(fig. 1.29) in a simplified version of the style Earl had established in the state.

The hesitancy of James Cogswell, Sr., to have Earl paint his portrait suggests that
the selection of an artist had as much to do with the values of the sitter as with the
availability and relative expense of a painter. Cogswell represented the most conservative element of Connecticut society. He rejected a highly popular artist in favor of a
less gifted imitator, but a man of similar values – a fellow minister, whom he described
in his diary in 1790 as "an amiable character . . . sensible, religious, candid – able in
prayer, agreeable in conversation & a very tender husband." [139] At the other end of the
spectrum, the Wadsworths, perhaps the wealthiest and most sophisticated family in
the state, chose John Trumbull to paint their family members. Trumbull's animated
portrait *Jeremiah Wadsworth and Son, Daniel Wadsworth* (fig. 1.30), painted in London
in 1784, is an accomplished rendition informed by the English conversation piece; it
includes an emblem of Jeremiah Wadsworth's commercial occupation, the ship in the
background. Earl's subjects fell between these two extremes, representing a broad segment of upper- and middle-class Connecticut society.

Earl's double portrait *Oliver Ellsworth and Abigail Wolcott Ellsworth* (cat. 41) reflects
the spirit of the Constitutional era and remains his masterpiece from this period in his
career. Painted at the Ellsworths' home in Windsor, just north of Hartford on the Connecticut River, the portrait symbolizes the important role both Oliver and Abigail had
played in bringing about the ratification of the new Constitution. A self-made man,
Oliver Ellsworth performed a crucial role in drafting, ratifying, and amplifying the
Constitution, a copy of which he holds in his hand. The document separates him from
his wife, perhaps symbolic of the lengthy separations the Ellsworths endured to bring
about its ratification. Abigail Ellsworth, who is visually linked to the couple's domestic world through Earl's depiction of their house and farmlands through the window,
managed to oversee the construction of their house and its later modernization in 1788
and 1789, to raise their nine children, and to maintain their extensive property while
her husband spent much of his time away from home engaged in public service. By the
ingenious inclusion of references to their public and private lives and by the faithful depiction of the toll Abigail's responsibilities took from her – she appears much older than
her thirty-six years – the portrait captures the pride they had in their respective accomplishments. Earl includes symbols of their hard-earned affluence, as well: the couple are
seated in newly acquired, Hartford-made, Federal shield-back chairs in their recently
built Palladian parlor, and their much-loved home, with its recently added south wing
and the surrounding lands, all accurately depicted, are seen through the window.

Earl continued to capture on canvas the beauty of the Connecticut River Valley.
Since his depiction of regional landscape features was innovative, his views of Hartford
are the earliest known. In the portrait of Col. Samuel Talcott (cat. 42), a prominent
Hartford citizen, Earl not only depicts the stoic visage of this elderly man and suggests

his puritan ancestry but also documents his status as a leading landowner by including a beautifully rendered view of his property in Hartford, which extended from Main Street to the Connecticut River. For his portrait *Mrs. William Moseley and Her Son Charles* (fig. 1.31), painted in Hartford in 1791, Earl placed his subjects—Laura, the daughter of Oliver and Laura Wolcott (cats. 25, 26), and her son—in a panoramic landscape setting, which included a distant view of Hartford.

At times, Earl's sitters expressed their impatience with the lengthy sittings required for his detailed compositions. For example, in a letter of September 1791 to her brother Frederick, Laura Moseley apologized for not writing sooner, explaining that her time had been taken up with extensive portrait sessions. "You ought to consider that my attention has been engrossed by Mr. Earl and that I have had enough to do, to acquire the grace of patience. I assure you I have nearly attained it, and probably in the course of two or three months shall arrive at a state of perfection in this virtue. Painting goes on steadily, though slowly and my portrait looks—I can't tell you how. Mr. Earl has two or three others in hand." [140]

A growing interest in the colonial history of the state inspired Earl's documentation of certain historic sites in several of his sitters' portraits. The famous Charter Oak Tree, where, according to legend, the original charter of Connecticut was hidden in 1687, stood on the Wyllys family property. The site came to symbolize for state inhabitants the spirit of independence that had brought about the American Revolution. During the 1790s, when the interest in the ancient tree and the Wyllys mansion arose, Earl became the first in a long succession of artists to paint them. Polly Wyllys Pomeroy, like her stepbrother, Samuel, was born in the Wyllys mansion. Earl's view of the oak and the mansion in his unfinished portrait *Polly Wyllys Pomeroy* (fig. 1.32) helped to promote their veneration. [141]

On other occasions, Earl first completed the portrait of his subject and returned later to fill in the landscape view he shows through the window. This was the case for his portrait of Samuel Wyllys Pomeroy (1792; Connecticut Historical Society), who had been raised in the Wyllys mansion in Hartford. The subject's aunt, who was then living in the house, wrote to him: "We have had your portrait in the room most of the winter— Mr. Earl brought it to take the prospect from the Hall window—it was very agreeable to Look at [but] yet it would add a higher degree of satisfaction to see the original." [142] Earl included an accurate view of the buildings seen from the Wyllys mansion to the Connecticut River.

With Mason Fitch Cogswell's assistance, Earl received commissions to paint several prominent citizens in nearby Middletown, a thriving port town, again using landscape features to convey aspects of importance in his subjects' lives. His penetrating portraits of one mother and daughter, *Mrs. Joseph Wright* and *Mrs. Richard Alsop* (cats. 44, 45), capture the strength of character of these two self-sufficient widows, who commissioned their portraits while they both served as the heads of their households following their husbands' untimely deaths. Once again, Earl includes a regional landscape out the window, in each case, a view of the Connecticut River (or its tributary, the Mattabeseck), representing the livelihood of this mercantile family.

After his two highly productive years in the Hartford area, Earl and his family traveled to the major port town of New London, on the Connecticut shore, where he painted a series of portraits of various members of the Shaw family in 1792 and 1793. Thomas Shaw (1739–95), commissioned six portraits of his family subsequent to the renovation and refurnishing of their home. [143]

The Shaw mansion was built in 1756 by Thomas Shaw's father, Nathaniel Shaw, Sr.

The house, situated on New London Harbor, had served as the first naval office during the Revolution. From there Thomas and his brother Nathaniel, Jr., directed U.S. Naval affairs. The house was extensively damaged during the raid on Long Island in 1781 by Benedict Arnold and his men. After the war, Thomas repaired the house and ordered new furnishings from the local cabinetmaker Patrick Robertson (b. 1751); his sofa and armchair appear in Earl's portraits of the family members.[144]

Following his established formula for Connecticut portraits, Earl painted accurate renditions of the Shaw family members and included in their portraits their locally made furnishings and references to the role the family and their house had played during the Revolution. Earl shows Thomas Shaw (fig. 1.33) seated in the Shaw mansion; he is placed near a window with a view of one of his many ships in New London Harbor, Fort Trumbull beyond it, flying an American flag. Earl received a total of fifty pounds eight shillings (approximately 170 dollars) for painting the six Shaw portraits.[145]

While established on the Connecticut shore, Earl took advantage of his close proximity to Long Island, returning there to paint several prominent families. Once again, his introduction was through Cogswell.[146] Just as the Connecticut River Valley retained a certain regional distinctiveness, so too did Long Island. The inhabitants of Long Island, like Connecticut's, were, for the most, farmers who also pursued other professional endeavors, though somewhat in isolation from a major urban center. In 1811, on a visit to East Hampton, Timothy Dwight commented on their character. "Living by themselves more than the people of most places, they became more attentive to whatever is their own, and less to the concern of others. Hence their own customs, especially those that have come down from their ancestors (and these are about all that exist among them), have a commanding influence on their conduct."[147]

As in Connecticut, Earl's patrons in this region were owners of large tracts of land. During the British occupation, however, many of these families suffered great personal loss. After the Battle of Long Island in August 1776, several thousand refugees fled to Connecticut. Upon their return after the war, they discovered their homes in ruins. Many of Earl's Long Island sitters commissioned him to paint portraits that celebrated the renewal of their lives as American citizens after surviving the devastation of the war.

Earl maintained his Connecticut portrait style for these works.[148] For example, his most distinguished Long Island patron, Col. William Floyd (cat. 46), is depicted in a defiantly proud pose, with a view of his recently rebuilt ancestral home in the distance. Floyd's neighbor Elizabeth Smith (cat. 47) is engaged, in her portrait, in a patriotic endeavor—the domestic production of silk thread. Earl portrays her unwinding silk cocoons.

In 1794, Earl returned to New York City, where he painted a series of portraits that, once again, clearly demonstrate his ability to deliberately alter his style to suit his patrons.[149] The return to a more elegant style is best exemplified by *Benjamin S. Judah* (cat. 48), the portrait of a prominent merchant and member of one of New York's most distinguished Jewish families. Here Earl concentrated on conveying the important social standing of his sitter: Judah is formally posed, dressed with flamboyant elegance, and his international trade connections are signified by a bill of sale in German marks. To achieve the desired effect, Earl returned to the use of more loosely executed brushwork, a subtle palette of pastel hues, and warm glazes.

This trip to New York proved to be his last. Perhaps Earl did not wish to compete with the growing number of artists who began to appear in the city in the 1790s. And his singular popularity in Connecticut provided him with the certainty of ample commissions. Of greatest importance to the artistic climate of New York was the pres-

1.32
Ralph Earl
detail of *Polly Wyllys Pomeroy*,
1791 or 1792
oil on canvas
38½ x 32 in. (97.8 x 81.3 cm.)
Courtesy, Wadsworth Atheneum,
Hartford, Conn.

1.33
Ralph Earl
Thomas Shaw, 1793
oil on canvas
59 x 48 in. (149.9 x 121.9 cm.)
New London County Historical
Society, Conn. Photograph by
Claire White-Peterson.

Facing page 1.31
Ralph Earl
*Mrs. William Moseley and Her Son
Charles*, 1791
oil on canvas
86⅞ x 68⅜ in. (220.7 x 173.7 cm.)
Yale University Art Gallery,
New Haven, Conn. Bequest of
Mrs. Katherine Rankin Wolcott
Verplanck.

1.34
Gilbert Stuart
Don Josef de Jaudenes y Nebot, 1794
oil on canvas
50¼ x 39½ in. (127.6 x 100.3 cm.)
The Metropolitan Museum of Art,
New York. Rogers Fund, 1907.
(07.75).

Earl's Landscape Paintings

1.35
Gilbert Stuart
*Matilda Stoughton de Jaudenes y
Nebot*, 1794
oil on canvas
50¼ x 39½ in. (127.6 x 100.3 cm.)
The Metropolitan Museum of Art,
New York. Rogers Fund, 1907.
(07.76).

ence of Gilbert Stuart, who arrived in 1793 and was still there when Earl returned. Stuart painted a series of portraits of leading figures, including *Don Josef de Jaudenes y Nebot* and *Matilda Stoughton de Jaudenes y Nebot* (figs. 1.34, 1.35), which rank among the most aristocratic images of the period. Stuart accented wealth and worldly rank in these portraits, working in the most up-to-date style. In his studio setting, Stuart brought to America his "painterly" style, which had developed out of the British portrait style of the 1780s. His rapid brushwork and blending of colors created an atmospheric effect.

One contemporary, William Dunlap, was impressed by the impact that this artist's arrival had upon the city, noting that as soon as Stuart opened "an atelier . . . all who admired the art or wished to avail themselves of the artist's talents, daily resorted [there]. It appeared to the writer as if he had never seen portraits before, so decidedly was form and mind conveyed to canvas." Stuart was the most sophisticated and highly regarded portrait painter of his generation. His influence on American artists was widespread, changing the fashion of portraiture in urban centers throughout the nation.[150] Certainly Earl responded to Stuart's presence in New York when he painted *Benjamin Judah*, returning to the style and technique he had absorbed during his London years. Earl may not have wished to switch to the new form of portraiture established by Gilbert Stuart, however, even though he was certainly capable of doing so.

"From a wilderness into a well-inhabited and well-cultivated country"
                                                              —Timothy Dwight, *Travels*

Following this brief interlude in New York, Earl returned to Connecticut, where he spent the next four years traveling to the towns where he had previously found success, as well as venturing for the first time to the northeastern region of the state. He discovered that during his absence other itinerant artists had appeared on the scene and the success of his portrait style had inspired a number of imitators. Earl responded by relying more consistently on his novel skill as a landscape painter.

For instance, on a return visit to Fairfield County in 1794, Earl painted portraits of the Bradley sisters (cats. 49, 50), focusing his attention on a view of the beaches of Long Island that could be seen from the Bradley farm in Greenfield Hill. When hung together, the portraits form one continuous panorama.

Earl was one of only a few American artists to receive commissions for landscape paintings in the 1790s. Landscape art had remained scarce in the American colonies until after the Revolution, for the most part appearing as decorative paintings on walls and over doors and mantles in imitation of more elaborate murals in royal and aristocratic English mansions.[151] In Connecticut, Winthrop Chandler had executed a number of overmantle paintings in the northeastern region of the state, only one of which was on canvas, *Homestead of General Timothy Ruggles* (fig. 1.36). Most were imaginary scenes based on English print sources, though Chandler frequently depicted the house of his patron in an imaginary setting, as in the Ruggles overmantle.[152]

While in England in the late 1770s and early 1780s, Earl had witnessed the rise of landscape art as a mode of high artistic expression that was practiced by such major artists as Richard Wilson (1714–82) and Thomas Gainsborough. When he returned to America, landscape art was taking on a new artistic and intellectual significance in the young nation. Along with the preoccupation with images of revolutionary war heroes, the American landscape emerged as a topic for nationalistic symbolism, as seen in both the writings and paintings of the Federal period. In the early 1790s Earl had already begun to include landscapes in the backgrounds of his subjects' portraits.

1.36
Winthrop Chandler
Homestead of General Timothy Ruggles, c. 1770–75
oil on canvas
31 ½ x 62 ¾ in. (80.0 x 159.4 cm.)
Collection of Miss Julia T. Green.
Courtesy, Worcester Art Museum, Worcester, Mass.

One way in which American landscape art was popularized was through the rising interest in "picturesque travel," which emerged as a popular pastime in Europe and America. After the Revolution, the New World became a favorite place to visit, and the travelers produced numerous illustrated accounts of their journeys. The proliferation of illustrated travel accounts in the 1790s coincided with the arrival in America of a number of British landscape painters, who worked mainly in and around Philadelphia, Baltimore, and New York.[153] They concentrated on natural wonders, such as Niagara Falls and the Natural Bridge in Virginia, as well as sites associated with historical events or personages, including West Point and Mount Vernon, city and town views, and country houses. None of these artists is known to have painted in New England.

Patronage by such nationally respected figures as George Washington and Thomas Jefferson helped to promote an interest in landscape art in America. These two men patronized one or more of the British immigrant artists.[154] In addition, instruction in landscape art became available for the first time. Archibald and Alexander Robertson opened their drawing academy, the Columbian Academy of Painting, in New York in the 1790s, one of the few places where aspiring artists could learn to paint landscapes.

John Trumbull was executing landscapes in Connecticut in the 1790s. While in the Hartford area in 1791, he produced several sketches along the Connecticut River, plus a number of oil paintings, including *View on the West Mountain near Hartford* (c. 1791; Yale University Art Gallery), which adhered to the eighteenth-century English tradition of the picturesque landscape.[155]

Ralph Earl had already provided a significant addition to the development of landscape art in New England through the inclusion of regional landscape features in his portraits. One of the first native-born American artists to focus on regional landscape subjects, Earl painted country houses, historic sites, town views, and his last and most ambitious project, a panorama of Niagara Falls. His landscapes were largely topographical recordings with the addition of some picturesque elements. By helping to establish a taste for landscapes among his sitters, Earl created a clientele for such paintings.

His paintings of his patrons' newly built houses, in the English tradition, owed their success to the generation of architects and housewrights that appeared in Connecticut after the war. Using academic pattern books and new building methods, these men were responsible for the substantial statewide increase in the construction of houses in the latest styles. Earl benefited from the increased activity in the building trade. In many ways, his portraits complemented the new Palladian style embraced by Connecticut architects, who, like Earl, adapted the style to suit regional conditions and tastes. They transformed this international style by diminishing its scale and ornament and by substituting wood and brick for stone.[156]

This building boom also affected the portrait trade, since many of Earl's Connecticut patrons commissioned him to paint their portraits after they enlarged their houses -- the Ellsworths are an example (cat. 41) – or completed new ones. Earl benefited from the new, grand parlors, which provided the necessary wall space for his large-scale portraits.

In his painting career, Earl closely followed two Connecticut architects in particular, who were responsible for a large portion of the new construction in the state. William Sprats (1747–1810) introduced the Palladian style to Connecticut in the 1790s, where he built and remodeled the houses of many of Earl's sitters, especially in Litchfield County, including those of Elijah and Mary Anna Boardman (cats. 29, 55) and Benjamin and Mary Tallmadge (cats. 37, 38).[157] Thomas Hayden (1745–1817), a Windsor, Connecticut, architect and builder, demonstrated the influence of Sprats when he embraced the Palladian style. A major figure in the building profession in the Connecticut River Valley, he also remodeled and built houses for Earl's sitters, including that of Oliver and Abigail Ellsworth (cat. 41).

Earl returned to Litchfield County in 1796, initiating one of his most productive years: he had sixteen portrait commissions and commissions for three landscapes including his patrons' newly built houses. In February he announced his return to Litchfield in the newspaper.[158] Later, upon his arrival in New Milford in May, his announcement was clearly aimed at discrediting his recent competition in that town.

> *Mr. Ralph Earl, the celebrated Portrait Painter, is now at New Milford; where he will probably reside for some time. As we profess a friendship for Mr. Earl, and are desirous that the public avail themselves of the abilities of this able artist, we feel a pleasure in making this communication; many gentlemen in this vicinity, having been disappointed of his services, and several of our friends being driven to accept the paultry* daubs *of assuming pretenders. Mr. Earl's price for a portrait of full length is* Sixty Dollars, *the small size* Thirty Dollars, *the painter finding his own support and materials.*[159]

He is probably alluding to the work of William and Richard Jennys, who had painted portraits in New Milford in 1794 and 1795.

The Jennyses provide an interesting contrast with Earl, for they found only modest success as itinerant portrait painters in New England. They adhered to a highly conservative style and were forced to pursue several other branches of the painter's trade, as well as teaching. Richard Jennys (active 1766–1801) and William Jennys (active 1793–1807), who are thought to have been father and son, executed severely plain and far less expensive likenesses than Earl's more detailed and more highly priced ones. The Jennyses were little influenced by Earl's work, instead practicing a divergent style of portraiture that reflected Richard's earlier work as an engraver in Boston; characteristic are the bust-length format, the surrounding spandrels (spaces they often delimned in the background), and the sharp contrasts of light and shade. Even the most basic details of the artists' lives remain unknown, although they were fairly prolific during their careers and collaborated on several occasions between 1795 and 1801.[160]

Approximately sixteen portraits executed in New Milford between 1794 and 1795

1.37
Richard and William Jennys
Lazarus Ruggles, 1795
oil on canvas
25 x 21 in. (63.5 x 53.3 cm.)
Courtesy, Kennedy Galleries,
New York.

1.38
Richard and William Jennys
*Mrs. Lazarus Ruggles (Hannah
Bostwick)*, 1795
oil on canvas
25 x 21 in. (63.5 x 53.3 cm.)
Courtesy, Kennedy Galleries,
New York.

have been assigned to Richard and William Jennys.[161] Of particular interest are the portraits they executed for Jared Lane, which are documented in Lane's account book for 1795. Lane sat for Ralph Earl the following year (cat. 51).

According to Lane's ledger, William and Richard Jennys painted six bust-length portraits (measuring 7 ½ x 9 ⅓ inches), the most expensive being that of Apphia Lane, Jared's wife (unlocated), at two pounds six shillings. In addition, Jared Lane paid the local cabinetmaker, Levi Knapp, for "5 small picture Frames," and one month later, he paid "Richard & Wm Jennys for Varnishing" his family portraits, along with the portraits of his parents-in-law, Capt. Lazarus Ruggles and Mrs. Hannah Ruggles (figs. 1.37, 1.38), also painted by the Jennyses.[162] Their severe style is demonstrated here in the sharply defined features of the subjects, the lack of ornamentation, and the stark brown background.

The Jennyses seemed to find their niche in the New England market for portraits by adhering to a plain, highly realistic style, executed quickly on a modest, bust-length scale that precluded the need to depict arms and hands. These portraits were relatively inexpensive. In spite of Earl's initial anxiety upon learning of the competition that had developed during his absence, he had little to fear, for he continued to appeal to those townspeople wishing for a somewhat grander image of themselves. In addition, his skill as a landscape painter came into play to a greater degree in these later years.

Earl received a series of commissions to paint portraits with accompanying landscapes in New Milford and Sharon in 1796. Jared Lane, a nurseryman and farmer, had recently built a house in the Still River Neck district of New Milford. Taking advantage of the presence of a more versatile and gifted painter than the Jennyses, he commissioned Earl to paint a portrait of himself and his wife, Apphia (cats. 51, 52), as well as a landscape of his newly completed house (cat. 53). While Earl completed these portraits, he and his wife boarded with Jared's father-in-law, Lazarus Ruggles, who lived on the same property. Jared Lane's detailed account books provide illuminating information on Earl's life as an itinerant artist, his drinking problem, and his working methods (cats. 51, 52; chapter 3) while painting for the Lanes – from May 23 to July 28.

In Sharon, Earl painted a similar series of portraits for the Lanes' relations Judson and Mabel Canfield, including a panoramic landscape of their house, *Landscape View of the Canfield House* (cat. 54). In his depictions of the Lane and Canfield houses, Earl followed the precedent of English country-house painting, framing the scene in a conventional fashion, the house placed in the middle ground surrounded by cultivated lands, a picturesque river in the foreground, and hills in the distance. The artist was careful to delineate the architectural features of these houses, which are striking in their similarity and which are built in the Palladian style of Sprats and Hayden.

At the same time, Earl painted additional portraits for the Boardman family, including a grand-scale portrait of Elijah Boardman's wife and son, *Mrs. Elijah Boardman and Son* (cat. 55), as well as ones of Elijah's parents, *Sherman Boardman* and *Mrs. Sherman Boardman (Sarah Bostwick)* (cats. 56, 57). Elijah also commissioned a landscape of his recently built house and shop in New Milford (cat. 58). Abandoning the conventions of English country-house painting, here Earl creates the sense of a prosperous town center with his close-up view of the mansion house, built by William Sprats in 1792–93, the new shop nearby, and the house to the north, which was also owned by Elijah Boardman and which had been the site of his first shop in New Milford. Earl was careful to include the elaborate Palladian features of the Boardmans' house, as well as the ornate fence and newly planted saplings that lined the main street.

The neatly constructed, well-situated mansion houses and the thriving village seen in Earl's three landscapes are bathed in the golden light of the artist's distinctive pink and blue sky. Like his portraits of the period, these landscapes reflect the hopes and promise of the young nation. Once again Timothy Dwight's writings, the product of his travels in New York State a decade later, complement Earl's landscapes. "It is questionable whether mankind has ever seen so large a tract changed so suddenly from a wilderness into a well-inhabited and well-cultivated country. A great number of beautiful villages have risen up as by the power of enchantment; and the road for one hundred and twenty miles is in a sense lined by a succession of houses, almost universally neat, and frequently handsome." [163]

Final Years

"View of the Stupendous Falls of Niagara" – Advertisement, *Hampshire Gazette*

In 1798, Earl left Connecticut, moving north to Vermont and Massachusetts in search of new portrait and landscape commissions. A variety of reasons can be offered for his move. He may have been hindered by the growing competition he faced from less gifted imitators. During the course of his ten-year stay in Connecticut, Earl had painted portraits in nearly every region of the state, so he may also have exhausted the audience he had catered to for so long. Indeed, in his later years Earl was forced to travel more frequently and more widely in search of commissions. Many of the portraits he painted in 1797 and 1798 are hastily executed; his 1798 painting of a Litchfield physician, *Dr. Seth Bird* (unlocated), is an example. [164] Earl's bouts of heavy drinking provide one explanation for the inferior quality of some of these later works. Finally, Earl's wife Ann and their two children, who until this time had traveled with the artist, suddenly moved permanently to Troy, New York.

During Earl's frequent visits to Litchfield, Ann Earl had developed a friendship with the local tavern owner and his wife, David and Rachel Buell. The family had stayed at the Buells' tavern while Earl painted the residents of the town. Earl also painted portraits of the Buells' daughters, *Mary H. Buell* (1796; Historic Deerfield) and

Sally Buell (1796; Historic Deerfield). In 1798 the Buell family, including David and Rachel, their daughter Sally, and her husband, Dr. John Bird, moved to Troy, New York. Ann Earl, who had undoubtedly grown tired of her rootless existence, followed the Buells the same year, settling in Troy with her daughter, Mary Ann.[165] Their son, Ralph (by this time between the ages of ten and thirteen), in contrast, was spending a great deal of time with his father, learning the art of portrait painting.

Presumably in an effort to remain close to his family, Earl traveled to Bennington, Vermont, in 1798, where he painted a series of impressive portraits and one landscape. As these works show, being in a new region renewed Earl's artistic vitality. This thriving town had been the site of a crucial battle in the war. In a contest that proved to be a military turning point, Gen. Horatio Gates, aided by thousands of New England militiamen, defeated Burgoyne at Bennington, a victory that was followed by Burgoyne's surrender at Saratoga in 1777. The historic significance of those events, which were still fresh in the minds of Bennington townspeople, provided inspiration for Earl's paintings.

In Vermont, Earl encountered a clientele as diverse as he had found in Connecticut. On a visit to Bennington ten years earlier, the Rev. Nathan Perkins of Hartford recorded his impressions in his journal. He found Bennington to be "a good town of land," its people "proud – scornful – conceited & somewhat polished," although a few appeared "countrified in manners, and without any elegance." The town itself had a "small meeting house" and was "considerably thick-settled, as many as can possibly get a living; – no stone; – no fencing timber; some elegant building; – a County town; – a tolerable Court-house & jail." Perkins also visited the "hill where ye Bennington battle was fought . . . a battle which will be greatly celebrated in ye history of America." [166]

Earl's Bennington sitters had close ties to the artist's Connecticut patrons. Noah Smith, a Connecticut native and Yale College graduate, was related to the Boardman family of New Milford and commissioned Earl to paint large portraits of himself and his family. As a leading attorney in the town, Noah Smith had given an address at the anniversary celebration of the Battle of Bennington in August 1778. In his full-length portrait (cat. 59), Earl depicts him holding a large map of the Bennington area. Earl also painted one of the most complex compositions of his career for the Smith family: a group portrait with full-length portrayals of Chloe Smith and her five children (cat. 59). The Smith portraits must have caused a sensation in this remote town, since Earl appears to have been the first artist to paint there.

Following his customary format, Earl painted lively portraits of the local tavern-keeper, Capt. Elijah Dewey and his wife, Mary Dewey (cats. 60, 61). Earl included a detailed rendition of the Dewey tavern through the window in the background of Elijah's portrait. Elijah Dewey was the son of the town minister and was celebrated as a hero of the revolutionary war. A landscape view of Bennington (cat. 62) that was commissioned by the Deweys is one of the artist's finest achievements. It was hung with their portraits in the tavern.

Earl's painting of Bennington provides an accurate record of the location of the houses and other buildings in the town. More importantly, Earl conveys the social structure of the town, emphasizing by his placement its most important sites and leading citizens. The center is dominated by three buildings: the mansion house of Gov. Isaac Tichnor, with its formal gardens and elaborate fencing; the newly built court-house; and the State Arms House. The site of the Battle of Bennington serves as a dramatic backdrop for the central buildings. Earl also includes Elijah Dewey's tavern, as well as the house of Elijah's parents, at the right. In the distance, the North Mountains loom above the town; they are softly depicted in a purplish tone with the golden pink light of the setting sun illuminating the entire scene. There is no hardship evident in this portrayal. Rather, the pastoral beauty of this idyllic scene, neatly laid out and appropriately structured, evokes the idealism of the republican era and takes on a nationalistic overtone.[167]

In *Landscape View of Old Bennington*, Earl chose to include a rare, perhaps unique, self-portrait. A small figure of the artist is shown seated under a tree, at the lower left; the figure, with a drawing pad in hand, is taking a sketch of the young boy standing before him. Earl appropriately depicts himself as a portrait painter. He may have used his son, Ralph, Jr. (who was with him during this period), as his model for the boy he shows himself sketching.

From Bennington, Earl traveled eastward to Northampton, Massachusetts, the fastest-growing commercial center in the upper Connecticut River Valley. Here Earl spent the last years of his career as both an artist and a teacher. Some of his portraits reflect a marked decline in quality and attention to detail. One explanation for their lack of finish may be that he used these works as teaching tools for his students. *Dr. Ebenezer Hunt* (1799; Historic Deerfield), a portrait of Northampton's leading physician and apothecary, is hastily executed and provincial in appearance; here Earl includes the tools of Hunt's profession on the table.

In the same year, 1799, Earl agreed to accept William Southgate (1782–1811) of Leicester, Massachusetts, as his student. The young man's father, Jonathan Southgate, was the artist's second cousin, and he sent a letter to Earl asking if his son might "spend some time under your tuition in the Art of Painting and Drawing . . . long enough to satisfy yourself and him whether it is worth his while to Indeavor to obtain your Art." He concluded by inviting Earl to visit him in Leicester and made reference to the Earl family's artistic heritage. "Some of your friends suppose my son has so much Earle Blood in him that he will not fail of making himself master of your Art if he applyes himself to it." Within two years, Jonathan noted that his son had attained "a surprising proficiency in portrait painting" under Earl's tutelage.[168]

Earl simultaneously taught his own son, allowing him on at least one occasion to collaborate on a portrait commission. In 1800 the Northampton clockmaker Isaac Gere commissioned portraits of himself, his wife, and his infant son. Earl, Sr., painted *Isaac Gere* (1800; private collection) and *Jemima Kingsley Gere* (1800; private collection), allowing his son to paint the portrait of Edward Gere (fig. 1.39), which is prominently signed and dated, in the manner of his father, using red vermillion: "R. E. W. Earl / Pinxt 1800." The portrait is a delightful rendition of the two-year-old boy, who holds a large cat in his arms. Employing his father's formula, Earl, Jr., includes a green curtain and a window view of a landscape to complete the composition.

Earl, Jr., continued to paint portraits in the Connecticut River Valley and in Troy, New York, until 1809, when he left for Europe. These early works continue to demonstrate a marked reliance on his father's example. Such portraits as *Reverend Ebenezer Porter* (cat. 63) and *Mrs. Ebenezer Porter (Lucy "Patty" Pierce Merwin)* (cat. 64), painted after Earl, Sr.,'s death, embody the aesthetic formula passed on by his father, including the use of such compositional elements as drapery, a red round-back chair, and objects that convey the interests of the sitters.

During his final years in Northampton, Earl, Sr., engaged in the most ambitious effort of his career. At the age of forty-eight, he became the first American artist to travel to Niagara Falls, where he took sketches of the "Stupendous Cataract" in preparation for painting a grand panorama of it. Earl was encouraged in this endeavor by

1.39
Ralph E. W. Earl
Portrait of Edward Gere, 1800
oil on canvas
22 x 18½ in. (55.9 x 47.0 cm.)
Location presently unknown. Copy
photograph from the William
Sawitzky Papers. Courtesy, The
New-York Historical Society,
New York.

two local men, Hezekiah Hutchins, a Northampton entrepreneur, and Jacob Wicker, an ornamental painter.[169]

When Earl undertook this venture, Niagara Falls had already become the most frequently described natural wonder in North America, appearing in numerous European engravings that illustrated published travel accounts, beginning in the late seventeenth century. In addition to its acknowledged aesthetic significance as America's most sublime scene, Niagara Falls acquired significance as the symbol of the most unique resource of the new nation – the seemingly limitless wilderness landscape.[170]

Aware of the possible commercial gain in promoting this natural wonder, Earl and his two assistants devised a plan to travel to the falls in October 1799. In a carefully orchestrated campaign to promote their venture, the men announced their departure from Northampton in newspapers from Litchfield, Connecticut, to Charleston, South Carolina. "Last week Messrs. Hutchins, Wicker and Earle, the celebrated portrait and landscape painters, left this town for Niagara, with a design of taking an accurate map of the falls at that place. The map, we understand, is to be 30 feet in length and 15 {feet} in width." [171]

The journey was extremely arduous, particularly for a man of Earl's age. Very few Americans had undertaken the trip; and the few who had attempted it chose to travel via Kingston, New York, along the Hudson River Valley to Albany, then across the

1.40
Daily Hampshire Gazette, March 5,
1800
Courtesy, American Antiquarian
Society, Worcester, Mass.

Mohawk River Valley to Genesee Falls, and finally to New Amsterdam (Buffalo). At this time, the roads across upstate New York to Buffalo virtually ended at Canandaigua. Earl and his companions may have chosen the late fall and winter months to travel so that they had the benefit of snow, which allowed for travel by sleigh. John Vanderlyn, who has traditionally been credited as the first "professionally trained" American artist to sketch the falls, made the journey in 1801, but even though a young man, he reached the falls only with considerable difficulty.[172]

Until well into the first decades of the nineteenth century, views of the falls were taken from the Canadian side, where there was an active portage road with transportation and accommodation facilities. The U.S. side remained largely unsettled. Thus it can be assumed that Earl and his associates traveled to the Canadian side to take sketches, as Vanderlyn and John Trumbull would do in the following decade. Over a month after the announcement of their departure, several newspapers reported the men's successful arrival at Niagara, where they were purportedly engaged in "taking an accurate painting of the Stupendous Cataract."[173]

Upon their return to Massachusetts, Earl, probably with assistance from Wicker, worked from his sketches to complete a large panorama of the falls, which measured approximately fifteen by thirty feet. The men worked on the huge canvas in the Tontine Building in Northampton, where the panorama was later exhibited. According to a nineteenth-century description of the building, it stood on the east corner of Bridge and Hawley streets and "was of wood, three stories high, and was occupied mainly by mechanics and traders." Most likely the panorama was executed and exhibited on the third floor, where there was a "dancing hall."[174] Among the various artisans with shops in the building were the clockmaker Isaac Gere and Earl's associate Jacob Wicker.

Upon the completion of the panorama, Hutchins and Wicker announced its exhibition. Their grand proclamation, which appeared in the newspaper throughout the month of March, expressed some familiarity with contemporary aesthetic ideas of the sublime, as defined chiefly by Edmund Burke in his popular treatise *A Philosophical Enquiry into the Origin of Our Ideas of the Sublime and the Beautiful* (1757). The announcement appears in figure 1.40.[175]

The panorama, last seen on view in London in the early nineteenth century, probably no longer exists. One Northampton resident, upon viewing the awe-inspiring canvas, did, however, record her impressions in a diary. The feelings invoked are a tribute to the artist's skill and his knowledge of contemporary landscape aesthetics. "This Morning {Friday, March 14, 1800}—went with Mrs. Edwards to see the painting executed by Mr. Earl representing the falls of Niagara. I was struck with the grandeur of the scene—the painting I think does credit to Mr. E.'s abilities. The view I presume is correct—I am sure it is majestic and noble. Contemplating the works of nature—our thoughts should be led up to Nature's God &—delighted with the scenery around us—we should adore the great author of it."[176] Earl's son Ralph would paint a sensitive portrayal of this Northampton woman two years later, showing her with her first baby, *Abigail Lyman Brackett and Child* (1802; private collection).

In early April 1800 the panorama was transported from Northampton to Philadelphia, where it was placed on view in the Peale Museum, located in the statehouse. Its popular success led to an announcement of the extension of the exhibition: "Painting of the Falls of Niagara, by the request of several Gentlemen, will be exhibited at the State House for one week longer."[177] Hutchins and Wicker then took the painting to New Haven, where it was exhibited in late June at the house of Earl's early collaborator, Amos Doolittle.

Prospectus View of the Falls of Niagara, one of the greatest Natural Curiosities in the known World, painted on the spot by the celebrated Ralph Earl, will be exhibited to view THIS DAY, between the hours of 8 in the morning and 6 in the evening, at the house of AMOS DOOLITTLE, College Street – This painting is 27' long and 14' wide, and will afford the spectator as just an idea of this stupendous Cataract as can be represented on canvas. Price admittance, 9d {pence}. [178]

Doolittle frequently hosted the meetings of the local Masonic Order in his house and thus must have had a room large enough to accommodate the panorama. After its New Haven presentation, the panorama was transported to London for exhibition. Unfortunately, there are no details of its reception in London, where it remained for a time. [179]

The idea for this ambitious venture was certainly inspired by the widespread popularity of panoramic exhibitions in England and America in the late eighteenth century. The circular panorama appeared at this time in England, a huge topographical picture that surrounded the viewer, offering a 360-degree vista. The English artist Robert Baker exhibited the first such view in London in 1787. Although not in the circular mode, several panoramas were exhibited in America in the 1790s, including William Winstanley's view of London, shown in New York in 1795, and Joseph Jefferson's "pantomime view of the city of Hartford," shown in that city in 1799. [180] The panoramic landscape mode used by Earl, which developed more fully in America in the nineteenth century, solved the problem of depicting the vast breadth of Niagara Falls; it would be employed later for this same subject by Vanderlyn, Trumbull, and many successive artists. [181]

This last great venture completed, Earl's artistic production slowed considerably. Approaching the end of his life, the artist took the opportunity to return to his native town, Leicester, Massachusetts, in 1800, presumably for the first time since his departure a quarter of a century earlier.

In Leicester, Earl painted a sensitive portrait of his cousin, a noted gunsmith, Thomas Earle (cat. 65). Using his standard format, he included a detailed view of his cousin's house and gun manufactory. Earl also painted a panoramic landscape for Col. Thomas Denny (1757–1814; cat. 66). The view represented the vista from the Denny family homestead and farm, situated on top of a high hill, looking toward Leicester and Worcester. Earl's bucolic landscape includes farmhands harvesting the fields in the foreground and the town centers in the distance. Like his *Landscape View of Old Bennington* (cat. 62), Earl's idyllic view of the region in which he was raised conveys a sense of well-being and the promise of America, seen in the seemingly limitless fertile fields and prosperous towns. This was a fitting work with which to end his career.

In 1801, Earl traveled to Bolton, Connecticut, where he sought medical treatment at the home of Dr. Samuel Cooley, a prominent local physician. [182] Suffering from ill health probably due to the debilitating effects of his heavy drinking, Earl may have learned about Cooley through his relationship with Cogswell. A modest obituary notice reported Earl's death in August at the Cooley home, noting that "he was a portrait painter, celebrated in America and respected in Europe, a pupil of Sir Joshua Reynolds." An entry in the diary of the local minister provides the cause of death. "Ralph Earle died Aug. 16, 1801 ae [age] 50 – intemperance – from Europe." [183] Earl apparently died penniless, for no gravestone has been found. Earl's problems with alcoholism, the rigors of his life of continual travel, and his separation from his family all contributed to his early death.

Ralph Earl and His Followers

"Assuming pretenders" – Advertisement, *Litchfield Weekly Monitor*

Because of its popular acceptance, Earl's Connecticut portrait style began to generate a number of imitators by the mid-1790s. This phenomenon is one measure of the artist's extraordinary success. Because his innovative portraits became accessible models for his less-trained, less-traveled contemporaries, his style has come to be associated with portraiture in the state. The artists working in Earl's style (as well as other styles, like the one practiced by the Jennyses) have recently been dubbed the Connecticut School.[184] In fact, through his successful promotion of portraiture, Earl was faced for the first time with competition right where he had previously been hailed as the first artist to cater to local needs.

The impact of Earl's portraits is most dramatically demonstrated in the works of Joseph Steward (1753–1822). Originally trained for the ministry, Steward abandoned this vocation in the early 1790s because of poor health and turned to portrait painting. Largely self-taught, he began painting in Hampton, Connecticut, eventually moving on to Hartford and traveling extensively throughout New England. Steward relied on the many examples of Earl's portraits that were available to him, imitating the artist's compositional elements, palette, and scale. Steward even adopted Earl's distinctive manner of signing his portraits, using red vermillion, as did a number of Earl's other followers. Steward was particularly inspired by Earl's monumental portrait *Oliver and Abigail Wolcott Ellsworth* (cat. 41), painted in Windsor in 1792. He reinterpreted this composition for his own first grand-scale portrait, *Reverend Eleazar Wheelock* (cat. 67), painted the following year for his alma mater, Dartmouth College.

In 1796, Steward opened a "painting room" in the newly constructed Hartford Statehouse, and there, in the following year, he opened the Hartford Museum to the public. In addition to natural curiosities and humanmade objects, Steward exhibited a number of paintings, many of which he executed himself, both history paintings and portraits of important people. One of his works, a portrait of Jeremiah Halsey (cat. 68), who had been instrumental in bringing about the completion of the Hartford Statehouse, hung in the museum and helped bring Earl's portrait style to a wider audience.

Steward's role in disseminating Earl's portrait style was enhanced by his role as the teacher of several local painters. The most gifted of Earl's imitators, John Brewster, Jr. (1766–1854), received early instruction in the art of portrait painting from Steward and later was directly influenced by Earl's work. Born deaf-mute, Brewster was the son of a prominent physician in Hampton, Connecticut. During the 1790s he created a simplified version of the compositions seen in the works of Earl and Steward. Most notable are his portraits *Comfort Starr Mygatt and His Daughter Lucy* (cat. 69) and *Lucy Knapp Mygatt and Her Son George* (cat. 70), painted in Danbury, Connecticut, in 1799. For these portraits, Brewster drew on the many exmaples of Earl's portraits that hung in the surrounding houses: he retained the grand-scale format but refined the composition to its simplest form. Brewster's portraits are profoundly direct images, set in austere surroundings. Like Earl, he puts his full-length subjects in Windsor chairs, which are placed on decorative, patterned floors, and he includes in one portrait, a view of the Mygatts' farm through the window. Brewster's disability seems to have provided him with a heightened visual sense, which is amply demonstrated in his serene characterizations.

A group of portraits painted in Suffield, Connecticut, in the 1790s demonstrates the diffusion of Earl's style among less-trained painters. The portrait of Deborah Richmond (cat. 71), by an unidentified artist who clearly lacked the benefit of formal instruction, contains many elements of Earl's compositional formula. In a lively, two-dimensional treatment, the painter has placed the subject in a chair, near a table, with the ubiquitous curtained window and landscape view of a house in the distance.

Earl's style spread up and down the Connecticut River Valley, as well as to the eastern and western regions of the state. Capt. Simon Fitch (1785–1835), who spent much of his life in Lebanon, Connecticut, painted portraits that appear to have been inspired by Earl. His masterly portraits *Ephraim Starr* and *Mrs. Ephraim Starr* (cats. 72, 73), painted in Goshen in 1802, best illustrate this point. Fitch used the formula of the room interior, found in many of Earl's portraits, placing his full-length subjects in Windsor chairs, near a table, on a decorative, patterned floor. Like his fellow Connecticut painters, he concentrated on the careful, unflattering delineation of his subjects' likeness.

The many portraits painted by Earl in Fairfield County – on nearly an annual basis from 1788 until 1798 – provided inspiration for at least one local painter, Jonathan Budington (1779–1823). Budington, who was born in Fairfield, began painting portraits of local people in 1796.[185] *George Eliot and Family* (cat. 74), which he painted in Killingworth (now Clinton), Connecticut, in 1796,[186] clearly shows Earl's influence. Budington adopted Earl's Connecticut portrait format, including his favored palette and stock compositional elements – red drapery, red upholstered round-back chairs, green-cloth-covered table, and shelves of books. Like Earl, he also conveys the personal and political interests and social pretensions of his sitters, and he even goes so far as to adopt Earl's flamboyant style of signing his portraits, in vermillion.

Earl's sustained presence in Connecticut inspired a surge of artistic energy that stamped his style on portraiture in the state for decades. Ironically, the popularity of his technique and format made it more difficult for Earl himself to obtain portrait commissions in his later years. Because of his versatility and skill, however, he could distance himself from his less-gifted competitors by focusing on his novel ability as a landscape painter.

Ralph Earl had begun his career as an artist on the eve of the American Revolution. For the next twenty-five years, he distinguished himself as a portrait and landscape painter of exceptional breadth and power. He symbolized in his own life the struggle all Americans faced during the war and the formative years of the new nation. Drawing on his own life experience, Earl captured on canvas the many faces of the young republic. A prolific painter of American patriots, loyal English subjects, citizens of the American republic, and American landscapes, Earl responded to the various people and places he painted with a strong and clear intelligence, conscious of the often-conflicting desires of his sitters. Guided by his entrepreneurial spirit, Earl was uniquely qualified to inspire the burst of pictorial production that occurred in Connecticut during his lifetime. His upbringing in rural New England and his innate artistic skill allowed him to transform the international portrait style he had absorbed in England into a form more suited to the aesthetic sensibilities of his New England patrons, making him one of the most talented and ingenious painters of his era.

Portraiture and Society
in Late Eighteenth-Century Connecticut

Richard L. Bushman

THE ARTISTIC CAREER of Ralph Earl raises a question about society and culture in the Connecticut River Valley at the end of the eighteenth century. Why was one limited area suddenly able to support a painter for more than a decade? Not until the 1760s did any professional artists, so far as is known, work in Connecticut itself. People wanting portraits went to New York or Boston until William Johnston (1732–72) moved to New London and New Haven, the major ports, for two years and subsequently painted in Middletown and Hartford in 1763 and 1764. Then he was gone. The visits of the peripatetic John Durand to New Haven and Norwich, once in 1768 and again in 1772, were even briefer, and Henry Pelham was in Connecticut only for two months in 1774. Winthrop Chandler (1747–90), born in Woodstock, Connecticut, painted a powerful if unpolished portrait of the Rev. Ebenezer Devotion (fig. 1.3), the pastor of Scotland Parish in Windham, in the 1770s and six other portraits for the family. Almost all of his other portraits were limited to relatives, friends, and neighbors (cats. 1, 2). He moved to Worcester, Massachusetts, in 1785, where he advertised as a house painter. His obituary in the *Worcester Spy* called him a man whose "native genius" was "not matured on the bosom of encouragement."[1]

Against this spotty background, Ralph Earl's success in painting a hundred portraits in Connecticut alone, nearly all between 1788 and 1798, comes as a surprise (fig. 2.1). Earl also painted farther north in the Connecticut River Valley in Northampton, Massachusetts, and Bennington, Vermont, as well as elsewhere in New England and New York (fig. 1.19). But for more than a decade the bulk of his customers came from a relatively limited area. Granted that Earl's talent surpassed Chandler's, it is nonetheless remarkable that suddenly the demand for portraits was sufficient to keep a portraitist busy for so long in a region where earlier artistic activity had been meager. Furthermore, Earl was not the only painter in the 1790s. William Jennys had a clientele (figs. 1.37 and 1.38), and Abraham Delanoy, Jr.'s three years in the state (1784–87) overlapped Earl's. In the same period, miniaturists practiced their art in Hartford.[2]

Not only the volume but also the geographical distribution of Earl's sitters is remarkable. Previous painters worked primarily in New Haven and New London, the

Detail of
Houses Fronting New Milford Green
(cat. 58).

centers of wealth and commercial activity, venturing up the Connecticut River Valley to a few of the most prosperous river towns. Earl himself naturally went to New Haven in 1774 to launch his career. Away from the coast in the country towns to the east and the west of the Connecticut River, there was little painting and few pictures. Only Winthrop Chandler found clients in the agricultural villages, and then primarily among his family and neighbors. Yet it was in just such towns that Earl thrived. Forty-eight of his one hundred Connecticut portraits were for clients in inland country towns, forty-six of those in towns in the Housatonic River Valley—Sharon, Litchfield, New Milford, Newtown, and Danbury. He painted another twenty-one portraits in western coastal towns—Fairfield and Stamford—not notable ports and previously not promising locales for painters. All told, sixty-nine of Earl's one hundred Connecticut portraits were for sitters from small towns off the main axes of culture and commerce, which extended down the Connecticut River and eastward along the coast to New London. It is not hard to understand why he found sitters in the established centers. The interesting question is, What did the demand for portraits in the smaller towns mean? Ellen Miles has estimated that between 1750 and 1776 approximately 1 percent of the colonial population sat for a portrait, virtually all of them great landowners and merchants, the provincial elite. What happened by 1790 that brought a substantial number of people in small Connecticut towns into the society of pictured people?[3]

To the end of the eighteenth century, the river and coastal towns outdistanced the inland country towns by virtually every measure of cultural achievement. Two lines of hills descend through Connecticut paralleling the Connecticut River. If the towns between those two ranges are considered valley towns and the towns adjoining Long Island Sound are considered coastal towns, two squares of inland country towns remain, one west of the line of hills in the northwest corner of the state (roughly Litchfield County) and the second east of the other line of hills in the northeast corner of the state (roughly Windham and Tolland counties). Litchfield County understandably lagged behind the river and coast culturally and socially because it was the last settled. A number of towns were not organized until 1740. Some were organized earlier, it is true—New Milford, for example, in 1712 and Litchfield in 1719—but by the end of the century the northwest towns still had not caught up.[4] Economically and culturally this was backcountry compared to the central river valley and coastal core.

For one thing, the valley and coastal towns dominated the upper reaches of politics. The most eminent colonial leaders came from these regions. Election to one of the high offices came to men notable for colonywide service, family distinction, substantial wealth, education, and cultural sophistication. Table 2.1 shows how people of this kind clustered along the cultural axes. Twenty-six of the seventy-two officials, 36 percent, came from just four towns: Hartford, New Haven, New London, and Fairfield, which charted on a map define the major lines of cultural power. The twenty-nine towns of the northwest region had produced just three such men by the time that Earl began to paint there in earnest in 1789.

Houses mirrored the eminence of their residents. Connecticut houses were known for their flamboyant doorways, the most ostentatious having a huge broken-scroll pediment mounted above the frame. Others had a triangular pediment, and even some doorways with flat tops were decorated with a high frieze. These doorways measured the elegance of the house and the cultural and social aspirations of the residents. Amelia F. Miller has located all the high-fashion doorways that remain from the eighteenth century, 128 of them. Of that number, only eleven are found on structures in the northwest, and of those, seven are on churches. Only four houses in the whole region

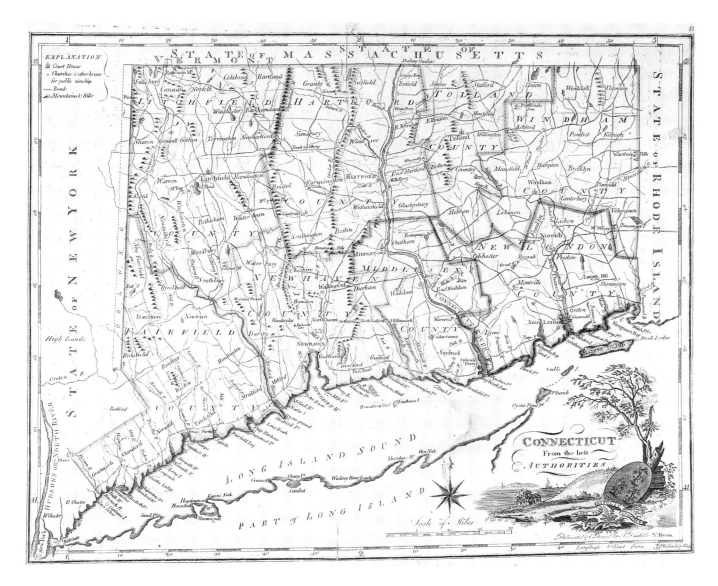

2.1
Amos Doolittle
Map of Connecticut, c. 1795
engraving
12 x 14¾ in. (30.5 x 37.5 cm.)
The Connecticut Historical Society, Hartford.

have a fancy doorway, a number nearly corresponding to the number of colony leaders from there.[5]

Miller had to depend on the extant houses for her survey, but contemporaneous tax lists tell the same tale. The valuation lists for 1796 counted fireplaces, dividing them into four ranks as a rough measure of the value of a house. First-rate fireplaces were assessed at four times the value of fourth-rate fireplaces. Again the great port towns were where residences with the best fireplaces were located (table 2.2).

The big towns stand out sharply in the matrix: Hartford with 0.62 first-rate fireplaces for every adult male, New London with 1.53, Norwich with 0.86, and New Haven with 1.75, whereas Litchfield, the only town in the northwest to make the cut, had only 0.08 first-rate fireplaces per adult male. New Milford, though falling short of thirty, is listed because Earl painted nineteen portraits there, nearly one fifth of his total Connecticut production, and yet the town had only seven first-rate fireplaces. There were more than three times as many first-rate fireplaces in Hartford alone as in all of Litchfield County.

Extrapolating from the fireplace figures, we must imagine the country towns in the northwest and northeast as having quite a number of log structures and many more low, unpainted frame houses with little decoration. Only here and there would we find four- or five-bay, painted, decorated houses with parlors worthy of the name, fea-

Table 2.1
Homes of Assistants, Deputy Governors, and Governors in Connecticut, 1701–1784

Region	Number of officials	Number of towns home to one or more officials	Number of towns in region
Valley	25	13	20
Coast	37	11	24
Northeast	7	5	24
Northwest	3	2	29

Source: Tabulated from figures in Bruce C. Daniels, *The Connecticut Town: Growth and Development, 1635–1790* (Middletown, Conn., 1979), 164.

Note: Towns divided from larger old coastal towns are included in the coastal group, as is Norwich, which has access to the sea by way of the Thames.

Table 2.2
Assessable Luxuries in Selected Connecticut Towns, 1796

Town	Polled adults 18–70	Fireplaces 1st-rate	1st-rate per capita	2d-rate	3d-rate	4th-rate	Total	Watches Total	Per capita	Carriages Total	Per capita
Hartford Co.	6,994	1,292	.18	1,927	4,954	3,215	11,388	510	.07	458	.07
Hartford	784	492	.62	318	416	29	1,255	134	.17	90	.11
East Hartford	468	57	.12	265	363	173	858	26	.06	48	.10
East Windsor	521	209	.40	159	502	129	999	28	.05	37	.07
Wethersfield	660	279	.42	379	435	124	1,217	51	.08	69	.10
Enfield	327	34	.10	32	172	190	428	12	.04	20	.06
Farmington	484	32	.07	116	287	424	859	47	.10	25	.05
Suffield	477	119	.25	244	331	115	809	29	.06	44	.09
Windsor	513	30	.06	168	483	257	938	27	.05	61	.12
New Haven Co.	5,324	1,405	.26	1,112	4,877	3,293	10,687	585	.11	293	.06
New Haven	622	1,089	1.75	271	492	84	1,936	172	.28	109	.18
Cheshire	340	30	.09	99	331	275	735	19	.06	13	.04
East Haven	175	42	.24	40	121	12	215	13	.07	11	.06
Hamden	279	98	.35	83	223	97	501	22	.08	21	.08
Wallingford	460	36	.08	110	548	201	895	56	.12	35	.08
Woodbridge	334	35	.10	34	202	361	632	34	.10	0	.00
New London Co.	3,751	1,263	.34	963	4,396	2,887	9,507	530	.14	125	.03
New London	332	509	1.53	61	35	0	605	53	.16	43	.13
Norwich	532	460	.86	295	474	271	1,500	165	.31	61	.11
Stonington	606	76	.13	93	848	210	1,227	35	.06	0	.00
Groton	539	46	.09	47	516	172	781	28	.05	0	.00
Lyme	597	47	.08	101	1,023	225	1,396	48	.08	8	.01
Windham Co.	4,145	134	.03	690	3,617	2,625	7,066	313	.08	57	.01
Pomfret	250	50	.20	19	250	70	389	14	.06	10	.04
Fairfield Co.	5,908	169	.03	681	5,555	3,772	10,177	287	.05	93	.02
Fairfield	591	73	.12	134	544	150	901	23	.04	24	.04
Litchfield Co.	6,451	153	.02	536	4,483	4,182	9,354	339	.05	25	.00
Litchfield	678	55	.08	46	933	132	1,166	46	.07	6	.01
New Milford	484	7	.01	34	373	396	810	27	.06	0	.00

Source: Calculated from "Grand List of the Polls and Rateable Estate of the Several Towns in the State of Connecticut for August 20th. 1796," Connecticut State Archives, Hartford.

Note: Listed here are all the towns with thirty or more first-rate fireplaces, plus New Milford, which had fewer.

turing fireplaces with paneled chimneybreasts and molded fireplace surrounds. Across the hills to the Connecticut River Valley, the frequency of decorated houses went up sharply, not just in Hartford but also in smaller towns along the river. All sorts of amenities and tokens of polite society increased commensurately, carriages being one such item listed in the tax valuation. Litchfield had only 6 carriages in 1796 and New Milford none, while Hartford had 90 and New Haven 109. In some ways, the two regions were different worlds.

With so much evidence of cultural deprivation in the northwest country towns, who were Earl's sitters? Who would be interested in a portrait when other marks of high culture were comparatively rare? To locate the sitters socially and culturally, we have to look more closely at the structure of leadership in the country towns.

The name River Gods applied to a handful of interwoven families who filled a high proportion of colony and county offices and who dwelt in elegant houses with the stupendous doorways that seemed to express their social and political pretensions.[6] Surrounding them was a much larger group of lesser leaders who were just as entrenched in the local sphere. Our fascination with the River Gods, or the Standing Order, as it was sometimes called in Connecticut, can divert attention from this group of second-rank leaders who had sprung up in virtually every town by the middle of the eighteenth century. In a study of thirty-three Connecticut towns, Bruce C. Daniels measured the frequency of family representation in the General Assembly between 1700 and 1780. That is, of all the deputies elected over the eighty-year period, how many had the same family name? Daniels found that on the average, five families in a town accounted for 66 percent of all the deputies chosen. In one town the percentage went as high as 87; in no town did it fall below 48. Although none of the towns in Daniels's sample were from the northwest (because of their late organization date), the country towns from the northeast followed the pattern, though on the low side of the range.[7] There is reason to believe, therefore, that a small group of leading families soon formed in virtually every town with a presumptive claim on local attention at election time. Considering the colony as a whole, with ninety-seven towns in the 1790s, this cadre of political families must have amounted to four hundred or five hundred names.

The significance of these people in town society comes into focus when we look at some of Earl's patrons in New Milford. To begin with, thirteen of the nineteen portraits of New Milford people were members of two families, the Taylors and the Boardmans. Both families were prominent in New Milford from the beginning. The father and grandfather of the Boardman sitters was the Rev. Daniel Boardman, called as the town's first minister in 1712. The town voted to construct a house for him forty by twenty-one feet in size, large for that time, and granted him rights to 1,100 acres of town land. He purchased another 400 acres to become the largest landowner in town. His son Sherman (cat. 56), the eldest of the Boardman sitters, did not go to college, but he was active in town affairs. He continuously held a town or state office from the age of twenty-one to the age of sixty-eight. He was elected New Milford's representative to the General Assembly twenty-one times. He was both deacon and captain of the militia. Sherman Boardman's son Daniel (cat. 28), another sitter for Earl, graduated from Yale in 1781, went into the mercantile business in New Milford, and was elected captain of an independent military company and later major. He doubtless would have assumed further responsibilities had his Connecticut political career not ended when he moved to New York City. Daniel's brother Elijah (cat. 29) studied with the local minister in preparation for college but instead enlisted in the army when the Revolution broke out. He apprenticed with New Haven merchants, went into the mercantile business in New Milford, was elected the New Milford representative six times, and served as both state senator and U.S. senator. Another brother, Homer, was the New Milford representative to the General Assembly three times and also state senator and justice of the peace. A sister, Esther, married Jonathan Burrall of nearby Canaan, a Yale graduate of 1781, frequent Canaan representative to the General Assembly, and a magistrate.

By 1789, when Earl first began painting Boardmans, they were entrenched local gentry who combined wealth, education, family tradition, and doubtless considerable wisdom born of long experience. All this enabled them to make their claim to political office and community leadership. They naturally married people of the same social stratum, joining the Boardman line to families of similar pretensions either in New Milford or elsewhere. The Taylors, who accounted for five of the New Milford portraits, linked themselves to the Boardmans when Nathaniel Taylor (cat. 31) married Tamar Boardman (cat. 32), daughter of Daniel, the first minister. Nathaniel, who graduated from Yale in 1745, then became the long-lived second minister in New Milford. One son, William, who graduated from Yale in 1785, became an amateur landscape painter, and another, Nathaniel, a colonel in the militia.[8]

The tale of the Boardmans and the Taylors could be told a hundred times over in eighteenth-century Connecticut towns. Even in New Milford, the Boardmans and the Taylors were not the only notable families. A Canfield was the wealthiest man in town in 1797, and the Bostwicks, who, like the Taylors, were related to the Boardmans by marriage (to Sherman Boardman), were leaders in various economic enterprises. Families like the Boardmans, Taylors, Canfields, and Bostwicks formed a network of interconnected social and political leaders spread across the colony just below the level of the River Gods.

Besides commanding the major political offices, these local gentry were the ones to benefit from economic opportunities after the Revolution. The prosperity of the 1790s did not compare to the wealth that accumulated after industrialization took hold in the early nineteenth century, but there were opportunities for people with capital and a habit of enterprise. The local gentry were in a position to use their land, their influence, and their good names to advantage. In Litchfield County, the influx of people by itself created opportunities, even without the development of new crops or industries. Between 1756 and 1790, the population of Connecticut as a whole increased by 83 percent, from 130,095 to 238,127. In the same period the population of Litchfield County grew from 11,827 to 38,755, an increase of 228 percent. In the face of such growth, the demand for land alone was an opportunity. Samuel Canfield, the richest man in New Milford in 1797, traded heavily in town lots. Others were speculating in more distant regions. Elijah Boardman and Ithamar Canfield bought lands in the Connecticut Western Reserve in Ohio, where the surplus population of the state spilled over in search of new farms. Fort Edward, New York, was another site for New Milford speculation.[9]

As population expanded, the town benefited from its position as a center of trade for the surrounding villages, which initially had no centers of their own. Until 1750, New Milford had little commerce at its center. The first store building did not appear until 1750, when William Sherman erected one that his brother Roger Sherman (cat. 5) ran until 1760. Another store went up in 1761. In 1781, Elijah Boardman opened his store, and Daniel Boardman joined him as a partner in 1782. Besides profiting from New Milford customers, the Boardmans prospered from people who drove in from surrounding towns. New Milford lay on one of the regular post roads from Boston to Philadelphia. (John Adams once passed through on his way to Congress.) People from nearby towns naturally flocked to it.[10] The Boardmans bid for their patronage by placing advertisements in the *Connecticut Courant and Weekly Intelligencer*, a Hartford paper that circulated widely through the northwest towns.

> *Daniel and Elijah Boardman, At their Store in New-Milford, have for Sale a very large and general Assortment of European, East & West-India Goods, On the most reasonable terms for Cash, Bills of Exchange, public Securities of all kinds, pot-Ash, Pork, Beef, Butter, Cheese, Wheat, Rye, Corn, Oats, Flax-Seed, Bees-Wax, Bar-Iron, Nail-Rods, Geese-Feathers, Hog's Lard, Tallow, and Furs of all kinds. N.B. Any of the above articles will be received on account, from those indebted, where speedy payments will be thankfully acknowledged.*[11]

Daniel accumulated enough from his New Milford venture to launch a successful mercantile business in New York City, where he eventually moved. Elijah remained in New Milford, prospered, and went on to his distinguished political career.

The entrenched gentry, were not, of course, the only ones to benefit from economic opportunities in Litchfield County. Another of Earl's New Milford sitters was Angus Nickelson (cat. 35), born in Scotland in 1735, who migrated to America in 1762 and arrived in New Milford in 1765. He went into the mercantile business, married a New Milford woman, and later opened a marble quarry and an ironworks. Nickelson represented another type of pictured people: the newcomer who prospered. These newcomers rose economically with the older gentry, though usually not achieving political eminence.[12] We can imagine both types emerging everywhere in Connecticut after the Revolution, elevated by the economy from their previous obscurity, ambitious for achievement, and eager to embrace the culture suitable to their position.[13] In the 1770s, Earl painted Roger Sherman, the highly ambitious New Milford surveyor, speculator, and storekeeper who moved to New Haven in 1760 and later won national political distinction. A decade later, the gentry who remained behind in New Milford were ready to be portrayed.

If this emerging elite thought of itself as challenging the River Gods for the leadership of Connecticut society and government, the cultural dimensions of the struggle did not take the form of a distinctly new mode of life. The wealthiest among the rising elite may have exceeded the older families in extravagance of architecture and aesthetic refinement, but both old and new drew their culture from the same well. Only one high culture was available to the Atlantic elites in the eighteenth century, the culture emanating from English and European capitals and epitomized in the English country house. The River Gods led the way in the Connecticut River Valley, setting the pattern of gentility for those who were to succeed them. The aim of the Boardmans was not to replace the older culture but to acquire it for themselves.[14]

According to the 1796 tax evaluation, only a few houses in New Milford had first-rate fireplaces, but one can be sure gentry families resided in them. As fast as they accumulated the means, the eminent families built houses of appropriate distinction. Already in the 1796 lists, New Milford residents owned nearly as many gold and silver watches per capita as older towns in the valley, 0.06 per adult male, a figure exceeding that for East Windsor, where there were 209 first-rate fireplaces. The twenty-seven owners of watches in New Milford were doubtless men of personal address who would soon seek a fitting residence and who in every other respect embraced the genteel culture that elites up and down the colonies had assimilated in the course of the eighteenth century. These people needed portraits to support their claims to social leadership.

The portraits were simply one element in this program of cultural improvement. The same impulses that made a painter useful to some families, decorated houses and refined the dress of others. The urge to improve worked its way into civic life and even into the appearance of the town. In the decade when Earl was painting in Connecticut, New Milford began to develop a recognizable center around a green (chapter-opening fig.). Before the Revolution there had been only a tavern, a store or two, and a few houses, and the green continued in rough form until later in the nineteenth century. Pigs and geese wandered at large, and the runoff from the nearby slope cut an ugly gully along which weeds and brambles grew. No fenced greensward appeared until after 1830. But despite the shaggy look, notable structures began to cluster near the green by the end of the eighteenth century. Three more stores were built near it in the 1780s, and the Episcopal minister's house stood in the vicinity after 1775, joining the home of the Rev. Nathaniel Taylor and his family, which was built there in 1759. The first Daniel Boardman had placed his residence on a hill overlooking the main street; by the 1780s the village center was drawing the finest residences. Around 1790, Beebe Hine built the two-story United States Hotel, believed by residents to be the finest hotel between New Milford and New York City. The upper room of another major residence became an assembly room for balls and socials. Along with the structures came cultural institutions: a private school, a singing school, and in 1796 the Union Library. By the 1790s the green was becoming a center of civilization as well as of commerce.

The first inklings of the urge to beautify the appearance of the town appeared in the same decade. Jared Lane (cat. 51), one of Earl's sitters, began raising fashionable Lombardy poplars for his own property and then for others in town. The town was beginning to be conceived as a landscape whose beautification was the responsibility of the landowners.[15] Elijah Boardman, for one, took the responsibility seriously. He was sufficiently proud of his own property to commission Earl in 1796 to paint his house and shop (cat. 58). The house had the prized pedimented doorway with a small portico and a fashionable venetian window above. Not stopping with the house, Boardman put a white fence around the yard, a gazebo in back, and trees in the corners to simulate a modest pleasure garden.[16]

There was even more of a cultural flowering in an immediately adjoining town, Litchfield, the county seat, where Earl found fourteen subjects. Litchfield led the northwest towns in assessable luxuries in 1796 with fifty-five first-rate fireplaces, forty-six watches, and six carriages (table 2.2). It had a tavern as early as 1782 with a small ballroom on the second floor. There was enough business that David Buell built another tavern in 1787 with the entire second floor devoted to a ballroom. A hotel followed in 1800. In 1798 a ball held in town ran up expenses to the sum of 160 dollars, a stupendous amount for the day. Yale students put on a theatrical performance in 1785, and a Shakespearean company visited in 1789. A newspaper began publication in 1784, and a public library was organized in 1798.[17]

Oliver Wolcott, a Litchfield citizen (cat. 25), whom Earl painted in 1789 along with two members of his family, was utterly smitten with the appearance of New Haven when he went there at age thirteen to consider attendance at Yale, and he brought back beautification ideas to Litchfield. "It took a long time to recount all the wonders I had seen," he later wrote, mentioning, among other things, "the grandeur of New Haven, its numerous Streets, beautiful Trees, Shrubbery and Flowers in the House Yards," and the vessels at Long Wharf. The elms James Hillhouse had planted in New Haven made their mark on Wolcott's imagination, and when he returned from college, he began to plant trees in Litchfield. First he set out thirteen sycamores along South Street to commemorate the thirteen colonies and, when these died, elms from the swamps to replace them. John C. Calhoun later did his part. While a student at Tapping Reeve's law school he planted trees in front of every house where he boarded. All of this put the

Litchfield town center a step or two ahead of the New Milford town center in forming a small locus of civilized life.[18]

The brightest star in Litchfield's firmament was Miss Pierce's Litchfield Female Academy. Sarah Pierce's brother Col. John Pierce directed his sister toward school-teaching after their father, not a wealthy man, died prematurely in 1783. Sarah needed to support herself, and John used part of the family's limited resources to send her to school in New York City when she was seventeen. He wrote her there in 1784 to urge her to make the most of every minute.

> *The short time you have and the many things you have to learn, occasions me to wish you would employ every moment for the purpose, I hope you will not miss a single danc-ing school, and that you will take lessons from Capt. Turner at other times, pray get him and Katy your friend, to instruct you in every thing in walking standing and sitting, all the movements of which tho' they appear in a polite person natural, are the effects of art. {Which} country girls never attend to and which you had best take the utmost pains, or you will never appear natural and easy in. I am somewhat fearful that your old habits at your age can not be so thoroughly removed, as to give place to a natural careless genteel air, and which totally hides all the art of it.*[19]

The message epitomizes Litchfield's cultural situation in the 1780s. Litchfield people prized the genteel arts and yearned to embody them, but as country people, they knew they fell short. Not having disciplined their bodies and minds from childhood, they could not easily assume the easy confidence of the well-bred. What they lacked in breeding, they had to make up for with studied effort.

By all accounts Sarah Pierce succeeded marvelously. She returned to Litchfield to open a school in her own dining room around 1792, first teaching local girls of aspiring families and later attracting young women from all over the country. Both Catherine and Harriet Beecher studied with her and admired her. As the chief justice of the state noted in 1851 at the Litchfield centennial, Sarah Pierce educated young women "as well for genteel as for useful life."[20] At the heart of the school, as all acknowledged, was her own self-discipline, her personal pursuit of improvement and culture.

Her life, it is not too much to say, exemplified the general desire of the Litchfield gentry for refinement. In his 1784 letter, John told Sarah, "I want you to study the fashions, the art of pleasing to advantage and for this purpose to spare no necessary ex-pense, and if you do not appear as genteel as any of the girls it will be your own fault."[21] Although recognizing the drawbacks of a country upbringing, Litchfield people as-sumed responsibility for meeting the standards of polite society – failure would be their own fault – and they were ready to spare no necessary expense. That compulsion cre-ated Earl's opportunity. The advertisement he placed in the *Litchfield Weekly Monitor* for June 21, 1790, after presenting his credentials, expressed the hope that "in this age of refinement, the well-born and well-bred of his countrymen will patronize him in the road to Fame."[22] And of course many did.

Although cultural ambition obviously underlay Earl's portrait business, we can easily misunderstand these village parvenus if we concentrate on ambition alone. It is easy to imagine that their aspirations knew no limit, that only restricted means held them back. Had they enjoyed greater wealth, they would have built ever-larger houses, furnished them ever more extravagantly, and cried their success by every means at hand. But to think of them that way misconstrues their cultural situation and actually obscures the meaning of the paintings.

Insofar as they absorbed gentility, their sensitivity to rank would have been heightened, not merely to their own exalted position at the top of village society but also to their middling location in a hierarchy of ranks that stretched far above them. Deference to superiors was at the very core of genteel culture. A great many of the conventions of polite conduct arose from respect for rank—everything from the breadth of staircases in a house and the placement of guests at a table or in a room, to the amount of white space around the salutary address in a letter. Gentility arose in the Renaissance courts, where regard for rank was essential to peace and harmony amid the snarl of ambition and intrigue. Every courtesy book, including the American favorites, instructed readers to honor rank, which meant avoidance of every pretension to privileges not due to one's position. According to the rules of gentility, it was of prime importance for all people, not just the humble members of society, to know their place. Overly extravagant houses and ostentatious table settings doubtless appeared in country villages, but they were a breach of the genteel code and betrayed a lack of taste. Insofar as upstarts exceeded a fitting expression of their true position in society, they failed in their wish to appear genteel.

Tokens of rank still remained in republican New England to remind the Litchfield citizenry that they occupied a place in a hierarchically ordered society. The solvent of American plentitude had not yet dissolved the traditional ordering of people. Litchfield and New Milford seated their meetinghouses according to rank, and everyone acknowledged the presence of "gentlemen," set apart from the rest.[23] Experience in the militia or army, the lot of nearly every adult male, also reminded people of the ordered ranking of society. These incontrovertible facts exerted their influence over those at the top as well as over those at the bottom. The acceptance of an order that placed them at the pinnacle of their village societies compelled the Litchfield County elite to recognize people of superior rank in the society beyond. All of these things imposed limits on the expression of cultural ambition.

On top of these restraints, in the 1780s, in the aftermath of Revolution, republican egalitarianism further dampened flagrant elitist behavior. At the very moment when the ascendant gentry were buying gold and silver watches, commissioning portraits, and contemplating the construction of a mansion, the break with monarchical government and the institution of democracy made the obliteration of rank in favor of republican equality the official ideology of the independent United States. The principle of political equality was not so powerful as to scourge every form of inequality from the new republic. The aristocratic practice of designating gentlemen as officers in the military and plebeians as enlisted men was never seriously brought into question. Nor did Litchfield Congregationalists debate the propriety of seating the meetinghouse according to rank. But the many contradictions notwithstanding, revolutionary egalitarianism cast a shadow on many forms of elitism because of the anxiety about privilege. Many Americans feared the institution of political or legal privileges and suspected that the socially and economically powerful desired such privileges. Those suspicions inhibited the gentry from adopting aristocratic extravagances even if they could have afforded them.

Popular jealousies were loudly voiced in 1783 and 1784 on the eve of Earl's return to Connecticut and reverberated in the background in succeeding years as he began to portray his well-bred sitters. In the disputes over the commutation of officers' pay and the organization of the Order of the Cincinnati, the widespread sensitivity about aristocratic privilege came to the surface. That revolutionary war officers were the target rather than the gentry in country towns did not obscure the point that any privileged group was suspect.

The trouble began in 1780 as soon as Washington proposed that the Congress promise officers a half-pay pension for life. The Congress had failed to come up with the money for their salaries, and the pension would be an inducement for them to reenlist. Connecticut was recalcitrant from the beginning. The legislators thought it unfair to offer the officers so much and nothing to the enlisted men and made their objections abundantly clear. Under pressure from the officers, the Congress in 1783 compromised with an offer to commute the half-pay pension to five years of full pay, but Connecticut was not appeased. The Massachusetts legislature wrote a letter to the Congress to denounce commutation as "inconsistent with the Equality which ought to subsist among Citizens of free and Republican States." Commutation was a measure "calculated to raise and exalt some Citizens in wealth and Grandeur, to the injury and oppression of others." The Connecticut House approved a similar letter, but the Council, the upper house of the legislature, blocked it, and the house had to be content with a refusal to approve a continental impost that would fund, among other things, the officers' pay.[24]

The citizens of the state were more vocal. The little northwest town of Torrington condemned the assembly for not taking a stand and called for a Litchfield County convention to demand redress. In the statement adopted in town meeting and published in the *Connecticut Courant and Weekly Intelligencer*, Torrington asked, "Are there not individuals in every state, who are endeavouring to saddle the people with pensions? Are there not many in the legislature of this State, who would see, with happiness, the establishment of pensions?" In Torrington's opinion, the wish for privilege in the form of a pension went beyond the military officers to many in the Connecticut legislature who were eager to feed at the public trough. "Can you brook the alarming idea, that the very bread, should be wrested from the hungry mouths of . . . infants, and given to support the luxury . . . of men already fattened by the treasure of their country? Will you, any longer, open your purses to those ravenous harpies, who perch, with whetted beaks and piercing eyes, watching the most favourable opportunity of preying on the public revenues?"[25] The rhetoric sounded alarmingly like the language of the Revolution, now turned on American officers and the Connecticut elite.

Torrington's obscurity among Connecticut towns did not stop the appeal from being heeded. Committees formed in Hartford, Wethersfield, Glastonbury, and Farmington, and the call went out for a convention in Middletown in September 1783, thirteen days before the election of nominees to the Council, where support for commutation centered. Perhaps because of the season and too little time for the towns to rally their forces, only twenty-eight sent delegates. That was enough to arouse conservatives, who filled newspaper columns with criticisms, a sign of their alarm. The fears proved founded when at the September elections six of the men nominated for the previous year lost their places, among them the governor and lieutenant governor. The nominees for the U.S. Congress were similarly decimated, including Eliphalet Dyer (fig. 1.7), the Connecticut representative who had caved in on commutation. The voters struck down men at the pinnacle of Connecticut society, men of wealth, education, and family distinction. These occasional barrages from the voters reminded the gentry that they were never out of range and that one sure way to incur popular wrath was to grant privileges to the elite. The commutation episode warned the gentry against reaching too high. There was danger in appearing aristocratic, and Earl's sitters could not avoid hearing that message.[26]

When the Middletown Convention met again in December 1783, it recommended that the state read Aedanus Burke's *Consideration on the Society or Order of Cincinnati*. The publication of the pamphlet twice in Hartford added to a newspaper campaign against the Cincinnati that opponents had been waging since the previous spring. The convention readily shifted from commutation to the Cincinnati because the two issues were so closely intertwined, both dealing with the officer corps and special privileges. The Order of the Cincinnati had been founded in May 1783, just when the army disbanded, as a fraternal and benevolent society for officers and their children. Members were to contribute one month's pay to a charitable fund. The order alarmed republicans because membership was hereditary and because the emblem they adopted, called the Institution and consisting of a gold eagle hung on a blue and white ribbon, resembled the medals of the European nobility so much. The ultimate aim of the officers, Burke thought, was nothing less than to create an American nobility. Although something short of that now, "the next generation will drink as deep of noble blood, and hereditary peerage be as firmly settled in each potent family, and rivetted in our government, as any order of nobility is in the monarchies of Europe." Peering into the future of the Cincinnati, Burke could see that "in less than a century it will occasion such an inequality in the condition of our inhabitants, that the country will be composed only of two ranks of men; the patricians or nobles, and the rabble." Members of the order "would soon have and hold an exclusive right to offices, honors and authorities, civil and military. And the whole country besides themselves, a mere mob of plebeians, without weight or estimation: degraded in the eyes of our patricians, as the Roman people were by their republican nobility." That tyranny could only end in civil war.[27]

The officers' request for retirement pay could not help but lend weight to Burke's perception of a scheme to create an order of nobles. It was the first of the privileges that would end at last in a distinct rank. A writer in the *Connecticut Journal and New Haven Post Boy* in April 1784 accused the Cincinnati of attempting "to be distinguished from the rest of the citizens, wearing the badge of peerage, and to be paid from the purse of the people." There were probably about 250 members of the order in Connecticut, but the critics thought the numbers would naturally enlarge. Burke believed the officers themselves would be "reinforced and firmly supported by all the potent families and leading first-rate men, in and out of the different legislatures and public bodies throughout America, whose influence and interest the deep policy of the Order has already determined to pre-engage as honorary members."[28] Burke implied, like the Torrington enemies of commutation, that many powerful people waited expectantly in the wings for the chance to acquire privileges. They would gladly join a conspiracy to create an American nobility. The suspicions cast over the Cincinnati fell on the ruling gentry, all of whom, so some believed, secretly wished to elevate themselves above the ordinary people.

Even though this particular tempest soon dissipated, the underlying issue of 1783 did not go away. The label aristocrat remained a term of political opprobrium, the code word for the dreaded alternative to republican government and society. For a generation or more, Americans did not forget that their republic stood alone among the prevailing monarchies of the world. Everywhere nobilities enjoyed special privileges under the reign of kings and queens. Labeling political enemies aristocrats, as American politicians freely did, evoked the specter of the European two-tiered system of ranks, patricians and the rabble, starkly contrasted to the equality of all citizens in a republic. The prevailing suspicions changed carriages and grand houses from well-earned marks of economic and social achievement into dangerous signs of an unrepublican desire for aristocratic distinction and made modesty in appearance not only a virtue but a political necessity.

The political controversies thus raised a question for the gentry: What is your proper place in a republican society? Were the gentry to live with the grandeur that was traditionally thought necessary to exercise effective authority, or were they to blend with the republican masses? An attempt to answer the question was made by a Connecticut man of letters who was himself a distinguished descendant of the mid-century River Gods, Timothy Dwight (fig. 2.2). Dwight was the son of an eminent Northampton merchant and landowner, Maj. Timothy Dwight, and Mary Edwards, daughter of Jonathan Edwards. He could not have had a more distinguished pedigree or a more favored career. Inheriting the Edwards intellect and ambition, at age fifteen, while a student at Yale, Dwight began studying twelve hours a day and limiting his dinners to twelve mouthfuls. He was in succession principal of a grammar school, tutor at Yale, chaplain of a Connecticut brigade in the Continental Army, and representative from Northampton to the Massachusetts legislature. In 1783, Dwight accepted a pulpit at Greenfield Hill in Stratford, a parish where Earl painted nine portraits during the years of Dwight's ministry. Earl had painted Dwight himself and his wife in 1777, when they still lived in New Haven. Dwight wrote poetry on topical themes, including an epic, *The Conquest of Canaan* (1785), in eleven books and the *Triumph of Infidelity* (1788). In 1795 he was elected president of Yale, where for twenty-one years he was the single most powerful intellectual influence in the Connecticut River Valley. In the final year of his parish ministry, 1794, Dwight published a lengthy pastoral poem called *Greenfield Hill* in which he described Connecticut society in detail, revealing how an established member of the provincial gentry coped with the issue of aristocracy.[29]

The remarkable thing about *Greenfield Hill* is the vehemence of the attack on privilege and the European system of rank. Dwight wrote with the barely suppressed rage of a republican radical. Comparing Greenfield Hill, Connecticut, to Europe, he dwelt on the cruelties of economic inequality in the Old World.

2.2
John Trumbull
Timothy Dwight, 1807
oil on canvas
30¼ x 24 in. (76.8 x 61.0 cm.)
Yale University Art Gallery, New
Haven, Conn. Gift of Timothy
Dwight Partridge, B.A. 1912,
1948.5.

> *No griping landlord here alarms the door,*
> *To halve, for rent, the poor man's little store.*
> *No haughty owner drives the humble swain*
> *To some far refuge from his dread domain;*
> *Nor wastes, upon his robe of useless pride,*
> *The wealth, which shivering thousands want beside;*
> *Nor in one palace sinks a hundred cots;*
> *Nor in one manor drowns a thousand lots;*
> *Nor, on one table, spread for death and pain,*
> *Devours what would a village well sustain.*

Those lines go beyond the commonplace criticisms of luxury and corruption heard so often in revolutionary rhetoric and attack unvarnished economic exploitation. What drew Dwight's wrath was the suffering that aristocrats inflicted on the poor.

> *Ah, yonder turn thy wealth-inchanted eyes,*
> *Where that poor, friendless wretch expiring lies!*
> *Hear his sad partner shriek, beside his bed,*
> *And call down curses on her landlord's head,*
> *Who drove, from yon small cot, her houshold sweet,*
> *To pine with want, and perish in the street.*
> *See the pale tradesman toil, the livelong day,*
> *To deck imperious lords, who never pay!*
> *Who waste, at dice, their boundless breadth of soil,*
> *But grudge the scanty meed of honest toil.*
> *See hounds and horses riot on the store,*

> *By HEAVEN created for the hapless poor!*
> *See half a realm one tyrant scarce sustain,*
> *While meagre thousands round him glean the plain!*
> *See, for his mistress' robe, a village fold,*
> *Whose matrons shrink from nakedness and cold!* [30]

Coming in the midst of the French Revolution, which was no triumph of liberty in the mind of the Federalist Dwight, this embittered attack on the European aristocracy was truly remarkable and seemingly contradictory. Did the scion of the Connecticut River Gods really wish to draw the attention of his readers to the vicious injustices of privilege? Was there not a danger that the condemnation of a European aristocracy would lash back at the gentry of his own Greenfield Hill? With the attacks on the Cincinnati only a decade behind him, how did Dwight dare to parade the unfeeling greed of European landlords before the eyes of Connecticut readers?

Dwight's confidence arose from his absolute assurance that Greenfield Hill was another world entirely. Here there were no kings and nobles, no imperious landlords, and for that matter no exploited poor.

> *Here every class (if classes those we call,*
> *Where one extended class embraces all,*
> *All mingling, as the rainbow's beauty blends,*
> *Unknown where every hue begins or ends)*
> *Each following, each, with uninvidious strife,*
> *Wears every feature of improving life.*

Competence was his word for Connecticut society, the economic independence that permitted each family to provide for itself with enough for emergencies and little left over for luxuries. "Oh Competence, thou bless'd by Heaven's decree, / How well exchang'd is empty pride for thee!" Under the administration of competence, "every farmer reigns a little king; / Where all to comfort, none to danger, rise; / Where pride finds few, but nature all supplies." [31]

This idyllic picture could be construed as an elaborate scam perpetrated by Dwight on behalf of the Connecticut gentry. To disguise the actual inequalities in Connecticut, *Greenfield Hill*, it could be argued, deflected the reader's gaze to the excesses of wealth and poverty in European society. It was a gambit to make the inequities of Connecticut disappear in the glare of the comparison. In Dwight's Greenfield Hill, there were no gentry, not even a kindly patron or an honored elder statesman. All were dissolved into the population of competent yeomen with their comfortable firesides and modest farms. There were no five-bay houses with pedimented doors, no carriages or gold watches, no portraits. Did he leave all these out to conceal the aristocracy that still flourished in Connecticut? Was Dwight stonewalling the critics of provincial gentility? [32]

The degree of Dwight's sincerity cannot now be measured, and in a sense it need not be. For the consequences of his vision of Greenfield Hill remain the same whether he believed his own words or not. The belief (or the pretense) that Connecticut society was essentially egalitarian imposed a discipline on the gentry. Along with the other influences that have been discussed – the genteel aversion to excessive display and the republican principle of equality – the poetic vision of a classless society kept aristocratic extravagance within bounds. The Connecticut gentry could not give themselves completely to the unfettered ornamentation of aristocratic houses. They had to retain some degree of simplicity in their self-presentation in compliance with the cultural restraints of their society. Stepping beyond some invisible line would bring them into the sphere of the nobles and kings who sacrificed the well-being of the populace to their own pride-ful pleasure. While groping for refinement and dignity, the gentry had to keep their feet firmly planted in Dwight's one extended class that supposedly embraced everyone in Greenfield Hill.

There were models for this mode of gentility. Earl's Connecticut patron and friend Mason Fitch Cogswell lived for a period with one of them, Samuel Huntington of Nor-wich (fig. 2.3). Huntington went from a modest farm in Windham to the governorship of the state. He was an ambitious lawyer and politician who in 1783 built a commodi-ous house in Norwich, reputed to be the finest in the town. Although adopting some of the tokens of gentility, Huntington carefully restrained himself. Tradition held that people attended dances in the mansion, but the dances "had little in them of the nature of a ball; there were no expensive dresses, no collations, no late hours. They seldom lasted beyond nine o'clock." Samuel's wife, Martha Devotion, the daughter of the Rev. Ebenezer Devotion, was said to be "a lady without any pretensions to style or fashion," who dressed simply all her life and was happy to take tea with the wife of a butcher. The inventory of Samuel Huntington's estate when he died listed few luxuries or orna-ments. His simplicity of life may partly account for the immense popularity that made him governor in 1786, in the very decade when commutation and the Cincinnati had made people sensitive to social inequality.[33] In the same vein, Elijah Boardman (cat. 29) in New Milford was noted for his urbanity and easy manner but chose to be portrayed with signs of his work plainly visible. The portrait said he was a merchant and store-keeper and, though refined and elegant, a working person, not a gentleman.

In view of all this, it can be seen how well Earl served his patrons. His dignified portraits announced the social position of his sitters with perfect clarity. They were people of achievement and refinement but not aristocrats. The very brushstrokes in the paintings, as Elizabeth Mankin Kornhauser has pointed out in chapter 1, distinguished Earl's Connecticut portraits from the more flamboyant ones he executed in England and New York. Connecticut people who wished for more ostentation could employ John Trumbull, as the Wadsworths did, or travel to a metropolitan center to sit for their portraits. For the modest gentry of the Connecticut country towns and little entrepôts, for people who had emerged into prominence after the Revolution and who respected the restraints of republican equality, Earl's hard-edged realism and simplicity of style accurately expressed their pride, their aspirations, and their limitations.

2.3
Charles Willson Peale
Samuel Huntington, 1783
oil on canvas
22 ½ x 18 in. (57.2 x 45.7 cm.)
Courtesy, Independence National Historical Park Collection, Phila-delphia.

III
Ralph Earl's Working Methods and Materials

Stephen H. Kornhauser

UNDERSTANDING THE PAINTING TECHNIQUES and materials used by Ralph Earl during his career may help to explain certain visual trademarks in his pictures and give insight into his virtuosity as an artist in both England and America. Although Earl left no written records about his craft, we are able to obtain a general understanding of his working techniques by studying the account book of one of his patrons, contemporary treatises on painting, and artists' correspondence and by analytically and empirically examining some of his portraits.

A stretcher or a strainer is a wooden frame on which an artist's fabric is stretched. A stretcher can be expanded at all four corners with wooden wedges, called keys, whereas a strainer is anchored at all four corners and cannot be expanded. The more technically advanced stretcher first appeared in Europe in the eighteenth century and had become more universally adopted by the beginning of the nineteenth century.[1]

Stretchers and Strainers

Most of Earl's paintings do not retain their original stretchers or strainers; they were lined with a secondary canvas support at a later date. Although no unlined English or New York paintings with original stretchers or strainers are known, five Connecticut examples have been found: *Squire Samuel Bradley* and *Mrs. Samuel Bradley* (cats. 49, 50), *Smith Booth* (1790; Wilton Historical Society, Wilton, Conn.), *Mrs. Guy Richards* (1793; Hartford Steam Boiler Inspection and Insurance Company), and the large-scale *Colonel Samuel Talcott* (cat. 42).[2] All five have strainers with half-lap corners that are anchored with nails. The strainer dimensions vary in width, thickness, and overall size. In the large portrait of Colonel Talcott, the fabric was also stretched over the strainer, but strips of wood were nailed along the four edges to reinforce it and prevent it from buckling.

An account book of one of the artist's patrons suggests that while Earl was working in the provincial areas of New England he ordered the easily made strainers from local cabinetmakers. Local construction would account for the variation of sizes in his Connecticut portraits. This New Milford patron, Jared Lane (cat. 51), noted on

Detail of
Colonel William Taylor
(cat. 33).

June 16, 1796, for example, "Paid Jonathan Mygatt for making a frame straining on the cloth . . . for Mrs. Lanes portrait."[3] Jonathan Mygatt was a New Milford furniture-maker.

Fabric Supports

Earl painted on canvas supports; the quality and width of his fabrics were probably determined by regional availability. In major cities such as London and New York, artists' materials were readily available. Colormen provided bolts of both primed fabric and standard-size prestretched canvases.[4] The original fabric used for the portrait of William Carpenter (cat. 10) bears what appears to be a colorman's inscription: "E U sq / c / c / 4." The fabrics Earl used for his English and New York portraits were simple in weave and finer and more uniform in texture than those used for his later New England works. For certain commissions, however, he did switch to a smoother twill fabric, as for *Baron von Steuben* (cat. 21), painted in New York City. Twill was almost twice as expensive as a normal fabric.[5]

Once Earl left the cosmopolitan areas, artists' supplies were less readily available. On at least three occasions Earl painted portraits on bed ticking, an unusual, yet not uncommon, support. In some instances, he used a very finely woven fabric, as for the *Canfield Children* (Litchfield Historical Society), painted in 1796. On his sojourns, Earl mainly relied on coarse, nappy, irregularly woven fabrics, almost like tow cloth. According to the Lane account book, Earl procured "1 ½ yards of Russia sheeting for Jared Lane's portrait." Russia sheeting is a strong coarse linen. Such fabrics impart a distinct texture to many of the Connecticut pictures. One early nineteenth-century artist noted that "a canvas somewhat coarser is even preferable because it holds the paint better,"[6] though Earl's choices probably depended more on regional availability.

A common characteristic of the fabrics used by Earl during his travels in New England was that they never measured more than a yard in width. Those pictures that are wider than thirty-six inches were painted on pieced canvases sewn from the reverse with a pressed-open seam, as in his portrait of Colonel Talcott (fig. 3.1). Winthrop Chandler, John Brewster, Jr., and other contemporaries of Earl who worked in provincial New England also used pieced canvases—further evidence that narrow bolts were more common to the region; see, for example, Chandler's Devotion portraits (cats. 1, 2) and Brewster's Mygatt portraits (cats. 69, 70). In the portrait of the Ellsworths (cat. 41), which is painted on three joined pieces of fabric in almost equal size, Earl deftly minimized the distortions by incorporating them into the window posts of the composition. There are no examples of pieced canvas among the portraits Earl painted in New York or England, even though he executed such grand-scale works as *Marinus Willett* (cat. 39), which is fifty-six inches in width.

Grounds and Primings

Earl used a variety of primings during the course of his career. Many of his English pictures have the more fashionable, smooth, cool white primings, which he continued to use on his return to New York City. At times he added a warm brown *imprimatura,* as in *Marinus Willett* (cat. 39). Analytical tests conducted on ground samples from the portrait of Benjamin Judah (cat. 48), painted in New York in 1794, found both lead and calcium. The presence of lead indicates that one pigment was lead white, a simple lead carbonate, which is a common white component of grounds, and the calcium most likely indicates the use of calcium carbonate.[7]

Recipes for white grounds were quite diverse at the end of the eighteenth cen-

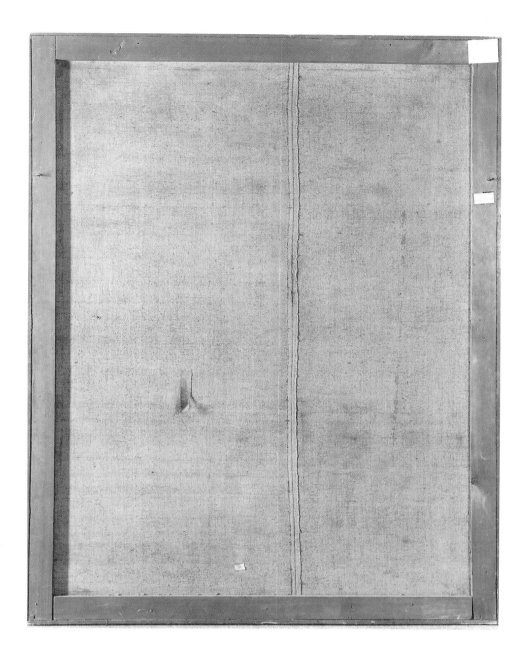

tury. For example, grounds on many of Hogarth's paintings contained a mixture of lead white and calcium carbonate. A seventeenth-century English technical writer, Edward Norgate, recommended a combination of lead white and calcium carbonate as an ideal ground. Another author, Edward Salmon, gave a recipe for a ground consisting of "whiting . . . size and a little honey."[8] Commercially prepared fabrics, according to another early author, were prepared with whiting. The prepared canvases were sold by colormen in white as well as light gray, pink, and the faintest pink flesh color.[9]

Once Earl left New York City and undertook his itinerant career in New England, he employed several canvas preparations. At times he retained the more stylish, cool white ground of his English years; at other times, a bluish red ground, an anachronistic practice more in keeping with mid-century American colonial painters. It is unclear whether Earl chose a white ground to enhance the lighter palette he frequently favored for the more fashionable works or whether time and availability were also factors.

In 1789 he completed *Elijah Boardman* (cat. 29) in New Milford, painted on a priming that was prepared in two layers, a thin red stain layer followed by a thick, cool, grayish white layer. According to pigment analysis, the dark red stain contains iron, most likely an iron oxide, and the upper layer is again a mixture of white lead and chalk. The use of layering shows that Earl had at least a nodding acquaintance with Robert Dossie's *Handmaid to the Arts*, published in London in 1758. The author recommended that cloth be well soaked with two to three coats of drying oil and red ochre (an iron oxide), covered with a white lead on oil, rendered gray, and polished with pumice or with glass pointers, called calendar stones.[10] In 1796, Earl painted the portrait of Jared Lane (cat. 51), for which he also used a white priming. The accompanying entry in Lane's account book noted purchases of "1 lb. of white lead" and "½ lb of glue for J. L. Portrait." The white lead would have been for the priming and the glue most likely for a fabric sizing.

Earl also employed a range of red-earth-colored ground preparations for his paintings. They varied from a thick and powdery priming to a thin reddish stain. They are more absorbent than the reflective white grounds, which give paint films a lean chalky appearance. When Earl prepared his canvas with a lean absorbent priming, as for the *Portrait of Ashahel Pomeroy*, painted in Northampton, Massachusetts, in 1799 (Forbes Library, Northampton), it caused light colors, such as those used for the flesh and sky, to take on an uneven grayish cast, because the oil paint medium was absorbed by the fabric.

An analysis of the reddish priming layer of Earl's *Colonel Samuel Talcott* (cat. 42), painted in Hartford in 1792, shows it to contain lead, calcium, iron, and barium. The pigments containing these elements, particularly the red iron oxide, create the deep reddish cast seen in the painting. The presence of barium most likely means that barite was added; the mineral form of barium sulfate was used by the pigment industry as an extender in grounds as early as the late seventeenth century, and it was also readily available to both artists and house painters.[11]

In his portraits *Oliver Ellsworth and Abigail Wolcott Ellsworth* and *Reverend Nehemiah Strong* (cats. 41, 36), Earl applied thin priming washes and then blocked in areas of localized color. The fabrics are tight and finely woven, which may have helped to retard the absorption of the oil paint film. Earl was not unique in using thin grounds; Sir Joshua Reynolds, for one, used thin grounds or no grounds at all, sometimes painting directly on unprimed canvas in a manner he thought to be Venetian. Another English painter, Sir Thomas Beechey, saw an unprimed canvas as assisting in the preservation of pictures. In *The Artist's Repository* (1784–86), it is noted that "portrait painters chose a very thin priming."[12]

Pigments

Although Earl used a limited palette, his choice and number of pigments was in keeping with contemporary portrait practices. For example, the palette of the English artist Thomas Bardwell consisted of white, a variety of earth reds, ochres, vermillion, red lake, blues, black, and browns. Reynolds used very few colors, stating that "lake, yellow ocher, blue and black are sufficient . . . to paint anything." Gilbert Stuart used Prussian blue, white, yellow, vermillion, crimson lake, burnt umber, and black.[13] In his account book, Jared Lane listed all the pigments Earl used to paint the Lanes' two portraits and one landscape (cat. 51).

Black: Again, Jared Lane's account book tells us that Earl received "1/ [oz] Ivory Black . . . for J. Lanes Portrait." Traditionally, black was used to cool or darken pigment mixtures and was recommended, along with Indian red, as an additive for shadows.[14] The analysis of the pigments used in painting the black shoes of Oliver Ellsworth and Colonel Talcott (cats. 41, 42) shows them to be composed primarily of a bone black. Ivory black may merely be a generic term.

Blue: Prussian blue was discovered early in the eighteenth century and was a major component of Earl's palette, as well as the palettes of many of his contemporaries. Known to be a good drier, it replaced other, more costly and unreliable blues, though it had a greenish cast. Not only artists but also house and ship painters commonly used it.[15] Earl ordered "½ oz Prussian Blue" for Jared Lane's portrait (cat. 51). Although the predominant color in the Lane portrait is green, pure green pigments were of such poor quality that painters usually achieved a green by combining ochre and Prussian blue.[16] Analysis of the blue taken from the skies in two of Earl's paintings and a sample from Oliver Ellsworth's jacket show them to contain elements found in combination only in Prussian blue.

Brown: Since umbers were common to the palette of late eighteenth-century portrait painters, Earl probably used them, although there is no written reference to his purchasing umbers, nor is there any conclusive analysis of their presence.

Green: Portrait painters rarely used pure green pigments because of their poor quality. Sir Joshua Reynolds, Mather Brown, and Thomas Sully all omitted them, relying more on simple admixtures of blue and ochre. The only green that was stable, according to Bardwell, was terre verte.[17] Verdigris and other greens used by house painters were not. Analysis of Earl's pigments shows green earth, or terre verte, in both the green waistcoat in *Benjamin S. Judah* (cat. 48) and the green carpet banding in *Colonel Samuel Talcott* (cat. 42).

Red: Earl used at least three types of reds in his pictures, a carmine or lake (observed), vermillion, and iron oxide. Carmine was common to English painters, yet relatively expensive. Earl used it in *Mary Ann Carpenter* (cat. 11), painted in England, and *Benjamin S. Judah* (cat. 48), done in New York. He did not appear to use it in his rural New England portraits. In those, according to chemical sampling, vermillion or cinnabar was the brilliant red component found in clothing, chairs, and draperies and flesh tones with warm red highlights. Jared Lane recorded that "1 oz vermillion" was purchased for his wife's portrait. Earl signed his New England paintings, beginning in 1788, with vermillion.

Red oxide is a general term for red earth pigments containing iron oxide, such as English red and Venetian red. Dossie mentioned light red and red ochre, which are iron bearing. Bardwell mentioned the importance of Indian red for flesh tones.[18] Samples of flesh tones in Earl's portraits indicate the typical presence of iron oxide.

White: Lead white was the traditional base for white pigments. It is commonly referred to as flake white, which may relate to a guarantee of purity. The contemporary term for a white lead mixed with calcium carbonate was ceruse.[19] Analysis of the whites used by Earl shows them to be an unmixed white lead.

Yellow: In the samples taken, the only yellow to appear is yellow ochre, the yellow artists predominantly used, although they sometimes used Naples yellow and orpiment.[20] Naturally occurring pigments like yellow ochre can vary considerably, thus providing the subtle variations an artist might need. Lane's account book indicates that Earl received "3 oz of stone yellow . . . for Mrs. Lanes Portrait." Stone yellow is a yellow ochre; the term itself is fairly obscure, however, and has been found only in a manual for house and ship painters and not in treatises on painting.[21]

Driers

A drier is a compound, such as red lead, cooked at high temperatures with an oil; it is used to accelerate the drying of an oil paint or varnish. Sugar of lead or lead acetate was a type of drying agent. It would have been mixed with pigments that were slow driers or used in small quantities as a resin varnish to facilitate drying. The Lane account book itemized "sugar of lead and spirits of turpentine for J. Lane's Portrait."

Final Coatings

The only references to Earl's varnishing material appear in Jared Lane's account book. On September 19, 1796, he wrote, "Paid Elijah Boardman for Copal Varnish for 2 portraits and one landscape," and on September 30, "Spirits of turpentine to pay some borrowed to varnish portraits."

Copal varnish was prepared by boiling a copal resin in oil, usually with a drier. The strong, amber-colored, durable varnish so produced had qualities sought by house and coach painters rather than by artists, though Sully mentioned that "some [artists] recommended copal varnish," and another of Earl's English contemporaries, Mather Brown, discussed how, once made, it should be diluted with turpentine. Reynolds used it only as a sealant for his fabrics or as a painting medium, not as a varnish.[22]

Earl's contemporaries followed a number of varnish recipes. Copley made a mastic with "whitest gum mastic 6 ounces, spirit of turpentine 7 ounces," as did Benjamin West. One of Reynolds's favorite final coatings was made with egg white. Two New England artists, Richard and William Jennys, who, like Earl, pursued itinerant careers, provided a recipe for varnish on the backs of two portraits – directions for the sitters to follow.

> *To varnish the portrait*
> *beat the white of an egg to a froth, add a small piece of loaf sugar*
> *and beat it again with two spoonfuls of gin, dust the picture with a piece of silk and put*
> *   on varnish with a rag*
> *to be varnished once a year.*[23]

It is likely that Earl normally used other types of varnish, but he may have used a copal varnish for Jared Lane's portrait because of its availability.

Both the materials and straightforward formal technique that Ralph Earl developed over the course of his career demonstrate a somewhat unorthodox mastery of portrait painting. A study of Earl's British and New York City portraits shows his awareness of the English portrait conventions of the late eighteenth century. For example he used a warm transparent imprimatura applied over a white ground in *Marinus Willett* (cat. 39) and some glazes in the portraits of the Carpenter children (cats. 10, 11) and *Benjamin S. Judah* (cat. 48), as well as a twill fabric for a cloth support in the portrait of Baron von Steuben in the collection of Yale University Art Gallery (cat. 21).

Once he returned to America and began to travel through the rural Northeast, Earl apparently distilled what he had learned while in London into a pragmatic and simplified formula. When possible, he would retain his sound habits, such as working with a limited palette, using traditional methods to prepare primings, and avoiding problem colors, such as green. At the same time, he modified his practices as need required.

For instance, his use of a fabric prepared with a dark priming may seem at first to be *retardataire* but upon closer examination it is evident that this technique was effective in creating a middle tone for his sober New England portraits.

Although Earl's painting skills were based on the available technical knowledge, he may have been restricted at times by the unavailability of certain artists' materials, as well as by his sitters' reluctance to pay the cost of procuring proper materials. It is of some interest that John Brewster, Jr., an itinerant contemporary of Earl's, purchased his materials from a house painter, including such pigments as verdigris and Spanish white that were more fitting for house exteriors than for easel paintings.[24] Earl sensibly resorted to seamed fabrics, locally constructed strainers, unorthodox pigments, such as stone yellow, and copal varnish in adapting to the New England towns in which he worked.

Notes

CHAPTER I: RALPH EARL

1. Emory Washburn, *Historical Sketches of the Town of Leicester, Massachusetts* (Boston, 1860), 359; Pliny Earle, *Ralph Earle and His Descendants* (Worcester, Mass., 1888); Earle, *Memoirs of Pliny Earle, M.D.* (Boston, 1898). Although the birth of Ralph Earl is recorded in the towns of both Shrewsbury and Leicester, it is likely that the artist was born in the house of his grandfather, William Earle, in Shrewsbury, where his parents were living at the time of their marriage on July 19, 1750. William Earle is listed in the Shrewsbury Town Records, in the Worcester County Courthouse, Worcester, Mass. as a "yeoman" and "joyner."

The town of Paxton was incorporated in 1765 from sections of Leicester and Rutland.

2. Although Ralph Earl changed the spelling of his name from Earll, to Earl when he began his career as an artist, his immediate family used the spelling Earll, and many of his relatives spelled their name Earle; see Franklin P. Rice, *Vital Records of Leicester, Massachusetts* (Worcester, Mass., 1903).

3. Rice, *Vital Records of Leicester*; Paxton Town Records, 1765–1790, Worcester County Courthouse; Office of the Secretary, Commonwealth of Massachusetts, *Soldiers and Sailors in the Revolutionary War* (Boston, 1899), 5:152. Ralph Earll inherited one half of his father's farm and lands in Paxton, which, when added to his other landholdings, made him one of the highest payers of real estate tax in the town.

4. Washburn, *Historical Sketches of Leicester*, 439–40.

An existing schoolbook, *The Youth's Instructor*, found in the Earll family home in Paxton in the 1950s, is inscribed with the artist's name and that of his youngest brother: "James Earll / Ralph Earll / 1768 / 1767." For photographs of the book and the Earl house, see William Sawitzky and Susan Sawitzky Papers, "Ralph Earl," Box 1, New-York Historical Society, New York.

For a discussion of child-rearing practices in eighteenth-century New England, see Philip Greven, *The Protestant Temperament: Patterns of Child-Rearing, Religious Experience, and Self in Early America* (1977; reprint, New York, 1979), 151–256.

5. Office of the Secretary, *Soldiers and Sailors*, 5:152.

6. Jonathan Trumbull, Sr., to William Kneeland, August 10, 1772, cited in Helen Cooper et al., ed., *John Trumbull: The Hand and Spirit of a Painter*, exhib. cat. (New Haven, Conn., 1982), 2. Neil Harris, *The Artist in American Society: The Formative Years, 1790–1860* (New York, 1966), discusses contemporary attitudes toward art and artists in America.

7. The most up-to-date discussion of James Earl's career appears in Robert G. Stewart, "James Earl: American Painter of Loyalists and His Career in England," *American Art Journal* 20, no. 4 (1988), 34–59; see also Harold Spencer, *The American Earls: Ralph Earl, James Earl, R. E. W. Earl*, exhib. cat. (Storrs, Conn., 1972), 32–47.

8. Harris, *Artist in American Society*, 56–90.

9. Elizabeth Mankin Kornhauser, *Ralph Earl: Artist-Entrepreneur* (Ann Arbor: University Microfilms, 1989), 13–14; Edgar P. Richardson, *Painting in America* (New York, 1956), 122.

10. *The Huntington Family in America* (Hartford, Conn., 1915), 549, quoted in Robert F. Trent with Nancy Lee Nelson, "New London County Joined Chairs, 1720–1790," *Connecticut Historical Society Bulletin* 50 (Fall 1985), 20.

11. Nina Fletcher Little, "Winthrop Chandler," *Art in America* 35 (April 1947), special issue; Little, "Recently Discovered Paintings by Winthrop Chandler," *Art in America* 36 (April 1948), 81–97.

12. Elizabeth Mankin Kornhauser and Christine Skeeles Schloss, "Painting and Other Pictorial Arts," in *The Great River: Art and Society of the Connecticut Valley, 1635–1820*, exhib. cat. (Hartford, Conn., 1985), 135–36, 143–46.

13. For a discussion of Johnston's Connecticut portraits, see ibid., 143; Richard H. Saunders and Ellen G. Miles, *American Colonial Portraits: 1700–1776*, exhib. cat. (Washington, D.C., 1987), 260–61. The use of British mezzotint prints by artists working in colonial America is discussed in Waldron Phoenix Belknap, Jr., *American Colonial Painting* (Cambridge, Mass., 1959); Trevor J. Fairbrother, "John Singleton Copley's Use of British Mezzotints for His American Portraits: A Reappraisal Prompted by New Discoveries," *Arts Magazine* 55 (March 1981), 122–30. On Durand's dates, see Kornhauser and Schloss, "Painting and Other Pictorial Arts," 147. On his portraits, see Belknap, *American Colonial Painting*, 296, 326.

14. *Worcester Spy*, July 29, 1790, reproduced in Little, "Winthrop Chandler," 88.

15. Ibid.

16. Washburn, *Historical Sketches of Leicester*, 276; John L. Brooke, *The Heart of the Commonwealth: Society and Political Culture in Worcester County, Massachusetts, 1713–1861* (Cambridge, Eng., 1989), 144–45, discusses the political tension that arose in the spring of 1774, in particular the town of Leicester's response to the Coercive Acts imposed by Parliament in the spring of 1774. The town drew up the Leicester Resolves, which were circulated in the surrounding towns and provided "a model for revolutionary language."

17. Thomas C. Barrow, *Connecticut Joins the Revolution* (Chester, Conn., 1973), 15.

18. Carol Troyon, *The Boston Tradition: American Paintings from the Museum of Fine Arts*, exhib. cat. (New York, 1980), 70.

19. The announcement appeared three times in the *Connecticut Journal and New Haven Post Boy*, on July 8, July 15, and July 22, 1774. A newspaper mistakenly called John Singleton Copley by another name entirely when he was in England – William Copeley; see Jules Prown, *John Singleton Copley*, 2 vols. (Cambridge, Mass., 1966), 2:49, 387.

20. My thanks to Marcia Hinckley for locating the following sources that identify Medad Lyman: Lyman Coleman, *Genealogy of the Lyman Family, in Great Britain and America* (Albany, N.Y., 1872), 392, 457; Medad Lyman, New Haven, probate docket 6545, Connecticut State Library, Hartford; New Haven Land Records, 17:133, Connecticut State Library. The land records indicate that Lyman purchased the New Haven homestead of Gideon Andrews in 1753, a property bounded south and west by town streets (probably York and George streets), north by land owned by Mary Atwater, and east by land owned by the heirs of James Colbert.

21. Four witnesses were present at the marriage ceremony, including Sarah's brother Daniel Gates and Ralph's brother Clark

Earll. The details of Earl's marriage, as well as his movements during the early years of his career, are illuminated in a deposition made by Sarah in 1815, after Earl died, when she was Sarah Earl Pierce. The deposition is recorded in Worcester District Registry of Deeds, Worcester, Mass., book 196, p. 293; a second deposition by Sarah's cousin Sarah Moore appears on p. 295. Kornhauser, *Ralph Earl*, 17–19, 32n.

Sarah Earl Pierce's testimony establishes Ralph Earl's presence in New Haven in the summer of 1774. Sarah states that she married him in Paxton in "September or October of 1774," and at the time, he "lived in New Haven from whence he came to Leicester to be married." She continues, "I understood his native place was Paxton where his father lived at the time of our marriage – he called Paxton his home, but worked some in Leicester, how long I do not know – I knew him three or four years before our marriage and was first acquainted with him when he worked in Leicester. . . . We began to keep house in November AD 1776 at New Haven, about two years after we were married and continued until the May following, which was all the time we kept house together." Quoted in Kornhauser, *Ralph Earl*, 17–18.

22.   In Charles O. Gates, *Stephen Gates of Hingham and Lancaster, Massachusetts, and His Descendants* (New York, 1898), 44.

23.   *Letters and Papers of John Singleton Copley and Henry Pelham, 1739–1776*, ed. Guernsey Jones (1914; reprint, New York, 1970), 266–67, 273. On securing commissions, see also ibid., 278. Pelham wrote letters from New Haven from November 18 until December 12, 1774.

24.   Henry Pelham to Adam Babcock, April 3, 1775, in "Copley/Pelham Correspondence," Public Record Office, Archives, London, in American Loyalist Claims, Series III (A.O. 13), Bundle 41.

25.   Pelham made "some Alteration in the Landscape which Mr. Copley said Mr. Pelham was to make" for the portrait of Benjamin Andrews. Andrews to Pelham, Monday, March 1773, in *Letters of Copley and Pelham*, 197.

26.   Barbara Neville Parker, *New England Miniatures, 1750 to 1850* (Boston, 1957), 11–12; see also Saunders and Miles, *American Colonial Portraits*, 307–8, for a documented miniature of *Stephen Hooper* (1773).

27.   Mabel M. Swan, "The Johnstons and Reas – Japanners," *Antiques* 47 (May 1943), 212, reproduces segments of the account books of Rea and Johnston, including the following outstanding bill for Ralph Earl: "July 15, 1778 To Sundries M'd Ralph Earl ¼." The entry was made two months after Earl's departure for England.

28.   Roger S. Boardman, *Roger Sherman: Signer and Statesman* (Philadelphia, 1938); John G. Rommel, *Connecticut's Yankee Patriot: Roger Sherman* (Hartford, Conn., 1979); Christopher Collier, *Connecticut in the Continental Congress* (Chester, Conn., 1973), 10.

29.   Quoted in Boardman, *Roger Sherman*, 133.

30.   Ellen D. Larned, *History of Windham County, Connecticut*, 2 vols. (Worcester, Mass., 1874–80), 1:458–59; William F. Willingham, *Connecticut Revolutionary: Eliphalet Dyer* (Hartford, Conn., 1976).

31.   According to the *Records of the Windham Free Library*, Windham, Conn., the portrait was damaged in a fire in the Windham Congregational Church in the late nineteenth century. The artist J. Alden Weir (1841–1926), a local resident, restored the painting. In the 1930s, Ralph Thomas, then director of the New Haven Colony Historical Society and a painting restorer, reported that this portrait had been badly damaged, having lost much of the outer right edge and bottom edge of canvas. He treated the painting and trimmed the edges. For his report, see Painting Files, Yale University Art Gallery, New Haven, Conn.

32.   Dunlap, *History of the Rise and Progress of the Arts of Design in the United States*, 3 vols. (1834; reprint, New York, 1969), 3:223–24. Dunlap became closely associated with the Dwights when he married Mary Woolsey Dwight's half sister, Elizabeth Woolsey. *Diary of William Dunlap, 1766–1839*, 3 vols. (New York, 1930), 3:808, makes a second reference to the portraits: "Mrs. Dwight tells me that Earl painted herself and husband in 1777."

33.   Nehemiah Strong to Ezra Stiles, August 30, 1790, Beinecke Rare Book and Manuscript Library, Yale University, New Haven, Conn.

34.   Dunlap, *History of Design*, 1:223.

35.   The Boston Massacre took place on March 5, and Pelham advertised his print *The Fruits of Arbitrary Power* in the *Boston Evening Post and Boston Gazette* on April 2, 1770, as "An Original Print, representing the late horrid Massacre in King Street, taken on the Spot." Pelham's colleague Paul Revere managed to publish a pirated version of Pelham's print one week earlier. See Wendy J. Shadwell, *American Printmaking: The First 150 Years* (New York, 1969), 27.

36.   Pelham to Singleton, May 16, 1775, in *Letters of Copley and Pelham*, 321.

37.   *Boston Prints and Printmaking, 1670–1775* (Boston, 1973), 52–54.

38.   John W. Barber and Lemuel S. Punderson, *History and Antiquities of New Haven, Conn.* (New Haven, Conn., 1856), 14.

39.   *Connecticut Archives, Revolutionary War*, microfilm, vol. 6, part 1, V-290, Connecticut State Library.

40.   *Connecticut Journal*, April 2, 1777.

41.   The claim is reproduced in John Marshall Phillips, "Ralph Earl, Loyalist," *Art in America* 37 (October 1949), 187–89. The original is in the Public Record Office, Archives, London, in American Loyalist Claims, Series III (A.O. 13), Bundle 41. For Ralph Earl's rank, see Office of the Secretary, *Soldiers and Sailors*, 5:152.

42.   Quoted in Phillips, "Ralph Earl," 187.

43.   Ibid., 187–88.

44.   *Records of the State of Connecticut, 1776–1778*, 1:187, Connecticut State Library.

45.   Phillips, "Ralph Earl," 188, 189.

46.   Dorinda Evans, *Benjamin West and His American Students*, exhib. cat. (Washington, D.C., 1980).

47.   Marcia Pointon, "Portrait-Painting as a Business Enterprise in London in the 1780s," *Art History* 7 (June 1984), 187–205. The quotation appears on p. 187.

48.   John Chambers, *History of Norfolk* (Norwich, Eng., 1826), 2:766: "Major Money had a narrow escape for his life in a balloon, at a time when aerial trips were reckoned great proofs either of a man's courage or his insanity." See also the *Norfolk and Norwich Remembrancer* (Norwich, Eng., 1801), 21, for an account of Money's rescue.

Money's military career is documented in John Philipart, *The Royal Military Calendar*, 2 vols. (London, 1815), 1:119–21. As a boy, Money joined the Norfolk militia. He later served as a cornet in the Sixth Regiment of Dragoons and, with his regiment, eventually went to Ireland in 1773 and to America in 1777. There he served as quartermaster general in General Burgoyne's army in Canada. On September 19, 1777, Money was ordered into action during Burgoyne's descent on Albany and was taken prisoner on October 8 of that year. He returned to England, with Earl, in April 1778.

49.   Walter Rye. *Norfolk Families* (Norwich, Eng., 1913), 561–

62. In a letter to the American artist John Trumbull, who was then in London, Ralph E. W. Earl wrote from Norwich: "General Money whom you have heard me mention was my father's friend and has become my friend, and have just finished a portrait of him to his satisfaction." Earl to Trumbull, February 18, 1810, Gage Family Papers, MS, American Antiquarian Society, Worcester, Mass. The portrait is unlocated.

50.   Phillips, "Ralph Earl," 188–89.

51.   Previous scholars have suggested an earlier date for Earl's presence in the London studio of Benjamin West, based solely on the portrait *Mrs. John Johnston* (cat. 20), which was erroneously dated 1782. See Evans, *Benjamin West*, 61; William Sawitzky and Susan Sawitzky, "Two Letters from Ralph Earl, with Notes on His English Period," *Worcester Art Museum Annual* 8 (1960), 22–23.

52.   W. F. Dickes, *The Norwich School of Painting* (London, 1906), 15.

53.   Trevor Fawcett, "Eighteenth-Century Art in Norwich," *Walpole Society, 1976–1978*, 46 (1978), 71.

54.   *Norwich Gazette*, March 4, 1712, reproduced in Fawcett, "Eighteenth-Century Art in Norwich," 72.

55.   *Norwich Mercury*, August 2, 1777, reproduced in Fawcett, "Eighteenth-Century Art in Norwich," 81.

56.   Fawcett, "Eighteenth-Century Art in Norwich," 79; R. H. Wilenski, *English Painting* (Boston, 1933), 160–61.

57.   W. Roberts, *Sir William Beechey, R.A.* (London, 1907), 21–22, reproduces segments of Beechey's notebook, describing a party he attended at Lord Orford's country house, in Houghton, on August 11, 1785, which also included the artists Henry Fuseli and Giovanni Battista Cipriani. Beechey notes "the rest of the company consisted of aeronauts, the Balloon makers, namely Major Money of Norwich . . . Captain somebody who rescued the Major from a watery death . . . as the company consisted of such gentry, it is natural to suppose that their conversation would turn on nothing but what makes the best gas, what ingredients make the best balloon varnish [etc.]."

58.   Ellis Waterhouse, *Painting in Britain, 1530–1790* (London, 1953), 227, 232.

59.   The most illuminating work on provincial British portraiture to date is Trevor Fawcett, *The Rise of English Provincial Art: Artists, Patrons, and Institutions outside London, 1800–1830* (Oxford, Eng., 1974); on Earl's career in Norwich, see Fawcett, "Eighteenth-Century Art in Norwich." Lillian B. Miller provides a parallel between Norwich and New England portraiture in "The Puritan Portrait: Its Function in Old and New England," in David D. Hall and David Grayson Allen, eds., *Seventeenth-Century New England* (Boston, 1984).

60.   British Art Photograph Archive, Yale Center for British Art, New Haven, Conn., includes photographs of the following portraits of Norwich-area subjects that include geometrically patterned carpets: attributed to Henry Walton (1746–1813), *A Gentleman at Breakfast* (c. 1775–80; collection of the Brooklyn Museum, New York), and Walton, *Group Portrait of Mr. and Mrs. Hayward with Their Children* (c. 1789; Christies, London, April 11, 1980, no. 157).

61.   Algernon Graves, *The Royal Academy of Arts: A Complete Dictionary of Contributors and Their Work from Its Foundation in 1769 to 1904*, 8 vols. (London, 1895), 3:2.

62.   Kornhauser, *Ralph Earl*, 253–343.

63.   Dunlap, *History of Design*, 1:233.

64.   Dunlap returned from England to America in 1787, and the following year he noted: "I derived much advantage intellectually from the society of the Rev. Timothy Dwight . . . who had married my wife's sister, and at whose house in Greenfield Hill I passed some of my happiest hours." Dunlap, *History of Design*, 1:267. Ralph Earl was painting portraits in Greenfield Hill that same year. In addition, a 1789 visitor to the Dwights' house noted that the "rooms are ornamented with paintings from the pencil of Mr. Dunlap, his brother-in-law." He also mentioned seeing Earl's portraits of "Dr. Dwight and Mrs. Dwight." Samuel Davis, "Journal of a Tour to Connecticut – Autumn of 1789," in *Proceedings of the Massachusetts Historical Society* (Boston, 1869–70), 18. Dunlap would later develop a friendship with Earl's guardian and friend, Mason Fitch Cogswell of Hartford. Dunlap, *History of Design*, 1:272–73.

65.   Earl to Trumbull, September 23, 1784, Historic Deerfield, Deerfield, Mass., reproduced in Sawitzky and Sawitzky, "Two Letters from Ralph Earl," 11–12.

66.   Prown, *John Singleton Copley*, 2:296.

67.   Dorinda Evans, *Mather Brown: Early American Artist in England* (Middletown, Conn., 1982), 122–23.

68.   Mather Brown wrote in 1782: "History painting is what I prefer to all others, as it [is] on a more extensive Plan, and requires the Advantage of Education united with the Luxuriance of a Fine Imagination." Quoted in Evans, *Mather Brown*, 28. Trumbull expressed a similar sentiment in a letter to his brother in 1785: "I wish to rise above the necessity of painting [portraits] & and there is a line . . . which offers me a more easy & elegant support if I can acquire the necessary powers of execution. . . . If I do succeed it makes me master of my time. & disengages me from all the trumpery & caprice & nonsense of mere copying faces – & places me the servant not of Vanity but Virtue." Quoted in Cooper et al., ed., *John Trumbull*, 98.

69.   Robert Rosenblum, "Reynolds in an International Milieu," in Nicholas Penny, ed., *Reynolds* (New York, 1989), 43–54.

70.   Robert O. Park, ed., *Sir Joshua Reynolds: Discourses on Art* (San Marino, Calif., 1959), 42.

71.   Graves, *Royal Academy of Arts*, 3:2; Laurence B. Goodrich, "Ralph Earl's First Royal Academy Entry," *Antiques* 75 (May 1959), 456–57. The subject's identity as George Onslow was discovered by an entry in Horace Walpole's copy of the Royal Academy catalogue for 1783.

72.   Horace Walpole, *Memoirs of the Reign of George III* (London, 1845), 3:116–17.

73.   *Dictionary of National Biography*, 22 vols. (London, 1882–1953), 218–19; Goodrich, "Ralph Earl's First Royal Academy Entry," 456–57.

74.   Goodrich, "Ralph Earl's First Royal Academy Entry," 456, reproduces the review that appeared in the *Morning Post and Daily Advertiser* (London), May 1, 1783, in a column featuring "the principle Pictures, Busts, Drawings, &c. now exhibiting at the Royal Academy."

75.   Quoted in Stephen Deuchar, *Noble Exercise: The Sporting Idea in Eighteenth-Century British Art*, exhib. cat. (New Haven, Conn., 1982), 28.

76.   Ibid., 45–47.

77.   Evans, *Benjamin West*, 66–67.

78.   Laurence B. Goodrich, "Ralph Earl's Portraits of Three Young English Ladies," *Antiques* 71 (November 1958), 418–19. For a discussion of portrait prices in London in the 1780s, see Pointon, "Portrait-Painting as a Business Enterprise," 200.

79.   Prown, *John Singleton Copley*, 2:259.

80.   Pointon, "Portrait-Painting as a Business Enterprise," 193–94; M. Kirby Talley, Jr., "'All Good Pictures Crack': Sir Joshua Reynolds's Practice and Studio," in Nicholas Penny, ed., *Reynolds*

(New York, 1989), 57. Farrington is quoted in Talley, " 'All Good Pictures Crack,' " 57.

81. The advertisement appeared in the New York section of the *Connecticut Courant and Weekly Intelligencer* (Hartford), May 10, 1785, and in *Thomas' Massachusetts Spy, or, the Worcester Gazette,* May 12, 1785.

82. Nina Fletcher Little discovered the following announcement, which appeared in the *Salem Gazette* (Mass.), May 24, 1785, and *Thomas' Massachusetts Spy*, May 26, 1785: "Boston, May 23   In the Neptune, Capt. Callahan, who arrived here since our last, in 30 days from England, were the following passengers: Mr. Joseph Trumbull, Worcester; Mr. Earl and lady, Worcester; Mr. Levi Williard, Lancaster. . . ." First reproduced in Sawitzky and Sawitzky, "Two Letters from Ralph Earl," 35–36.

83. For example, Prown, *John Singleton Copley*, 1:93, says that in May 1775, Copley's wife, Susannah, paid seventy pounds to Capt. John Callahan (later shipmaster for Earl's voyage) for passage for herself and her three children from Boston to London.

84. See Kornhauser, *Ralph Earl*, 83–84. The Callahan family portrait is now in three fragments; the first section, which would have been to the viewer's left, is a portrait of John Callahan (Massachusetts Historical Society, Boston); the second section, which would have appeared in the center, is of the two Callahan daughters (private collection); the third section, which depicted their mother, Lucretia Callahan, is unlocated. The Callahan portrait was first attributed to Earl by William Sawitzky; see Sawitzky and Sawitzky, "Two Letters from Ralph Earl," 40, 41n.

Earl is not the only artist known to have painted a portrait during a voyage. William Dunlap noted in his diary that on August 1, 1787, "the weather had permitted me to set up my esel [sic] in the cabin, and I painted two portraits of our captain [Mr. Watson] during the voyage." *Diary of William Dunlap*, 3:265–66.

85. "The Last Will and Testament of Joseph Trumbull," August 25, 1823, Case 59956, Series A, Probate Office, Worcester County Courthouse. When Trumbull died in 1824, he bequeathed the Callahan portrait to the Callahans' eldest son. "I give to Mr. Callahan, a large family Painting being the Portraits of his late Father Capt. Callahan, his mother now living and some of his sisters, given to me by his said father and mother as a token of friendship."

86. It is not likely that Earl attempted to visit his family in Worcester County, since he is not known to have ever been legally separated from his first wife, Sarah. See Nancy F. Cott, "Eighteenth-Century Family and Social Life Revealed in Massachusetts Divorce Records," in Nancy F. Cott and Elizabeth H. Peck, eds., *A Heritage of Her Own* (New York, 1979), 121–22, which indicates that in the eighteenth century women who wished to divorce waited an average of five years before actually petitioning for a divorce. There is no record of a divorce between Sarah and Ralph Earl. Soon after Earl's return with his wife Ann, Sarah married Oliver Pierce of West Boylston, Massachusetts. The marriage probably took place in 1786; they had a son, Levi Pierce, on January 17, 1787.

87. Carol Troyon, *Boston Tradition*, 70.

88. Swan, "Johnstons and Reas–Japanners," 212.

89. Henri Marceau, "A Recently Discovered Portrait by Ralph Earl," *Gazette des Beaux-Arts* 23 (April 1943), 251–55. The portrait of Talbot was previously thought to be by Benjamin West; see Henry Tuckerman, *Book of the Artists* (New York, 1867), 101. For one sitter's account book see cats. 51, 52. In comparison, John Johnston, a less accomplished artist, received eighteen pounds in 1780 for painting a portrait of Gen. Joseph Warren; see Swan, "Johnstons and Reas–Japanners," 212.

90. *Hartford Courant*, May 10, 1785; G. H. Hollister, *The History of Connecticut*, 2 vols. (Hartford, Conn., 1855), 2:550–51. My thanks to Robert G. Stewart, senior curator, National Portrait Gallery, Washington, D.C., for bringing the Seabury portrait to my attention and providing information on its provenance; see Kornhauser, *Ralph Earl*, 86, 315.

91. Delanoy to Abraham Beekman, March 10, 1783, Beekman Papers, Box 17, New-York Historical Society. Abraham Delanoy, Jr., was born in New York and studied in London with West around 1766. When he returned to America the following year, he worked principally in New York but also in Charleston, South Carolina, possibly in the West Indies, and from 1784 to 1787, in New Haven as a general painter. In poor health during the 1780s, he died in Westchester County, New York. See Susan Sawitzky, "Abraham Delanoy in New Haven," *New-York Historical Society Quarterly* 41 (January 1957), 193–206; Saunders and Miles, *American Colonial Portraits*, 273–74.

92. Jerry Patterson, *The City of New York* (New York, 1978), 85.

93. *Independent Journal: or General Advertiser* (New York), November 26, 1785; Isaiah Thomas, *The History of Printing in America* (1810; reprint, New York, 1970), 478–80; *The New-York Historical Society Portrait Catalog*, 2 vols. (New York, 1974), 2:665.

Charles Willson Peale benefited greatly from the artistic community that centered around Rivington's bookstore in Philadelphia. Around 1763, when Peale visited the painter Christopher Steele, he wrote of "Rivington who then kept a Bookstore at the Corner of Market & front street in who's store Mr. Steele was often seated. At this store I bought the [book entitled] hand maid to the arts." Peale to Rembrandt Peale, October 28, 1812, quoted in Saunders and Miles, *American Colonial Portraits*, 38.

94. The portrait bears an inscription on the stretcher: "Thos Barrow. AETAT 50. May 5, 1786. New York"; see Sawitzky and Sawitzky Papers, Box 24.

95. Barrow married Sarah Moore of New York, the sister of Bishop Benjamin Moore of Trinity Episcopal Church. He served as a vestryman of the church and executed a watercolor view entitled *The Ruins of Trinity Church after the Great Fire in 1776* (1776; Museum of the City of New York). William Kelby, "Notes on Trinity Church Yard Families, 1841–1878," MS, New-York Historical Society; Dunlap, *History of Design*, 2:31–32.

96. Dunlap, *History of Design*, 2:31–32. Dunlap noted that during the Revolution, Barrow "was the only dealer in good prints." Barrow's numerous advertisements are reproduced in Rita Susswein Gottesman, *The Arts and Crafts of New York, 1777–1799: Advertisements and News Items from the New York City Newspapers* (New York, 1954), 276, 339, 346, 913.

97. Levi Williard was the son of Col. Levi Williard, a prominent merchant in Lancaster, Massachusetts (not far from Earl's native town of Paxton), and Catherine Chandler Williard, the sister of the artist Winthrop Chandler. Levi and Catherine Williard were painted by Chandler around 1775; see Little, "Winthrop Chandler," 117.

98. The court minutes document the various litigations involving Ralph Earl. Levi Williard first sued Earl on August 3, 1786. At the first hearing of the trial, the sheriff announced that the defendant, Earl, was "not found," and the trial was postponed until October 26. The sheriff then assigned an officer to serve Earl with a writ for his arrest. Almost concurrently with his own trial, Earl sued Samuel Campbell, a bookseller whose shop was located at 41 Hanover Street on September 6, 1786. In turn, on the same day, John Lockwood, a merchant, brought suit against Earl. As a result of this second suit against Earl, it was ordered

that "the sheriff bring in the body of the defendant [Earl] sitting in the court or [Earl would] be ordered forty shillings and that the defendant plead in seven days after the declarations filed or judgement" would be made, see "Minutes of the Mayor's Court," 286. Following this case, Williard's suit was brought to court for the second time, on October 26, 1786, and it was recorded that Earl had already been "taken on [a] like motion," indicating that the artist was already jailed, evidently unable to pay the forty shilling fine from the suit brought by Lockwood. "Minutes of the Mayor's Court," October 17, 1785 to June 26, 1787, County Clerk's Office, County Courthouse, New York. Kornhauser, *Ralph Earl*, 90-104, discusses the trial in detail and the portraits of individuals later painted by Earl who were involved in his trial.

99.   *New York City Directory, 1785-1786* lists the merchant John Lockwood.

Earl was later released from prison through a law passed in 1786 that enabled those imprisoned for debts of less than twenty-five dollars to be released after thirty days. *A Sketch of the Origin and Progress of the Humane Society of the City of New-York. Together with the Act of Incorporation and By-Laws, Inc.*, pamphlet (New York, 1814). An index of the inventories of insolvent debtors is in the Historical Documents Collection, Queens College, City University of New York, but no mention of an inventory for Ralph Earl has been found there.

On the suit against Campbell, see "Minutes of the Mayor's Court," 241. On October 26, 1786, although Earl was already imprisoned, his lawyer, Mr. Willocks, brought suit a second time against Samuel Campbell, and a "writ of inquiry" was issued.

100.   William Bowen, *Centennial History of New York* (New York, 1892), 13.

101.   Mary L. Booth, *History of the City of New York* (New York, 1867), 623.

102.   *Sketch of the Humane Society*. The society changed its name to the Humane Society of the City of New York in 1803.

103.   Ibid., 2. Details of the act are also given in *Sketch of the Humane Society*.

104.   I. N. Stokes, *The Iconography of Manhattan Island, 1498-1909* (New York, 1926), 5:1284.

105.   See "Minutes of the Mayor's Court," 314. John Clark sued Ralph Earl while Earl was imprisoned, on November 8, 1787. Clark had previously sued a Thomas Field for nonpayment of fifty pounds for "meat, drink, washing, lodgings and other necessities" for Field's wife and child. Clark apparently made a similar charge against Earl. Clark is identified in New York City directories for the years 1787 and 1789 as running a "boarding house" and as a "Bookseller." The New York City directories for 1785, 1786, and 1787 list an "Ann Earl shopkeeper" at 31 Broadway during the years of Earl's imprisonment; however, after his release, the directories continue to list an "Ann Earle widow shopkeeper" at various addresses on Broadway, making it unclear as to whether this was indeed Earl's wife. The listing recurs through 1797, perhaps in an effort to avoid payment of taxes. Her name is dropped in 1798, the year she established a residence with her daughter, Mary Ann, in Troy, New York.

Ralph E. W. Earl's birth date is unknown. Mary Ann Earl's birth date is verified by an inscription on her headstone in the Presbyterian Churchyard, White Plains, New York, which reads "August 31, 1787."

106.   George Colton, Diary, August 16, 1801, MS, Connecticut Historical Society, Hartford.

107.   Evans, *Benjamin West*, 48-51; Monroe H. Fabian, *Joseph Wright: American Artist, 1756-1793* (Washington, D.C., 1985).

Joseph Wright, who had been a student of West's in the 1770s and early 1780s, painted in Philadelphia from 1783 to 1786. When he arrived in New York, the following announcement appeared in the *Daily Advertiser* (April 7, 1786). "New York bids fair to outvie the sister states in becoming the seat of the Arts. Today we are informed of the arrival of Joseph Wright of Philadelphia . . . [and] as he means to follow his profession as a Limner here, we are tempted to believe every encouragement will be given his genius."

108.   Dunlap, *History of Design*, 1:266.

109.   The portraits of Earl's New York prison years are more fully discussed in Kornhauser, *Ralph Earl*, 90-105; the Catalogue includes representative examples from this period. Members and honorary members of the Society of the Cincinnati who commissioned portraits of themselves or a family member include Maj. Gen. Baron Friedrich von Steuben, Col. William North, Col. Robert Troup, Maj. James Fairlie, Matthew Clarkson, Col. Richard Varick, James Duane, and Col. Marinus Willett. Members of the debtors' relief society who patronized Earl include Col. Robert Troup, Matthew Clarkson, James and Mary Duane, Alexander and Elizabeth Hamilton, James and Abigail Cogswell, Joseph and Mary Winter, Col. Marinus Willett, and Dr. Mason Fitch Cogswell.

110.   James Duane, Daybook F, Duane Papers, MS, New-York Historical Society.

111.   Minor Myers, Jr., *Liberty without Anarchy: A History of the Society of the Cincinnati* (Charlottesville, Va., 1983).

112.   Kornhauser, *Ralph Earl*, 97-99. The portraits are *Major Matthew Clarkson* (1787; Gilcrease Institute of American History and Art, Tulsa, Okla.), *Major James Fairlie* (1786-87; FIGGIE International, Richmond, Va.), *Major William North* (1786; private collection), *Colonel Robert Troup* (1786; private collection), *Colonel Richard Varick* (1787; Albany Institute of Art), and three portraits of *Baron von Steuben* (cat. 21).

113.   My thanks to Christopher Gilbert, Temple Newsam House, Leeds, England, for his comments on the chair type used frequently in Earl's portraits. It appears to be an English chair, usually with leather upholstery. Earl's detailing of the seat-corner nailing patterns are very accurate, whereas the arm pads extended to the elbow are an eccentric feature.

114.   The following appeared in the *New-York Morning Post, and Daily Advertiser* on January 18, 21, and 28: "Notice is hereby given, by the petitioning creditors of Ralph Earl, an insolvent debtor, that they do appear before John Wylley, Esq., one of the Judges in the Mayor's Court of the City of New York at his office on Nassau Street on Monday, the 28th instant, at ten o'clock in the morning to show cause, if any they have, why an assignment of the estate of the said Ralph Earl should not be made for the benefit of all his creditors, and the said Ralph Earl discharged, pursuant to the directions of the legislature of the State of New York, entitled, 'An Act for the Relief of Insolvent Debtors,' passed the 13th day of April, 1786. Dated the 18th day of January, 1788. Ralph Earl."

The court ordered that Earl's "goods and chattels, Effects, Debts, and Demands due and owing unto Ralph Earl . . . [be] assigned and conveyed unto Mason Fitch Cogswell." Mason Fitch Cogswell Papers, MS, Connecticut Historical Society.

115.   These portraits include *Mrs. Abraham Beach* (1788; Museum of the City of New York), *Jacob Isaacs* (1788; unlocated), *Robert Boyd* (1788; Brooklyn Museum), and *David and Sarah Hubbell* (1788; unlocated); see Kornhauser, *Ralph Earl*, 256, 263, 292, 296.

116.   Harris, *Artist in American Society*, 21-25; Charles Coleman Sellers, *Mr. Peale's Museum* (New York, 1980); Jules Prown, "His-

tory Painting," in Helen Cooper et al., ed., *John Trumbull*, 22–42; Edgar P. Richardson, *Gilbert Stuart: Portraitist of the Young Republic*, exhib. cat. (Providence, R.I., 1967).

117. Cogswell to Rev. James Cogswell, March 10, 1791, reproduced in Frances Root Cogswell, ed., *Father and Daughter: A Collection of Cogswell Family Letters and Diaries, 1772–1801* (West Hartford, Conn., n.d.), 47.

118. Edward M. Cook, *Fathers of the Towns* (Baltimore, Md., 1976), 155, 174, 177; Ellen Strong Bartlett, "Extracts from the Diary of Dr. Mason Fitch Cogswell," *Connecticut Magazine* 5 (January–December, 1899), 532–37, 562–71. For a complete discussion of Cogswell's network of family ties, see Kornhauser, "Ralph Earl as an Itinerant Artist: Pattern of Patronage," in Peter Benes, ed., *Itinerancy in New England and New York: Annual Proceedings of the Dublin Seminar for New England Folk Life, 1984*, vol. 9 (Boston, 1986), 172–90.

119. Mason Fitch Cogswell to Rev. James Cogswell, July 15, 1791, reproduced in Cogswell, ed., *Father and Daughter*, 47; Account Books, Mason Fitch Cogswell Papers, Connecticut Historical Society; Kornhauser, "Ralph Earl as an Itinerant Artist." On Cogswell as a tastemaker, see Kornhauser and Schloss, "Painting and Other Pictorial Arts," 136–37, 152.

120. Quoted in George William Sheldon, *Recent Ideals in American Art* (New York, 1890), 57–58, reproduced in Colleen Cowles Heslip, *Between the Rivers: Itinerant Painters from the Connecticut to the Hudson* (Williamstown, Mass., 1990), 23.

121. Mary Breed to Mason Fitch Cogswell, February 18, 1795, Mason Fitch Cogswell Papers, Connecticut Historical Society. It is not known if Mary Breed had her portrait taken.

122. Earl was boarded at the Litchfield tavern run by David Buell while painting portraits of the Seymour family in 1789. According to an entry for June 10, 1789, in the account books of Moses Seymour (1710–95), David Buell was paid "9 pounds for Mr. Ralph Earl." Also recorded is a payment of six pounds to Earl and, on August 31, 1789, a charge to Earl for "6 yd. calico," perhaps a purchase for his wife. Moses Seymour, Account Books, Litchfield Historical Society, Litchfield, Conn.

123. My thanks to Elizabeth McClintock and Marcia Hinckley for gathering and interpreting the probate inventories for the majority of Earl's Connecticut sitters. These inventories, cited in the catalogue entries, clearly demonstrate the accuracy of Earl's depictions of the lands, houses, furnishings, libraries, and personal possessions of his sitters.

124. De Warville, *New Travels in the United States of America Performed in 1788* (New York, 1792), 74.

125. Cogswell had visited these same families a few months before Earl's arrival; see Kornhauser, *Ralph Earl*, 121–23.

126. A graduate of Yale College in 1732, Abraham Davenport married Elizabeth Huntington; he served as a judge in Fairfield County. Mason Fitch Cogswell's brother, James Cogswell, married the Davenports' daughter, Elizabeth Huntington Davenport, while working as an army surgeon during the Revolution. See Kornhauser, *Ralph Earl*, 123, 279–80; Franklin Bowditch Dexter, *Biographical Sketches of the Graduates of Yale College* (New York, 1907), 3:376–78; Painting Files, Yale University Art Gallery.

127. Margaretta M. Lovell, "Reading Eighteenth-Century American Family Portraits: Social Images and Self-Images," *Winterthur Portfolio* 22 (Winter 1987), 255–59; Nancy F. Cott, *The Bonds of Womanhood* (New Haven, 1977), 63–101.

128. Kornhauser, "Ralph Earl as an Itinerant Artist," 178–79.

129. Kornhauser, *Ralph Earl*, 273–74; Dexter, *Biographical Sketches of Yale*, 3:250–51. Champion's probate inventory, Litch-

field, 1810, reel 678, no. 1397, Connecticut State Library, indicates that he owned over forty volumes.

130. Samuel Orcutt, *History of the Towns of New Milford and Bridgewater, Connecticut, 1703–1882* (Hartford, Conn., 1882), 55–59.

131. William H. Gerdts, "American Landscape Painting: Critical Judgments, 1730–1845," *American Art Journal* 17 (Winter 1985), 29.

132. Waterhouse, *Painting in Britain*, 231–32.

133. Strong to Stiles, August 30, 1790, Beinecke Rare Book and Manuscript Library.

134. *Litchfield Weekly Monitor*, June 21, 1790.

135. Paul D. Schweizer, *Masterworks of American Art from the Munson-Williams-Proctor Institute* (New York, 1989), 19; Robert L. Harley, "Ralph Earl, Eighteenth-Century Connecticut Artist, Comes into His Own," *American Collector* 14 (November 1945), 10–13.

About the sitter's costume, Aileen Ribeiro has commented that it is "sober, neat, and seemly, but with no pretensions to fashion. Earl's portraits of elderly women have faint echoes of Dutch seventeenth-century portraits of old women of the ruling class. Bethia Watson wears a gown of black silk with old-fashioned elbow-length sleeves. The fichu crossed over her bosom and her sleeve ruffles are embroidered muslin. Black was a suitable color for elderly women, and it was also the color of mourning, which was strictly observed, particularly by older people, in God-fearing New England communities of the sort where Earl painted. Watson's status as a widow is also demonstrated by the black band around her linen mobcap, which modestly hides her hair and ties under the chin."

136. Kornhauser, *Ralph Earl*, 141, 277. Earl painted *Mrs. Timothy Conklin* (1791; Witte Memorial Museum, San Antonio) in Huntington, Long Island.

137. Richard H. Saunders with Helen Raye, *Daniel Wadsworth: Patron of the Arts* (Hartford, Conn., 1981); Kornhauser and Schloss, "Painting and Other Pictorial Arts," 135–41.

138. Dr. James Cogswell to Mason Fitch Cogswell, October 23, 1791, Cogswell Family Papers, Beinecke Rare Book and Manuscript Library; Mason Fitch Cogswell to Rev. James Cogswell, December 28, 1791, reproduced in Cogswell, ed., *Father and Daughter*, 49; Mason Fitch Cogswell to Rev. James Cogswell, March 15, 1792, reproduced in Cogswell, ed., *Father and Daughter*, 51.

139. Rev. James Cogswell, Diary, May 2, 1781–September 17, 1791, MS, Connecticut Historical Society, quoted in Thompson R. Harlow, "The Life and Trials of Joseph Steward," *Connecticut Historical Society Bulletin* 46 (October 1981), 132.

140. Moseley to Frederick Wolcott, September 28, 1791, in Samuel Wolcott, *Memorial of Henry Wolcott, One of the First Settlers of Windsor, Connecticut, and Some of His Descendants* (New York, 1881), 149–50.

141. The Wyllys land had been granted to Gov. George Wyllys (1598–1644 or 1645) in 1636 and descended in the male line of the family for four generations. The Wyllys family held prominent political positions throughout the seventeenth and eighteenth centuries. When the line began to die out in the early nineteenth century, the house and Charter Oak Tree became revered for their historic value. For more on the cult, see Robert F. Trent, "The Charter Oak Artifacts," exhib. cat., *Connecticut Historical Society Bulletin* 49 (Summer 1984), 124–30. For a discussion of the interest in colonial Connecticut history, see Christopher Kent Wilson, "The Landscape of Democracy: Frederic Church's West Rock, New Haven," *American Art Journal* 18, no. 3 (1986), 20–39.

Earl first painted the portraits of Gen. Samuel Wyllys and his wife, Ruth Wyllys, who lived in the Wyllys mansion, in 1791 or 1792. These portraits were later destroyed in a fire; see George Dudley Seymour, *Captain Nathan Hale – Major John Palsgrave Wyllys* (New Haven, Conn., 1933), 126–27.

See Amelia Wyllys Adams to Maria Pomeroy, April 12, 1827, Wyllys Family Papers, Connecticut Historical Society, for Polly Wyllys Pomeroy's birthplace. In this letter from the subject's niece to her cousin, the writer indicates that Earl left *Polly Wyllys Pomeroy* unfinished. The figure in the portrait was repainted at a later time by an amateur artist, but Earl's landscape view of the Charter Oak Tree and the Wyllys mansion remains intact. See Kornhauser, *Ralph Earl*, 310–11.

Several artists depicted the tree and house, including Earl's follower Joseph Steward (cat. 67), who painted a portrait of George Wyllys (c. 1790; Connecticut Historical Society), shown seated in the Wyllys mansion with a copy of the original charter. The Hartford native Frederic Church also painted several views of the Charter Oak in 1846–47. See Trent, "Charter Oak Artifacts."

142.   Susanna Wyllys Strong to Pomeroy, March 16, 1792, Wyllys Family Papers, Connecticut Historical Society.

143.   Kornhauser, *Ralph Earl*, 178–81, 309–10, 313, 317–18, discusses the Shaw family portraits, including *Judge Elias Perkins* (1793; New London County Historical Society); *Mrs. Elias Perkins (Lucretia Shaw Woodbridge)* (c. 1793; New London County Historical Society); *Mrs. Guy Richards (Elizabeth Harris)* (1793; Hartford Steam Boiler Inspection and Insurance Company); *Thomas Shaw* (1792; New London County Historical Society); *Thomas Shaw* (1793; private collection); *Mrs. Nathaniel Shaw (Temperance Harris)* (1792–93; New London County Historical Society).

144.   Minor Myers, Jr., and Edgar Mayhew, *New London County Furniture, 1640–1840*, exhib. cat. (New London, Conn., 1974), 80–81. For a history of the Shaw mansion, see Ernest E. Rogers, *Connecticut's Naval Office at New London during the War of the American Revolution, Including the Mercantile Letter Book of Nathaniel Shaw, Jr.* (New London, 1933); Frances Manwaring Caulkins, *History of New London County, Connecticut* (New London, 1852), 512–13; Sara Emerson Rolleston, *Historic Houses and Interiors in Southern Connecticut* (New York, 1974), 150–51.

145.   Thomas Shaw, Ledger, Nathaniel and Thomas Shaw Papers, Box 23, Ledger 27, MS, Sterling Memorial Library, Yale University. The entries indicate that Earl received between thirty and fifty-five dollars for each painting, prices that are consistent with his advertisements; there he suggests thirty dollars for half-length and sixty dollars for full-length portraits. The ledgers also indicate that Earl's wife Ann was with him in New London.

146.   Kornhauser, *Ralph Earl*, 182; Kornhauser, "Ralph Earl as an Itinerant Artist," 172–90.

147.   Timothy Dwight, *Travels in New England and New York* (London, 1823), 3:297. See Dean F. Failey, *Long Island Is My Nation*, exhib. cat. (Setauket, N.Y., 1976), for a discussion of Long Island in the eighteenth century.

148.   Kornhauser, *Ralph Earl*, 181–85.

149.   Ibid., 185–87.

150.   Dunlap, *History of Design*, 1:195–96. See Dorinda Evans's forthcoming monograph on Gilbert Stuart, which will deal with Stuart's impact on portraiture in America in the post-revolutionary era.

151.   Edward J. Nygren, "From View to Vision," in Nygren with Bruce Robertson et al., *Views and Visions: American Landscape before 1830*, exhib. cat. (Washington, D.C., 1986), 13–17; Edward Croft-Murray, *Decorative Painting in England, 1537–1837*, 2 vols. (London, 1962).

152.   Little, "Winthrop Chandler," 149.

153.   Bruce Robertson, "The Picturesque Traveler in America," in Nygren with Robertson et al., *Views and Visions*, 187–211. See *Views and Visions* for a discussion of these artists: John James Barralet (c. 1747–1815), George Beck (c. 1748–1812), William Birch (1755–1834), Thomas Birch (1779–1851), William Groombridge (1748–1811), Francis Guy (1760–1820), George I. Parkyns (1749–1800), Archibald Robertson (1765–1835), Alexander Robertson (1772–1841), and William Winstanley (active 1793–1806).

154.   Nygren with Robertson et al., *Views and Visions*, 285; James T. Flexner, "George Washington as an Art Collector," *American Art Journal* 4 (September 1972), 224–25.

155.   Bryan Wolf, "Revolution in the Landscape: John Trumbull and Picturesque Painting," in Cooper et al., ed., *John Trumbull*, 206–30.

156.   William N. Hosley, "Architecture," in *The Great River: Art and Society of the Connecticut Valley, 1635–1820*, exhib. cat. (Hartford, Conn., 1985), 66–67.

157.   William L. Warren, "William Sprats, Master Joiner: Connecticut's Federalist Architect," *Connecticut Antiquarian* 9 (December 1957), 14–20.

158.   *Litchfield Weekly Monitor and Agricultural Register*, February 24, 1796: "Arrived in town a few days since, Mr. Ralph Earl, the celebrated Portrait Painter; who holds rank with the most distinguished pupils of the great WEST. His paintings will do honor to any country, in any age."

159.   *Litchfield Weekly Monitor*, May 18, 1796.

160.   What little is known concerning these artists appears in William L. Warren, "The Jennys Portraits," *Connecticut Historical Society Bulletin* 20 (October 1955), 97–128; Warren, "A Checklist of Jennys Portraits," *Connecticut Historical Society Bulletin* 21 (April 1956), 33–64. More recent findings on the artists' collaboration, as well as a discussion of their style, appears in Kornhauser, *Ralph Earl*, 191–96.

161.   Kornhauser, *Ralph Earl*, 193, 37n, and 38n.

162.   Jared Lane, Account Book, private collection. See Kornhauser, *Ralph Earl*, 194–95.

163.   Dwight, *Travels*, 3:373, quoted in Nygren with Robertson et al., *Views and Visions*, 227.

164.   Kornhauser, *Ralph Earl*, 211.

165.   The Gage Family Papers contain a series of letters between Ralph E. W. Earl and his mother, Ann, and sister, Mary Ann Earl Higbie, that document the family's friendship with the Buells, as well as their presence in Troy, New York, beginning in 1798.

166.   Nathan Perkins, *A Narrative of a Tour through the State of Vermont, 1789* (Rutland, Vt., 1964), 18–19.

167.   See John R. Stilgoe, "Smiling Scenes," in Nygren with Robertson et al., *Views and Visions*, 211–27, for a discussion of nationalistic themes in early American landscape.

168.   Southgate to Earl, September 14, 1799, Gage Family Papers; Southgate to John Southgate, Jr., June 4, 1801, Gage Family Papers. Both letters are copies; see Box 3, Folder 18. For additional information on William Southgate, see Kornhauser, *Ralph Earl*, 224–25; Gage Papers; Washburn, *Historical Sketches of Leicester*, 397; George C. Groce and David H. Wallace, *The New-York Historical Society's Dictionary of Artists in America* (New Haven, Conn., 1957), 594.

169.   Hutchins was a large landowner who had invested considerable money in the Northampton Aqueduct Company; Office of the Secretary, *Soldiers and Sailors*, 580; James Russell Trum-

bull, *History of Northampton*, 2 vols. (Northampton, Mass., 1898), 2:559–60, 632.

Wicker worked as an ornamental painter in Northampton and is known to have painted and gilded two frames for the portraits of Dr. William Stoddard and his wife, Mary Stoddard, painted by William Jennys; see Warren, "A Checklist of Jennys Portraits," 62.

170.   Elizabeth McKinsey, *Niagara Falls: Icon of the Sublime* (New York, 1985). For a history of images of Niagara Falls, see Jeremy Elwell Adamson, "Frederic Edwin Church's 'Niagara': The Sublime as Transcendence" (Ph.D. diss., University of Michigan, 1981); Adamson et al., *Niagara: Two Centuries of Changing Attitudes, 1697–1901*, exhib. cat. (Washington, D.C., 1985).

171.   The announcement appeared in the *Carolina Gazette* (Charleston), November 14, 1799, and in the *Litchfield Weekly Monitor*, November 9, 1799.

172.   My thanks to Jeremy Adamson for providing information on the conditions of the journey to the falls in the period of Earl's trip.

A detailed account of Vanderlyn's arduous journey is contained in William Townsen Oedel, "John Vanderlyn: French Neoclassicism and the Search for an American Art" (Ph.D. diss., University of Delaware, 1981), 181n. According to Vanderlyn's contemporary Thomas B. Thorpe, whom Oedel quotes, "Vanderlyn . . . used sometimes to speak of his long, dreary journey to the 'great falls' travelling steadily for ten days to reach his . . . destination, and, for want of better conveyance, doing some distance on foot, carrying his paint-box and canvas strapped to his back."

173.   *Thomas' Massachusetts Spy, or, the Worcester Gazette*, November 20, 1799; *Federal Gazette and Baltimore Daily Advertiser*, November 18, 1799. For the information on the portage road, I am indebted to Jeremy Adamson, letter to the author, November 30, 1983.

174.   *Hampshire Gazette* (Northampton), September 6, 1886, quoted in Leigh Keno, "The Windsor-Chairmakers of Northampton, Massachusetts," MS, Historic Deerfield.

175.   This advertisement appeared in the *Hampshire Gazette* on March 5, 12, 17, and 19, 1800. Newspapers in New York and Boston also ran abbreviated versions of this announcement, adding that the view "will be exhibited in several cities of the United States." *Daily Advertiser*, March 1, 1800.

176.   Journal of Abigail Brackett Lyman, Northampton, Mass., 1800, private collection.

177.   *Philadelphia Gazette and Universal Daily Advertiser*, April 9 and April 28, 1800.

178.   *Connecticut Journal*, June 25, 1800.

179.   In an obituary notice in 1856 for Earl's son from his first marriage, Capt. John Earl, Earl's artistic accomplishments are discussed at length, and the Niagara Falls panorama is reported to have been "exhibited in all parts of the country, and was carried to London, where it was in existence but a few years ago." *Worcester Palladium* (Mass.), April 30, 1856.

180.   Nygren with Robertson et al., *Views and Visions*, 304; *The Great River: Art and Society of the Connecticut Valley, 1635–1820*, exhib. cat. (Hartford, Conn., 1985) 139.

181.   McKinsey, *Niagara Falls*, 74–76.

182.   Kornhauser, *Ralph Earl*, 237.

183.   *Connecticut Courant*, August 24, 1801; George Colton, Diary, Connecticut Historical Society. For biographical information on Colton, see Dexter, *Biographical Sketches of Yale*, 2:408–9.

184.   Earl and his followers were first dubbed the Connecticut School in an exhibition organized by Samuel M. Green at Wesleyan University in 1953; see his article "Uncovering the Con-

necticut School," *Art News* 51 (January 1953), 38–41, 57–58. See also Green, *American Art: A Historical Survey* (New York, 1966), 98–102, 157–62. I dealt with the regional portrait styles in Connecticut more recently in Kornhauser and Schloss, "Painting and Other Pictorial Arts," 135–85.

185.   Kornhauser, *Ralph Earl*, 267–68, 292–93, 307–8.

186.   Paula B. Freedman, "In the Presence of Strangers: Jonathan Budington's *Portrait of George Eliott and Family*," *Yale University Art Gallery Bulletin* 40 (Spring 1988), 22–30. My thanks to Paula B. Freedman for sharing information on this painter.

CHAPTER II: PORTRAITURE AND SOCIETY

1.   Quoted in Richard H. Saunders and Ellen G. Miles, *American Colonial Portraits: 1700–1776*, exhib. cat. (Washington, D.C., 1987), 306.

2.   This problem was posed in the essay by Elizabeth Mankin Kornhauser and Christine Skeeles Schloss, "Painting and Other Pictorial Arts," in *The Great River: Art and Society of the Connecticut Valley, 1635–1820* (Hartford, Conn., 1985), 136–37. On Delanoy, see Saunders and Miles, *American Colonial Portraits*, 274; on the miniaturists, Kornhauser and Schloss, "Painting and Other Pictorial Arts," 138–39.

3.   Saunders and Miles, *American Colonial Portraits*, 43–44.

4.   The organization dates of Connecticut towns are graphically presented in Bruce C. Daniels, *The Connecticut Town: Growth and Development, 1635–1790* (Middletown, Conn., 1979), 25, 33, 42.

5.   Amelia F. Miller, *Connecticut River Valley Doorways: An Eighteenth-Century Flowering* (Boston, 1983), 21–105.

6.   Kevin M. Sweeney, "Mansion People: Kinship, Class, and Architecture in Western Massachusetts in the Mid Eighteenth Century," *Winterthur Portfolio* 19 (Winter 1984), 231–55.

7.   Daniels, *Connecticut Town*, 198–99.

8.   John F. Schroeder, ed., *Memoir of the Life and Character of Mrs. Mary Anna Boardman* (New Haven, Conn., 1849), 392–407; Elizabeth Mankin Kornhauser, *Ralph Earl: Artist-Entrepreneur* (Ann Arbor, Mich., 1989), 150, 327, 329.

9.   Samuel Orcutt, *History of the Towns of New Milford and Bridgewater, Connecticut, 1703–1882* (Hartford, Conn., 1882), 273–74, 292.

10.   Orcutt, *History of New Milford*, 447, 495–96, 503; *Two Centuries of New Milford, Connecticut: An Account of the Bi-centennial Celebration of the Founding of the Town Held June 15, 16, 17 and 18, 1907, with a Number of Historical Articles and Reminiscences* (New York, 1907), 16.

11.   *Connecticut Courant and Weekly Intelligencer* (Hartford), January 21, 1788.

12.   Kornhauser, *Ralph Earl*, 307.

13.   For an illuminating account of Gov. Samuel Huntington's rise in Norwich, see Larry R. Gerlach, *Connecticut Congressman: Samuel Huntington, 1731–1796* (Hartford, Conn., 1976).

14.   Richard L. Bushman, "American High-Style and Vernacular Cultures," in Jack P. Greene and J. R. Pole, eds., *Colonial British America: Essays in the New History of the Early Modern Era* (Baltimore, Md., 1984), 345–84.

15.   Orcutt, *History of New Milford*, 290, 296, 488, 498, 499, 500, 504; *Two Centuries of New Milford*, 14.

16.   Kornhauser, *Ralph Earl*, 288.

17.   Alain C. White, *The History of the Town of Litchfield, Connecticut, 1720–1920* (Litchfield, 1920), 95, 96, 97, 121, 123, 138. Litchfield was one of six Connecticut towns to support a news-

paper through the entire decade of the 1790s. The only other towns with a persistent newspaper were Hartford and Middletown in the Connecticut River Valley, and New Haven, New London, and Norwich along the coast. A few others had sporadic papers. Edward Cannery Latham, *Chronological Tables of American Newspapers, 1690–1820: Being a Tabular Guide to Holdings of Newspapers Published in America through the Year 1820* (Barre, Mass., 1972), 23.

18.   White, *History of Litchfield*, 95, 96, 97, 121, 123, 138, 144 (quotation), 168, 169, 170.

19.   Emily Noyes Vanderpoel, *Chronicles of a Pioneer School from 1792 to 1833: Being the History of Miss Sarah Pierce and Her Litchfield School*, ed. Elizabeth C. Barney Buel (Cambridge, Mass., 1903), 347.

20.   Ibid., 6, 8 (quotation), 448.

21.   Ibid., 347.

22.   Quoted in Kornhauser, *Ralph Earl*, 156.

23.   Elijah Boardman helped seat the meetinghouse in 1797. Orcutt, *History of New Milford*, 260.

24.   Quoted in Richard Buel, *Dear Liberty: Connecticut's Mobilization for the Revolutionary War* (Middletown, Conn., 1980), 297–303, 304 (quotation), 305.

25.   *Connecticut Courant*, July 15, 1783.

26.   Buel, *Dear Liberty*, 306–9, 313.

27.   Aedanus Burke, *Considerations on the Society or Order of Cincinnati; Lately Instituted by the Major-Generals, Brigadier-Generals, and Other Officers of the American Army. Proving That It Creates a Race of Hereditary Patricians, or Nobility. Interspersed with Remarks on Its Consequences to the Freedom and Happiness of the Republic. Addressed to the People of South-Carolina, and Their Representatives. By Cassius* (Philadelphia, 1783), 2–6.

28.   *Connecticut Journal and New Haven Post Boy*, quoted in Wallace Evan Davies, "The Society of the Cincinnati in New England, 1783–1800," *William and Mary Quarterly*, 3d ser., 5 (January 1948), 4, 6 (quotation); Burke, *Considerations*, 10.

29.   Kenneth Silverman, *Timothy Dwight* (New York, 1969); *The Major Poems of Timothy Dwight (1752–1817) with a Dissertation on the History, Eloquence, and Poetry of the Bible*, ed. William J. McTaggart and William K. Bottorff (Gainesville, Fla., 1969).

30.   *Greenfield Hill*, in *Major Poems of Timothy Dwight*, 399–400.

31.   Ibid., 400, 402.

32.   These issues are related to broader American cultural traditions in Sacvan Bercovitch, *The American Jeremiad* (Madison, Wis., 1978), 154–57.

33.   Gerlach, *Connecticut Congressman: Samuel Huntington*, 28, 103.

CHAPTER III: RALPH EARL'S WORKING METHODS AND MATERIALS

1.   A. A., *Handbook of Young Artists and Amateurs in Oil Painting* (New York, 1856), 115.

2.   *Portrait of Mrs. Guy Richards* has been lined, but the original stretcher has been saved. Knowledge of the strainer for *Colonel Talcott* is based on an old photograph of the reverse. Painting Files, Wadsworth Atheneum, Hartford, Conn.

3.   Jared Lane, Account Book, "Sundry Paintings &c. Charged in Acct." (private collection), henceforth cited in the text as the account book.

4.   A. A., *Handbook*, 166.

5.   M. Kirby Talley, Jr., "'All Good Pictures Crack': Sir Joshua Reynolds's Practice and Studio," in Nicholas Penny, ed., *Reynolds* (New York, 1989), 58.

6.   A. A., *Handbook*, 116.

7.   I am indebted to Henry A. DePhillips, Jr., Vernon K. Krieble Professor of Chemistry, Trinity College, Hartford, Conn., for the analysis and for assistance with the interpretation of the pigment samples. He performed the tests using an electron microscope with an energy dispersive X-ray accessory in the research labs at the Loctite Corporation, Newington, Conn.

8.   On Hogarth, see David Bomford and Ashok Roy, "Hogarth's Marriage à la Mode," *National Gallery Technical Bulletin* 6 (1982), 60; on Norgate, see R. D. Harley, *Artist's Pigments* (New York, 1970), 154; on Salmon, see M. Kirby Talley, Jr., and K. Groen, "Thomas Bardwell and His Practice of Painting: A Comparative Investigation between Described and Actual Painting Technique," *Studies in Conservation* 20 (May 1975), 56.

9.   Robert Dossie, *The Handmaid to the Arts* (London, 1758), 1:201; A. A., *Handbook*, 116.

10.   Dossie, *Handmaid to the Arts*, 201.

11.   Tally and Groen, "Thomas Bardwell," 58.

12.   Talley, "'All Good Pictures Crack,'" 66.

13.   On Bardwell, see Talley and Groen, "Thomas Bardwell," 66; on Reynolds, see Talley, "'All Good Pictures Crack,'" 66; on Stuart, see Thomas Sully, *Hints to Young Painters* (Reprint, New York, 1965), xxi.

14.   Thomas Bardwell, *The Practice of Painting and Perspective Made Easy: In Which Is Contained, the Art of Painting in Oil, with the Method of Coloring* (London, 1756) 32.

15.   Hezekiah Reynolds, *Directions for House and Ship Painting* (1812; reprint, Worcester, Mass., 1978), 16.

16.   Bardwell, *Practice of Painting*, 32.

17.   Sully, *Hints to Young Painters*, xxi; Dorinda Evans, *Mather Brown: Early American Artist in England* (Middletown, Conn., 1982), 178; Talley, "'All Good Pictures Crack,'" 65.

18.   Bardwell, *Practice of Painting*, 23.

19.   Harley, *Artist's Pigments*, 154.

20.   Talley, "'All Good Pictures Crack,'" 65.

21.   Reynolds, *Directions for House Painting*, 18.

22.   Sully, *Hints to Young Painters*, 48; Evans, *Mather Brown*, 176; Talley, "'All Good Pictures Crack,'" 65.

23.   Sully, *Hints to Young Painters*, 68; Talley, "'All Good Pictures Crack,'" 65. The recipe appears in *The Great River: Art and Society of the Connecticut Valley, 1635–1820*, exhib. cat. (Hartford, Conn., 1986), 165; punctuation added.

24.   The following references to artists' materials for Brewster are found in Nathaniel F. Martin, *Account Book*, Connecticut Historical Society: "1792, Sept. Frame for painting," "1798 June ½ oz. verdigris 3 lb. 6 oz. Spanish White, Kings Yellow, etc.," and "Sept. 1803 1 qt. boiled oil ⅔, 3 lb. White lead at 11, etc." My thanks to James and Janet Robertson for providing this reference.

Catalogue

Elizabeth Mankin Kornhauser wrote the entries. Aileen Ribeiro (AR) prepared the notes on costume based on direct observation of Earl's portraits or, in most instances, on photographs and slides. Elizabeth McClintock and Marcia Hinckley researched the subjects of the portraits in the exhibition.

Ralph Earl's works are arranged chronologically, but paired portraits are inverted to show them as they were intended to hang; paintings by his contemporaries and followers are inserted where appropriate. In the footnotes for each entry, the following short titles and abbreviations are used.

CHS The Connecticut Historical Society, Hartford.
CSL The Connecticut State Library, Hartford.
DAB *Dictionary of American Biography*. New York, 1926–36.
DNB *Dictionary of National Biography*. 22 vols. London, 1882–1953.

1

2

1 Judge Ebenezer Devotion, 1772

Winthrop Chandler (1747–90)

Oil on canvas

70 x 44 ½ in. (177.8 x 113.0 cm.)

Technical note: the canvas is in two pieces, attached with a horizontal seam

Lyman Allyn Museum, New London, Conn.

On extended loan from the Scotland Historical Society

2 Mrs. Ebenezer Devotion (Eunice Huntington) and Eunice Devotion, 1772

Oil on canvas

52 ¾ x 36 ½ in. (134.0 x 92.7 cm.)

Technical note: the canvas is in two pieces, attached with a horizontal seam

Lyman Allyn Museum, New London, Conn.

Gift of Margaret Thomas Bower

Winthrop Chandler painted portraits of Judge Ebenezer Devotion (1740–1829) and his wife, Eunice Huntington Devotion (1742–1827), in 1772. An open ledger on the slant-top desk in Judge Devotion's portrait provides the date of the paintings; it is inscribed "1772 (194) LDS / Jany 13th." The powerful imagery and directness of approach seen in these portraits, which were painted in the rural Connecticut town of Scotland, demonstrate Chandler's ingenious response to the conservative aesthetic of his local patrons.

Chandler was the son of William Chandler and Jemima Bradbury Chandler of Woodstock, Connecticut. After his father died in 1754, Chandler was placed under the guardianship of his brother-in-law, Samuel McClellan. He purportedly "studied the art of portrait painting in Boston," and although there is no documentary evidence of artistic training, his portraits strongly suggest that he was at least exposed to the works of such Boston painters as John Singleton Copley.[1] In fact, Copley painted a portrait of Chandler's cousin, *Mrs. John Murray (Lucretia Chandler)*, in 1763.[2]

Chandler began his career in Woodstock in 1770 by painting Judge Devotion's parents, the Rev. Ebenezer and Martha Devotion (figs. 1.3, 1.4), also of Scotland. These are his earliest known portraits. Two years later he painted Judge Ebenezer Devotion and his wife and their daughter, as well as three bust-length portraits of their sons, Ebenezer, Jr., John, and Jonathan (private collection).[3] The portraits are recorded in the judge's will as "the seven Family

Pictures painted by Chandler," to be "divided as justly as possible among my four surviving children."[4]

A graduate of Yale College, Ebenezer Devotion was a prominent farmer and storekeeper in Scotland. As an eminent politician and ardent patriot, he was commissioned justice of the peace in 1774 and representative to the General Assembly in 1775.[5]

In this full-length portrait of his distinguished subject, Chandler creates the illusion of an actual room. He has placed Ebenezer in his study, leaning casually against a desk and writing in his ledger. The desk is against a wall, indicated at the left. Above his head can be seen the bottom section of a shelf of books, and beneath the desk are a dog and a box stool. The shelf of books may represent a chimney cupboard, which would explain its location high on the wall.[6]

Eunice Devotion is also shown at full length; she is seated in a locally made chair holding her daughter Eunice (1770–1854) on her lap and a fan in her right hand. Next to her is a tea table. The daughter of Jonathan Huntington and Elizabeth Rockwell Huntington of Scotland, Eunice Devotion was the cousin of Samuel Huntington (fig. 2.3), president of the First Continental Congress, signer of the Declaration of Independence, and governor of Connecticut in 1786. She married Ebenezer Devotion in 1764 and had nine children.[7]

The ambitious scale and complex compositional elements of these portraits were likely inspired by Copley.[8] Merchants, lawyers, and businessmen were commonly shown at ease in their working capacity in American eighteenth-century portraiture, particularly in the colonial works of Copley. After the Revolution, Ralph Earl took this tradition one step further by showing his subjects with their merchandise, as in *Elijah Boardman* (cat. 29), the portrait of a New Milford shopkeeper.

What Chandler lacks in technical ability is made up for by his masterly rendition of details, such as the lines of the locally made desk and chair and the fabric of Mrs. Devotion's dress. As an inventory left by Judge Devotion indicates, the furnishings and decorative objects in the portraits represent items that the couple actually owned.[9]

Chandler also skillfully captures faithful likenesses of his subjects, devoid of flattery. He shows the large mole on Ebenezer Devotion's somber visage and the familial resemblance of mother and child, seen in their penetrating dark eyes and stern mouths.

The year Chandler completed these portraits, 1772, he married Mary Gleason, with whom he had five children. In spite of his considerable talent, Chandler's career was a constant struggle, requiring that he turn his hand to house painting and other odd jobs. A year before his death in 1790, Chandler was described as "poor, diseased, insolvent."[10] His obituary of July 29 in the *Worcester Spy* alludes to the difficulties Chandler and other rural painters of the era faced. "Died at Woodstock, Mr. Winthrop Chandler of this town; a man whose native genius has been serviceable to the community in which he resided. By profession he was a house painter, but many good likenesses on canvas show he could guide the pencil of the limner. . . . The world was not his enemy, but as is too common, his genius was not matured on the bosom of encouragement. Embarrassment, like strong weeds in a garden of delicate flowers, checked his enthusiasm and disheartened the man."

1. William Lincoln, *The History of Woodstock, Connecticut* (Hartford, Conn., 1862), 78.

2. Nina Fletcher Little, "Winthrop Chandler," *Art in America* 35 (April 1947), 79.

3. Ibid., 82.

4. Ebenezer Devotion, Windham, 1829, Reel 1550, Pkt. 1106, CSL.

5. Ellen D. Larned, *History of Windham County, Connecticut*, 2 vols. (Worcester, Mass., 1874–80), 1:47; Franklin Bowditch Dexter, *Biographical Sketches of the Graduates of Yale College* (New York, 1907), 2:578–79.

6. Chandler painted a trompe l'oeil *Shelf of Books* (1769 or after; Shelburne Museum, Shelburne, Vt.) as part of the chimneybreast of a room in the house of Gen. Samuel McClellan in South Woodstock, Connecticut.

7. Robert F. Trent with Nancy Lee Nelson, "New London County Joined Chairs, 1720–1790," *Connecticut Historical Society Bulletin* 50 (Fall 1985), 145–51. Ibid., 100.

8. Judge Devotion's portrait relates strongly to *James Tilley* (1757; unlocated), a work at one time thought to be by Copley; see Barbara Neville Parker and Anne Bolling Wheeler, *John Singleton Copley: American Portraits in Oil, Pastel, and Miniature, with Biographical Sketches* (Boston, 1938), 248, plate 128. Tilley's portrait includes a tall desk and, underneath it, a box stool and a sleeping dog.

9. Ebenezer Devotion, Windham, 1829, Reel 1550, Pkt. 1106, CSL. The inventory lists the following: "2 round Tea-Tables $3.25," "2 desks $1.00," "1 Book-case $4.50," numerous chairs, 78 books, and 14 magazines.

10. Little, "Winthrop Chandler," 88; a tax abatement applied for in 1789 described him thus.

3   Mrs. Adam Babcock, 1774

John Singleton Copley (1738–1815)

Oil on canvas

50 x 40 in. (127.0 x 101.6 cm.)

National Gallery of Art, Washington, D.C.

Gift of Mrs. Robert Low Bacon, 1985

Washington, D.C., only

In the early 1770s, the sophistication of American portraiture reached new heights in the works of John Singleton Copley. Copley began his career in Boston in the 1750s and rapidly became the most important colonial artist in America. As his career flourished, he managed to maintain a neutral political position, catering to both Whig and Tory patrons alike. With the sudden increase in political conflict in the early 1770s, however, Copley's future as the leading artist in his native country became untenable, and he made plans to continue his career in Europe.[1]

Shortly before his departure for Europe on June 10, 1774, Copley painted portraits of Adam and Abigail Babcock, most likely in Boston, making these works among the artist's last American portraits. In a letter to Copley's half brother, Henry Pelham, the following year, Joshua Wentworth of Portsmouth, New Hampshire, complained that Copley had interrupted work on his wife's portrait to undertake "a Portrait for a Mrs. Babcock" before he left for England.[2] (Pelham had previously executed miniature portraits of Adam Babcock [fig. 1.5] and other members of his family during a visit to New Haven in 1774.)

The son of Joshua Babcock and Hannah Stanton Babcock, Adam Babcock (1740–1817) was born in Westerly,

Rhode Island, and settled in New Haven. There he married Abigail Smith (1744–77) in 1764 and became a prominent merchant and shipowner. A leading patriot, he supplied the Continental Army with a variety of goods during the war. Having raised three sons, the Babcocks spent their final years in Boston.[3]

John Singleton Copley
Adam Babcock, c. 1774
oil on canvas
46⅛ x 36⅛ in. (117.2 x 91.8 cm.)
National Gallery of Art, Washington, D.C. Gift of Henry A. and Caroline C. Murray, 1978.

3

In the portrait of Abigail Babcock, Copley shows his subject seated on a dark blue sofa with brass tacks. Both her costume and her detached and pensive gaze relate this work to Copley's *Mrs. Thomas Gage (Margaret Kemble)* (1771; Timken Art Gallery, San Diego), an equally sophisticated portrait.[4] Adam Babcock, in the other portrait, wears a dark red waistcoat with brass buttons and is seated on a greenish blue upholstered chair with brass tacks. He leans forward toward a green-cloth-covered table holding a pen in one hand and a ledger in the other. Both portraits demonstrate the dramatic effects of light, muted colors, strong characterizations, and careful attention to detail that so impressed Ralph Earl. Earl clearly demonstrated the seriousness of his artistic ambition when he chose these highly sophisticated portraits by Copley as a model for his earliest known works.

Costume Notes   Abigail Babcock is dressed in an imaginary quasi-Oriental costume. She holds a beautifully depicted garnet bracelet in her hands.   AR

1.   Jules Prown, *John Singleton Copley*, 2 vols. (Cambridge, Mass., 1966); *Letters and Papers of John Singleton Copley and Henry Pelham, 1739–1776*, ed. Guernsey Jones (1914; reprint, New York, 1970); Trevor J. Fairbrother, "John Singleton Copley's Use of British Mezzotints for His American Portraits: A Reappraisal Prompted by New Discoveries," *Arts Magazine* 55 (March 1981), 122–30.
2.   Wentworth to Pelham, April 7, 1775, in *Letters of Copley and Pelham*, 313.
3.   Stephen Babcock, *Babcock Family Genealogy* (New York, 1903), 68; Barbara Neville Parker and Anne Bolling Wheeler, *John Singleton Copley: American Portraits in Oil, Pastel, and Miniature, with Biographical Sketches* (Boston, 1938), 29–31.
4.   Richard H. Saunders and Ellen G. Miles, *American Colonial Portraits: 1700–1776*, exhib. cat. (Washington, D.C., 1987), 241–43.

4 Mrs. Henry Daggett (Elizabeth Prescott), c. 1774–75

Attributed to Ralph Earl

Oil on canvas

29 x 25 in. (73.7 x 63.5 cm.)

Stowe-Day Foundation, Hartford, Connecticut

The portraits of Henry and Elizabeth Daggett were painted after Earl's arrival in New Haven in the summer of 1774 and surely before his early masterpiece, *Roger Sherman*, of 1775 or 1776. Both Daggett portraits are clearly based on Copley's *Adam Babcock* and *Mrs. Adam Babcock* (cat. 3), painted in 1774, which hung in the Babcocks' home in New Haven. As a letter from Henry Pelham to Adam Babcock suggests, Earl was familiar with the Babcock portraits.[1]

Henry Daggett (1741–1830) graduated from Yale College in 1771 and became a prosperous merchant in New Haven.[2] An ardent patriot, he served, with his associate Adam Babcock, on various town committees during the Revolution and fought as a captain in the militia.[3] After the war, he became a state legislator and an alderman for New Haven. Daggett was related to Earl's important patron, Roger Sherman (cat. 5): Henry Daggett's wife, Elizabeth Prescott (1752–1813), was the sister of Rebecca Prescott, who married Roger Sherman in 1763. Elizabeth met Henry through the Shermans, and after their marriage in 1771, the Daggetts lived near the Shermans, on the corner of Chapel and High streets in New Haven, where they raised their ten children. Several Daggett family members, including Elizabeth and Henry (private collection), were later painted by the New Haven artist Reuben Moulthrop (1763–1814).[4]

Earl's portrait of Henry Daggett remains unlocated, known only through a photograph and a description by the art conservator Sheldon Keck in 1957 that indicates the

Attributed to Ralph Earl
Henry Daggett, c. 1774–75
oil on canvas
Unlocated. William Sawitzky Papers. Courtesy, The New-York Historical Society, New York.

4

painting had been extensively overpainted.[5] In the portrait, Daggett is shown in a pose similar to that of Babcock: seated, with a book in his hand, and presented in a somber palette against a plain, dark background. The resemblance between the portraits of Abigail Babcock and Elizabeth Daggett is far more striking. Not only are the poses similar but Elizabeth wears a simplified version of Abigail's fashionable attire. Both women have a detached and pensive gaze, more successfully limned in Copley's portrait, rather than look directly out at the viewer, as was more typical of Copley's poses. Earl's lack of training and experience can also be seen in his depiction of Elizabeth's costume and in the crudely rendered hand, holding what appears to be an orange. In both Daggett portraits, Earl attempts Copley's use of strong contrasts of light and shade.

Mrs. Henry Daggett descended to the subject's daughter, Elizabeth Daggett Hooker, in 1813. It remained in the Hooker family until 1963, when as part of the Katherine Seymour Day collection, it entered the collection of the Stowe-Day Foundation.[6]

Costume Notes   Elizabeth Daggett wears a costume invented by the artist to promote a timeless and slightly exotic image. The only item of real-life clothing is the linen shift, or chemise (the basic item of female underwear throughout this period), peeking out around the neckline. Over it is worn a bulky square-necked blue gown, which is quite shapeless when compared to the stylish, albeit imaginary, dress depicted in Copley's *Mrs. Babcock*; there the body is clearly defined, mainly by means of a classical jeweled girdle that supports the bust.

The silk of the Copley is recognizable taffeta, and the fur is ermine, with the distinctive black-tipped tails sewn in. Earl's portrait of Elizabeth Daggett, in contrast, shows a poor imitation of the fur seen in the Copley, fur that is clearly not copied from life. The jewelry in the Earl is poorly depicted, without the detail of the bracelet or the jeweled, gold or leather belt in the Copley. Daggett's turban can be described only as a white fabric, whereas that worn by Abigail Babcock is clearly spotted muslin trimmed with pearls. Daggett's hairstyle places the date of the portrait between the early and mid-1770s. Both the turban and the ermine lining to the mantle were inspired by the vogue for *turquerie,* very popular in eighteenth-century England.[7]

The girdle Babcock wears, called a *zone,* from the Greek, produces a high-waisted effect then thought to be antique. From the 1760s onward there was a growing vogue for classical dress in portraiture and genre painting, but classical dress was often confused with Turkish costume (understandably, since Greece was under Turkish rule). Hence we often find a mixture of the classical (high waist, loose drapery, zone) and the Oriental (turban, fur linings and trimmings, fringed sashes) in a single portrait, as in

Mrs. Babcock. The ermine also added an air of nobility, for in Europe it had been limited by sumptuary legislation to royalty and aristocracy for many hundreds of years.

Avoiding a direct copy of the Copley costume, Earl has removed the zone and added the asymmetrically draped chain. The brooch with two strands of pearls that loop over the left breast derives, albeit remotely, from a portrait by Rubens of Helena Fourment (early 1630s; Gulbenkian Collection, Lisbon), which was a fertile source of inspiration for artists in the eighteenth century, as well as for people seeking a masquerade costume.[8]   AR

1.   Pelham to Babcock, April 3, 1775, in "Copley/Pelham Correspondence," Public Record Office, Archives, London.

2.   According to a personal inventory, Henry Daggett owned a substantial "dwelling house, Barn & Garden" on the corner of Chapel and High streets, as well as an office and two shops on Chapel Street. He owned pew 9 in the "Meeting House of the United Society" and at the time of his death, the value of his estate totaled $16,932.32. Daggett, New Haven, 1830, Reels 827 and 3201, CSL.

3.   *Connecticut Journal and New Haven Post Boy*, September 17, 1777.

4.   William Prescott, *The Prescott Memorial: A Genealogical Memorial of the Prescott Families in America* (Boston, 1870), 93; Samuel Bradlee Daggett, *Daggett Family History* (Boston, 1894), 87; Franklin Bowditch Dexter, *Biographical Sketches of the Graduates of Yale College* (New York, 1907), 3: 411–13; Christine Skeeles Schloss, *The Beardsley Limner and Some of His Contemporaries*, exhib. cat. (Williamsburg, Va., 1972), 42–43.

5.   When the portrait of Henry Daggett was owned by Mrs. William McElroy of New York and East Haddam, Connecticut, in 1949, it was severely damaged in a fire. It was sold to a Mrs. Cramp, who in 1957 had the painting examined by Sheldon Keck, a conservator at the Brooklyn Museum. Keck indicated that the painting had been extensively overpainted and that it had a monogram, "R. E.," which had been reinforced by an earlier restoration. William Sawitzky and Susan Sawitzky Papers, Box 22, New-York Historical Society, New York.

6.   My thanks to Renee Williams, curator, Stowe-Day Foundation, for this information.

7.   Aileen Ribeiro, "Turquerie: Turkish Dress and English Fashion in the Eighteenth Century," *Connoisseur* 200 (May 1979), 17–23.

8.   See J. Steegman, "A Drapery Painter of the Eighteenth Century," *Connoisseur* (June 1936), for a comprehensive discussion; see also Aileen Ribeiro, *Dress in Eighteenth Century Europe, 1715–1789* (New York, 1984), 170, 183, 184. Some art historians think the Rubens portrait is of Susanna Fourment, Helena's sister.

5 Roger Sherman, c. 1775–76

Oil on canvas
64⅝ x 49⅝ in. (164.2 x 126.1 cm.)
Yale University Art Gallery, New Haven, Conn.
Gift of Roger Sherman White, B.A. 1899, LL.B. 1902

Ralph Earl's portrait of Roger Sherman (1721–93) was the most important commission the artist received during his early years in New Haven. Sherman was born in Newton, Massachusetts, and after the death of his father, a cordwainer, in 1743, moved to New Milford, Connecticut. There he served an apprenticeship under a cobbler and eventually became a wealthy landowner. In 1755, Sherman was admitted to the bar and later represented New Milford in the General Assembly. A self-educated man, he received an honorary degree from Yale College in 1768 and acted as treasurer of the college from 1768 to 1776. Sherman's impressive record included participation at the Continental Congress in Philadelphia in 1774, when he signed the Articles of Association. Later, as a member of the Congressional Committee, Sherman helped draft the Declaration of Independence, which he also signed. He debated the pros and cons of the Articles of Confederation from 1776 to 1777, and finally, in 1787, acted as an influential participant at the Philadelphia constitutional convention.[1]

Sherman chose to commemorate his service in Philadelphia as a member of the First Continental Congress, from which he had just returned. In his simple yet monumental portrait, Earl successfully captures the Yankee virtues that Sherman represented: self-control, honesty, frugality, piousness, and industry. Sherman was not an elegant figure; his Connecticut colleague Silas Deane detested him as a boor. But as one author has pointed out, "It was Sherman, more than any other man at the First Continental Congress, who epitomized the American character of the day."[2] Earl's depiction embodies the spirit that brought about the American Revolution.

Sherman is portrayed at full length. He is seated in a green Windsor armchair with a red seat, the only decorative prop; it was important to the sitter because it was of a regional type found in Philadelphia.[3] Earl places his subject in a defined space, adding the suggestion of a room corner behind him and dark shadows, which emanate from his legs and from the legs of the chair. The background is completely plain with the exception of a drapery that hangs on the left wall.

Most of Earl's patrons have no listing of their portraits in the inventory of their effects at the time of their death, since the portraits held no exchange value. Sherman's inventory of effects, however, lists "1 Portrait" at one pound four shillings. His inventory also reflects the breadth of Sherman's knowledge as seen in the over one hundred volumes listed from his private library.[4]

The Sherman portrait remained in the family until 1918, when it was given to the Yale University Art Gallery.[5] The portrait inspired a series of copies and engravings in the nineteenth century, notably a full-length oil portrait (1854; Connecticut Historical Society, Hartford) by the New Haven artist Nathaniel Jocelyn (1796–1881) in which the artist substituted contemporary furnishings. Nathaniel's brother, Simeon S. Jocelyn (1799–1879), produced the earliest engraving, in 1823, reproduced in John Sanderson's *Signers of the Declaration of Independence* (1823). Both Jocelyn and Sanderson credited Earl as the artist of the original Sherman portrait.[6]

Costume Notes   The clothing Sherman wears is in keeping with the austere simplicity of his physical appearance. The suit is a garnet-colored wool; the somewhat old-fashioned color and the worn patch on the right knee indicate an outfit some years old. Only those of a conservative nature wore coat, vest, and breeches made of the same material; only the sternly unfashionable wore a plain fringed muslin cravat and shirt sleeves unadorned with any kind of ruffle. The outfit is completed by black worsted stockings and black leather shoes, which are fastened with large oval buckles probably of polished cut steel.

The sobriety of the costume is completed by the sitter's lack of a wig. His short hair could, of course, be worn under a wig (long hair would be impractical), but many American men deliberately dispensed with wigs as an egalitarian gesture, a rejection of the Old World. They chose to have themselves painted this way, which gave them a Roman gravitas and anticipated the neoclassical hairstyles of the French Revolution.

1.   Roger S. Boardman, *Roger Sherman: Signer and Statesman* (Philadelphia, 1938); John G. Rommel, *Connecticut's Yankee Patriot: Roger Sherman* (Hartford, Conn., 1979).
2.   Lillian B. Miller, *"The Dye Is Now Cast": The Road to American Independence, 1774–1776*, exhib. cat. (Washington, D.C., 1975), 28.
3.   My thanks to Nancy Goyne Evans, Winterthur Museum, Newark, Del., for her assistance in identifying this chair.
4.   Roger Sherman, Special Estate File, Probate Records, New Haven, 1793, no. 9247, CSL.
5.   Registrar Files, Yale University Art Gallery, New Haven, Conn.
6.   Elizabeth Mankin Kornhauser, *Ralph Earl: Artist-Entrepreneur* (Ann Arbor, Mich., 1989), 319–20, provides a complete listing of engravings after Earl's Sherman portrait.

5

6 The Battle of Lexington, 1775

Amos Doolittle (1754–1832), after Ralph Earl
Engraving, handcolored on laid paper
13¾ x 19½ in. (34.9 x 49.5 cm.)
Inscribed at the lower right margin: "A. Doolittle Sculpt."
The Connecticut Historical Society, Hartford

7 A View of the Town of Concord, 1775

Engraving, handcolored on laid paper
13¾ x 19 in. (34.9 x 48.3 cm.)
Inscribed at the lower right margin: "A. Doolittle Sculpt."
The Connecticut Historical Society, Hartford

8 The Engagement at the North Bridge in Concord, 1775

Engraving, handcolored on laid paper
13¾ x 19 in. (34.9 x 48.3 cm.)
Inscribed at the lower right margin: "A. Doolittle Sculpt."
The Connecticut Historical Society, Hartford

9 A View of the South Part of Lexington, 1775

Engraving, handcolored on laid paper
13¾ x 19½ in. (34.9 x 49.5 cm.)
Inscribed at the lower right margin: "A. Doolittle Sculpt."
The Connecticut Historical Society, Hartford

Ralph Earl and Amos Doolittle began their careers in New Haven on the eve of the Revolution, Earl as a portrait painter and Doolittle as an engraver. Unlike Earl, Doolittle worked at a variety of trades, including that of silversmith, jeweler, and engraver; he produced book illustrations, bookplates, music scores, maps, diplomas, portraits, currency, and historical prints.[1]

Among Doolittle's first and most important efforts were the four large copperplate engravings of the Battle of Lexington and Concord that he produced with Ralph Earl. The details of the production of the prints have remained vague, and Earl's role has at times been questioned.[2] Contemporary accounts provide, however, a fairly clear tale of the collaboration, which is verified by the known facts.

The Battle of Lexington and Concord occurred on April 19, 1775, shortly before Doolittle's twenty-first birthday. Several records attest to his advocacy of the American cause.[3] When news of the battle reached New Haven on April 21, 1775, Doolittle marched with Capt. Benedict Arnold's militia company, the Governor's Second Company of Guards. He arrived in Cambridge on April 29 and returned home three or four weeks later. Shortly after the battle, Doolittle and Earl met at the battleground, where Earl took sketches. Doolittle then worked on the engravings for several months in New Haven; and upon their completion eight months later, he placed an advertisement in the *Connecticut Journal and New Haven Post Boy*.

In the 1830s the New Haven engraver and historian John Barber (1798–1885) first gave Earl and Doolittle public recognition for the engravings. Barber was closely acquainted with Doolittle, first as his student and later as a colleague. In *History and Antiquities of New Haven, Connecticut* (1831), Barber reproduced Doolittle's original advertisement for the prints and noted: "The above prints were drawn by Mr. Earl, a portrait painter, and were engraved by Mr. Amos Doolittle. . . . Mr. Doolittle is living and from him the above information is obtained."[4] In two subsequent histories, published in the 1830s, Barber added to the details of Earl and Doolittle's collaboration and verified the story, stating: "The author of this work . . . was personally acquainted with Mr. Doolittle, and has conversed with him repeatedly upon the subject of these drawings."[5] Finally in a revised edition of his 1831 New Haven history, Barber provides the most detailed account: "According to the statement of Mr. Doolittle, he acted as a kind of model for Mr. Eàrl to make his drawings, so that when he wished to represent one of the provincials as loading his gun, crouching behind a stone wall when firing on the enemy, he would require Mr. D. to put himself in such a position."[6]

Only one inaccuracy exists in Barber's account of Earl's role; he states that Earl marched with the militia from New Haven to Cambridge. In fact, Earl refused to join a militia company and by 1777 was a notorious Loyalist. At the time of the engravings, however, he managed to maintain a neutral stance. Most likely, Earl went to the battleground directly from Boston (having visited Henry Pelham's studio a few weeks before the battle) or traveled from New Haven to Cambridge on his own.

The collaboration of Earl and Doolittle resulted in highly accurate renditions of the events of the battle, despite their somewhat crude technique. In 1935, William Sawitzky claimed to have discovered one of Earl's four original paintings of the battle, *A View of the Town of Concord* (Concord Historical Society). A technical examination of the painting strongly suggests that the work was done after the Doolittle print,[7] which is verified by the Brooks family of Concord, in which the painting descended.[8] Sets of the engravings hung in houses throughout the area and in turn inspired copies of the famous battle scene,[9] including a

The Battle of Lexington, April 19.ᵗʰ 1775. Plate 1.

1 Major Pitcarn at the head of the Regular Grenadiers.   4 Regular Companies on the road to Concord.
2 The Party who first fired on the Provincials at Lexington.   5 The Meetinghouse at Lexington.
3 Part of the Provincial Company of Lexington.   6 The Public Inn.

A. Doolittle Sculp.ᵗ

6

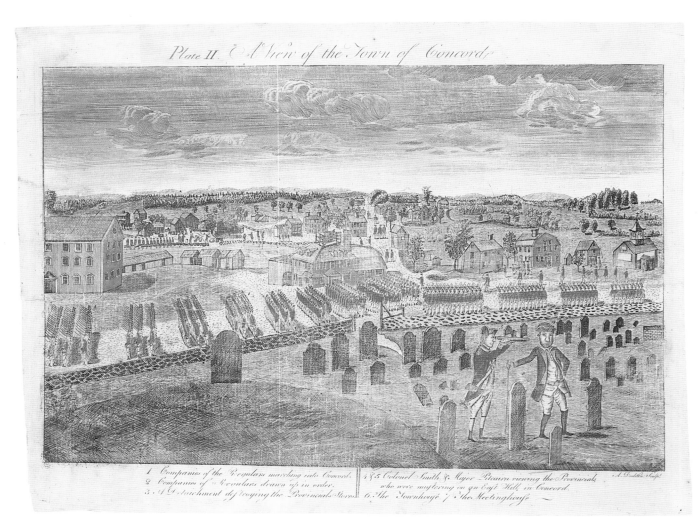

Plate II. A View of the Town of Concord.

1 Companies of the Regulars marching into Concord.   4 & 5 Colonel Smith & Major Pitcarn viewing the Provincials
2 Companies of Regulars drawn up in order.   who were mustering on an East Hill in Concord.
3 A Detachment destroying the Provincials Stores.   6 The Townhouse. 7 The Meetinghouse.

A. Doolittle Sculp.ᵗ

7

Plate III. The Engagement at the North Bridge in Concord.

1. The Detachment of the Regulars who fired first on the Provincials at the Bridge   2. The Provincials headed by Colonel Robinson & Major Buttrick. 3. The Bridge

A. Doolittle Sculp.

8

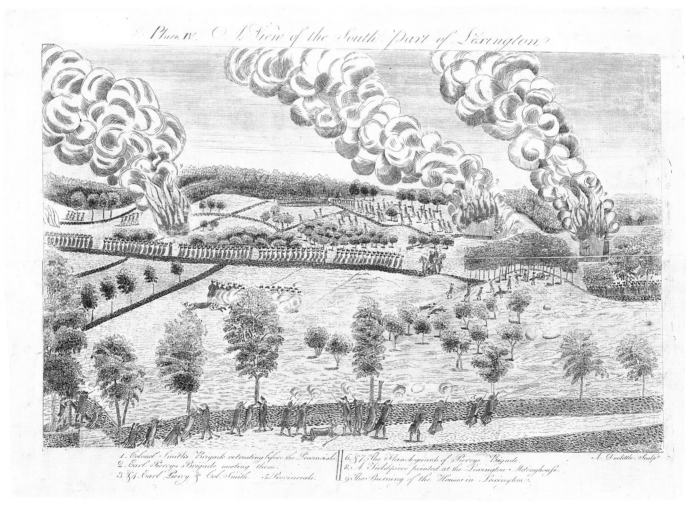

Plate IV. A View of the South Part of Lexington.

1. Colonel Smith's Brigade retreating before the Provincials. 2. Earl Percy's Brigade meeting them. 3 & 4. Earl Percy & Col. Smith. 5. Provincials. 6. & 7. The Flankguards of Percy's Brigade. 8. A Fieldpiece pointed at the Lexington Meetinghouse. 9. The Burning of the Houses in Lexington.

A. Doolittle Sculp.

9

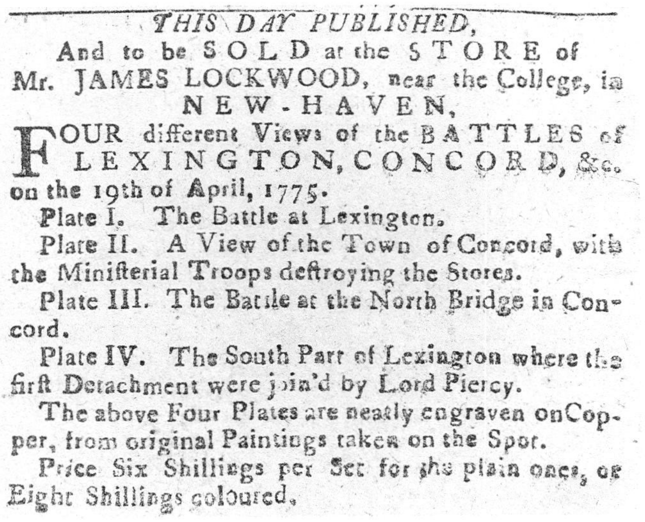

THIS DAY PUBLISHED,
And to be S O L D at the S T O R E of
Mr. JAMES LOCKWOOD, near the College, in
NEW-HAVEN,
FOUR different Views of the BATTLES of
LEXINGTON, CONCORD, &c.
on the 19th of April, 1775.
    Plate I. The Battle at Lexington.
    Plate II. A View of the Town of Concord, with
the Ministerial Troops destroying the Stores.
    Plate III. The Battle at the North Bridge in Con-
cord.
    Plate IV. The South Part of Lexington where the
first Detachment were join'd by Lord Piercy.
    The above Four Plates are neatly engraven on Cop-
per, from original Paintings taken on the Spot.
    Price Six Shillings per Set for the plain ones, or
Eight Shillings coloured.

Connecticut Journal and New Haven Post Boy, December 13, 1775
The Beinecke Rare Book and Manuscript Library, Yale University,
New Haven, Conn.

Anonymous
Amos Doolittle, c. 1795–1800
oil on canvas
36 x 28 in. (91.4 x 71.1 cm.)
Lyman Allyn Museum, New London, Conn.

watercolor executed in 1777 by the Yale student and amateur artist St. John Honeywood (1763–98), entitled *The
Ever Memorable Battle of Lexington*.[10]

    Because of the relationship between Earl and Doolittle,
a portrait of Amos Doolittle has been traditionally ascribed
to Ralph Earl.[11] The style and composition of Earl's Connecticut works are similar, it is true, but the portrait is
by a less gifted hand; the painting lacks Earl's attention to
detail, and only little stylistic or factual evidence supports
the attribution.

1.   William A. Beardsley, "An Old New Haven Engraver and His Work:
Amos Doolittle," *Papers of the New Haven Colony Historical Society* 7 (1914):
132–50; *DAB*; William F. Doolittle, *The Doolittle Family in America* (Cleve-
land, Ohio, 1901–8).
2.   For the most detailed account of the events that led to the production of the prints and the various questions about Earl's role, see Ian M. G.
Quimby, "The Doolittle Engravings of the Battle of Lexington and Concord," *Winterthur Portfolio* 4 (1968): 83–108.
3.   For example, Doolittle's signature appears on a petition of March 2,
1775, to the General Assembly of Connecticut calling for the establishment of an independent military company; see *Second Company Governor's
Foot Guards; Souvenir History. 150th Anniversary, 1775–1925* (New Haven,
Conn., 1925), opp. 8.
4.   Barber, *History and Antiquities of New Haven, Connecticut* (New Haven,
1831), 83.
5.   Barber, *Historical Collections of Massachusetts* (Worcester, Mass., 1839),
398–99; Barber, *Connecticut Historical Collections* (New Haven, Conn.,
1836), 14.
6.   Barber and Lemuel S. Punderson, *History and Antiquities of New Haven,
Conn.* (New Haven, 1856), 14.
7.   William Sawitzky, "Ralph Earl's Historical Painting: A View of the
Town of Concord," *Antiques* 28 (September 1935), 97–100; Elizabeth Mankin Kornhauser, *Ralph Earl: Artist-Entrepreneur* (Ann Arbor, Mich., 1989),
33–34.
8.   Quimby, "Doolittle Engravings," 102–5.
9.   See Lemuel Shattuck, *A History of the Town of Concord* (Boston, 1835),
114; Edward Jarvis, "Houses and People in Concord, 1810–1820," MS
(1882, Concord Public Library), 114–63. Both references document the
presence of a set of the Doolittle prints in the home of Reuben Brown of
Concord. In addition, Samuel Davis, in his "Journal of a Tour to Connecticut – Autumn of 1789," in *Proceedings of the Massachusetts Historical Society*
(Boston, 1869–70), 12–13, noted having seen a set of "prints engraved by
Doolittle of New Haven" in a house in Wilbraham, Massachusetts.
10.   See Quimby, "Doolittle Engravings," fig. 97.
11.   Laurence B. Goodrich, *Ralph Earl: Recorder for an Era* (Oneonta,
N.Y., 1967), 40, ill. 41.

10 William Carpenter, 1779

Oil on canvas

47 ⅞ x 35 ⅝ in. (121.6 x 90.5 cm.)

Signed and dated at lower center: "R. Earl Pinx 1779"

Worcester Art Museum, Worcester, Massachusetts

Museum purchase, 1916

11 Mary Ann Carpenter, 1779

Oil on canvas

47 ¼ x 35 in. (120.0 x 88.9 cm.)

Signed and dated at lower left: "R. Earl 1779"

Worcester Art Museum, Worcester, Massachusetts

Museum purchase, 1916

The Carpenter portraits are the first known signed and dated works from Earl's English years and represent William (1767–1823) and Mary Ann Carpenter (b. 1766), the children of William Carpenter, a yeoman, and his wife, Mary Carpenter, both of Aldeby, Norfolk. The Carpenters were neighbors of John Money of Norwich, now a colonel, who may have aided in obtaining this portrait commission for the artist.[1] The subjects are identified by the labels attached to the stretchers on each portrait: "This picture is a likeness of William Carpenter Esquire late of Toft Monks, in the County of Norfolk, when a boy about 12 years old, he was the only son of William Carpenter Esquire of Adelby, of the adjoining Parish of Adelby and was born in the year 1767, and died March 14th 1823, aged 56 years[.] This picture was renovated by Mr. Sands, an Artist in Norwich, in the year 1860, and at the expense of Philip Samuel Carpenter"; and "This picture is a likeness of Mrs. Foster, the wife of Thompson Foster, Esquire of London, and senior surgeon of Gay's Hospital, in London; and was the daughter of William Carpenter Esquire of Aldeby in Norfolk; it is a likeness of her, when a girl about 14 years old, and her maiden name was Mary Carpenter, and only sister of William Carpenter, Esquire of Toft Monks. This picture was renovated by Mr. Sands, an Artist in Norwich, in the year 1860, and by the order and expense of Philip Samuel Carpenter."

Although the portraits retain many of the elements apparent in Earl's New Haven works, they also demonstrate some improvement in his technical ability and composition. In *William Carpenter*, Earl repeats many of the features found in his earlier portrait *Roger Sherman* (cat. 5): he presents the subject at full length, seated on a simple wooden stool, with shadows emanating from the legs of the subject and the chair. William is placed in the corner of a room defined by light—which falls on the left side of his face—while the right side of the room is in shadow. Earl employs more brilliant colors than in his New Haven years and paints with greater expertise, as we can see in the anatomical features of his subject, particularly the hands, and his convincing treatment of fabric textures. Finally, Earl has created a slightly more animated pose for this portrait; William pauses while reading a book to look out at the viewer.

The portrait of Mary Ann Carpenter, aged thirteen, shows similar advancements in technique but appears somewhat stiff and provincial. Here Earl attempts a full-length, frontal pose; the figure leans awkwardly toward a table, on which her arm rests. He again uses a partially shaded wall to delineate space while bathing the figure in light. A more subtle palette is evident here, along with many of the decorative devices found in Earl's later American works and first introduced together in this portrait, including red drapery, a green-cloth-covered table, a round-backed chair with brass tacks, and a multicolored, geometric-patterned carpet.

Mary Ann Carpenter underwent restoration at the Worcester Art Museum in 1972, at which time extensive overpaint was removed; perhaps it was applied by the Mr. Sands referred to in the inscriptions on the backs of the canvases. Sands may have been the Norwich painter Anthony Sandys (1806–83).[2]

The two Carpenter portraits were sold at Christies, London, on June 23, 1915, to J. Leger, London, which in turn sold the portraits to Charles Henry Hart of New York. The Worcester Art Museum acquired the paintings from Hart in 1916.[3]

Costume Notes William's suit is of a startlingly bright scarlet wool, painted with great attention to the rather coarse, three-dimensional feel of the fabric.[4] Although somewhat provincial in color and deliberately unfashionable in the uniformity of its constituent parts, the suit is stylish in cut, particularly the coat with its curved front edges. The vest, open to midchest, reveals the shirt ruffle, and the coat collar is almost covered by the open linen shirt collar, a comfortable informal style, characteristically English, that was worn by boys until their late teens. Also typically English is the hairstyle; the hair is allowed to curl naturally on the neck and cut straight across the forehead in a fringe. Foreign visitors often commented on a welcome contrast to the more formal hairstyles seen on boys in continental Europe; one such traveler in 1782 noted that English boys had "their hair cut on their forehead, whilst behind it flows naturally in ringlets."[5] The white stockings are probably cotton; the black leather shoes fastened with large square buckles, possibly of pinchbeck, an alloy of copper and zinc (named after a Fleet Street watchmaker) imitating gold. On the table in front of William is a fantail hat, cocked on three sides, the

back cock standing up straight and the peak in front; the hat is worn with a braid loop on the lefthand side, and the hat band is decorated with a matching tassel.

Mary Ann wears a style of dress intermediate between the simple white frock of childhood and adult costume, usually adopted around the age of sixteen. It consists of a bodice and skirt of cream silk; the skirt has a pattern of tiny woven sprigs. The bodice, which is decorated with ruched silk ribbon in dark green and pink, is long and pointed in the front. It fastens at the back, laced tightly (it is easy to see the horizontal lines at the side where the silk is stretched over a boned underbodice), a style that pulled the shoulders back as an aid to good deportment. Mary Granville, Mrs. Delany, a great eighteenth-century letterwriter and arbiter of female gentility, argued for the retention of back-fastening dresses to counteract "anything that drags the shoulders forward at the growing time [which] is a great disadvantage."[6] The long pointed bodice also helps to keep the apron in place; this is a fine striped-silk gauze, the same fabric as the V-shaped stomacher pinned into the bodice. The skirt is decorated with a band of ruched cream silk at the hem, but only in the front.[7] The unpowdered hair is arranged in loose ringlets that fall on the shoulders; the crown of the head is decorated with a white feather.   AR

1. William Sawitzky and Susan Sawitzky, "Two Letters from Ralph Earl, with Notes on His English Period," *Worcester Art Museum Annual* 8 (1960), 8–41; H. M. L., "Portraits of William Carpenter and Mary Carpenter," *Bulletin of the Worcester Art Museum* 7 (July 1916), 8–10.

2. Sawitzky and Sawitzky, "Two Letters from Ralph Earl," 39.

3. *Pictures by Old Masters, the Property of the Late Lord Huntingfield and Others*, sale cat. (Christies, Manson, and Woods, June 25, 1915), no. 30; Painting Files, Worcester Art Museum.

4. It is always difficult to be precise about the identification of fabrics in painting, but Earl depicts very clearly the nap of this fabric, which might be witney, a coarse wool (from Witney, Oxfordshire) usually scarlet in color.

5. *Travels of Carl Philipp Moritz in England in 1782*, ed. P. E. Matheson (London, 1924), 81.

6. *Autobiography and Correspondence of Mary Granville, Mrs. Delany*, ed. Lady Llanover, 6 vols. (London, 1861–62), 3:582. Delany also comments on the popularity of fringes, or bangs, for girls in the 1770s, a fashion she disliked for it made them "look like dowdies"; Mary Ann Carpenter (or her mother) seems to have agreed with this advice, for her hair is swept up off her forehead.

7. A skirt was usually so decorated only when worn under an overdress, known as an open gown, or robe; then only the front hem of the skirt would be visible. It was, however, customary for adult clothing to be recycled for children, so it is quite likely that Mary Ann wears a skirt that was once part of a formal open gown owned by her mother.

12   Admiral Richard Kempenfelt, 1782 or 1783

Oil on canvas

50¼ x 39 in. (127.6 x 99.1 cm.)

Signed and dated along the anchor, at the lower left: "R. Earl Pinxt 178[3?]"

National Portrait Gallery, London

Admiral Kempenfelt's pose is generally recognized as based on that in Thomas Gainsborough's *Augustus John, Lord Hervey, Later Earl of Bristol* (1768, National Trust, Ickworth, Sussex), which was engraved by J. Watson in 1773. Gainsborough's *Lord Hervey* helped to popularize the iconography of portraits of naval officers. In his rendition of Kempenfelt, Earl borrowed from Gainsborough's portrait the unaffectedness of the figure's pose, as well as the large anchor to denote an association with the sea. Gainsborough's work inspired similar elements in Copley's *Midshipman Augustus Brine* (1772; Metropolitan Museum of Art) and John Trumbull's *Patrick Tracy* (1784 to 1786; National Gallery of Art, Washington, D.C.).

A freshness and vitality in Earl's likeness of Richard

Kempenfelt (1718–82) suggests the portrait was painted from life and completed after Kempenfelt's untimely death. Kempenfelt drowned with eight hundred others when his ship, the *Royal George*, sank suddenly at anchor off Spithead, England, in August 1782. Earl's meticulous depiction of Kempenfelt's uniform also suggests that he must have been looking at an actual uniform.

The man-of-war in the background of Earl's portrait was taken from an engraving of Admiral Kempenfelt after a portrait by the English artist Tilly Kettle (1740–86). Kettle's portrait, which was painted in 1781 to 1782, celebrates Kempenfelt's victory off Ushant, France, in 1781; it was engraved in mezzotint by Richard Earlom.[1]

Earl's portrait of Kempenfelt was with Henry Graves and Company, London, by 1889. It was purchased by the National Portrait Gallery, London, in 1912 from Leggatt Brothers, which had acquired it the previous year from the dealer John Glen of London.[2]

Costume Notes   If the portrait is dated 1783 (as the most recent restoration at the National Portrait Gallery claims) then it is likely that the head was painted from life.[3] Kempenfelt wears the wig style of his youth, with regimented side curls, or buckles (the contemporary word comes from

Tilly Kettle
Admiral Richard Kempenfelt, c. 1782
oil on canvas
96 x 60 in. (243.8 x 152.4 cm.)
National Maritime Museum, Greenwich, London.

the French *boucles*), and the back hair tied into a bag behind; it is a formal powdered wig, suitable both to his age and his rank.

Kempenfelt was promoted to rear admiral of the blue in 1780, and in this portrait he wears the full-dress uniform of a flag officer in the Royal Navy: a blue coat faced with white and laced with gold braid, a white vest also laced with gold, and white breeches. The uniform of naval officers was established in 1748 and based on the general popularity of blue in the navy; in style it followed the fashions of the day.[4] Modifications and extensions to the uniform were introduced in 1767 and 1774, and in 1783 new uniform regulations were introduced for flag officers; the different grades of admiral, for example, were indicated by the number of rows of braid on the coat cuffs. Kempenfelt, however, is painted in the pre-1783 uniform. It is painted so accurately, down to the exact detail of the button patterns and design of the gold braids, that it must have been painted from a surviving uniform, possibly placed on a dummy. An identical surviving uniform of the period, that of Adm. Sir James Douglas, exists in the Scottish United Services Museum, Edinburgh. In Gainsborough's *Lord Hervey*, the subject wears the uni-

form of a naval captain. In the Kettle portrait, Kempenfelt wears the undress (or everyday) uniform of a flag officer.

There is some controversy over the blue flag on the ship in the Earl, where it is shown on the main mast; strictly speaking, only the admiral, not the rear admiral, was entitled to fly a blue flag. But Kempenfelt is known to have experimented with the placement of flags, and its appearance here does not necessarily reflect an error on the part of the artist.[5]   AR

1.   Laurence B. Goodrich, "Ralph Earl's Debt to Gainsborough and Other English Artists," *Antiques* 78 (November 1960), 464–65. Kempenfelt's brother, Gustavus Adolphus Kempenfelt, was in possession of the Kettle portrait when he gave it to the National Maritime Museum in 1828. It has been suggested that Gustavus commissioned Earl's portrait of the admiral for his house, Ladye Place, at Hurley. See Painting Files, National Portrait Gallery, London.
2.   My thanks to Jacob Simon, curator, National Portrait Gallery, London, for this information.
3.   National Portrait Gallery Archive, London.
4.   On the subject of naval uniforms, see C. King, "The Evolution of British Naval Uniform," *Connoisseur* 103 (April 1939); W. E. May, *The Dress of Naval Officers* (London, 1966).
5.   My thanks to the staff of the National Portrait Gallery Archive, London, and to Patricia Blackett Barber of the National Maritime Museum, London, for their help.

Richard Earlom after Tilly Kettle
Admiral Richard Kempenfelt, 1782
mezzotint
14¼ x 11 in. (36.2 x 27.9 cm.)
Yale Center for British Art, New Haven, Conn.
Gift of Mr. and Mrs. J. Richardson Dilworth.

13   A Master in Chancery Entering the House of Lords, 1783

Oil on canvas

49 ½ x 39 in. (125.7 x 99.1 cm.)

Signed and dated at lower left: "R. Earl Pinxt 1783"

Smith College Museum of Art, Northampton,
    Massachusetts

Museum purchase, 1956

Earl exhibited this portrait at the Royal Academy exhibition of 1784 with the above title. It shows Earl's improving technical skills, as seen in his use of delicate glazes to illuminate the face, his skillful handling of gradations of gray and black in the costume, and his creation of a convincing receding space, which includes a stairway that rises behind the figure. Although the artist commonly used vermillion for his signature in his later Connecticut works, here he uses black, in keeping with the somber palette.

The subject's identity has remained elusive, in part because information concerning masters of Chancery is lacking. One possibility for the identity of the subject, however, may be Henry, second earl Bathurst (1714–94).[1] The son of Allen, first earl Bathurst, Henry served in Parliament from 1735 to 1754, when he was appointed chief justice of common pleas. Later appointed lord chancellor, he was raised to the peerage as Baron Apsley in 1771, and has been described as "the least efficient Lord Chancellor of the eighteenth century."[2]

Bathurst was an avid supporter of Lord North's ministry. The subject of Earl's portrait carries a scroll under his arm that is inscribed with portions of two bills written by Lord North and supported by Bathurst. The bills, which were passed and repealed in 1775, were intended to restrict trade with the northern and southern colonies in America. Earl inscribed the scroll as follows: "An Act to restrain / Trade of Massach / Rhode island Con / Virginia South Ca / North America."

In addition to biographical information, Bathurst's identity as the subject of Earl's portrait is suggested by its similarity to a drawing of Bathurst taken by Copley in 1779 in preparation for his history painting *The Death of the Earl of Chatham* (1779; Tate Gallery, London). Earl seems to have softened the effects of age, making Bathurst—if it is he—look younger than sixty-nine. A portrait of Bathurst in his robes as lord chancellor by Nathaniel Dance (1770s; Lord Bathurst collection, Cirencester, England) also presents him with a thinner, more aged face.[3] Although the identity of the subject remains in question, the portrait represents one of Earl's finest English works.

The portrait was purchased in England by the John Nicholson Gallery, New York, and then sold to Vose Galleries, Boston. Smith College Museum of Art acquired the portrait from Vose Galleries in 1956.[4]

Costume Notes   In the eighteenth century, masters in Chancery acted as legal functionaries in the court of Chancery and in the House of Lords, though their duties with regard to legislation are not altogether clear. The subject of this portrait wears legal costume over a formal, official black velvet suit and black silk vest. We can see the artist's skill in depicting the different blacks. Earl solves the problem of painting the hands by incorporating the gesture, so characteristic in formal portraiture of the eighteenth century, of placing one hand under the vest at midchest level; this was intended to show off the fine sleeve ruffles, usually of lace, but here of fine muslin.

The legal dress consisted of white linen bands, a style derived from the mid-seventeenth-century collar known as a falling band, and a gown of black silk. The subject's wig is the shorter full-bottomed style, dating to the early eighteenth century but retained thereafter by high-up legal officers of the Crown.[5] This type of legal undress, or everyday working costume, was worn in the eighteenth century not only by masters in Chancery but also by serjeants-at-law, King's Counsel, the speaker of the House of Commons, and the lord chancellor.

Although Bathurst could have been portrayed in this kind of legal undress (as he is in his bust by Joseph Nollekens in the Church of St. John the Baptist, Cirencester, England), it is unlikely that a formal portrait would show him without any visual tribute to his former legal eminence as lord chancellor, the top of the English legal profession. Furthermore, there is no evidence that Bathurst served as a master in Chancery.[6]   AR

1.   The subject's identity as Lord Bathurst was first suggested by Helen Davey, whose extensive research is contained in the Painting Files, Smith College Museum of Art, Northampton, Mass. For biographical information, see *DNB*, 407–8; John Lord Campbell, *Lives of the Chancellors* (London, 1857), 7:138; Edward Foss, *The Judges of England* (London, 1864), 8:240.

2.   *DNB*, 408.

3.   *Catalogue of Political and Personal Satires* (London), 5:628. There is a half-length version of this painting in Lincoln's Inn, London.

4.   Painting Files, Smith College Museum of Art.

5.   Linen bands were also worn by clerics (see Earl's portrait of the Rev. Nathaniel Taylor, cat. 31) and academics in the eighteenth century. They are still part of English legal dress today. Lawyers lower down on the social scale wore gowns of prunella, a light worsted fabric. When lawyers were promoted to King's Counsel, they were entitled to silk gowns, as in the Earl portrait. The custom, called "taking silk," continues to this day, when barristers become Queen's Counsel. A similar but longer version of this wig is still worn today by judges on formal occasions, the speaker of the House of Commons, and the lord chancellor.

6.   J. H. Baker, St. Catherine's College, Cambridge, to Aileen Ribeiro, May 1990. Baker, an eminent legal historian, said that Bathurst was never a master in Chancery. He also said that in the Earl portrait, "the wig is distinctly shorter in front than Bathurst's [in the known portraits] . . . [which] argues against the two sitters being the same person." My thanks to J. H. Baker for his comments on the portrait.

13

John Singleton Copley
Head of the Earl of Bathurst, Lord Chancellor, 1779–80
black and white chalk on gray-blue paper
26 x 19½ in. (66.0 x 49.5 cm.)
M. and M. Karolik Collection of Eighteenth Century American
Arts. Courtesy, Museum of Fine Arts, Boston.

14 Reclining Hunter, c. 1783–84

Oil on canvas

45 ½ x 59 ½ in. (115.6 x 151.1 cm.)

Collection of Drs. Caroline and Peter Koblenzer,
Philadelphia

In addition to demonstrating the great strides Earl made while in Benjamin West's studio, this enigmatic sporting spoof shows Earl indulging in his own considerable wit. A gentleman resembling a cockney squire reclines on a bank beneath some trees, grinning superciliously. He is dressed in a fine silk waistcoat and dress shirt. Having shot everything in sight, including a cow and donkey in the far field and a pile of nongame birds nearby, he now sits at his ease, holding a shotgun in his left hand, with his mushroom-filled hat beside him. In the foreground, the artist has added the broken clay pipe used to load the packets of shot, one of which is inscribed "fine" and the other "common gun powder."

The subject of this sporting spoof remains unidentified. At one time it was offered for sale as *Portrait of Captain Hallett*, attributed to Thomas Gainsborough. More recently, the portrait has been assigned to Ralph Earl and was included as such in the major exhibition Benjamin West and His American Students.[1]

Costume Notes The satirical nature of this portrait is reflected in the wholly impractical, if elegant, silk costume. Unlike an artist such as Pompeo Batoni, who costumed some of his English sitters (gentlemen on the Grand Tour) in fanciful hunting attire,[2] Earl shows off his unidentified subject in real-life clothing, although not clothing worn for sport. The sitter wears his own hair, pomaded and powdered, with the single side curl of the 1780s. His costume consists of a French frock coat of blue silk with intricately chased buttons, a vest of cream silk edged with gold braid, black silk knee breeches, and white silk stockings. Earl is concerned to include such details as the way the stockings wrinkle when caught by the knee band of the breeches and the clock (patterned insert from the foot to the ankle) of the stocking. The black leather shoes have huge gilt or silver buckles, known as Artois buckles (after the comte d'Artois, brother to the French king Louis XVI and a great leader of fashion), which were very popular in the 1780s. By then, lace was out of fashion except on formal occasions, when light needle laces on a fine mesh ground were preferred to the dense, allover patterns popular earlier in the century. In this portrait, the sitter is wearing a shirt frill and sleeve ruffles of Alençon, a French needle lace, or of fine embroidered muslin. Either would be impractical for hunting wear.   AR

1.   The portrait was in the collection of Capt. Charles Romer Williams of London by 1920, when it sold at auction, at Christies, London, on June 11, 1920, as *Portrait of Captain Hollett, {by} Thomas Gainsborough*. Information on the provenance of this portrait was kindly supplied by Sidney F. Sabin, London, who owned the portrait in the 1980s. The portrait was first attributed to Ralph Earl by Sidney F. Sabin and was included in Dorinda Evans, *Benjamin West and His American Students*, exhib. cat. (Washington, D.C., 1980), 67.

2.   See, for example, Batoni's *Sir Humphrey Morice* (1762; Sir Brinsley Ford collection); the subject reclines in a woodland setting, dogs and the day's bag at his side, dressed in a suit of shot silk in a somewhat arcadian style. This portrait is in *Pompeo Batoni and His British Patrons*, exhib. cat. (London, 1982), cat. 16.

14

15   A Gentleman with a Gun and Two Dogs, 1784

Oil on canvas

86⅞ x 57⁷⁄₁₆ in. (220.7 x 146.4 cm.)

Signed and dated at lower left: "R. Earle Pinxt 1784"

Worcester Art Museum, Worcester, Massachusetts

Museum purchase, 1921

Hartford only

Earl demonstrates his mastery of conventional English por-traiture in both composition and technique in this accurate rendition of a hunter with his two dogs. This unidentified gentleman in proper hunting attire is formally posed in a skillfully painted parklike setting. As the hunter's out-stretched arm, holding a hat, points in the distance, his two dogs follow the gesture with their rivetted eyes. Earl's subtle palette and delicate brushwork add to the accomplished effect of this portrait.

The portrait was in an estate in Brighton, England, in the nineteenth century and was sold to Sulley and Com-pany, London. Daniel H. Farr of Philadelphia acquired the portrait and sold it to Ehrich Gallery, New York, in 1921. It was purchased in the same year by the Worcester Art Museum.[1]

Costume Notes   Earl's subject wears a real hunting costume, which consists of a brass-buttoned coat of hunting pink (actually red) whose densely textured woollen cloth is cut away at the sides and slopes to the hem, a double-breasted vest, and leather breeches. The coat, an English frock with a turned-down collar and slit-buttoned cuffs, was of a type popular for wearing outdoors, as well as on more formal occasions. By the 1780s the dividing line between formal and informal dress for men was increasingly blurred, and the frock coat, which had originally begun as a hunting gar-ment, was accepted everywhere except at court – it is basi-cally the same coat that we see, for example, in Earl's *Dr. Joseph Trumbull*, *Dr. David Rogers*, and *Colonel William Taylor* (cats. 18, 23, and 33) – but the fabrics varied according to the occasion.

Here the unknown hunter's vest, orange edged with gold braid, adds another note of bright color; in 1774 Horace Walpole referred to this shade of orange as Barri, presumably named after the mistress of Louis XV, Madame du Barry. The breeches are cut in the characteristic eighteenth-century way, rather low on the hips. The boots, known as French top boots, are black leather with brown tops. From the 1780s on, boots were increasingly worn not just outdoors, as here, but indoors as well. Instead of the formal three-cornered hat, the hunter holds out a new style, the round hat, uncocked and with a flattish, shallow crown. Although his hair – powdered and tied in at the back – seems to contradict the informality of his costume, it is his own, not a wig.[2]   AR

1.   Research Files, Worcester Art Museum, Worcester, Mass.
2.   During this period of transition from the formality of the powdered wig to the informality of natural hair, men could choose, according to pref-erence and occasion, a wig, hair dressed in the style of a wig, or their own hair *au naturel*.

16

17

16   Marianne Drake, 1783

Oil on canvas
50¼ x 40¼ in. (127.6 x 102.2 cm.)
Signed and dated at lower left: "R. Earl pinxt / 1783"
Count Charles de Salis, Switzerland

17   Sophia Drake, 1784

Oil on canvas
50½ x 40¼ in. (128.3 x 102.2 cm.)
Signed and dated at lower left: "R. Earl Pinixt 1784"
Count Charles de Salis, Switzerland

Marianne (1764–1849) and Sophia Drake (1765–1803) were the only children of Adm. Francis William Drake (1724–1797), a descendant of the celebrated Sir Francis Drake, who married his first cousin Elizabeth Heathcote Drake (d. 1797). The Drakes resided at Deal, on the English coast, and later at Hillingdon Place, Middlesex, on a substantial property.[1]

The Drake daughters attended a number of schools in Deal and London, and according to family correspondence, either one or both daughters attended the Dutton sisters' boarding school at Windsor.[2] Earl probably received the commission to paint their portraits at that time. The Drake parents showed much concern for the proper education of their daughters, as a letter from a family relation implies. "I am glad Miss Drake [Marianne] is placed so much to your wish, but I imagine the time she passes with Lady Macclesfield [her aunt] is that in which she makes most improvements; as I think one parental precept has more weight than a thousand from those commonplace gentry that keep schools."[3]

Earl's portraits of the Drake sisters complement one another in compositional settings and successfully convey the young women's accomplishments. Sophia is placed in the English countryside, seated on a moss-covered ledge. She looks up at the viewer, interrupted while reading a book inscribed "History." Marianne, in contrast, is seated in a room between an ornate baroque harpsichord, representing her musical accomplishments, and a pembroke table that holds her watercolor box, palette, and water glass, which is reflected on the tabletop. She holds up for the viewer to admire a landscape with a river, a barge, and a church steeple.

In 1792, Marianne married Thomas Evance of Lambeth, recorder of the borough of Kingston. After his death in 1830, she married John McIntosh. In 1797, Sophia married Jerome de Salis, Count of the Holy Roman Empire.[4]

The two portraits have descended in the de Salis family to the present day.

Costume Notes   In these two portraits the artist has used dress to emphasize the different situations of the sitters; Sophia, seated outdoors, wears informal white-checkered muslin, and Marianne, indoors, more formal silk taffeta. Sophia's costume, a simple gown cut low in the neck and fastened around the waist with a blue silk sash, is suitable for what the French call a *jeune fille,* a young girl who is not yet a young woman. Paradoxically, however, such a costume was in anticipation of the styles worn at the end of the century, when, with the cult of youth promoted by the French Revolution, women of all ages adopted what had hitherto been regarded as childish dress: the simple, white, all-in-one frock worn by girls. The blue sash of Sophia's gown echoes the silk ribbons in her leghorn hat. This arcadian simplicity attracted much comment from visitors to England, among them the American Abigail Adams. Adams was somewhat critical of the negligence of English dress, which she noted in the summer of 1784. "A common straw hat, no cap, with only a ribbon upon the crown, is thought dress sufficient to go into company. Muslins are much in taste."[5]

Marianne's appearance is more formal. Her hair is frizzed and pomaded to achieve the rather bushy look popular in the 1780s; a piece of fine muslin (similar to that worn by her sister) is pinned on the crown of her head and falls forward over her left shoulder. The gown is a light taffeta, possibly a popular summer silk known as lustring, which had an extra shine and was particularly light and floating; it appears in a number of Earl's portraits of English and American sitters, a reflection of fashionable taste in the late eighteenth century. Here the gown is worn with a wide pink fringed sash, also probably of lustring.[6]   AR

1.   My thanks to Count Charles de Salis for providing genealogical information on the Drake family and making the portraits available for examination.
2.   Gilbert Heathcote to Elizabeth Drake, October 16, 1782 (Count Charles de Salis collection). This letter from Elizabeth Drake's brother-in-law inquires about paying Miss Dutton, who has a boarding school at Windsor, on behalf of his sister.
3.   Lady Knight to Elizabeth Drake, May 9, 1780, reproduced in *Lady Knight's Letters from France and Italy, 1776–1795,* ed. Lady Eliott-Drake (London, 1905); my thanks to Count de Salis for providing this reference.
4.   Lady Eliott-Drake, *The Family and Heirs of Sir Francis Drake* (London, 1911), 2:323; Laurence B. Goodrich, "Ralph Earl's Portraits of Three Young English Ladies," *Antiques* 71 (November 1958), 418–19.
5.   *New Letters of Abigail Adams, 1788–1801,* ed. S. Mitchell (Boston, 1947), 174.
6.   Samuel Johnson's *Dictionary* (1755) describes lustring as "a shining silk, commonly pronounced lutestring"; both spellings appear in the eighteenth century.

18   Dr. Joseph Trumbull, 1784

Oil on canvas

30⅛ x 25 in. (76.5 x 63.5 cm.)

Historic Deerfield, Deerfield, Massachusetts

Ralph Earl's friend Dr. Joseph Trumbull (1756–1824) was an apothecary-doctor from Worcester, Massachusetts, who made frequent trips to Europe. Earl wrote to Trumbull in September 1784 while he was a part of Benjamin West's entourage of family and students at Windsor, England. He directed the letter to Trumbull's current London address to establish a date for a first portrait sitting, instructing Trumbull to "meet earley [sic] in the morning to proceed to business."[1] Trumbull often traveled to London to purchase drugs and other items from the "most reputable Medicinal Warehouses" for his apothecary shop in Worcester and, later, in Petersham, Massachusetts. A man of the world, his family remembered him as a "brilliant wit" whose "society was much courted."[2]

The portrait shows Trumbull at the age of twenty-eight. Earl has captured a lively image of his young friend, who is shown leaning against a moss-covered ledge in a relaxed pose. Earl teased his friend – a handsome man – regarding his looks. "I am under constant feeris and apprehentions that your lookes may some day or other prove fatiol to You."[3] Earl uses loose, painterly brushwork for the costume details and background foliage and short, delicate strokes to depict the facial features of his subject. His improved technical ability is clearly seen in this and other later English portraits.

Trumbull wrote a long and poetic will in which he left his "half-length portrait, painted in London in 1784 . . . and also the gold burnished frame," to his son, George Augustus Trumbull. The portrait descended in the Trumbull family until 1955, when Vose Galleries in Boston purchased the portrait and the accompanying letter from Earl to Trumbull of September 23, 1784, from the estate of Mary Louisa Trumbull Cogswell Roberts. The portrait and letter entered the collections of Historic Deerfield in 1956.[4]

Costume Notes   There is a somewhat Romneyesque feel to this portrait, but with perhaps greater attention to textiles than the English artist usually gives. Earl is good at the texture of textiles and accessories – the tan woollen cloth of the English frock coat, with its plain pewter buttons, the satin of the vest with its gold braid and wide lapels, and the fine pleated muslin of the billowing shirt ruffle and the ruffles at the wrist. The sitter wears his own hair brushed into a curl at each side and lightly powdered.   AR

1.   Earl to Trumbull, September 23, 1784, Historic Deerfield, Deerfield, Mass., reproduced in William Sawitzky and Susan Sawitzky, "Two Letters from Ralph Earl, with Notes on His English Period," *Worcester Art Museum Annual* 8 (1960), 9, 11.

2.   George Augustus Trumbull, "Trumbull Genealogy," MS, Trumbull Family Papers, 1773–1896, American Antiquarian Society, Worcester, Mass. For biographical information, see Trumbull Family Papers; J. Henry Lea, *A Genealogy of the Ancestors and Descendants of George Augustus and Louisa Clap Trumbull* (Worcester, Mass., 1886), 13–14. Trumbull placed advertisements for his store in *Thomas' Massachusetts Spy, or, the Worcester Gazette*, June 23, 1785.

3.   Earl to Trumbull, September 23, 1784.

4.   "The Last Will and Testament of Joseph Trumbull," August 25, 1823, Case 59956, Series A, Probate Office, Worcester County Courthouse, Worcester, Mass.; Registrar Files, Historic Deerfield.

18

19

19 Ann Whiteside Earl, 1784

Oil on canvas

46⅝ x 37⅞ in. (118.4 x 96.2 cm.)

Signed and dated at lower left: "R. Earl Pinixt 1784"

Mead Art Museum, Amherst College, Amherst,
    Massachusetts

Gift of Herbert L. Pratt, Class of 1895

This portrait of Earl's second wife ranks among his most sensitive portrayals. Ann Whiteside Earl (1762–1826) was the daughter of Eleazer Whiteside of Norwich, England. The portrait was painted in 1784, less than a year before Earl returned to America with his new bride; in Earl's portrait, the couple's journey is suggested by the globe turned to North America. Ann and Ralph Earl's son, Ralph Eleazer Whiteside Earl (1785 or 1788–1838), later wrote of his visit to his grandfather's farm: "My Grandfather lives within a Mile of the General's [John Money] on a small farm pleasantly situated on a River heading to Yarmouth, the produce of which is sufficient to support him through life." [1]

This portrait displays the subtle coloring, graceful pose, and facile brushwork that provide a tribute to the lessons Earl learned during his stay in England. His intensity of feeling for his subject adds to the tenderness of his portrayal.

Ann and her husband (they were presumably married before their departure) arrived in Boston on May 23, 1785. She led a difficult life, following her husband from New York City to various towns in New England for the next thirteen years. The Earls did not establish a permanent residence and frequently boarded at taverns or in the homes of Ralph's clients. Ann gave birth to a daughter, Mary Ann Earl, on August 31, 1787, during her husband's imprisonment for debt in New York City. Their second child, Ralph Eleazer Whiteside Earl, was born between 1785 and 1788, the year of Earl's release from debtors' prison. Ann eventually left her husband to travel on his own; in 1798 she settled with her daughter in Troy, New York, where she remained until the end of her life. According to family tradition, Earl's intemperate habits brought about this separation. The Earls' son spent time with his father learning the art of portrait painting. Ann was cared for by her daughter, who married Benjamin Higbie of Troy in 1807. [2]

This portrait was in the collection of Sir Lionell Phillips of Tynley Hall, Winchfield, England, in the nineteenth century. It was purchased from Sir Lionell in 1913 by Thomas Agnew and Sons, London, as a "Portrait of the Artist's Wife" and sold to Messrs. Robinson and Farr of London. In 1921, William G. Warden of Philadelphia sold the painting to M. Knoedler and Company, New York, and in 1922, Herbert L. Pratt of Glen Cove, Long Island, purchased it. Pratt gave it to Amherst College in 1936. [3]

Costume Notes   This portrait has a very English feel in terms of both style of painting and the features of the sitter. Ann Earl was not beautiful but evidenced what Madame Roland called on her visit to England in 1784 a characteristic "maiden and affecting look." [4] The costume shows the stylish simplicity so typical of English dress in the 1780s. Ann wears a long-sleeved dress of creamy white silk taffeta; the bodice of the gown is almost hidden by a fichu-bodice of worked muslin whose frilled collar is held together by a tiny jeweled pin. Girdling the dress is a yellow silk sash, and around her shoulders she wears an *écharpe* cloak, a long broad scarf, almost reaching to the ground, of black silk edged with embroidered net. The hairstyle, ultrafashionable, consists of an allover frizz of hair, stiffly pomaded and powdered, and wide flat curls, or rolls, of hair falling to the shoulders. An artificial style like this (false hair was often used to eke out the sitter's own) took many hours to arrange, as can be seen from contemporary letters and diaries and such popular hairdressing manuals as *The Art of Hair-Dressing* (1788) by Alexander Stewart of Berkeley Square.   AR

1.   Earl to John Trumbull, February 18, 1810, Ralph E. W. Earl Papers (1810–38), American Antiquarian Society, Worcester, Mass.

2.   The headstone on the grave of Mary Ann Earl Higbie provides her birth date as August 31, 1787, and death date as February 19, 1866. Presbyterian Church Cemetery, White Plains, New York. Biographical information on Ann Whiteside Earl and her daughter is contained in the Gage Family Papers and the Ralph E. W. Earl Papers, American Antiquarian Society; see in particular Mary Ann Higbie to Ralph E. W. Earl, January 23, 1828, and Ralph E. Prime to Thomas Hovey Gage, February 28, 1914. Also see Ralph E. Prime, *The Descendants of James Prime* (Yonkers, N.Y., 1895); William Sawitzky and Susan Sawitzky, "Two Letters from Ralph Earl, with Notes on His English Period," *Worcester Art Museum Annual* 8 (1960), 31–38; Harold Spencer, *The American Earls: Ralph Earl, James Earl, R. E. W. Earl*, exhib. cat. (Storrs, Conn., 1972), 14–15.

3.   Painting Files, Mead Art Museum, Amherst College, Amherst, Mass.

4.   *A Trip to England, 1784*, from *The Works of Jeanne-Marie Phlipon-Roland* (London, 1800), 184.

20 Mrs. John Johnston
(Martha Spear), 1785

Oil on canvas
30 ¼ x 25 ½ in. (76.8 x 64.8 cm.)
Signed and dated at the lower left: "R. Earl Pinxt 1785"
Anderson House, Washington, D.C.
Courtesy, Society of the Cincinnati

Mrs. John Johnston was traditionally thought to represent a pivotal early work from Earl's English years and assigned an erroneous date of 1782.[1] Based on the stylistic advancement seen in this portrait over that of the Carpenter portraits of 1779 (cats. 10 and 11), Earl was thought to have entered West's studio by 1782. In fact, the portrait is dated 1785 (the digit five is hidden under the rabbet of the frame). Furthermore, Martha Johnston is not known to have ever been in England. Rather than representing an early turning point in his English career, this portrait signifies the strides Earl made during his seven-year stay in England and his intention of carrying this formal English portrait style to post-revolutionary America.

This portrait is the first work Earl painted upon his return to America. Although little is known about the subject other than that she was the daughter of Nathan Spear, a Boston merchant, and Grace Willis Spear,[2] the portrait is significant, since Martha Spear married an acquaintance of Earl, the Boston artist John Johnston, in 1773.[3]

John Johnston (c. 1753–1818) was the son of Thomas Johnston, an engraver who also worked as a japanner and heraldic painter in Boston, and the half brother of William Johnston the portrait painter. After serving an apprenticeship to John Gore, a coach and heraldic painter, John Johnston took over his father's successful business in partnership with his brother-in-law Daniel Rea, Jr. Rea and Johnston worked as artisan-painters from 1777 to 1789, when their partnership dissolved. Johnston then turned to portrait painting, working in a style derived from his exposure to Copley's pre-revolutionary Boston portraits, such as *Man in a Gray Coat* (c. 1788; Museum of Fine Arts, Boston). Until Gilbert Stuart's arrival in Boston at the turn of the century, Johnston was one of the few portrait painters working in the city.

Johnston interrupted his career during the revolutionary war, fighting valiantly in the Continental Army. He received an honorary discharge in 1777 after being seriously wounded and taken prisoner in the Battle of Long Island in August 1776. He became a founding member of the Massachusetts branch of the Society of the Cincinnati.[4] Johnston apparently overlooked Earl's earlier Tory sympathies when he commissioned the portrait of his wife, and may have welcomed the opportunity to view firsthand Earl's recently attained British portrait style.

Earl's portrait of Martha Johnston demonstrates his mastery of fashionable British portraiture. Compared to his earlier American works, the modeling is softer, the hues subtler, the brushwork more facile, and the approach far less linear. Earl chose a Romneyesque pose for his subject, who gracefully inclines her head toward the viewer, clasping her delicately portrayed hands, as she reclines on a green upholstered English-style chair with brass tacks. This type of chair is frequently seen in Earl's more formal American portraits, particularly those painted in New York City.

The portrait descended in the Johnston family to Parker Soren, who gave it to the Anderson House Museum in 1981.[5]

Costume Notes   Earl has perfectly captured here the floating, hazy quality of female costume in the 1780s. Even the frizzed hair has a kind of blurred feel to it. This is a romantic, lyrical portrait. The problem is therefore to analyze what the sitter is wearing. It is a formal, open gown of pink silk, but the only clear feature, apart from the wrist-length sleeves, is the ruched silk, known as the robing, that vertically trims the front of the open gown, which is worn over a separate skirt. The prevailing line in 1780s fashion was a large, softly billowing skirt, the fullness often created by hip pads and a kind of bustle in the back. When women were seated, their skirts would be bunched up and voluminous in the way that Earl shows in this and other portraits. The construction of the bodice front cannot be seen because of the vast gauzy scarf, the *buffon,* crossing her bosom. The same floating and insubstantial fabric decorates Martha Johnston's hair. These English gauzes were all the rage in the 1780s, and it was a source of great annoyance to fashionable American women when they could only be obtained with the greatest difficulty during the war with England.   AR

1.   William Sawitzky and Susan Sawitzky, "Two Letters from Ralph Earl, with Notes on His English Period," *Worcester Art Museum Annual* 8 (1960), 22. This important early article on Earl's English career dated the portrait to 1782 and placed Earl in Benjamin West's circle then because of the accomplished look of the work. Successive scholars accepted the chronology; see Laurence B. Goodrich, *Ralph Earl: Recorder for an Era* (Oneonta, N.Y., 1967), 6; Robert C. Alberts, *Benjamin West: A Biography* (Boston, 1978), 133; Harold Spencer, *The American Earls: Ralph Earl, James Earl, R. E. W. Earl*, exhib. cat. (Storrs, Conn., 1972), 4.
2.   Verne Raymond Spear, *The Descendants of George Spear, Who Settled Braintree, Massachusetts, 1642–1988* (West Springfield, Mass., 1988).
3.   Mabel M. Swan, "The Johnstons and Reas – Japanners," *Antiques* 47 (May 1943), 212.
4.   William Dunlap, *History of the Rise and Progress of the Arts of Design in the United States* (1834; reprint in 3 vols., New York, 1969), 311; Swan, "Johnstons and Reas – Japanners"; Carol Troyon, *The Boston Tradition: American Paintings from the Museum of Fine Arts*, exhib. cat. (New York, 1980), 70–71; Frederick W. Coburn, "The Johnstons of Boston," *Art in America* 21 (December 1932), 27–36; Nina Fletcher Little, "The Good Samaritan: Symbol of the Boston Dispensary," *Antiques* 70 (October 1956), 360–62.
5.   John Kilbourne, *Anderson House Museum Director's Report* (Washington, D.C., 1981), 35.

20

21

21 Baron von Steuben, 1786

Oil on canvas
48½ x 40 in. (123.2 x 101.6 cm.)
Signed and dated at lower left: "R. Earl Pinxt 1786"
New York State Historical Association, Cooperstown

While in debtors' prison, Earl received an important commission to paint Friedrich Wilhelm Ludolf Gerhard Augustin von Steuben (1730–94). The commission was instigated by the baron or by his friend, the mayor of New York, James Duane, who kept the portrait in his possession.[1] Duane had overseen Earl's trial at the Mayor's Court and later came to Earl's assistance as a leading member of the Society for the Relief of Distressed Debtors.

Born in Magdeburg, Prussia, Baron von Steuben served as aide-de-camp to Frederick the Great during the Seven Years' War, which lasted from 1756 to 1763. He came to America in 1777 to offer his services to the Continental Army and was given the rank of major general. Von Steuben entered into an agreement with the Second Continental Congress that if the American army won the war, he would be compensated, and if the British prevailed, he would not seek compensation. He succeeded in reorganizing the army on the European model, introducing strong discipline.

Von Steuben lived at what is now Fifty-seventh Street in New York when this portrait was painted. As a founding member and, at this time, presiding officer of the Society of the Cincinnati, von Steuben pressed the Congress concerning compensation for his wartime services.[2] After considerable controversy, Alexander Hamilton, a champion of the baron, eventually, in 1790, secured from the Congress a sum of seven thousand dollars and an annuity of two thousand dollars. Von Steuben later moved to his land grant (sixteen thousand acres) in Oneida County, New York, where he remained until his death.[3]

Earl painted a formal military portrait of von Steuben in the year that he was elected president of the New York branch of the Society of the Cincinnati. He is shown at three-quarter length, standing in a landscape. Von Steuben turns his left shoulder outward, displaying the eagle badge of the society on the facing of his coat, and he rests his outstretched right hand on the silver hilt of a sword (now in the Mabel Brady Garvan Collection, Yale University Art Gallery) that was presented to him by members of the Congress "for Military Merit."

Earl painted two portraits, and possibly a third, of von Steuben. This version, the only one signed and dated, includes a military encampment in the background, beyond the loosely painted foliage of the tree. This portrait hung in the mansion of James Duane at Duanesburg, New York, and descended to Duane Featherstonaugh, who through

Macbeth Gallery, New York, sold the portrait to Stephen Clark in 1946. Clark gave the painting to the New York State Historical Association in 1957.[4]

A second version of *Von Steuben*, likely painted in the same year, remained in the sitter's possession and was bequeathed to Maj. William North, von Steuben's adopted heir and former aide-de-camp.[5] (North was also painted by Earl in the same year, 1786; private collection.) The background in this version includes a river, sailboats, and two fortresses.

A third version (on loan to the Brandywine River Museum, Chadds Ford, Pa.) descended in the family of Benjamin Maverick Mumford (1772–1843), who was related through marriage to the James Duane family. This version, again with slight variations in the background, also appears to be by Ralph Earl. A question remains: Which of the three is the original?[6]

A copy of one of Earl's portraits of von Steuben was painted by Gherlando Marsiglia (1792–1850) and is owned by the Art Commission of the City of New York.[7]

Von Steuben was one of the most widely painted heroes of the war. In 1780, Charles Willson Peale painted his portrait (Pennsylvania Academy of the Fine Arts, Philadelphia). Joseph Wright painted a portrait (c. 1786–90; private col-

Ralph Earl
Baron Frederick Wilhelm von Steuben, c. 1786
oil on canvas
49¾ x 41⅜ in. (125.4 x 105.1 cm.)
Yale University Art Gallery, New Haven, Conn. Gift of Mrs. Paul Moore in memory of her nephew Howard Melville Hanna, Jr., 1931S.

lection) that is closely related to Earl's; it was commissioned by Stephen Van Rensselaer for his manor house near Albany, New York. Wright's portrait was probably painted after Earl's versions and before Wright's departure from New York in 1790. It is not nearly as flattering a depiction of this valiant soldier, showing von Steuben as an older and less fit soldier.[8]

Costume Notes This is a portrait of dignity and formality, both in the elegance of the pose – one hand on a sword, the other holding a pair of kid gloves – and the proudly decorated uniform. According to German military custom (more formal than that of the American army), von Steuben wears a powdered wig. His uniform, that of the Continental Army's general staff, consists of a coat of dark blue faced with buff. He wears a black military stock, or necktie (civilians wore white), over which the shirt collar is folded; the epaulets denote his rank as major general. The portrait demonstrates the sitter's pride in his military achievements and the honors given him. Besides the badge of the Society of the Cincinnati he wears an eight-pointed star suspended from a ribbon around his neck and a star on his chest clearly inscribed FIDELITAS, both of the Order of Fidelity founded in 1715 by the margrave of Baden-Durlach and given to von Steuben in 1769. AR

1. The Registrar Files, Yale University Art Gallery, New Haven, Conn., contain correspondence from Harriet Mumford Greene, great-granddaughter of James Duane, saying that Duane commissioned three portraits of von Steuben, one of which he kept.
2. *The First Federal Congress, 1789–1791* (Washington, D.C., 1989), 162.
3. Frederick Knapp, *The Life of Frederick Wilhelm von Steuben Major General of the Revolutionary Army* (New York, 1859); John McAuley Palmer, *General von Steuben* (Port Washington, N.Y., 1966).
4. Painting Files, New York State Historical Association, Cooperstown, N.Y.
5. Theodore Sizer, "Earl's Portrait of Steuben," *Bulletin of the Associates in the Fine Arts at Yale University* 9 (June 1939), 13–14.
6. William Sawitzky felt that the Yale picture, the second version discussed, was "a finished replica of [the] more sketchily treated life picture [the first version, at Cooperstown]." Painting Files, Yale University Art Gallery.
7. William Dunlap, *History of the Rise and Progress of the Arts of Design in the United States* (1834; reprint in 3 vols., New York, 1969), 2:296.
8. Monroe H. Fabian, *Joseph Wright: American Artist, 1756–1793* (Washington, D.C., 1985), 120, ill. 121.

22 Mrs. Alexander Hamilton (Elizabeth Schuyler), 1787

Oil on canvas

31¾ x 26⅞ in. (80.7 x 68.3 cm.)

Signed and dated at lower left: "R. Earl pinx / 1787"

Museum of the City of New York

Gift of Mrs. Alexander Hamilton and General Pierpont
Morgan Hamilton

Raised in great wealth, Elizabeth Schuyler (1757–1853) was the daughter of Philip Schuyler, one of George Washington's favorite generals, and Catherine Van Rensselaer Schuyler, member of an equally distinguished New York family. Alexander Hamilton, the leading New York Federalist, was acquainted with Philip Schuyler through his service as an aide to Washington. Hamilton met and married Schuyler's daughter in 1780. Tench Tilghman, upon meeting Elizabeth Schuyler in 1775, described her as "a Brunette, with the most good-natured, lively dark eyes that ever I saw, which threw a beam of good temper and benevolence over her entire countenance. Mr. Livingston told me I was not mistaken. . . . She was the finest Tempered Girl in the World." [1]

After her marriage, Elizabeth Hamilton lived in a modest house on Broadway near her husband's place of work, where the couple raised their eight children. She supported Alexander's political career, frequently revising drafts of his state papers. At the age of ninety-two, she recalled the years of the young republic when her illustrious husband was a member of Washington's cabinet. "I had little of private life in those days [although] I had a passionate love of home and domestic life. . . . I was fond of dancing and usually attended the public balls. . . . I was at the inauguration ball – the most brilliant of them all. . . . On that occasion every woman who attended the ball was presented with a fan prepared in Paris, with ivory frame, and when opened displayed a likeness of Washington in profile." [2]

According to family tradition, Elizabeth Hamilton's portrait was taken while Earl "was imprisoned for debt. . . . In [its] coming to Mrs. Hamilton's knowledge she went to the prison and sat for the portrait there. Others hearing of the action followed her example and Earl was soon released." [3] In spite of the circumstances, Earl painted a sensuous and elegant portrait of his charming subject. Taking great care to convey her social status, Earl placed her in his stock upholstered English armchair with gilt arms, which is also found, in less elaborate forms, in his later Connecticut portraits.

The portrait was a gift to the Museum of the City of New York from the subject and Gen. Pierpont Morgan Hamilton.

Costume Notes This is a stylish portrait of a sitter dressed in the latest English fashions of the 1780s. The hair is powdered and piled high, frizzed *à l'hérisson,* like a hedgehog; wide, unraveling roll curls fall onto the shoulder. Greatly powdered hair could give any face a washed-out look, so the discreet use of makeup was often advocated. Here I think the sitter has applied a modest dusting of pearl powder, with maybe a slight touch of rouge on the cheeks; the aim, however, was to make the face look as natural as possible, whereas women in Europe, especially the French, wore much more visible makeup. [4] Black silk necklaces and bracelets like the ones shown here (bracelets were featured in many of Earl's portraits) showed off the whiteness of the face, neck, bosom, and hands. The gown is white silk taffeta, possibly lustring, the neckline covered by a collar of embroidered muslin or net; a pink silk sash is tied around the waist. AR

1. Quoted in Noemie Emery, *Alexander Hamilton: An Intimate Portrait* (New York, 1982), 54.

2. Interview between the historian Benson J. Lossing and Elizabeth Hamilton, 1848, reproduced in Katherine Schuyler Baxter, *A Godchild of Washington: A Picture of the Past* (New York, 1897), 224.

3. Philip Schuyler to Charles Henry Hart, January 19, 1897, Charles Henry Hart Papers, Roll 929, Frame 1481, Archives of American Art, Irvington, N.Y.

4. On eighteenth-century cosmetics, see Aileen Ribeiro, *Dress in Eighteenth Century Europe, 1715–1789* (New York, 1984); Ribeiro, *The Female Face* (London, 1987).

22

23 Dr. David Rogers, 1788

Oil on canvas

34⅛ x 29 in. (86.7 x 73.7 cm.)

Signed and dated at lower left: "R. Earl / Pinxt / 1788"

National Gallery of Art, Washington, D.C.

Gift of Edgar William and Bernice Chrysler Garbisch,
1965.15.8

24 Martha Tennent Rogers and Daughter, 1788

Oil on canvas

34⅛ x 29 in. (86.7 x 73.7 cm.)

Signed and dated at lower left: "R. Earl / 1788"

National Gallery of Art, Washington, D.C.

Gift of Edgar William and Bernice Chrysler Garbisch,
1965.15.9

Ralph Earl began painting the friends and relatives of
Dr. Mason Fitch Cogswell in Fairfield County, Connecticut,
following his release from debtors' prison in 1788. Among
his first subjects were Dr. David Rogers (1749–1824), a
friend and colleague of Cogswell's, and his wife, Martha
Tennent Rogers (1751–1813 or 1829), with their child.
In these portraits, Earl began to modify his more formal
style, creating compositions more appropriate for his rural
Connecticut subjects and using landscape settings.

David Rogers studied medicine with his father, Dr.
Uriah Rogers, and, like Cogswell, served as a surgeon for
the Continental Army during the Revolution. In 1772 he
married Martha Tennent of Greenfield Hill, whose father
and brother were Congregational ministers in the town. The
couple had twelve children.[1] The doctor is portrayed in his
professional capacity, seated in a red upholstered armchair
with shelves of medical books in the background. As was
his custom in his Connecticut portraits, Earl inscribed the
spines of the books—in this instance, with the names of the
major authors of medical treatises of the period, including
"Sydenham," "Boerhave," "Cullen," and "Smellie."[2]

Martha Rogers and her daughter are placed in a landscape setting of loosely executed foliage. She sits, her
daughter standing before her, in a chair similar to the one
seen in her husband's portrait, a variation of the form seen
in Earl's English and New York portraits; her chair is more
suited to a gentleman's study or library, as in David Rogers's
portrait, than to the outdoors. Although the brass nails over
the seams in this and other chairs by Earl are accurately depicted, the front ends of the arms on these chairs vary and
do not appear to be accurate. Here the extended arms are
eccentric, perhaps an attempt by the artist to personalize
the furniture in his portraits.[3]

The two portraits descended in the Rogers family to
Mrs. George Reed. The family sold the paintings around
1960. They were purchased by Col. Edgar William and
Bernice Chrysler Garbisch from the Hirschl and Adler Galleries, New York, in 1963 and entered the National Gallery
of Art in 1965.[4]

Costume Notes   David Rogers's hairstyle is a compromise between the formal European wig and the natural locks of an
American democrat; the hair is the sitter's own, powdered
and arranged to fall somewhat carelessly on the shoulders
(the back hair, in a more formal situation, would be tied
or contained in back). It was quite acceptable for the loose
powder to be shown on the coat collar, as here. The coat, a
frock coat in the English style, is brown wool and has the
high collar of the later 1780s. Also popular in that decade
were buttons, here of stamped brass or copper. The yel-
lowish vest may be made of nankeen, a cotton fabric (originally from Nanking but also made in India and, by the late
eighteenth century, in England and America) popular for
summer wear. The shirt ruffles on chest and sleeve are plain
muslin, and the shirt collar is hidden by a stock, or made-up
linen neckcloth fastening at the back of the neck.

Martha Rogers's attire is a modest, middle-class costume with no pretensions to high fashion. The long-sleeved
dress is brown, possibly poplin, and much of the bodice
is hidden by a large muslin scarf crossed over the bosom.[5]
The plainness of the dress is mitigated by an indoor cap of
embroidered net tying under the chin with a blue silk ribbon; caps of linen or muslin were de rigueur in England and
America for middle-class married women, particularly in

households with strong Protestant beliefs.⁶ The daughter wears a pink dress with elbow-length sleeves (more practical than the adult wrist-length type) and a blue sash at the waist, tying in a bow at the back. Her hair, ash blonde, is cut across the front and curls naturally; English informality in the treatment and the clothing of children was largely followed in America.   AR

1. *History and Genealogy of the Families of Old Fairfield*, 2 vols. (Fairfield, Conn., 1932), 2:790–91; Herbert Thoms, ed., *The Heritage of Connecticut Medicine* (New Haven, Conn., 1942), 8–9, 179, 180.

2. See Samuel C. Harvey, "Surgery in the Past in Connecticut," in Thoms, ed., *Heritage of Connecticut Medicine* (New Haven, Conn., 1942), 179.

3. An example of the type of chair on which Earl based the chair that appears in his portraits is seen in the English leather-upholstered armchair of about 1780 in the collection of the Victoria and Albert Museum, London, number W.8-1955. My thanks to Christopher Gilbert, director of art galleries, Temple Newsam House, Leeds, England, for bringing this example to my attention. My thanks to Morrison H. Heckscher, curator, Department of American Decorative Arts, Metropolitan Museum of Art, New York, and Christopher Gilbert for their valuable comments on the chairs in Earl's portraits.

4. Painting Files, National Gallery of Art, Washington, D.C.

5. A fabric with a silk warp and a woollen weft, poplin was more hard-wearing than pure silk and was thus popular in thrifty households.

6. Biblical injunctions for women to cover their heads and not reveal their hair were strictly interpreted in some Protestant societies in Europe and America.

24

23

25 Oliver Wolcott, c. 1789

Oil on canvas
54 x 44 in. (137.2 x 111.8 cm.)
Museum of Connecticut History, Hartford

Earl's portrait of Oliver Wolcott, Sr. (1726–97), successfully conveys the prominent role Wolcott played in the politics of his country. The artist creates the sense of dignity appropriate for Wolcott's elevated position by relying on the traditional prop of a column, quoted from European grand manner portraiture.[1] Seated in an elegant red brocade chair, Wolcott rests his hand on a copy of the new Constitution of the United States, whose ratification he had been instrumental in obtaining. Earl avoided overtly military symbols, suitable for a man who had served as major general of the Connecticut troops, and instead dresses Wolcott as a gentleman, with a local reference, a view of the gentle Litchfield hills, seen through the window.

Beginning with Oliver's father, Roger Wolcott, who served as governor of Connecticut from 1750 to 1754, the Wolcott family had long dominated state political power. Oliver began his upward climb in public office when his father appointed him sheriff of Litchfield County after his graduation from Yale College in 1747. A signer of the Declaration of Independence, Wolcott served as a member of the Continental Congress along with Roger Sherman and Eliphalet Dyer (cat. 5; fig. 1.7). After the war, Wolcott returned to Litchfield, serving as lieutenant governor from 1786 until 1796, when he was elected governor, remaining in that office until his death the following year. His son Oliver Wolcott, Jr. (1759–1833), became the third-generation Wolcott to serve as governor of the state.[2]

When Earl's guardian, Mason Fitch Cogswell, first arrived in Hartford in 1789, he was warmly received by the Wolcott family. Oliver, Jr., who was then studying law with Oliver Ellsworth (cat. 41) in Hartford, received a letter from a fellow member of the Connecticut Wits, Joseph Trumbull, who noted: "I received yours by Dr. Cogswell, who appears a sensible agreeable young man, and I am glad that he proposes to settle in Hartford. Indeed our circle of friends wants new recruits." Various members of the Wolcott family would later appear as patients in Cogswell's account book.[3]

Earl's portraits of the Wolcotts were in the possession of their son Oliver, Jr., at the time of his death and are listed in his inventory as follows: "1 Painting Oliver Wolcott the Elder . . . $15.0 / 1 Mrs. Wolcott do . . . $15.0."[4]

Oliver, Jr., highly valued the portrait of his father. When John M. Sanderson wrote to him requesting a portrait of his father from which to make an engraving for his nine-volume series *Biography of the Signers of the Declaration of Independence* (1823–25), Oliver, Jr., recommended the por-

trait by Earl as "a good likeness of his person" and suggested that Sanderson use the "reduced copy from my Picture . . . made by my daughter [Laura Wolcott Gibbs] and sent to Mr. Delaplaine in the Year 1819."[5] In fact, it was this copy by his daughter, an amateur artist, that hung in Joseph Delaplaine's Gallery in Philadelphia and from which successive engravings were made.[6] In addition, Laura Gibbs apparently repainted the face of the Earl portrait, softening the features to match the reduced copy. At a later date, the overpaint was removed to reveal Earl's original rendition.[7]

The portrait descended in the Wolcott family to the subject's grandson, Dr. John S. Wolcott, who presented it to the State House in Hartford. The portrait was later transferred to the Connecticut State Library. Earl's follower Joseph Steward painted a copy (c. 1796; Connecticut Historical Society, Hartford) of Earl's portrait of Wolcott for display in the Hartford Museum, which opened to the public in 1797.

Costume Notes　Oliver Wolcott wears a gray frock coat, probably silk, cut fashionably narrow with tight sleeves, a style not very comfortable for a corpulent man. The silk buttons, crossed to form a pattern of four quarters, were known as death's-head buttons; they were not intended to fasten, and indeed, the artist seems to have omitted buttonholes. The vest, of white satin, fastens with some difficulty over the belly, and is open at midchest so that the hand may, in the characteristic gesture of the eighteenth century (see cat. 13), be inserted there to show off the wrist ruffle. The breeches are black satin, fastened at the knee with an oval buckle of cut steel; the costume, sober and unflashy, is finished off with white silk stockings. Wolcott's powdered hair appears to be his own.　AR

1.　The column appears frequently in the works of Sir Joshua Reynolds, Benjamin West, and John Singleton Copley, with all of whom Earl frequently advertised that he had trained.

2.　Franklin Bowditch Dexter, *Biographical Sketches of the Graduates of Yale College* (New York, 1907), 2:137–38; Ellsworth S. Grant, "From Governor to Governor in Three Generations," *Connecticut Historical Society Bulletin* 39 (July 1974), 69–79; John M. Sanderson, *Biography of the Signers of the Declaration of Independence* (Philadelphia, 1823–25), 3:63–77; Samuel Wolcott, *Memorial of Henry Wolcott, One of the First Settlers of Windsor, Connecticut, and Some of His Descendants* (New York, 1881), 149–96.

3.　Trumbull to Wolcott, December 9, 1789, in Wolcott, *Memorial of Henry Wolcott*, 149; Account Book, Mason Fitch Cogswell Papers, CHS.

4.　Oliver Wolcott, Jr., Probate Inventory, Litchfield, 1833, Reel 714, no. 6566, CSL.

5.　Wolcott to Sanderson, November 28, 1822, Oliver Wolcott Papers, CHS.

6.　Engraving of Oliver Wolcott by James Longacre "from a Painting in Delaplaine's Gallery," CHS; Sanderson, *Biography of the Signers*, 3:75.

7.　Elizabeth Mankin Kornhauser, *Ralph Earl: Artist-Entrepreneur* (Ann Arbor, Mich., 1989), 338–39; Frederick F. Sherman, "The Paintings of Ralph Earl," *Art in America* 27 (October 1939), opp. 167. Sherman reproduces before and after restoration photographs, though he misinterprets the restoration.

25

26

26   Mrs. Oliver Wolcott
(Laura Collins), c. 1789

Oil on canvas

53 ½ x 43 in. (135.9 x 109.2 cm.)

Virginia Museum of Fine Arts, Richmond

Museum purchase: The Adolph D. and Wilkins C.
    Williams Fund, 1976.25

Earl used elements of heightened formality from British portraiture in his *Mrs. Oliver Wolcott*, including voluminous red drapery and a fluted column, to signify his subject's prominence. Laura (or Lorraine) Wolcott (1732–94) was remembered by her family as "a woman of remarkable courage, masculine judgement, and business character." [1] Whereas her husband spent most of the war years in Philadelphia, Laura raised and educated their four children, as well as managed the family farm and businesses. She had her husband's complete confidence; as he said in a letter to her, "Your own Prudence in the Direction of [these matters] I have no doubt of." [2] In the extensive correspondence between the Wolcotts during his prolonged absence, Oliver wrote of his respect and concern for his wife, frequently providing encouragement. "The Roman and Grecian matrons not only bore with magnanimity the Suspensions of Fortune, but Various kinds of adversity, with amazing Constancy, an American Lady instructed in sublimer Principles I hope will never be outdone by any of these illustrious Examples if she should be called to the Exercise of the greatest female Heroism." [3]

Because of Laura's role as manager of the family's domestic affairs, it is fitting that Earl depicted the Wolcott mansion in the distant landscape—a charming detail, if illogical, since the subject is seated in the house represented in the landscape. The house (which still stands on South Main Street in Litchfield, Connecticut) is flanked by tall trees.

As the wife of a leading statesman, Laura Wolcott is suitably attired in elegant clothing. She is portrayed much the way her relation and friend Abigail Ellsworth is a few years later (in a double portrait that includes her husband; cat. 41). Earl symbolically relates the figures of the two women to their domestic worlds. In 1935 the portrait of Laura Wolcott descended to her great-great-grandson Roger Wolcott. It remained in the family until it was acquired by Childs Gallery, Boston, and was sold to the Virginia Museum of Fine Arts in 1976. [4]

Costume Notes   The dress is made of fine lustrous silk, with rather formal, old-fashioned elbow-length sleeves terminating in ruffles of French needle lace. It is girded around the waist with a wide black belt, which echoes the black silk ribbon tied at the neck. The front of the bodice is largely covered by a buffon, the starched white kerchief puffed up over the bust. From the late 1780s, women wore a variety of shawls to help create the floating, billowing look so popular then. Here Wolcott is up-to-date in her large square yellow shawl, folded in half to create a triangle and draped over the shoulders; it is probably fine wool and has a decorative border. The elbow-length gloves, of white silk, were not only de rigueur on formal occasions but also practical, for they kept the hands and arms white, smooth, and untouched by the sun.

The most striking part of Wolcott's costume is the large headdress of muslin—pleated, spotted, striped, and starched—known as a French nightcap; [5] it curves down from a bow on the top, leaving the front hair and forehead exposed. The style first appeared in the 1770s and was equally popular on both sides of the Atlantic. During the 1770s and 1780s the hair was built up high on the top and at the sides, and when a starched cap was worn, as here, the head often looked disproportionately large compared to the rest of the body.   AR

1.   Laura Wolcott Gibbs made this statement at her grandmother's funeral, reproduced in Samuel Wolcott, *Memorial of Henry Wolcott, One of the First Settlers of Windsor, Connecticut, and Some of His Descendants* (New York, 1881), 217; Wolcott to Wolcott, January 1777, reproduced in ibid., 167.
2.   My thanks to Marcia Hinckley for locating and reading Wolcott family correspondence. See Wolcott, *Memorial of Henry Wolcott*, 160, 165, 217, 223, 237, for additional letters between Oliver and Laura Wolcott.
3.   Wolcott to Wolcott, May 11, 1776, reproduced in Ann Van Devanter, "The Signers' Ladies," *Antiques* 63 (July 1975), 120.
4.   My thanks to Elizabeth McGarry, Collections Division, Virginia Museum of Fine Arts, for this information.
5.   In the eighteenth century a nightcap could be a headdress worn during the day, as well as a simpler form of cap worn in bed. Similarly, a popular eighteenth-century dress was known as a nightgown, a word that also referred to what we would now call a dressing gown or a house gown.

27 Mariann Wolcott, 1789

Oil on canvas

46 x 34 in. (116.8 x 86.4 cm.)

Signed and dated at lower left: "R. Earl / Pinit 1789"

The Litchfield Historical Society, Litchfield, Connecticut

Earl painted Mariann Wolcott (1765–1805) in 1789, the year of her marriage to the prominent Hartford lawyer Chauncey Goodrich. The youngest child of Oliver and Laura Wolcott (cats. 25 and 26), she was described as "one of the most distinguished beauties of her time," "as bright and witty as she was beautiful."[1] Mariann had a lively and independent intelligence, which is evidenced by her feminist attitudes toward marriage. For example, she spurned her brother Oliver, Jr.,'s advice concerning her role as a new wife, given one month after her marriage. "As for being obedient and dutiful, tell [Oliver] it is not in my creed." Well versed in radical feminist writings, she would later ask her sister-in-law to inform her brother, "I mean to get Mrs. Wollstonecraft's book, and make Mr. Goodrich read it aloud in the Family."[2] Earl emphasizes Mariann's charm and sophistication by posing her gracefully in the Litchfield landscape; the composition is reminiscent of Earl's earlier English portraits of young women of fashion such as Sophia Isham (fig. 1.18); and her elegant attire, the fashion of a young woman, complements that worn by her mother in her portrait.

Earl painted Mariann's sister, Laura Wolcott Moseley (fig. 1.31), two years later in Hartford. *Mariann Wolcott* descended in the family to Roger Wolcott; in 1965 it was given to his brother, Oliver Wolcott, Sr., and in 1967 to Oliver Wolcott, Jr. The Litchfield Historical Society acquired the portrait in 1983 from Hirschl and Adler Galleries, New York.

Costume Notes   Mariann Wolcott's light brown hair is curled all over the head, with a wide fall of hair at the back and two thick ringlets falling over the shoulders at the front. The dress, with the characteristic bounce and fullness of the 1780s (probably created by hip pads and/or a back bustle vulgarly known as a bum roll) is white cotton. It is bound around the waist with a sash of blue silk fringed with gold, and the same silk is made into bracelets at the wrist, a stylish touch. A shawl of white spotted muslin hides most of the bodice front but does not obscure a bunch of pink roses at the bosom. To preserve their freshness, posies like this one were placed in a tiny tin funnel covered with green ribbon, which was filled with water and either placed in the cleavage or hidden beneath the drapery of the dress or collar.

So that no bit of the arm or hand was exposed to the sun (a suntan indicated those of the working class), gloves were worn outdoors; here Mariann's are white kid with a scalloped decoration at the wrist. Women, as well as men, carried canes; a fashionable alternative for women in particular was an umbrella, or parasol, which protected the complexion from the sun, as well as giving shelter from the rain. Umbrellas, usually made of oiled silk on a wooden frame, appeared in the American colonies in the 1760s. Boston newspapers advertised "umbrilloes," sold either ready-made or as "sticks or forms" that women could cover with their own choice of silk.[3]   AR

1. Samuel Wolcott, *Memorial of Henry Wolcott, One of the First Settlers of Windsor, Connecticut, and Some of His Descendants* (New York, 1881), 150–51; Christine Skeeles Schloss, *The Beardsley Limner and Some of His Contemporaries*, exhib. cat. (Williamsburg, Va., 1972), 39. Mariann was the second wife of Chauncey Goodrich (1759–1815), a graduate of Yale College who went on to become a senator of the United States, lieutenant governor of Connecticut, and mayor of Hartford; see Franklin Bowditch Dexter, *Biographical Sketches of the Graduates of Yale College* (New York, 1907), 3: 609–11.

2. Mariann Wolcott to Elizabeth Stoughton Wolcott, November 15, 1789, reproduced in Wolcott, *Memorial of Henry Wolcott*, 233–34; Mariann Wolcott Goodrich to Abigail Wolcott, March 30, 1793, reproduced in Wolcott, *Memorial of Henry Wolcott*, 249. Here Mariann refers to the radical feminist treatise by Mary Wollstonecraft, *A Vindication of the Rights of Women*, published in England in 1792, in which Wollstonecraft advocated an emphasis on women's moral and intellectual powers rather than their "mere animal" capacities.

3. A. M. Earle, *Costume of Colonial Times* (New York, 1894), 251. Semantically speaking, both a parasol and an umbrella protect against the sun, the latter word coming from the Italian *ombrellino*, or something that gives shade. In 1721, Nicholas Bailey's *Etymological English Dictionary, Being Also an Interpreter of Hard Words* defined an "umbrello" as "a sort of skreen that is held over the head for preserving from the sun or rain."

In America, as in England, umbrellas were not wholly accepted for men until the nineteenth century, and those carrying them risked being accused of effeminacy. See Aileen Ribeiro, "Men and Umbrellas in the Eighteenth Century," *Journal of the Royal Society of Arts* (September 1986), 653–56, a paper given at a commemorative symposium on the life of the philanthropist Jonas Hanway, credited with introducing the umbrella into England in 1756. In spite of the hostility that initially greeted the umbrella, by the time of Hanway's death (1786) such items were increasingly accepted, and there were thriving umbrella manufacturers in London that exported their products to the United States.

Exaggerated claims were made by umbrella advocates; in the 1770s, Philadelphia newspapers poked fun at the faddish physicians who "recommended them to keep off vertigoes, epilepsies, sore eyes, fevers, etc." E. McClellan, *A History of American Costume* (1904; reprint, New York, 1969), 230.

27

28 Daniel Boardman, 1789

Oil on canvas

81 ⅝ x 55 ¼ in. (207.3 x 137.8 cm.)

Signed and dated at lower left: "R. Earl Pinxt 1789 –"

Technical note: the canvas is in two pieces, with a
vertical seam

National Gallery of Art, Washington, D.C.

Gift of Mrs. W. Murray Crane, 1948.8.1

Earl painted a magnificent series of portraits of the Boardman family of New Milford between 1789 and 1796. He
painted Daniel, the eldest son of Sherman and Sarah Boardman (cats. 56 and 57) at full length, elegantly dressed,
leaning on an ivory-capped cane, and gracefully posed in a
landscape. In the background Earl includes a detailed rendition of New Milford, viewed from the southeast, with
the Housatonic River winding toward the town center. Earl
accurately depicts some of the major houses in the town and
the Congregational meetinghouse. Farther in the distance
are the rolling foothills of the Berkshire Mountains.

Daniel Boardman (1757–1833), served in the Connecticut militia, graduated from Yale College in 1781, and
received a master's degree from Yale in 1784 (having certainly encountered Mason Fitch Cogswell, who graduated
the previous year). In 1782, while still a student, Daniel
joined his brother Elijah (cat. 29) in operating a drygoods
store in New Milford in 1782, located in the southern half
of the Bostwick House. The brothers also jointly owned
a considerable amount of land and real estate in town but
dissolved their partnership in 1793, the year after Elijah's
marriage. After running the store himself for two years,
Daniel moved to New York City, where he became a partner of Henry Hunt in the wholesale drygoods business. He
married Hetty More of New York in 1797 and continued to
prosper, acquiring real estate in New York and considerable
land in Georgia.[1]

The predominant landscape setting of the portrait may
symbolize the various properties Daniel owned at the time
his portrait was taken. Earl skillfully conveys the growing
prosperity of New Milford, including the large two-story
house with a fenced yard and the meetinghouse. Whereas
the portrait of Daniel makes reference to the brothers' sizable landholdings, the complementary portrait of Elijah
shows their prosperous drygoods store.[2] Neither brother
was married when their portraits were painted; they may
have continued to live with their parents. Both portraits
emphasize the local prominence of the Boardman family
following the Revolution.

Daniel's sister-in-law Mary Anna Boardman recalled
that he "was a large man, of strong frame, said to resemble
his grandfather, the Rev. Daniel Boardman. His personal
appearance was dignified, and his manners rather distant
and formal."[3] Earl painted Daniel Boardman as a young
man of thirty-two, adeptly capturing his handsome features. Further enhancing his attractive appearance was his
attire.

After his departure for New York, Daniel wrote to his
brother Elijah requesting his portrait. 'Mrs. Boardman is
frequently solliciting [sic] me to send for my portrait. You
will therefore tell Sims Carpenter to make a case for it and
screw it in fast that it will not chafe the gilding[;] send it the
first sleighing by one of your teamsters to Newfish[;] direct
them to be careful of it."[4] The portrait descended in the
Boardman family and was given by Mrs. W. Murray Crane
to the National Gallery of Art in 1948.

Costume Notes   The pose and costume are the epitome of
restrained Anglo-American elegance; the prevailing image
is one of unostentatious wealth and established position.
Daniel Boardman wears his own hair, powdered and frizzed
out at the sides; the back hair, not visible here, would be
tied in a knot club, or queue. He wears a frock coat with a
high collar, cut to curve away at the sides; the buttons are
merely decorative, for the coat is cut so narrow that they
cannot be used as fastenings. The color of the coat, an inky
blue, was very popular in England and America. The vest is
white silk, double-breasted, and cut straight across at the
waist; it is trimmed with gold braid, as are the small horizontal pockets, which are probably fake – the smooth line
would be spoiled if anything was carried in them.

The breeches are buff silk; the stockings are shining
white silk, with a discreet patterned insert, or clock, shown
off as Daniel stands, one leg crossed in front of the other, in
the pose seen in fashionable European portraiture. This pose
also serves to show off the fine cut-steel Artois buckles on
his shoes. Other items of clothing that announce a man of
wealth and status include the shirt ruffles of pleated muslin,
the white linen cravat tied *à l'anglaise* in a bow in the front,
and the hat of expensive black beaver. By the eighteenth
century men's jewelry was limited to buckles (on the knee
breeches and the shoes) and the bunch of seals hanging from
the waist, here from a chain of cut steel. The cane was a
fashionable accessory for walking outdoors; even in Europe
by the late eighteenth century it had largely replaced the
sword.[5] In America, a country with no nobility, swords were
considered inappropriate for civilians.   AR

1. Samuel Orcutt, *History of the Towns of New Milford and Bridgewater, Connecticut, 1703–1882* (Hartford, Conn., 1882), 495–96; Charlotte Goldthwaite, *Boardman Family Genealogy, 1525–1895* (Hartford, Conn., 1895), 331–32; John F. Schroeder, ed., *Memoir of the Life and Character of Mrs. Mary Anna Boardman* (New Haven, Conn., 1849), 397–99.

2. Land Records, Town Clerk's Office, New Milford, vol. 21, p. 420, indicate that Daniel owned a substantial amount of property in New Milford. In 1785, Daniel's father, Sherman Boardman, deeded him five acres of land on Onapis Island, north of the town. In addition, by 1789, Daniel and Elijah ran their shop in the "Long house" purchased from the estate of Daniel Bostwick. Daniel Bostwick's widow, Hannah Bostwick, lived in the northern half of the house until her death. Several other properties are listed as well.

Land records also indicate that Daniel and Elijah Boardman jointly owned over two hundred acres of land in various locations in New Milford. In 1789 their property and professional taxes, which came to fifty pounds altogether, were among the highest in town; see Tax Lists, 1789, Town Clerk's Office, New Milford.

3. Schroeder, ed., *Memoir of Mary Anna Boardman*, 399.

4. Boardman to Boardman, January 24, 1799, Carl Boardman Cobb Collection, Aurora, Ohio; my thanks to Carl Cobb for bringing this letter to my attention.

5. A cane identical to the one seen in Daniel Boardman's portrait is in the collection of Carl Boardman Cobb; it is inscribed "E. Boardman 1785."

29 Elijah Boardman, 1789

Oil on canvas

83 x 51 in. (210.8 x 129.5 cm.)

Signed and dated at lower left: "R. Earl Pinxt 1789"

Technical note: the canvas is in three pieces, with a vertical and a horizontal seam

The Metropolitan Museum of Art, New York

Bequest of Susan W. Tyler, 1979

Earl's portrait of the young shopkeeper from New Milford, Connecticut, *Elijah Boardman*, ranks among his finest works and epitomizes the entrepreneurial spirit of the new republic. As one of five shopkeepers in this prospering town, Elijah had recently established his drygoods business in partnership with his brother Daniel Boardman (cat. 28). In his portrait, he is shown in an unconventional setting, at work in his shop, near his counting desk, with a view of his high-quality merchandise in the back room.

Elijah Boardman (1760–1823) was the third son of Sherman Boardman and Sarah Bostwick Boardman (cats. 56 and 57). As a young man, he studied with the town minister, the Rev. Nathaniel Taylor (cat. 31), and served in the Connecticut militia during the revolutionary war. After the war, Elijah trained for a career as a shopkeeper by working as a clerk in the New Haven store of Elijah and Archibald Austin. He opened his own store in New Milford in 1781, in the southern half of the house owned by Daniel Bostwick on Town Street. His brother Daniel was his partner in the business for the next eleven years.

At the time of his marriage to Mary Anna Whiting (cat. 55) in 1792, Elijah built a mansion house and a new shop next to the old Bostwick house. All three buildings are depicted in Earl's *Houses Fronting New Milford Green* (cat. 58) of about 1796. In 1795, Elijah became a member of the Connecticut Land Company, purchasing extensive lands in the Ohio Western Reserve. The towns of Boardman, Palmyra, and Medina made up his Ohio landholdings. As one of New Milford's major landowners, Elijah eventually assumed his father's prominent position in the town. He became active in state and national politics, serving in the legislature and as a U.S. senator from 1821 until his death.[1]

Elijah's portrait is remarkable in a number of respects. The artist's best achievement of trompe l'oeil illusionism, this depiction of a full-length figure in a domestic setting draws its inspiration from such colonial works by John Singleton Copley as *Mrs. Jeremiah Lee* (1765; Wadsworth Atheneum), a portrait intended to be hung on the staircase landing of the Lees' recently built mansion, so that the subject appeared to be ascending the staircase. Winthrop Chandler also created illusionary effects in such life-size portraits as *Judge Ebenezer Devotion* (cat. 1). Earl's *Elijah Boardman* is more persistent in its effort to fool the eye, however, going beyond the more subtle effects found in Copley's and Chandler's works. Here Earl creates a life-size figure who seemingly steps off the floorboards and out of the picture plane into the viewer's space. In addition, the shop setting is ingeniously conceived, with two doors at the left creating the illusion of two rooms — one opens into the front room, the other back toward the storage room to reveal Boardman's inventory. There Earl painstakingly renders the multipatterned stack of domestic and imported fabrics. The bottom bolt of cloth is unrolled to reveal a British tax stamp.

This portrait suggests an antecedent for Charles Willson Peale's notable work of illusionism *Staircase Group* (1795; Philadelphia Museum of Art). During their years in England, both Peale and Earl may have known life-size trompe l'oeil–painted rooms and people, used to decorate seventeenth-century English homes. Earl shared with Peale the, by this time, old-fashioned belief that the measure

29

of his artistic power could be judged by the success of his illusionism.[2] Shortly after he completed *Elijah Boardman*, the Litchfield County newspaper stated: "[Earl's] paintings are admirably finished; and display the similarity and expression, as would seem to start them into life – though inanimate they speak."[3]

This portrait is also remarkable for its disarming directness in not just portraying Elijah's profession but actually showing him working in his shop and displaying his merchandise to the viewer. Again parallels can be made to the portraits of merchants by Copley and Chandler, who occasionally portray their subjects informally, standing near tall desks and holding business receipts in their hands. Earl's depiction of a small-town shopkeeper working at his trade is unique in the eighteenth century. The inclusion of merchandise makes the painting function, at some level, as an advertisement for Boardman's shop.

Earl's portrait beautifully captures the handsome visage and ambitious aspirations of this young shopkeeper. Elegantly attired, Elijah wears the gold chain and seals that indicate his ownership of a gold watch (one appears in his inventory with a value of one hundred dollars). He leans against an upright desk of an unusual design, probably the "high counting room desk" also listed in his inventory.[4] The lower portion of the desk has shelves of books, including works by Shakespeare, Milton's *Paradise Lost*, and a volume of Samuel Johnson's *Dictionary*, an indication of his broad cultural interests. Again, his inventory, which lists these volumes among nearly two hundred others on religion, theater, foreign language, literature, American politics, history, and philosophy, verifies his ownership of these books; and by virtue of their presence in his portrait, the books have an obvious importance to Elijah as proof of his intellectual interests. Finally, Earl's careful depiction of the merchandise underscores Elijah's pride in his selection of fabrics, revealed in his many advertisements for his shop; the following appeared in 1790: "furnished (as usual) with an extensive assortment of European and India Goods suitable for all seasons."

Elijah Boardman clearly valued his portrait throughout his life. It is listed in his inventory of effects and assigned a value of twenty-five dollars.[5]

Costume Notes Elijah Boardman, dressed with formal elegance, is a visible sartorial testimony to the fine fabrics on sale in his shop. His beige frock coat with its fashionable slim-line cut and tight sleeves is made of silk; the gilt basket-weave patterned buttons look identical to those in the portrait of his brother (cat. 28). Nor is Elijah's vest unlike that worn by his brother, but here it is single-breasted and buttons right over left in what we now think of as the feminine practice.[6] The breeches are black silk, the stockings white silk, and the shoe buckles faceted cut steel like those worn by Daniel. Elijah wears a stock, not a cravat, at his neck, a style that allows the fine shirt frill of pleated muslin to be seen to better advantage. A tiny stickpin is fastened to the shirt ruffle, a last and modest echo of the often flamboyant jewels that men wore earlier in the century. Distinguishing real hair from a wig is often difficult at this point in the eighteenth century, but it seems likely that in keeping with the formality of his attire, Elijah wears a wig. This style of wig was known as a club wig, or Catogan, and consisted of a wide fall of hair tied up on itself at the back; it first appeared in the 1770s in England and was soon adopted by men of fashion in America.[7]

The materials that Elijah appears so proud of include silks, wools, mixed fabrics (mainly silk-wool blends), printed cottons, and linens. Some of the fabrics on display can be seen in other portraits by Earl, including the checkered white muslin (cat. 19), the spotted muslin (cat. 27) and possibly the fine coral silk (worn by Elijah's wife in her portrait, cat. 55). It is impossible to estimate how many of these fabrics were of American manufacture. By the end of the century the United States was virtually self-sufficient in all but the most expensive and luxurious fabrics, like the high-quality wools and silks. The manufacture of cottons flourished there, set on a firm footing during the 1780s by English and American entrepreneurs with the aid of the new machinery resulting from the Industrial Revolution in England. Many fabrics, however, continued to be imported from Europe; there was a social cachet attached to the wearing of foreign goods in spite of attempts by patriotic Americans to promote their own products – snobbery and the demands of fashion have always been more powerful than the dictates of politics or ideology. AR

1. Samuel Orcutt, *History of the Towns of New Milford and Bridgewater, Connecticut, 1703–1882* (Hartford, Conn., 1882), 495–96; Charlotte Goldthwaite, *Boardman Family Genealogy, 1525–1895* (Hartford, Conn., 1895), 334–35; John F. Schroeder, ed., *Memoir of the Life and Character of Mrs. Mary Anna Boardman* (New Haven, Conn., 1849), 309–405.

2. M. L. d'Otrange Mastai, *Illusion in Art, Trompe l'Oeil* (New York, 1975), 136, 137, 139–41, 190; Theodore E. Stebbins, Jr., Carol Troyen, and Trevor J. Fairbrother, *A New World: Masterpieces of American Painting, 1760–1910* (Boston, 1983), 204.

3. *Litchfield Weekly Monitor*, June 21, 1790.

4. Elijah Boardman, Probate Inventory, New Milford, 1824, no. 288, CSL.

5. Ibid.

6. Some women buttoned their coats and jackets left over right in the eighteenth century, particularly garments borrowed from the masculine wardrobe, such as the riding habit and the greatcoat.

7. The club wig was popularized in the 1770s by English macaronis, or fops, who wore highly exaggerated versions of fashionable costume. Their style of clothing is satirized in the song "Yankee Doodle."

30 Esther Boardman, 1789

Oil on canvas
42 ½ x 32 in. (108.0 x 81.3 cm.)
Signed and dated at lower left: "R. Earl pint 1789"
Edith and Henry Noss

Earl painted the daughter of Sherman and Sarah Boardman (cats. 56, 57) in the same year that he painted the portraits of her two elder brothers, Daniel and Elijah (cats. 28, 29). Esther Boardman (1762–1851) is portrayed seated in a landscape setting, with a northwest view of New Milford. The scene is much like the one in the portrait of Daniel Boardman, including the Congregational meetinghouse and several prominent houses in the town center. The significance of the particular view of New Milford included in these portraits has remained elusive beyond the fact that it represents the prospering town that the Boardman family had been instrumental in settling. Esther's portrait was taken three years before her marriage to Jonathan Burrall, a merchant and iron manufacturer from Canaan, Connecticut, who had been a classmate of her brother Daniel at Yale College.[1] Esther presumably sat for her portrait while living with her parents in the Boardman house, northwest of the town center at Boardman's Bridge, on the Housatonic River.

Esther Boardman is as stylishly dressed as her two brothers, and Earl has taken great care to enhance her image. Although capturing a strong likeness of his lovely young subject, he softens the effect with delicate pink flesh tones, which are offset by a palette dominated by various shades of green. The portrait of Esther Boardman has remained in the Boardman family.

Costume Notes   Characteristic of the 1780s was the trend toward informality in dress. One of the new styles was a wraparound gown called a *lévite,* which the sitter wears here; hers is of green silk lined with grayish silk and ties around the waist with a white fringed sash. Such styles were especially suitable for young women, but they still attracted a certain amount of censure; in 1779, Horace Walpole decried the dress as "a man's nightgown bound around with a belt."[2] The headdress is composed of black and white feathers. The black silk bands at the wrists show off the whiteness of the hands, just as the powdering of the hair on the top and at the sides heightens the pale complexion. The ringlets and the chignon (a wide flat loop of hair falling down the back – the term comes into use in this period) remain unpowdered and may be false; contemporary newspapers often have advertisements for fake hairpieces that could be pinned or woven into the natural hair. In the same way, the eyebrows that look so striking against the pallor of the face may be artificial; mouseskin was made into false eyebrows throughout the eighteenth century.   AR

1.   Charlotte Goldthwaite, *Boardman Family Genealogy, 1525–1895* (Hartford, Conn., 1895), 333–34; John F. Schroeder, ed., *Memoir of the Life and Character of Mrs. Mary Anna Boardman* (New Haven, Conn., 1849), 405–6.
2.   Walpole, *Letters Addressed to the Countess of Ossory, 1769–1797,* ed. R. V. Smith (London, 1848), 379. *Lévite,* first used in the late 1770s, derives from a popular production of Racine's Old Testament play, *Athalie,* in which the actresses playing Levites wore loose gowns girdled at the waist. The American-born Lady Cathcart, writing from London to her native land in 1781, noted the rage for "a dress they call a Levete which is a kind of gown and Peticote with long sleeves . . . and worn with a sash tyed on the left side." Quoted in A. M. Earle, *Costume of Colonial Times* (New York, 1894), 152.

In 1798, Abigail Adams described the levite gown in a letter from Philadelphia as a dress "made to have only one side come forward and that is confined with a belt round the waist." But she decreed the style too youthful for herself. *New Letters of Abigail Adams, 1788–1801,* ed. S. Mitchell (Boston, 1947), 145. Elsewhere she calls it a "drapery gown"; the loose folds and casual ties or fastenings appeared too informal for those, like Adams, of conservative sartorial tastes.

30

31

31   Reverend Nathaniel Taylor, c. 1790

Oil on canvas

47¾ x 37 in. (121.3 x 94.0 cm.)

Addison Gallery of American Art, Phillips Academy,
    Andover, Massachusetts

Nathaniel Taylor, the son of Daniel Taylor and Elizabeth
Benedict Taylor of Danbury, graduated from Yale College
in 1745. He became the second Congregational minister
in New Milford in 1748, and in 1749 he married Tamar
Boardman, the daughter of his predecessor, the Rev. Daniel
Boardman (cat. 28). An ardent supporter of the Revolution,
he was chaplain to a regiment of Connecticut troops. In
addition to serving as minister, Taylor maintained a grammar school for young men in New Milford, preparing many
to attend Yale College. He retired from the ministry after
fifty-two years and devoted the rest of his life to farming,
having a particular interest in the cultivation of fruit trees.
After the death of his first wife, he took a second, marrying
Zipporah Strong of Long Island, widow of Daniel Bennett
and, before that, of the Rev. Benjamin Tallmadge.[1]

Taylor was highly respected and beloved. His colleague
the Rev. Thomas Robbins of Hartford would later recall
that "as a preacher . . . he held high rank. His preaching was
generally of a plain and practical cast, fitting to edify both
the humbler and the more intelligent classes. . . . He had
a fine manly voice, and his manner in the pulpit, while it
was free from all artificial airs, was well fitted to awaken and
hold the attention. . . . No one was more earnest than he in
enjoining habits of temperance and industry."[2] In keeping
with his demeanor, his portrait shows him conservatively
dressed.

Earl chose a highly conservative format for his portrait
of the Rev. Nathaniel Taylor (1722–1800). Painted shortly
after his retirement, he is shown in an austere depiction:
dressed in a minister's black attire, standing at the pulpit of
his meetinghouse, he is resting his hands on a red tasseled
cushion on which lies a book of Scripture. Taylor is placed
against a backdrop of red drapery and a large pane-glass
window with a view of a blue, cloud-filled sky, perhaps a
reference to Heaven. The window is shut, enclosing him in
the meetinghouse. This was an unusual device for the artist, who more customarily created open window views of
the landscape beyond, thereby linking his subjects to the
outside world. In addition, the minister is shown standing
at the pulpit, in contrast to Earl's more worldly depiction
of the Rev. Judah Champion (fig. 1.25) of Litchfield, who is
shown in a lavish, secular setting.

This portrait may have inspired a similar composition
by Earl's follower Joseph Steward, in his portrait *Reverend
Samuel Moseley* (c. 1790–91; private collection).[3]

Taylor's portrait descended in the Taylor family to
Harriet Taylor of New Milford. It was purchased by
MacBeth Gallery, New York, then acquired by the Addison
Gallery of American Art.

Costume Notes   Nathaniel Taylor's hair is his own, either
naturally gray or powdered; it is worn long and straight,
with no fashionable wave or curl that might indicate vanity.
Many Nonconformist ministers regarded vestments as
superstitious and popish and deliberately wore secular
clothing, albeit of a sober and conservative kind. Most
chose to wear the sober black cloth suit of the professional
man, clerical bands, and sometimes (although less so in the
United States than in England) the black Geneva gown.[4]
The clerical bands (sometimes known as Geneva bands)
were two pieces of white linen fastened round the neck;
they indicated that the minister was attached to a particular and recognized congregation. Not until the middle of
the nineteenth century were they largely replaced by the
round collar popularly known as the dog collar. On certain
formal occasions, the Geneva bands are still worn by some
Protestant clergy in Britain.   AR

1.   Franklin Bowditch Dexter, *Biographical Sketches of the Graduates of
Yale College* (New York, 1907), 5:63–65; William Sprague, *Annals of the
American Pulpit* (New York, 1857), 1:467–69.
2.   Sprague, *Annals of the American Pulpit*, 1:469.
3.   See Thompson R. Harlow, "The Life and Trials of Joseph Steward,"
Connecticut Historical Society Bulletin 46 (October 1981), 119, ill. 147.
4.   By the late eighteenth century the black suit was the uniform of the
middle-class professional man. Jane Austen noted that the clergy in England congratulated themselves that their dress was no different from that
of any gentleman; see J. Laver, "The Undress of the Clergy," *Country Life
Annual* (1955).
    The Geneva gown was originally adopted by John Calvin in the six-
teenth century (from the academic gown of the time). See J. Mayo, *A
History of Ecclesiastical Dress* (London, 1984), 72, 102, 154. In spite of this
worthy provenance, Nonconformist clergy in America sometimes preached
sermons against it as a kind of vestment, an overt sign of rank, even of
episcopalianism.

32 Mrs. Nathaniel Taylor (Tamar Boardman), c. 1789–90

Oil on canvas

47 ¾ x 36 ¾ in. (121.3 x 93.4 cm.)

The Newark Museum, Newark, New Jersey

Museum purchase, Sophronia Anderson Bequest
    Fund, 1947

Earl's portrait of Tamar Taylor (1723–95) equals that of her husband in its literal depiction of the subject. The daughter of New Milford's first minister, the Rev. Daniel Boardman, and the sister of Sherman Boardman (cat. 56), Tamar Boardman married the Rev. Nathaniel Taylor in 1749. She had three children, all of whom, along with their respective spouses and children, were painted by Ralph Earl; the portraits include *Colonel Nathaniel Taylor* (1796; New Milford Historical Society), *Mrs. Nathaniel (Ann Northrup) Taylor* (1796; New Milford Historical Society), *The Taylor Children* (1796; Toledo Museum of Art, Ohio), *Colonel William Taylor* (cat. 33), *Mrs. William Taylor and Son Daniel* (cat. 34), *Nicholas Shelton Masters* (c. 1796; The Litchfield Historical Society), and *Mrs. Nicholas (Tamar Taylor) Masters* (c. 1796; The Litchfield Historical Society).[1]

    Whereas Earl's portraits of her children and grandchildren are handsome portrayals of prosperous young families, Tamar Taylor's portrait is somewhat severe in its truthfulness. Earl did little to flatter his subject's homely visage but succeeded in suggesting the stature this woman must have had in the community. The portrait is enlivened by the view through the window, which includes a rendition of her husband's meetinghouse and what appears to be the house the Taylors built in 1759, north of the meetinghouse. Although the placement of the church and house is not accurate, Earl may have wished to include the view of the meetinghouse as it appeared from the window of the Taylor house, with an illogical reference to their house in the distance. The house may also represent the one the Taylors built for their elder son, Nathaniel Taylor, Jr., just south of the meetinghouse.[2] Earl includes an unusual detail in his portrait of Tamar Taylor: a broken pane of window glass, which may be one more example of his efforts to impress his rural subjects with his virtuosity at creating trompe l'oeil effects. Broken glass was a traditional motif of trompe l'oeil still-life painters.[3]

    The portrait descended in the Taylor family to Nathalie Taylor Stewart and was purchased by the John Levy Gallery, New York. It was acquired by the Newark Museum in 1947.[4]

Costume Notes   Tamar Taylor's dress is gray silk, and because the rather old-fashioned sleeves reach only to the elbow, her lower arms have to be protected by black silk mittens. Over her shoulders she wears a black silk mantle edged with embroidered net. On her head is a white linen mobcap edged with lace; around her neck, a white fichu collar edged with a frill of lace or patterned net.   AR

1.   Elizabeth Mankin Kornhauser, *Ralph Earl: Artist-Entrepreneur* (Ann Arbor, Mich., 1989), 305, 327–29.

2.   Samuel Orcutt, *History of the Towns of New Milford and Bridgewater, Connecticut, 1703–1882* (Hartford, Conn., 1882), 504. Nathaniel Taylor's last will and testament, New Milford, 1801, no. 2558, CSL, describes his property: "my House & Barn & home Lot Lying for five acres Situate in said New Milford, lying between the Meeting house and Common Burying place." The will further specifies its disposition: "I have given unto my eldest son Nathaniel half an acre of Land including his dwelling house."

3.   M. L. d'Otrange Mastai, *Illusion in Art, Trompe l'Oeil* (New York, 1975), 237, 244, 285.

4.   Painting Files, Newark Museum, Newark, N.J.

32

33 Colonel William Taylor, 1790

Oil on canvas
48½ x 38 in. (123.8 x 96.5 cm.)
Signed and dated at lower left: "R. Earl Pinxt 1790"
Albright-Knox Art Gallery, Buffalo, New York
Charles Clifton Fund, 1935

34 Mrs. William Taylor and Son Daniel, 1790

Oil on canvas
48¾ x 38⅛ in. (123.8 x 96.8 cm.)
Signed and dated at lower left: "R. Earl Pinxt 1790"
Albright-Knox Art Gallery, Buffalo, N.Y.
Charles Clifton Fund, 1935

Earl's fashionable portrait of Col. William Taylor, a prosperous farmer and merchant in New Milford, is a sharp departure from the soberness of his portrayal of William's father, the town minister (cat. 31). William is shown pursuing his avocation as an amateur landscape painter, a rare early illustration of the practice of this genre in America. As one of the earliest landscape painters, Earl may have furnished him with some instruction in the art. In his portrait, William is seated in an unusual leather-upholstered corner chair, taking a view of the landscape that is seen through the window. Holding a pen in one hand and an artist's maulstick in the other, the subject invites the viewer to see his unfinished sketch, which is propped up on the table before him.

William Taylor (1764–1841) was the second son of Nathaniel and Tamar Taylor (cats. 31, 32). He served in the Continental Army during the Revolution and graduated from his father's alma mater, Yale College, in 1785, where he received a master's degree in 1788. After his marriage to Abigail Starr of Danbury, Connecticut, in 1786, he built a house in New Milford near his father and brother.[1]

Earl's delightful rendition of Abigail Taylor (1768–1845) and the first of her five children, Daniel Starr Taylor (1788–1807), conveys warm maternal affection. Earl devised an informal composition that allowed the elegantly attired mother to keep her child quiet during lengthy sittings: seating him in a child's Windsor high chair, so that the heads of the two figures are aligned. The mother gently holds her son's bare foot, and the child is further occupied by the family's pet cat in his arms.

Both portraits remained in the Taylor family until they were acquired by M. Knoedler and Company in New York in 1931 and 1932 respectively from the great-granddaughter of William Taylor. They were purchased by the Albright-Knox Museum in 1935.[2]

Costume Notes *Colonel William Taylor* is perhaps the most stylish portrait Earl painted of a gentleman. The sitter wears a brown frock coat (possibly made of camlet, a wool and silk mixture) with the large round brass buttons popular throughout the 1780s and into the 1790s. His knee breeches are black silk, fastened with buckles of paste brilliants (imitation diamonds), and his stockings are white silk. By the end of the 1780s, coats were increasingly sober in color, giving vests a new importance as a focus for color; here the vest is striped black and white silk, double-breasted, and with wide lapels formed by the unbuttoning of the vest at the top, allowing the shirt frill of pleated muslin to be admired. The sitter wears his own hair, lightly touched with powder and tied with a black silk bow at the back.

Abigail Taylor wears a greatcoat dress of light gray silk with long sleeves and a Vandyke collar edged with silk braid. Women adopted the style of the man's greatcoat, with its wide collar, during the 1780s. Sometimes they wore the greatcoat as an outdoor garment (a fine example in dark blue broadcloth edged with gold braid is worn by Laura Moseley (in fig. 1.31). Worn as a dress, sometimes with a wraparound front, it was tied at the waist with a sash. Here frilled muslin scarf, or fichu, fills in the neckline. The hair is piled high; on top of it is placed a hat of ostrich feathers. Around her neck Abigail wears a black silk band to which tiny brilliant stars are pinned; similar bands encircle her wrists, also decorated with paste ornaments.[3]

The boy Daniel, in his white figured muslin frock tied around the waist with an embroidered ribbon, is dressed according to fashionable theories on the upbringing of children, originally derived from John Locke's *Thoughts on Education* (1693), an advocation of a relaxed and individualized regime that included lightweight clothing and exercise during infancy.[4]   AR

1.   Samuel Orcutt, *History of the Towns of New Milford and Bridgewater, Connecticut, 1703–1882* (Hartford, Conn., 1882), 774–75; Franklin Bowditch Dexter, *Biographical Sketches of the Graduates of Yale College* (New York, 1907), 4:442; Harold Spencer, *The American Earls: Ralph Earl, James Earl, R. E. W. Earl*, exhib. cat. (Storrs, Conn., 1972), 20–23; Col. William Taylor, Probate Inventory, New Milford, 1842, Reel 1045, no. 2561, CSL. The main street of New Milford was Town Street.
2.   Robert T. Buck et al., *Painting and Sculpture from Antiquity to 1942* (New York, 1979), 286–87.
3.   On the fashion for paste, see Aileen Ribeiro, "Eighteenth-Century Jewellery in England," *Connoisseur* 199 (October 1978), 75–84. Paste came in a variety of forms (including fine opaline paste, which Abigail may be wearing on her bracelets), imitating precious and semiprecious stones. Real jewelry was considered too opulent to wear on any but the most lavish occasions, so paste was increasingly the democratic fashion alternative.
4.   These ideas were popularized during the second half of the eighteenth century by a number of English and French philosophers, of whom the most famous was Jean-Jacques Rousseau; his book *Emile* (1762) promoted breast-feeding, loose-fitting clothes for children, fresh air and cold baths, and a healthy diet—all of which found wide acceptance in Europe and the United States in the last decades of the eighteenth century, particularly among progressive middle-class families.

33

35   Angus Nickelson and Family, c. 1790

Oil on canvas

42 ½ x 58 in. (108.0 x 147.3 cm.)

Technical note: the canvas is pieced in two sections, with a
vertical seam at the corner of the room

Museum of Fine Arts, Springfield, Massachusetts

Gift of Robert L. Munson, 1969.01

In the same period that Earl paid tribute to the prominent
founding families of New Milford, the Boardmans and the
Taylors, he painted a group portrait of the Scottish immigrant Angus Nickelson (also Nicholson) and his family. The
intimate scale of this portrait is a striking departure from
the life-size renditions favored for his New Milford subjects.
The full-length presentation of the Nickelson family on a
small scale relates the work to the by-now-antiquated conversation piece, a popular genre of English family portraiture.[1] Earl's patron, who would have been familiar with the
conversation-piece format during his earlier years in Scotland and England, may have suggested the format. In addition, Earl had seen examples of conversation pieces while in
Norwich, England, where they continued to be painted as
late as the 1780s by such local artists as Sir William Beechey,
Philip Reinagle, and Henry Walton.[2]

Angus Nickelson (1735–1804) was born on the island of
Islay, Argyll, Scotland, and immigrated to America in 1762.
He had established himself as a merchant in New Milford
by 1765; he acquired a considerable amount of land and,
by the time his portrait was painted, owned and operated a
marble quarry and an ironworks. He placed frequent advertisements, such as the following: "Marble lately discovered
by Mr. Nicholson at New Milford in this state, little inferior
if not equal to the Italian variety in goodness and variety of
colors. The curious and tasty may be immediately supplied
with Tomb-Tables, Headstones, Hea[r]ths, Mantlepieces
and Jam[b]s or any other matter."[3] As the town historian,
Samuel Orcutt, commented, he "gave himself wholly to
business enterprises."[4]

Angus Nickelson married Sarah Platt (1750–1820) of
New Milford in 1767, shortly after his arrival. Their portrait
by Earl includes seven of their surviving children: Barbara
(b. 1771), Ann (b. 1773), Sarah (b. 1777), Samuel Malcolm
(b. 1781), Mary Ann (b. 1784), Angus (b. 1786), and
Donald (b. 1789). The Nickelsons had this family portrait
painted at the height of Angus's success as a businessman.
Land and tax records indicate that he had one of the highest tax assessments in the town in the late 1780s and early
1790s, but by the middle of the decade, his taxes dropped
sharply, and he began to sell off his extensive landholdings.[5]

Although not dated by the artist, this portrait was likely
painted in 1790, when Earl is known to have been in New
Milford. The date is substantiated by the ages of the various
family members, in particular the baby, Donald, who posed
when he was one year old and died the following year. The
Nickelson family also had a family register and coat of arms
(now with the Connecticut Historical Society) engraved on
silver by Richard Brunton at about the same time that their
portrait was painted.[6]

Earl's composition appears antiquated when compared with his more fashionable portraits of the Boardman
and Taylor families. Angus Nickelson is seated at the left,
presenting his business card to the viewer; it is inscribed
"Angus Nicholson / merchant / New Milford." The subjects
fail to interact with each other, yet Earl varies the poses
of the stiffly placed children, with some seated and others
standing, each occupied with an object in his or her hands.
The two standing figures are less successfully proportioned.
The room itself is elaborately furnished with a desk and a
bookcase, curtained windows with the shutters closed, a
pair of oval mirrors (we can see where Earl had originally
placed a smaller mirror higher up on the wall), a fashionable
cabriole sofa with a squab cushion, and a patterned carpet.
Earl completed the work with a convincing trompe l'oeil
frame; the frame, now partly lost, originally consisted of a
painted, gold-beaded molding with a wide outer member
and a dark green liner.[7]

The portrait descended in the Nickelson family to
Angus Nickelson's great-great-grandson Robert Lewis
Munson, who gave the portrait to the Museum of Fine Arts
in 1969.[8]

Costume Notes   A merchant proud of his wealth and what it
could buy, Angus Nickelson wears a sober costume that is
a deliberate foil to the elegant dress of his womenfolk, his
daughters in particular. He wears a dark frock coat, double-
breasted vest, beige silk knee breeches, white silk stockings,
and black leather shoes with square buckles. His son Angus
wears the double-breasted trouser suit which boys were
given when "breeched" at the age of three or four years of
age; before that time, little boys dressed in white frocks, as
does Donald, at his mother's knee. Next to the father stands
his eldest son, Samuel Malcolm, in a red cutaway coat, a
striped vest, and long trousers of cream-colored cotton or
nankeen.

On the right of the group sits Sarah Nickelson, dressed
in brown silk. The front of her gown is covered by an embroidered muslin scarf; she wears a mobcap of starched,
pleated muslin trimmed with ribbon. Both of the older
girls, seated on the sofa, wear formal open gowns of pastel
silk; the one on the right wears plain white silk, the one on
the left a figured white silk over a spotted pink petticoat.
Both girls wear starched muslin fichus, pinned to form a

kind of overbodice. Their hair is frizzed and powdered to achieve a fashionable rigidity of appearance; on top of their hair perch scarves of gauze, one spotted, one striped. The youngest daughter, on the far right, wears a frock with a pink sash. The other, standing at the back, her hair still dressed as children wear it, has on a white gown, lifted (by way of inside tapes) into a bustle at the back; this was a style known as a polonaise, first appearing in the late 1770s and somewhat provincial by around 1790.   AR

1.   Ellen G. D'Oench, *The Conversation Piece: Arthur Devis and His Contemporaries*, exhib. cat. (New Haven, Conn., 1980); chap. 2 provides an excellent definition of this genre.
2.   Trevor Fawcett, "Eighteenth-Century Art in Norwich," *Walpole Society, 1776–1978*, 46 (1978), 71–87; Ellis Waterhouse, *Painting in Britain, 1530–1790* (London, 1953), 231, 232.
3.   *Hartford Courant*, October 1784.

4.   Samuel Orcutt, *History of the Towns of New Milford and Bridgewater, Connecticut, 1703–1882* (Hartford, Conn., 1882), 740.
5.   Ibid., 364–65, 740; Frederick F. Sherman, "The Angus Nickelson Family," *Art in America* 23 (October 1931), 154–58.
        From 1789 to 1792, Nickelson was paying from 104 to 144 pounds per year in taxes; in 1795 his assessment dropped to 52 pounds, and after that time, he was no longer taxed. Angus Nickelson, Tax Lists, Land Records, Town Clerk's Office, New Milford; my thanks to Elizabeth McClintock for gathering these data. In spite of an exhaustive search, no probate inventory has been found for Angus Nickelson; however, a modest personal inventory for Sarah Nickelson lists assets worth $770.05, largely a dowry from her family. Sarah Nickelson, Probate Inventory, New Milford, 1820, no. 1039, CSL.
6.   Albert C. Bates, *An Early Connecticut Engraver and His Work* (Hartford, 1906), ill. opp. 28, 32–33.
7.   *Bulletin* (Museum of Fine Arts, Springfield, Mass.) 35 (June and July 1969), 24.
8.   Painting Files, Museum of Fine Arts, Springfield, Mass.

36   Reverend Nehemiah Strong, 1790

Oil on canvas
67¾ x 38¼ in. (172.1 x 96.5 cm.)
Signed and dated at lower left: "R. Earl Pinxt 1790"
Yale University Art Gallery, New Haven, Connecticut
Gift of the artist

Earl first painted a portrait of the Rev. Nehemiah Strong (unlocated) while a young artist in New Haven, during the mid-1770s, when Strong was a tutor at Yale College. This portrait was placed in the college library. Strong, who later moved to Newtown, Connecticut, became aware of the great improvement in Earl's abilities and had a second portrait painted to replace the earlier work. He wrote of the portrait to his former associate, then president of Yale College, Ezra Stiles.

Mr. Earl the Limner, who formally drew my Portrait now in the College Library . . . returned from Europe, where he had been employed about twelve years, and made great improvements in the Business of his profession. Since his return, he has for about one year past, been chiefly employed in this and Litchfield County – Pursuant to his own proposal, he has gratis, *drawn my Effigie* de novo, *with this view only, that it may be placed in the College Library as a substitute to the former; which performance he now, by me, gratuitously, presents to the College, as a* Fairer Specimen of his Skill and improvement in his Art. – *In duty therefore to him, and as a grateful acknowledgement of his Generosity, I have considered myself as under obligation to endeavor that his Design may be carried into execution. . . .*

P.S. . . . Should the President order the placing of the Effigie himself, it is wished by mr Earl & myself, that its situation may be favorable in respect of Light *and* Shade; *as otherwise the performance may suffer in abatement from its Genuine Likeness.*

    For this purpose mr Earl recomends the west end of the Library appartment, where, formerly, the portrait of K. George *was placed.*[1]

Although the portrait was accepted by Yale College in 1790, President Stiles did not respond favorably to the suggestion that Earl's portrait of Strong replace that of King George. Strong hastened to comment: "When I mentioned it as mr. Earl's choice, that it might be set where K. George formerly stood, Neither he nor I had any conception of composing any Design of *Dithroning his Majesty;* But only ascending that former throne, which of late (tho perhaps before the President came to preside) he had abdicated."[2] There may have been some tongue-in-cheek humor in this exchange, for Earl had been a notorious Loyalist and Strong was at one point questioned concerning his own Tory leanings. Additionally, while Stiles was president of the College, Strong was forced to resign his professorship (in 1781), because of the college's lack of funds.

Earl's portrait of Nehemiah Strong is startling in its realism. Strong evidently suffered from a severe skin disease that caused red discoloration of his skin and hands, which Earl has clearly indicated. One wonders about the earnestness of Earl and Strong's concern that the portrait had to be hung in a well-lit location to fully appreciate the "Genuine Likeness." Perhaps the concept of a true likeness was so widely accepted in Connecticut that the realistic portrayal was considered appropriate.

Nehemiah Strong (1728–1807), the son of Nehemiah

36

Strong and Hannah French Strong of Northampton, Massachusetts, led a life filled with nearly as many twists and turns as Earl's. He studied theology while a student at Yale College, from 1757 to 1760, and became a minister of the Congregational parish in Granby, Connecticut. While there, he met and married Lydia Smith Burr. Lydia Burr had divorced her first husband after his disappearance at sea, but he returned a year after Lydia's marriage to Nehemiah and had the marriage annulled. This embarrassment, as well as other financial difficulties, led to Strong's dismissal from his parish post in 1767. Although he was able to obtain an unendowed professorship of mathematics and natural philosophy at Yale College in 1770, he was forced to resign this position in 1781 because of a lack of funds, as well as suspicion concerning his Loyalist sympathies. Strong eventually settled in Newtown, Connecticut, where he married the widow Mary Thomas (d. 1807). He studied law and passed the bar, and represented Newtown in the 1784 General Assembly. He also founded a school for young men in 1790 and later kept an academy in New Milford. Strong compiled a series of almanacs from 1775 to 1809 and was considered one of the most skillful astronomers in New England. In 1803 he moved to Bridgeport to teach, and he died there, leaving an estate worth only $680.[3]

In addition to providing a startling likeness, Earl's portrait of Strong focuses on his subject's intellectual interests, particularly in astronomy, as shown by the partially titled astronomy and mathematics books in the bookcase and by the astronomical globe on which he rests his right hand. These items are all listed in his will.[4] This portrait is reminiscent of the portrait of Strong's associate Ezra Stiles (1770–71; Yale University Art Gallery), painted twenty years earlier by Samuel King. King surrounded Stiles with labeled volumes of books and various symbols of Stiles's wide-ranging interests, which included astronomy. Stiles would write later in his diary, "These Emblems are more descriptive of my Mind, than the Effigies of my Face."[5] Strong's attire also emphasizes his academic background.

The portrait of Strong was placed in the Yale College library in 1790. If Earl had hoped that it might gain him additional commissions in New Haven, he was disappointed. Although he managed to find success in nearly every other major region of Connecticut, Earl is not known to have painted in New Haven in the 1790s.

Costume Notes   The sitter wears a powdered wig with rigid side curls, the style of an elderly and rather conservative man. His Tory sympathies might be discerned in the excessive formality of his wig! He wears a black silk suit, plain and untrimmed, as befits a cleric and an academic. His vest is white satin, unbuttoned to midchest so that the pleated shirt ruffle can be seen. Strong allows himself a touch of fashionable informality with his morning gown of lilac shot silk. Such a gown was worn in the mornings over vest and breeches to eat breakfast and receive friends, and would be an appropriate working costume for an academic. Morning gowns, as well as being comfortable and dignified, had a slight air of the exotic about them, not surprisingly, since the fashion came from Asia, originally in the seventeenth century. There was a timelessness about such styles (the basic T-shape changed very little) that appealed to those who claimed to be weary of the incessant changes of fashion in European dress. For all these reasons, morning gowns were popular with a wide range of men, the fashionable, the artistic, the intellectual, and the professional.   AR

1.   Strong to Stiles, August 30, 1790, Beinecke Rare Book and Manuscript Library, Yale University, New Haven, Conn.

2.   Strong to Stiles, September 8, 1790, Beinecke Rare Book and Manuscript Library.

3.   Franklin Bowditch Dexter, *Biographical Sketches of the Graduates of Yale College* (New York, 1907), 2:383–88; Painting Files, Yale University Art Gallery; *The Literary Diary of Ezra Stiles*, ed. Franklin Bowditch Dexter (New York, 1901), 94; Nehemiah Strong, Probate Inventory, Stratford, 1807, no. 1443, CSL.

4.   Nehemiah Strong, Will Stratford, 1807, no. 1443, CSL. Earl labeled the books as follows: "Gravesend Theosophy," shorthand for Willem Jacob van Gravesende, *Mathematical Elements of Natural Philosophy Confirm'd by Experiments* (1737); "Martin's Philosophy," for Benjamin Martin, *Biographia Philosophica, Being an Account of the Lives, Writings, and Inventions, of the Most Eminent Philosophers and Mathematicians* (1764); "Newton," for Isaac Newton, *Opera Quae Extant Omnia* (1728); "Whiston," for William Whiston, *Astronomical Lectures* (1728); "Ward's Mathe," "Ferguson Astrono," for James Ferguson, *Astronomy Explained upon Sir Isaac Newton's Principles* (1778); and "Leadbett Astrono," for Charles Leadbetter, *Astronomy; or the True System of Planets Demonstrated* (1727). The globe shows the sun's orbit and the equator intersecting at the vernal equinox and the third zodiacal constellation, I Gemini.

5.   *Literary Diary of Ezra Stiles*, 132–33. The portrait is reproduced in Charles F. Montgomery and Patricia E. Kane, *American Art: 1750–1800 towards Independence* (Boston, 1976), 90, ill. 91.

37 Colonel Benjamin Tallmadge and Son William Tallmadge, 1790

Oil on canvas

78 ¼ x 54 ½ in. (198.8 x 138.4 cm.)

Signed and dated at lower center: "R. Earl Pinxt 1790."

Technical note: the canvas is in two sections, pieced with a vertical seam

The Litchfield Historical Society, Litchfield, Connecticut

38 Mrs. Benjamin Tallmadge and Son Henry Floyd and Daughter Maria Jones, 1790

Oil on canvas

79 ½ x 55 ½ in. (201.9 x 141.0 cm.)

Signed and dated at lower left: "R. Earl Pinxt 1790."

Technical note: the canvas is in two sections, pieced with a vertical seam

The Litchfield Historical Society, Litchfield, Connecticut

Earl's portraits of the Tallmadges are the most elaborate displays of wealth and position found in his Connecticut works. The Tallmadges both came from prominent Long Island families and moved to Litchfield after the war. They maintained close ties with the Jeremiah Wadsworth family (fig. 1.30) in Hartford, with whom they shared an equal social and financial rank.

Col. Benjamin Tallmadge (1754–1835) was the son of the Rev. Benjamin Tallmadge of Setauket, Brookhaven, Long Island. Following in his father's footsteps, he graduated from Yale College in 1773. Benjamin entered the army at the outbreak of the Revolution and, by virtue of his daring exploits and ingenuity, was made chief of the intelligence service. After identifying Maj. John Andre as a spy for the British, he became deeply attached to him during André's imprisonment. After the war, Benjamin married Mary Floyd (1763–1805), daughter of Col. William Floyd (cat. 46), also of Brookhaven, Long Island.

The couple settled in Litchfield in the house Benjamin had purchased two years earlier, where they raised seven children (the house still stands on North Street). There Benjamin joined his brother John in the firm of B. Tallmadge and Company, quickly becoming the leading merchants in the region. Through his connections with such prominent capitalists as Jeremiah Wadsworth, Benjamin developed international trade connections, offering the finest goods "at a very small advance for pay in hand, or on a short credit." [1] He parlayed his business into money lend-

ing, investment in stocks and securities, land speculation in the Mohawk River Valley and Ohio, and later banking. Benjamin was elected to the Congress and served there from 1801 to 1817. Henry Ward Beecher later recalled the town's distinguished citizen with awe. "How well do we remember the stately gait of the venerable Colonel of Revolutionary memory! We don't recollect that he ever spoke to us or greeted us, – not because he was austere or unkind, but from a kind of military reserve. We thought him good and polite, but should as soon have thought of climbing the church steeple as of speaking to one living so high and venerable above all boys!" [2]

For the Tallmadge portraits, Earl abandoned any sense of restraint, creating monumental images of his affluent and eminent subjects. In *Colonel Benjamin Tallmadge and His Son William Tallmadge*, Earl depicts Benjamin elegantly posed, seated on an upholstered chair, holding a business paper in hand. His intellectual interests, evidenced by his valuable library, are indicated by the many shelves of books in the background.[3] His illustrious military career is symbolized by the badge of the Society of the Cincinnati (he was president of the Connecticut chapter), worn on his left lapel. His elder son, William Smith (1785–1822), stands near his father, his hand resting near an exquisite button on his father's coat cuff.

Mary Tallmadge is equally elegant; she is shown in a similar room, with a view of the Litchfield landscape, dominated by the church steeple, in the distance. She holds her infant daughter, Maria Jones (1790–1878), on her lap, with her son Henry Floyd (1787–1854) at her feet; he is engaged with a toy carriage. The Tallmadges actually owned a fine carriage, so the toy is another indication of their elevated status.[4] The couple's social position is clearly indicated in Mary's attire as well.

Earl's depiction of the multicolored carpet and green drapery serves to unite the grand-scale portraits, which are imposing when hung together. The Tallmadge portraits were given to the Litchfield Historical Society by the subjects' granddaughter, Mary Floyd Tallmadge Woodruff Seymour, in 1917.[5]

Costume Notes   Benjamin Tallmadge, with his elegant silk costume and powdered wig, is the epitome of ancien régime grandeur. His costume consists of a pale green silk frock coat, an embroidered silk vest, silk knee breeches, and stockings. The coat is particularly stylish with its elaborate buttons made of either diamond paste or marcasite (faceted crystalized iron pyrites) to glitter in candlelight. The coat and the vest of white silk embroidered in a flower design look French, as indeed may be the beige silk breeches fastened at the knee with small gilt buttons. His son William, with his loose, flowing natural hair and English-influenced costume, is a startling contrast; in its sober practicality, his costume, a green double-breasted cloth jacket and trousers, points the way toward masculine dress in the nineteenth century.[6]

The portrait of Mary Tallmadge is monumental in every way; the costume is almost regal in tone.[7] The sitter wears a formal open gown and matching petticoat (the contemporary word for a skirt) of lustrous blue satin. The robings, the vertical trimmings to the open gown, are made of gathered satin with cords and buttons; the hem of the petticoat is also trimmed with loops and buttons. There is a white fringed girdle round the waist, and around the neck, a collar of embroidered muslin with a deep frill. The blue and white of the dress complement the blue and white of the ribbon of the badge worn by her husband. Her hair is frizzed and pomaded so stiffly that it acts as a cushion for the pearls and jeweled ornaments pinned in it and the white ostrich feathers on top.

Her son Henry, his hand on his mother's half-open ivory fan, is dressed in his white baby gown of embroidered muslin and a cap to protect his head from the cold. Her daughter, Maria, also wears a white muslin gown, tied at the waist with a black sash.   AR

1. The advertisement appeared in the *Litchfield Weekly Monitor and Agricultural Register*, November 7, 1792.

2. Beecher, *Litchfield Revisited* (Litchfield, Conn., 1856), 95. For biographical information, see Tallmadge Papers, Litchfield Historical Society, Litchfield, Conn.; Benjamin Tallmadge, *Memoirs of Colonel Benjamin Tallmadge* (New York, 1905); Franklin Bowditch Dexter, *Biographical Sketches of the Graduates of Yale College* (New York, 1907), 4:506–7; Alain C. White, *The History of the Town of Litchfield, Connecticut, 1720–1920* (Litchfield, 1920), 87–91, 130–37; Charles Swain Hall, *Benjamin Tallmadge: Revolutionary Soldier and American Businessman* (New York, 1943).

3. Benjamin Tallmadge, Probate Inventory, Litchfield, 1835, Reel 708, CSL, indicates that his library, listed in a separate catalogue, was valued at $542.61.

4. The probate inventory of Benjamin Tallmadge lists "1 four wheel carriage and harness" worth $150.

5. My thanks to Lisa Kightlinger, Litchfield Historical Society, for this information.

6. Mrs. Papendiek (who worked at the English court under Queen Charlotte) described the breeching of her son Frederick in 1790, when he switched from a white cotton frock to the kind of costume seen here. "A total change of dress it was then for a boy. The shirt was made like a man's except that the collar was large and frilled and turned over the jacket instead of being buttoned up. The jacket and trousers were of cloth." *Court and Private Life in the Time of Queen Charlotte*, ed. V. D. Broughton (London, 1887), 2:230–31.

7. The portrait suggests Elisabeth-Louise Vigée-Lebrun's images of Marie Antoinette, including one of the French queen in blue satin, with white ostrich feathers in her headdress (1783; Versailles), and one in which she wears blue velvet, with a blue and white headdress (1788; Versailles). Also at Versailles is a Vigée-Lebrun portrait of Marie Antoinette with a baby on her lap (1787).

38

39

39 Marinus Willett, c. 1791

Oil on canvas
91 ¼ x 56 in. (231.8 x 142.2 cm.)
The Metropolitan Museum of Art, New York
Bequest of George Willett Van Nest, 1917 (17.87.1)

Earl's striking change in composition and technique from one region to the next is amply seen in his portrait of Marinus Willett (1740–1830). At the time this portrait was painted, Earl had already established his restrained Connecticut portrait style, a sharp departure from the more sophisticated New York portraits of his prison years, which drew on his English experience for their inspiration. Now that he was back in New York, painting a sitter he had known when in prison, Earl once again switches to a more formal and technically accomplished style.[1]

Born in Jamaica, Long Island, Willett led a varied career as a soldier and public servant. He attended Kings College (later Columbia College), then worked for a time in New York City as a cabinetmaker, eventually becoming a wealthy merchant with extensive real estate holdings. Willett had entered the army as a young man and later became a prominent member of the Sons of Liberty in New York. The Congress presented him with the sword (now in the Metropolitan Museum of Art) seen in his portrait for his bravery in a skirmish against the British at Fort Stanwix in the Mohawk River Valley in 1777.

Earl first encountered Willett at his own trial, where Willett was the sheriff of New York County, an office he held from 1784 until 1788. As a leading member of the Society for the Relief of Distressed Debtors, Willett later wrote of his concern for these prisoners to Mayor De Witt Clinton of New York. "Since my arrival here I paid a visit to the prison – the wretchedness there is past my power to attempt a description – If distress ever claimed Legislative assistance, the melancholy situation of the confined debtors in this place demand attention."[2]

Earl's full-length portrait of Willett commemorates his greatly celebrated role in negotiating a treaty with the Creek Indians, an assignment given to him by George Washington, which he completed on August 7, 1790. Willett was in favor of establishing peaceful solutions to successive disputes with other tribes, writing in 1792: "It has been uniformly my opinion that the United States ought to avoid an Indian War. . . . The intercourse I have had with these people, [and] the treatment I have myself received . . . make me an advocate for them. To fight with them would be the last thing I desire."[3] When Washington appointed Willett to the new rank of brigadier general in the same year, he refused it. "The honor . . . of fighting and beating Indians, is what I do not aspire after. If in any way I could be instrumental in effecting and maintaining peace with them, it would be to me a source of great satisfaction."[4]

Willett was a member of the Society of the Cincinnati in New York. Later, turning to a political career, he succeeded De Witt Clinton as mayor of New York in 1807.[5]

Earl reverts in this portrait to the more fluid, loaded brushwork evident in his English and earlier New York works. The figure is gracefully posed in a formal stance derived from such British prototypes as Joseph Wright of Derby's *Portrait of a Gentleman* (c. 1771–72; private collection).[6] Willett stands in an accomplished landscape setting. To commemorate Willett's success with the Creeks, Earl includes three Indians, placed in nonthreatening poses, crouched behind a hill, and holding rifles.

Earl's portrait of Willett was exhibited at the Stuyvesant Institute, New York, in 1838 at the Exhibition of Select Paintings by Modern Artists, a benefit for the family of William Dunlap. Listed as "No. 148 Portrait of Colonel Marinus Willett by Earle of Connecticut," it was lent by Marinus Willett's third wife, Margaret Bancker Willett. The portrait descended in the Willett family to George Willett Van Nest, who bequeathed it to the Metropolitan Museum of Art in 1917.

Costume Notes The elegant uniform, that of the New York militia, makes a great impact. The very dark blue coat, faced and buttoned back with white (the buttons are of pewter), is lined with white silk, and on the lefthand facing hangs the badge of the Society of the Cincinnati. The vest of white, with flapped pockets, and the breeches are of the same cloth. The knee-high black leather boots are fashionable civilian and military wear. His military career is signaled in the choice of accessories. In his black beaver hat (a bicorne with a brim turned up high in front and behind, a fashionable sporting and military style) he wears the black and white Federal cockade, ordained in 1780 to symbolize the unity of the American and French armies.[7] AR

1. William Sawitzky first suggested a date of 1791 for this portrait because Earl was in New York in this year painting other works, as well as because the painting makes reference to Willett's treaty with the Creeks, accomplished in August 1790. William Sawitzky and Susan Sawitzky Papers, New-York Historical Society, New York.

2. Willett to Clinton, March 11, 1791, reproduced in I. N. Stokes, *The Iconography of Manhattan Island, 1498–1909* (New York, 1926), 5:1284.

3. Quoted in Wiley Sword, *President Washington's Indian War: The Struggle for the Old Northwest, 1790–1795* (Norman, Okla., 1985), 213.

4. Willett to Washington, April 14, 1792, reproduced in *A Narrative of the Military Actions of Colonel Marinus Willett, Taken Chiefly from His Own Manuscript*, prepared by William N. Willett (New York, 1831).

5. For biographical information, see *Narrative of the Military Actions of Willett*; Howard Thomas, *Marinus Willett* (New York, 1954); Albert Ten Eyck Gardiner and Stuart P. Feld, *American Paintings: A Catalogue of the Collection of the Metropolitan Museum of Art* (New York, 1965), 1:72–74.

6. See Benedict Nicholson, *Joseph Wright of Derby: Painter of Light* (New York, 1968), 2:80, cat. 79.

7. Such cockades were sometimes worn by women to demonstrate their political loyalties. This may also explain the popularity of black and white for women's headdresses during the 1780s (as in Earl's *Esther Boardman*, cat. 30), although it was also a fashionable color combination.

40   Dr. Mason Fitch Cogswell, 1791

Oil on canvas

37 ⅛ x 31 ¾ in. (94.3 x 80.7 cm.)

Signed and dated at lower left: "R. Earl Pinxt / 1791"

The Museum of Fine Arts, Houston

The Bayou Bend Collection

Museum purchase with funds provided in memory of
  Miss Ima Hogg by her friends

This portrait of Mason Fitch Cogswell owes much of its impact to the sitter's close relationship with the artist. Earl's sympathetic portrayal of his friend and court-appointed guardian conveys Cogswell's kind nature and intelligent professionalism.

Cogswell (1768–1830), the son of the Rev. James Cogswell (fig. 1.29) and Alice Fitch Cogswell, was born in Saybrook, Connecticut. Upon Alice's death the family moved to Scotland, Connecticut, where James Cogswell succeeded the Rev. Ebenezer Devotion (fig. 1.3) as minister of the Congregational Church and married his widow, Martha Lathrop Devotion (fig. 1.4). As a young man, Mason was sent to live with his uncle, Samuel Huntington of Norwich, who would become a signer of the Declaration of Independence and the governor of Connecticut from 1786 to 1796.

After graduating from Yale College in 1780, Mason lived with his older brother, Dr. James Cogswell, Jr., and his wife, Elizabeth Huntington Davenport Cogswell, in Stamford. There he studied medicine with his brother, who was then the examining surgeon of volunteers for the Continental Army. In 1783 the brothers moved to New York City, where they established a medical partnership. As founding members of the Society for the Relief of Distressed Debtors, they became aware of the plight of Ralph Earl, who was then imprisoned for debt. Upon Earl's release in January 1788, the court appointed Mason Earl's guardian. Mason helped Earl to reestablish his artistic career by using his impressive connections to provide Earl with an entrée to a new region. When Mason moved his medical practice to Hartford in 1789, he encouraged the artist to follow him to Connecticut, where Earl painted his friends, relations, and patients for the next ten years.[1]

One of the leading members of his profession, Mason Fitch Cogswell achieved prominence as a physician and surgeon, becoming a founder of the Connecticut Medical Society in 1792. Although he refused the appointment, he was selected to be the first professor of surgery at Yale College. Cogswell gained fame for his introduction of the first successful operation for cataracts. As a local philanthropist, he was instrumental in founding the Connecticut Asylum for the Education of Deaf and Dumb Persons (now the American School for the Deaf) in Hartford in 1817, the first institution of its kind in America.[2]

Like Earl, Cogswell's profession demanded constant travel throughout the state, as reflected in his physician account books. Because he dealt with people at times of birth, illness, and death, all appropriate occasions for portraits to be taken, he was often asked to recommend appropriate painters. Cogswell was well suited to the role he came to play as a tastemaker in the state, because he was on intimate terms with many American artists who worked in Connecticut. Several, including Earl, John Trumbull, Joseph Steward (cats. 67, 68), John Brewster, Jr. (cats. 69, 70), and the Hartford miniature painters, William Verstille, Isaac Sanford, and William Wadsworth, had painted Cogswell family members and relations.[3]

Cogswell commissioned Earl to paint his portrait during the artist's two-year stay in the Hartford area. As Cogswell's physician ledger indicates, the portrait was painted in exchange for medical attention.[4] Although fashionably attired, Cogswell chose to be depicted in a professional capacity, seated in a Windsor chair with a writing arm, his hand on an open book. Cogswell's expression exudes the kindness and good humor he was noted for possessing and also conveys the artist's fondness for his subject. Cogswell's extensive library of medical books, listed in his inventory of effects, is implied by the partially titled books in the bookcase, including references to William Cullen's *First Lives of the Practice of Physic* and Benjamin Fell's *System of Surgery*, as well as *System of Anatomy* and *Malaria Medica*.[5] The chair Cogswell is seated in was made by the Hartford cabinetmaker Stacey Stackhouse, who is listed in Cogswell's ledger as having received medical treatment in exchange for "a writing chair."[6]

One attraction of Hartford for Cogswell was the Connecticut Wits, a group of politically conservative satirists who attacked popular politics in such poems as Dr. Lemuel Hopkins's "The Anarchiad" of 1786–87.[7] As an amateur poet, Cogswell became a peripheral member of this group, having already become familiar with them at Yale. Earl's portrait of Cogswell, seated in a Hartford Windsor chair, may have inspired the use of a similar prop in two portraits by John Trumbull of fellow Connecticut Wits, *Dr. Lemuel Hopkins* (Yale University Art Gallery) and *John Trumbull* (Detroit Institute of Arts), a painting of the artist's second cousin, both executed in Hartford in 1793. Trumbull placed his subjects in green Windsor chairs, which, for him, was an unusual prop.[8]

The portrait descended in the Cogswell family to the subject's great-grandson, Ledyard Cogswell, Jr., who sold the portrait through Vose Galleries, Boston, to the Museum of Fine Arts in Houston in 1976.

Costume Notes   The sitter wears the sober dress of the professional man, but one who was not indifferent to fashion. The costume consists of a suit of black silk cut fashionably with a high collar and tight sleeves—the artist has care

40

fully depicted the slit cuff on the arm resting on the chair. Cogswell is clearly a man of some refinement, wearing a fine linen pleated shirt ruffle and a fringed silk cravat at his neck. His black silk breeches are fastened at the knee with silk rosettes and oval diamond paste buckles. His hair is his own, brushed out to a fashionable frizz at the sides and just touching the top of his collar. Altogether, the costume is a harmony of black and white; even the dog is a fashionable accessory.[9] AR

1.   Elizabeth Mankin Kornhauser, "Ralph Earl as an Itinerant Artist: Pattern of Patronage," in Peter Benes, ed., *Itinerancy in New England and New York: Annual Proceedings of the Dublin Seminar for New England Folk Life* (Boston, 1986), 172–90.

2.   For biographical information, primary sources include the Rev. James Cogswell Papers and Mason Fitch Cogswell Papers, CHS; Cogswell Family Papers, Sterling Memorial Library, Yale University, New Haven, Conn.; Cogswell Family Papers, Beinecke Rare Book and Manuscript Library, Yale University. Secondary sources include Frances Root Cogswell, ed., *Father and Daughter: A Collection of Cogswell Family Letters and Diaries, 1772–*

1801 (West Hartford, Conn., n.d.); Edward R. Lamson, "Mason Fitch Cogswell," *Yale Journal of Biology and Medicine* 3 (October 1930), 1–9.

3.   Elizabeth Mankin Kornhauser and Christine Skeeles Schloss, "Painting and Other Pictorial Arts," in *The Great River: Art and Life of the Connecticut Valley, 1635–1820*, exhib. cat. (Hartford, Conn., 1985), 138–39, 152, 170–71; Kornhauser, *Ralph Earl: Artist-Entrepreneur* (Ann Arbor, Mich., 1989), 145.

4.   On July 29, 1791, and April 29, 1792, Earl was treated for "sundries," in the amount of five shillings six pence, which was covered "by painting in full." Mason Fitch Cogswell Papers, Physician Ledgers, CHS.

5.   Mason Fitch Cogswell, Probate Inventory, Hartford, 1832, CSL, indicates "234 Medical Books," as well as an additional 348 books and pamphlets.

6.   "1790 Stacey Stackhouse . . . By a writing chair 1 pound." For information on Stackhouse, see Phyllis Kihn, ed., "Connecticut Cabinetmakers," Part 2, *Connecticut Historical Society Bulletin* 33 (January 1968), 19–20.

7.   Charles W. Everest, *The Poets of Connecticut* (Hartford, 1843).

8.   Oswaldo Rodrigues Roque, "Trumbull's Portraits," in Helen A. Cooper et al., ed., *John Trumbull: The Hand and Spirit of a Painter*, exhib. cat. (New Haven, Conn., 1982), 125.

9.   For a portrait in which the sitter, dressed in black and white, has a pet to match (a cat), see John de Critz's painting *Henry Wriothesley, Third Earl of Southampton* (1603; collection of the Duke of Buccleuch and Queensbury).

41   Oliver Ellsworth and Abigail Wolcott Ellsworth, 1792

Oil on canvas

76 x 86¾ in. (193.0 x 220.4 cm.)

Signed and dated at lower left: "R. Earl Pinxt 1792"

Technical note: the canvas is in three sections, pieced with two vertical seams that run along the outer window moldings

Wadsworth Atheneum, Hartford, Connecticut

Gift of the Ellsworth heirs, 1903.7

With great elation, Oliver Ellsworth reported to his wife, Abigail, on June 7, 1790, that "the Constitution is now adopted by all the States, and I have much satisfaction & perhaps some vanity in seeing at length a great work finished for which I have long labored incessantly."[1] Two years later, the Ellsworths commissioned Earl to paint a monumental double portrait of themselves that celebrated their respective roles in the formation of the new nation – Oliver as an ardent patriot and leader of the new republic and Abigail as the keeper of their domestic world. One of Earl's greatest efforts, this portrait is an icon of the Constitutional period and served as a model for many Connecticut painters of the period.[2]

Oliver Ellsworth (1745–1807), the second son of a Windsor, Connecticut, farmer, attended Yale College in preparation for the ministry. After his expulsion from Yale at the end of his sophomore year, he completed his education at Princeton College in 1766. Eventually rejecting a career in the ministry in favor of the law, he rapidly emerged as one of Connecticut's most powerful political figures and successful lawyers. He further strengthened his position by marrying into a prominent family in the state when, in 1772, he wed Abigail Wolcott (1756–1818), second cousin of Oliver Wolcott, Sr. During the revolutionary war he served as delegate to the Continental Congress, and after the war his service would ascend to a national and international level.

At the Constitutional Convention, Oliver Ellsworth was instrumental in securing the famous Connecticut Compromise, which ended the struggle between large and small states over representation, and he was also responsible for the use of the term United States in the Constitution. He published a series of letters using the pseudonym A Landowner in favor of ratification. When his portrait was painted, he was an active member of the U.S. Senate, responsible for drafting the Judiciary Bill and an up-and-coming leader of the Federalist party. He abandoned his seat in the senate when Washington appointed him chief justice of the Supreme Court in 1796. In 1800, at the request of President John Adams, he served as a special minister in Paris, charged with preventing a Franco-American war.[3]

The Ellsworths were painted at their home in Windsor, which had been built between 1781 and 1783 by Samuel Denslow.[4] During the 1780s, while active in national politics, Oliver managed at the same time to improve his modest financial situation by building a thriving law practice, acquiring lands and real estate on speculation, and lending money.[5] When their portrait was painted, the Ellsworths were able to have their house enlarged and modernized by the local architect Thomas Hayden.[6] Originally painted red, the house, and the newly added south wing, was painted white, as Earl's rendition shows. Oliver and Abigail are seated in two of a set of six Federal shield-back chairs (Ellsworth Homestead and Wadsworth Atheneum collections) designed by Aaron Chapin of Hartford and recently acquired for their new Palladian-style parlor. The chairs are the earliest datable examples of neoclassical seating furniture in the Connecticut River Valley. Their portrait, which hung in the fashionably furnished new parlor, was the final symbol of their ascendancy to a position of political and social leadership.

Earl's ingenious composition combined many elements found in his earlier portraits of the Ellsworths' relations, Oliver Wolcott and Laura Wolcott (cats. 25, 26). Rather than making a reference to Ellsworth's current position as a U.S. Senator, here Earl celebrates Oliver Ellsworth's role in drafting, ratifying, and amplifying the Constitution. Staring boldly out at the viewer with his piercing blue eyes, he holds a copy of the new Constitution in his left hand; on it Earl has inscribed passages from the last two articles. Behind the figure, red drapery is drawn back to reveal shelves of books, a reference to Oliver's extensive library, one of the largest in the state. When he died, he owned 632 volumes, most dealing with law and political philosophy.[7]

Earl portrays Abigail Wolcott with a stern visage, contrasting sharply with her rich surroundings. Although she was only thirty-six when Earl painted her portrait, Earl shows the effects of her arduous life in this truthful likeness – she had borne the last of her nine children the year before and appears much older than her years. In addition to tending to her children, Abigail was left to arrange the construction and later renovation of the house and the maintenance of their property and gardens, because Oliver was away from the family home for extended periods of time. His letters to his wife, particularly in the 1780s, when he was in Philadelphia for lengthy periods, express occasional alarm at her "low spirits"[8] and indicate the conflict between his love for his wife and children and his desire to serve the public.

Earl has softened somewhat the severity of Abigail's likeness by using voluminous red drapery as a backdrop. Symbolically, he relates her figure more directly than her husband's to the detailed view through the window of their newly renovated house and cultivated fields, using perspective to direct the viewer's eye from her figure to the landscape beyond and using the window molding to cut Oliver's figure off from the landscape. In addition, the drapery encompasses both the figure of Abigail Ellsworth and the view of the house and property. (An artistic alteration can be seen behind the figure of Oliver – Earl originally placed red drapery there but changed the backdrop to a bookcase.)

Earl painted Abigail in a pose nearly identical to the one seen in the portrait of Laura Wolcott. Both wives are associated with the family homestead, which they had, with difficulty, maintained during their husbands' long absences. In

the Ellsworth portrait the copy of the Constitution is placed between the couple, symbolizing the personal sacrifices each had made to bring about its ratification.

Earl's view of their house, called Elmwood, an illogical but charming addition to the portrait, accurately represents the recently built south wing. The neatly painted fences, sapling elm trees "set out by [Ellsworth's] hand," and the distant view of the houses on the eastern bank of the Connecticut River complete the scene.[9] Toward the end of his life, Oliver expressed his great sense of regional pride, a pride that Earl beautifully communicates in this portrait. "I have been in all the states, and Connecticut is the best state. Windsor is the pleasantest town in the state of Connecticut, and I have the pleasantest place in Windsor. I am content to die on the banks of the Connecticut."[10]

Costume Notes Oliver Ellsworth wears a dark blue frock coat decorated with brass buttons, a white silk vest, black silk breeches, white silk stockings, and black leather shoes with the large Artois buckles first seen in fashionable footwear in the 1780s and now worn by most men. The coat has an unusual feature (for American dress) – a red collar. Dark blue coats with red collars were popular in England during the 1770s; in 1778, George III introduced the Windsor uniform at court, a coat of dark blue with a collar and cuffs of red. Whether a sartorial reference here links the Windsor uniform to Oliver's coat in a visual play on his much-loved home in Windsor, Connecticut, is not clear. At first glance it might seem unlikely, for Oliver was a great American patriot. But sometimes Earl subtly uses color in dress in exercises in wit, so this theory may not be altogether fanciful.

Abigail Ellsworth's costume is slightly old-fashioned but with some modish features. Her rather formal open gown is white silk, possibly lustring, a fabric that during the 1790s had largely replaced heavier silks; it consists of a robe (the contemporary word) with long tight sleeves to the wrist and a skirt of matching silk.[11] The bodice front cannot be seen behind the starched muslin collar tucked into the waist sash. Such a collar served to cover the décolletage of the dress; during the day many middle-aged women also wore a chemisette, or modesty piece, of muslin pinned under the neckline of the bodice and covering the neck and bosom. Over her gray hair – either naturally so, or with a pale dusting of powder – Abigail wears a starched muslin mobcap; this type of headdress was virtually a uniform among women of her age and class.   AR

1. Ellsworth to Ellsworth, June 7, 1790, Oliver Ellsworth Papers, CHS.

2. Elizabeth Mankin Kornhauser and Christine Skeeles Schloss, "Painting and Other Pictorial Arts," in *The Great River: Art and Society of the Connecticut Valley, 1635–1820*, exhib. cat. (Hartford, Conn., 1985), 137, 154–55.

3. For biographical information, see William C. Brown, *The Life of Oliver Ellsworth* (New York, 1905); Ronald John Lettieri, *Connecticut's Young Man of the Revolution: Oliver Ellsworth* (Deep River, Conn., 1978).

4.   See Adams and Roy, Consultants, *Oliver Ellsworth Homestead, Windsor, Connecticut, Historic Structure Report: Physical Investigation Prepared for the Ellsworth Memorial Association* (Portsmouth, N.H., 1990), and Samuel Denslow and Oliver Ellsworth, Articles of Agreement, February 2, 1781, private collection, which outline the details of the house construction. My thanks to Rose-Marie Ballard, curator, Oliver Ellsworth Homestead, who is engaged in overseeing a major research and renovation project of the Ellsworth Homestead and has provided updated reports on the house.

5.   Oliver Ellsworth's estate at the time of his death totaled the very high sum of $126,674.32.

6.   See also Architectural Drawings by Thomas Hayden (private collection; photoduplicates in the Connecticut River Valley Archive, Wadsworth Atheneum). See also Kornhauser and Schloss, "Painting and Other Pictorial Arts," 113; Oliver Ellsworth, Account Book, private collection, which contains receipts itemizing the expenses for Hayden's renovation in 1788 and 1789, as well as lists furniture Hayden made for the house. Again, my thanks to Rose-Marie Ballard for bringing this information to my attention.

7.   Oliver Ellsworth, Probate Inventory, Windsor, 1807, Reel 509, CSL. A catalogue in the inventory lists each book, providing a fascinating document of Oliver Ellsworth's intellectual interests. The books are valued at $806.62.

8.   Ellsworth to Ellsworth, February 3, 1779, Ellsworth Papers.

9.   John W. Barber, *Connecticut Historical Collections* (New Haven, Conn., 1836), 129. This source also includes an engraving of the house. According to family tradition, Ellsworth planted thirteen elm trees to signify the thirteen original states.

10.   The Oliver Ellsworth Homestead has a facsimile of the quote by Oliver Ellsworth that was handed down from the nineteenth century; the original source remains unlocated.

11.   Even Abigail Adams, conservative in her sartorial tastes, mentions a white lustring gown and petticoat in 1799; she found the fabric, although light, to be more modest than the muslins that were all the rage among younger women. *New Letters of Abigail Adams, 1788–1801*, ed. S. Mitchell (Boston, 1947), 218, 242.

42   Colonel Samuel Talcott, c. 1791–92

Oil on canvas

71 ¼ x 53 ¾ in. (181.0 x 136.5 cm.)

Technical note: the canvas is in three sections, pieced with two vertical seams; the original frame was tacked directly to the canvas surface

Wadsworth Atheneum, Hartford, Connecticut

The Ella Gallup Sumner and Mary Catlin Sumner Collection, 1963.32

Earl's penetrating depiction of this aged Hartford gentleman is a tribute to his ability to convey the conservative and pious values held by many of his Connecticut subjects. Col. Samuel Talcott (1711–97), a member of the third generation of a distinguished and wealthy family, was the son of Joseph Talcott, who had served as the colonial governor of Connecticut from 1724 to 1741. Samuel graduated from Yale College in 1733 and six years later married into an equally affluent and prominent family when he wed Mabel Wyllys, the daughter of Hezekiah Wyllys. He inherited his father's mansion house on Main Street and Talcott Lane in Hartford, where he and his family (which eventually included eight children) lived, along with extensive landholdings. Although he served in various public offices, he devoted much of his time to managing his estate. At the time of his death, he owned sixteen hundred acres of land and five houses besides the "Old Mansion house."[1]

Earl seems to have taken pleasure in capturing Talcott's stern New England visage, which is locked in a humorless scowl. He is stiffly seated in Earl's stock red upholstered armchair, with what appears to be an arthritic right hand resting on the chair arm. A well-educated man, Talcott's sizable library is indicated by the bookcase behind him.[2]

Earl devoted a large portion of the canvas to an elaborate landscape, seen through the window, which depicts Talcott's property, extending from his house on Main Street to the Connecticut River. Earl put sailboats on the river and dotted the distant eastern bank with houses. In 1761, Talcott granted a right of passage through his property to the main street of Hartford for the town's inhabitants.[3] The fenced path in the foreground of Earl's view of Hartford may represent this public thoroughfare. Talcott was a strict Congregationalist, insinuated by Earl's inclusion of two church steeples in the landscape; neither was visible from Talcott's house when this portrait was painted.

The portrait descended in the Talcott family to Col. Phillip S. Wainwright and his heirs, from whom it was purchased by the Wadsworth Atheneum in 1963.

Costume Notes   The sitter is almost Puritan in the austerity of his costume and in his defiantly inelegant pose; here is a man whose plainness of attire is almost a creed. The suit of black silk velvet is formal and rather old-fashioned; the buttons are silk, quartered in the death's-head style. The white linen cravat is plain, knotted round the neck and poking through the vest, which is unbuttoned at midchest; the style dates from the middle of the eighteenth century. The wig also dates from the 1750s – the style was fashionable in Talcott's youth. Known as a physical wig, it has a wide frizz of hair standing out around the sides and back of the head from above the ears to the shoulders. The style was usually preferred by members of the learned professions, especially medicine. It would have been extremely old-fashioned when Earl painted this portrait. The wig is heavily powdered, much of the powder falling onto the shoulders of the coat. Talcott wears plain white silk stockings (no fine embroidery here) and plain silver buckles on breeches and shoes.   AR

1.   S. V. Talcott, *Talcott Pedigree in England and America* (Albany, N.Y., 1876), 39, 46, 85–86; William G. Wendell, "Colonel Samuel Talcott and His Portrait by Ralph Earl," *Wadsworth Atheneum Bulletin* 5 (Winter 1963), 23–25. Samuel Talcott, Probate Inventory, Hartford, 1797, Reel 601, CSL, indicates that his total estate was valued at 9,447 pounds 19 shillings plus $120.25.

2.   According to Talcott's probate inventory, he owned ninety-four books.

3.   John R. Campbell, "Governor Talcott's Mansion and the City of Hartford's Claim," *Connecticut Magazine* 6 (July–August 1900), 359–61.

42

43

43 Captain John Pratt, 1792

Oil on canvas
46½ x 38½ in. (118.1 x 91.4 cm.)
Signed and dated at lower right: "R. Earl 1792"
Dallas Museum of Art
Gift of the Pauline Allen Gill Foundation, 1990

Earl's portrayal of Capt. John Pratt is surprisingly pretentious when compared to the artist's other Connecticut portraits. In spite of his modest rank, Pratt is shown in full military regalia, formally posed and holding a sword in his right hand. Although Earl rarely included references to his Connecticut subjects' membership in the Society of the Cincinnati (commonly thought of as an elitist organization), here Pratt is shown wearing the society's badge on his left lapel. He is placed in a landscape with a dog by his side and an impressive Palladian structure in the distance, which may, in fact, be imaginary.

John Pratt (1753–1824) was a native of Hartford, the son of Zachariah Pratt and Abigail Cook Pratt and a good friend and patient of Dr. Mason Fitch Cogswell. During the Revolution, he served as an assistant commissary general under Gen. James Clinton, and he continued to pursue a military career after the war. He fought against the Indians in Ohio and other western localities. In 1791, President Washington appointed him a captain of the First Regiment of the U.S. Army, in which role, Pratt was ordered by Gen. Henry Knox to head the army recruiting service for the state of Connecticut with "the principal rendezvous . . . at Middletown."[1] Because of his new assignment, Pratt settled in Middletown either in 1792 or 1793; in the latter year, he purchased a farm from Eli Butler for one thousand pounds. The property, located in the North Society of Middletown and bordering the lands of Mary Alsop (cat. 45), consisted of a large, five-bay, two-and-a-half-story house with a central chimney built around 1734 and located on 118 acres of land.[2]

Pratt managed to operate his substantial farm, which he called Troy Farm, with the help of a tenant farmer and a slave named Cuff.[3] He married Elizabeth Cooper of Middletown in 1795 and became a prominent figure in local politics, serving as a magistrate and a representative in the state legislature.

Earl's portrait of Pratt celebrates his military career and his membership in the Society of the Cincinnati. He is shown in the regimental uniform of the Continental Army. In 1791, Pratt ordered a "Regimental coat" from a New York tailor, for which he paid fifteen pounds one shilling five pence.[4] In his left hand, Pratt holds a paper inscribed "Inspection returns 1791," a reference to his military work. A dog, either a pet or a fashionable addition to the landscape,

looks up at his master. The most puzzling element in Earl's portrait is the Palladian house, which is not the house Pratt purchased in Middletown in 1793 but presumably the property he referred to as Troy Farm.[5] Because Earl tended to be accurate in his depictions of houses and other elements in his Connecticut portraits, this structure must have had an important significance to the sitter, though no information about this particular house has come to light.

There are several copies of this portrait, including one by Junius Brutus Stearns, *Captain John Pratt* (1862; Wadsworth Atheneum), painted for the Pratt family. The portrait by Earl descended in the Pratt family of Hartford to James T. Pratt and Porter Pratt. It was acquired by Vose Galleries, Boston, from the family in 1976 and was with R. H. Love Gallery, Chicago, in 1980 when it entered the Moss collection. It was acquired by the Dallas Art Museum in 1990.

Costume Notes   In 1783 the Continental Army was put into a uniform coat of blue faced with red, and this is what Pratt wears, with white vest and breeches; the red sash round his waist is fastened to one of his vest buttons to keep it in place.[6] His rank is denoted by one epaulet on his shoulder, as specified by a general order on uniform that Washington issued in 1779. Among the other military elements are the sword and the black silk stock at Pratt's neck. The elements of fashion include the pleated muslin shirt ruffle and the matching sleeve ruffles. His own hair, powdered, is quite long and tied in the back.   AR

1.   Charles Whittlesey, *Ancestry of John Pratt* (Hartford, Conn., 1900), 46; J. B. Beers, ed., *History of Middlesex County* (New York, 1884), 82.
2.   Property Deed, April 4, 1793, Eli Butler of Middletown to Capt. John Pratt of Hartford, Capt. John Pratt Collection, 2 vols., CSL; Judith E. Johnson and William H. Tabor, *History and Architecture: Cromwell* (Middletown, Conn., 1980), 216, ill. 217. My thanks to Elizabeth McClintock for gathering information on Pratt's landholdings and house.
3.   Capt. John Pratt to Mr. Roberts, June 13, 1793, Pratt Collection, 2:158; Bill of Sale of Negro Cuff from Capt. Jabez Hall to Capt. John Pratt, August 25, 1791, Pratt Collection, 2:156. In the letter to his tenant farmer, Mr. Roberts, Pratt issued instructions for the running of his "Plantation" and warned: "The House is large and valuable. The two Northeast rooms are reserved for my use and mustn't be occupied by anyone whatsoever."
4.   Bill of Sale from the New York Tailor Christian Baehr: "To making [sic] a Regimental Coat – 15 1 5 pounds / December 12, 1791, New York." Pratt Collection, 2:156.
5.   Johnson and Tabor, *History and Architecture*, ill. 217, illustrates the house Pratt purchased from Eli Butler.
6.   In 1794 a clothier from Wiltshire, England, visited New England and noted the clothing of an American officer whom he saw near Hartford: "a blue coat of superfine cloth with scarlet facings and cuffs; a buff cassimere waistcoat and breeches." Henry Wansey, *Journal of an Excursion to the United States of America in the Summer of 1794* (Salisbury, Eng., 1796), 61. Cassimere or Kerseymere was a fine woollen cloth.

44 Mrs. Joseph Wright, 1792

Oil on canvas

46 x 36½ in. (116.8 x 92.7 cm.)

Signed and dated at lower center: "R. Earl Pinxt. 1792"

Inscribed on the back of the canvas: "Hannah Wright 1792 / AE – 74"

National Museum of American Art, Smithsonian Institution, Washington, D.C.

Museum purchase and gift of Joseph Alsop, 1975

45 Mrs. Richard Alsop, 1792

Oil on canvas

45⅝ x 36⅛ in. (115.9 x 91.8 cm.)

Signed and dated at lower center: "R. Earl Pinxt / 1792"

Inscribed on the back of the canvas: "Mary Alsop 1792 / AE.ͭ / 52"

National Museum of American Art, Smithsonian Institution, Washington, D.C.

Museum purchase and gift of Joseph Alsop, 1975

Earl's portraits of Hannah Wright and her daughter Mary Alsop were unusual in having been requested and paid for by two widows, both of whom were highly independent and self-sufficient. Hannah Gilbert (1718–1804) married the Middletown, Connecticut, merchant Joseph Wright, notable for founding one of the first brickyards in the state and instrumental in developing Middletown as a thriving port. She lived with her husband in a large house (built from the bricks of Joseph Wright's brickyard) on Main Street, and they operated a farm in the Westfield section of town. Her husband died in 1775, leaving Hannah Wright to manage the substantial estate.[1]

Earl captures a penetrating characterization of his elderly subject, reminiscent of such earlier works by Copley as *Mrs. Humphrey Devereaux* (1770–71; on loan at the National Art Gallery, Wellington, New Zealand).[2] Wright is seated in Earl's stock red upholstered armchair holding a book; she is placed against a backdrop of red drapery. Next to her, Earl depicts a large window view of the Connecticut River (or possibly a tributary, the Mattabeseck River), symbolizing the Wright and Alsop families' mercantile interests, which depended on river access to the sea.

Mary Wright Alsop (1740–1829) was the only child of Hannah and Joseph Wright. In 1760 she married her father's friend and business associate Richard Alsop (1726–76), also a leading Middletown merchant. Both families had close ties through their mercantile interests, as well as through their membership in the Episcopal Church. Mary

Alsop became a widow at the age of thirty-six, one year after the death of her father. She was left with eight children to raise, the eldest being fifteen and the youngest, an infant. Although her husband left an enormous estate, valued at 34,812 pounds 17 shillings, it consisted of widely scattered assets, including ships, dry goods, real estate holdings, and notes and bonds. Mary Alsop was left to sort out the estate as well as run the international mercantile business – a formidable task, since there was little readily available cash. It took her fourteen years, but she finally acquired the income from collecting and distributing the estate to free herself of the grave financial restrictions under which she had lived.[3]

With the benefit of their mother's guidance, all eight children distinguished themselves; the most famous child was her son Richard Alsop, Jr. (1761–1815), a prominent member of the Connecticut Wits. During her lifetime, she was acclaimed for her needlework, of which there are several surviving examples that demonstrate her skill.[4]

Earl's portrayal of this remarkable woman successfully captures her fortitude, intelligence, and strength of character. Tradition holds that she is seated in her parents' Westfield, Connecticut, house, with a view of the Mattabeseck River seen through the window.[5] She rests her left hand on what appears to be a silver snuffbox, reflected in the surface of the round-topped table (again reminiscent of Copley). In the eighteenth century women commonly used snuff; however, it is an unusual prop for a woman's portrait.[6]

The portraits descended in the Alsop family to Joseph Alsop, from whom they were acquired by the National Museum of American Art in 1975.[7]

Costume Notes In the portrait of Hannah Wright the costume brings out but does not overwhelm the character of the sitter, who is depicted with great affection and insight. The dress is clearly Wright's best, a formal and rather old-fashioned open gown of mushroom-colored damask; the large-scale stylized floral pattern is very much out of fashion for the 1790s, but it is an expensive silk, probably English, and the apron is swept aside to reveal more of it.[8] There are many elegant and individualistic touches in her costume: a shawl of black embroidered net, mittens of black knitted silk, and pale coral beads. Yet the head, always the most sensitive fashion barometer, reveals the age and status of the sitter. Instead of the large frizzed hairstyles and gauzy headdresses of high fashion, we see a modest mobcap of plain linen with side wings, tying in a bow under the chin.

To a European observer, there is in much of American portraiture of this period a curious dichotomy between the often plain features of many sitters (which the artists made no attempt to gloss over) and their expensive dresses (which the artists depicted with lavish detail). The mode for realistic portrayal and artistic honesty account for the artists' approach, as do the wishes of the sitters and a culture that exalted prosperity gained by hard work and self-reliance. Mary Alsop comes across as a tough businesswoman who enjoys one reward of hard work – fine clothing. She wears a dress of dark green watered silk[9] (dark colors were both fashionable and suitable to her age and status as a widow) and a collar and apron of embroidered muslin, whose painting is a tour de force – every detail of the flowers, flower baskets, and tassels can be picked out. Two pins keep the collar in place. Pins were an essential part of female attire in the eighteenth century, and their wardrobe budgets always included pin money. Unlike the modest mobcap worn by her mother, Alsop's version is a balloon of starched muslin edged with pleated, embroidered frills and trimmed with a white silk ribbon.   AR

1.   Curtis Wright, *Genealogical and Biographical Notices of Descendents of Sir John Wright of Kelvedon Hall, Essex, England; in America* (Carthage, Mo., 1915).

2.   This portrait is illustrated in Jules Prown, *John Singleton Copley*, 2 vols. (Cambridge, Mass., 1966), 1, plate 283.

3.   "Richard Alsop," MS, Alsop Family Papers, Box 1, Sterling Memorial Library, Yale University, New Haven, Conn.

4.   Jane Nylander, "Textiles, Clothing and Needlework," in *The Great River: Art and Society of the Connecticut Valley, 1635–1820*, exhib. cat. (Hartford, Conn., 1985), 402–3.

5.   Margaret Jackson, "Some Old Mattabeseck Families," *Connecticut Magazine* 8 (March–April 1901), 473–82.

6.   Catherine Jestin, *Powder Celestial: Snuff Boxes, 1700–1880* (New Haven, Conn., 1990), 5.

7.   Correspondence, Painting Files, National Museum of American Art, Smithsonian Institution, Washington, D.C.

8.   For much of the eighteenth century, fashions changed slowly, and because silks were expensive, they were sometimes kept for many years before they were made up. In America prized silks from England were often kept for some time before they were turned into gowns; there was also some residual Puritan feeling that to wear silks straight off the ships might be thought rather vulgar. The kind of silk that Wright wears would have been fashionable in the 1730s and for decades thereafter. By the 1770s such patterns had been increasingly replaced by plain silks and silks with small patterns; and the introduction of fashion plates in the 1770s accelerated changes in dress.

9.   Watered silk is a corded silk pressed between heated rollers so that the crushed cords reflect the light in wavelike patterns.

45

44

46 Colonel William Floyd, 1793

Oil on canvas

47 ⅛ x 35 ½ in. (119.7 x 90.2 cm.)

Signed and dated at lower right: "R. Earl 1793"

Technical note: a strip of canvas along the bottom has been trimmed off, thus obscuring a segment of the artist's signature

Independence National Historical Park, Philadelphia, 1973

Washington and Hartford only

During the 1790s, when his time was spent mainly in Connecticut, Earl made occasional trips to Long Island, where he received commissions to paint portraits of subjects who had some connection to Mason Fitch Cogswell and who were frequently related to Earl's Connecticut sitters. His most important commission on Long Island was for a portrait of Col. William Floyd (1734–1821), a signer of the Declaration of Independence and the member of a very wealthy family. The son of Nicoll Floyd and Tabitha Smith Floyd of Mastic, William became a major land proprietor at the age of eighteen, when he inherited the family's four-hundred-acre estate, Brookhaven. He spent seventeen years in public service—as a delegate to the Continental Congress, as a New York State senator, and as a representative to the U.S. Congress.[1]

With the British occupation of Long Island in 1776, the Floyd family fled to Connecticut. In 1780, William sent a memorial to the Connecticut Assembly documenting his great personal loss, claiming that Tories had seized his property and "[taken] on my estate a Considerable Quantity of Stock of Different kinds, the Greatest part of my Household furniture, and all my farming utensils."[2] Floyd returned to Mastic in 1783 and repaired the Floyd family farmhouse, and outbuildings, which had been built by his ancestors. The following year, Floyd's daughter, Mary, married Col. Benjamin Tallmadge, and the couple was later painted by Earl in Litchfield (cats. 37, 38). The artist also painted William Floyd's sister, Anna Smith (1792; private collection) of East Moriches, Long Island.[3]

Although Earl's portrait of Floyd is reminiscent of *Captain John Pratt* (cat. 43), painted the previous year, it is far less pretentious. Floyd assumes a commanding pose, standing on his property, with a full view of his ancestral home in the background, but the only signs of his affluence are the gold seals at his waist and his gold-topped cane.

In keeping with the simplicity of Floyd's taste, his mansion house is ancient in appearance, reflecting its original date of construction, thought to be 1724. Earl included the figure of a woman standing in the open doorway and two black servants in the front of the house.[4] The portrait celebrates Floyd's distinguished political role during the Revolution, as well as his determination to preserve the seventy-year-old Floyd estate. Floyd's grandson, William, later wrote to his father suggesting that the artist Samuel Waldo (1783–1861) be commissioned by the family "to paint out the old house in the background of grandfather's portrait." Fortunately, Earl's rendition of the house remained intact.[5]

The artist's signature and date at the lower right of the canvas was partially removed during an early restoration of the painting; however, William Sawitzky documented the signature and date before its partial removal.[6]

Asher B. Durand produced an engraving after Earl's portrait in 1818 for Joseph Delaplaine's *Pamphlet of Delaplaine's National Panzographia for the Reception of the Portraits of Distinguished Americans* (Philadelphia, 1818). The American artist Edward L. Henry (1841–1919) painted a copy of the portrait (Independence National Historical Park) in 1875. It descended in the Floyd family until given to the National Park Service in 1973 by Mrs. David Weld.

Costume Notes   The colonel is self-confident in his homespun, rather old-fashioned suit with coat, vest, and breeches of the same fabric, a green brown woollen stuff, possibly of American manufacture.[7] By the early 1790s the frock coat, with its high collar, was cut away at the sides, almost forming a swallowtail at the back. The vest was usually cut straight across at the waist; here the flapped pockets and diagonally cut lower skirts of the vest indicate a man of conservative tastes. There is not a single piece of trimming or adornment to the costume; under the high shirt collar is a plain linen stock, and only the smallest amount of shirt ruffle (also plain) can be seen. The bunch of gold seals hanging from the waist are for practical use and not for adornment. The hair, Floyd's own, is a compromise: the short crop on the top and at the sides (a style popularized during the revolutionary years in America and taken up in revolutionary Europe) is functional, and the longer curled hair in the back echoes the more formal styles of his youth. This portrait is impressive in its dignity and restraint and is as eloquent as any of Earl's depictions of dashing military officers; here the cane replaces the sword as an elegant accessory.   AR

1.   B. J. Lossing, *Biographical Sketches of the Signers of the Declaration of Independence* (New York, 1848), 63; *DAB*, 5:484; Louis Fanelli, "William Floyd," MS, Independence National Historical Park, Philadelphia.

2.   Quoted in Dean F. Failey, *Long Island Is My Nation*, exhib. cat. (Setauket, N.Y., 1976), 151.

3.   Elizabeth Mankin Kornhauser, *Ralph Earl: Artist-Entrepreneur* (Ann Arbor, Mich., 1989), 275, 322; which also documents Floyd's relation to Mason Fitch Cogswell's sister-in-law, Abigail Floyd Cogswell.

4.   It is not known that Floyd owned slaves.

5.   William Floyd to Nicoll Floyd, 1832, quoted in a facsimile of the original letter, Painting Files, Independence National Historical Park.

6.   William Sawitzky and Susan Sawitzky Papers, "Ralph Earl," New-York Historical Society, New York.

7.   By this time, woollen cloth was woven in a number of places in the area, including Hartford, Connecticut, where Jeremiah Wadsworth had helped to found the Hartford Woollen Manufactory in 1788.

46

47 Mrs. Charles Jeffery Smith, 1794

Oil on canvas

48 x 42 in. (121.9 x 106.7 cm.)

Signed and dated at lower left: "R. Earl pinxt 1794"

Technical note: a four-inch strip of canvas is attached at the
      top and bottom with seams

The New-York Historical Society, New York

Bryan Fund, 1975.28

While on Long Island in 1794, Earl painted Colonel Floyd's
(cat. 46) friend and neighbor Elizabeth Smith (1736–1816).
She was the daughter of Platt Smith and Mary Woolsey
Smith of Southhold, Long Island, and married her first
cousin, the Rev. Charles Jeffery Smith of Brookhaven in
1767. A graduate of Yale College (1757), Charles Smith was
a noted missionary, teacher, and minister.[1] After his death in
1770, Elizabeth cared for her only child, Elihu Platt Smith,
who was also painted by Earl (1794; private collection).
Elizabeth had close associations with many of Earl's Long
Island and Connecticut sitters: her sister, Abigail Smith
married Adam Babcock (cat. 3), and she was related to
Timothy and Mary (Woolsey) Dwight and to Mason Fitch
Cogswell's sister-in-law, Abigail Floyd Cogswell.[2]

   As was his custom in his Connecticut portraits, here
Earl did little to flatter his middle-aged subject. Instead,
he concentrated on commemorating Elizabeth Smith's role
in promoting silk manufacturing in Long Island. Seated in
Earl's stock red upholstered side chair, she is unraveling silk
cocoons. Her spectacles and red leather case are placed on a
round-topped table near a basket filled with cocoons, some
of which are already unraveled.

   The production of silk was promoted after the Revolution as a patriotic endeavor – a means of making the new
nation more independent of Britain. Connecticut took the
lead in the manufacture of silk thread. President Ezra Stiles
of Yale College promoted the planting of mulberry trees and
kept a diary of his own experiments in sericulture from 1763
to 1790. To further encourage the production of silk thread,
in 1784 the Connecticut legislature offered a bounty of ten
shillings for every one hundred mulberry trees and three
pence per ounce for raw silk.[3]

   The portrait remained in the Woolsey family until 1975,
when it was acquired by the New-York Historical Society.

Costume Notes Elizabeth Smith is shown in rather conservative dress, as befits a widow of her class. Her hair, a chestnut
color, unpowdered, is arranged rather carelessly under a
white muslin mobcap of moderate proportions – not the
close-fitting kind worn by elderly women (such as Hannah
Wright; cat. 44) nor the vast, puffed-out sort chosen by
younger women or those more interested in fashion (such
as Mary Alsop and Laura Wolcott, cats. 45 and 26). The
crossed-over fichu and sleeve ruffles are plain cotton. Over
Smith's shoulders is a mantle of black net threaded with red
ribbon, a slightly frivolous touch. The dress is a plain green
silk without any distinguishing characteristics.

   Smith's occupation in this portrait is perhaps more
interesting than her costume. She is stringing cocoons of
silk, which will then be unraveled preparatory to being
reeled into silk thread. Smith's introduction of sericulture
to her region was one of a number of experiments, some successful, in this field. The Wiltshire clothier Henry Wansey
noted, in 1794, that there were mulberry trees (on which
silkworms feed) at Wallingford, near Hartford, Connecticut. "At one house where I stopped, a young woman told
me that herself and sister had last year raised silk enough
to make eighteen yards of florentine [a light taffeta]."
Altogether, he said, the local community made three hundred yards a year.[4] It is not clear whether the silk was woven
locally or – as was usually the case – the reeled silk fibers
[raw silk] were sent to England for weaving.   AR

1.   Franklin Bowditch Dexter, *Biographical Sketches of the Graduates of Yale
College* (New York, 1907), 2:495–97.

2.   Elizabeth Mankin Kornhauser, *Ralph Earl: Artist-Entrepreneur* (Ann
Arbor, Mich., 1989), 275–76, 321–22.

3.   L. P. Brockett, *The Silk Industry in America* (Philadelphia, 1876), 30–
31; Albert H. Heusser, *The History of the Silk Dyeing Industry in the United
States* (Paterson, N.J., 1927), 93–99.

4.   Wansey, *Journal of an Excursion to the United States of America in the
Summer of 1794* (Salisbury, Eng., 1796), 64.

47

48

48 Benjamin S. Judah, 1794

Oil on canvas

48⅝ x 34½ in. (123.5 x 87.6 cm.)

Inscribed on the original stretcher: "Ralph Earl pinxt 1794"

Wadsworth Atheneum, Hartford, Connecticut

The Ella Gallup Sumner and Mary Catlin Sumner
    Collection, 1985

Once again Earl altered his style upon one of many return trips to New York by practicing a more formal manner in his portrait of this prominent city merchant. Benjamin Judah (1760–1831) was born in New York City, the son of Samuel Judah and Jessie Simcha Jonas Judah (Jessie Judah was also painted by Earl in 1794).[1] The Judahs were one of the most notable Jewish families in the city. Benjamin's paternal grandfather, Baruch Judah (1678–1774), helped to establish the first synagogue in New York, Congregation Shearith Israel. His father, Samuel, was a successful merchant and ardent patriot. Benjamin expanded the family trade connections established by his father and was a member of the prestigious Marine Society of New York. His extensive mercantile business was nearly destroyed during the War of 1812.[2]

In the portrait of Benjamin Judah the artist is concerned with establishing the prominence of his subject. Judah is formally posed, seated on a red damask upholstered side chair. Rather than depicting regional attributes, Earl creates a generalized effect, as seen in the landscape through the window. The receipt on which Judah rests his right hand, which is inscribed "Exchange for / 16507 Marks / The Usance of this Bill is . . . ," makes reference to the subject's international trade connections. Judah's urbanity is echoed in his stylish attire.

The portrait descended in the Judah family to Hildegard Whitehead Reed, the sitter's great-great-granddaughter. The portrait was purchased from the family by the Wadsworth Atheneum in 1984.

Costume Notes   This man of fashion has a touch of flamboyance in his appearance. His own personal taste must have dictated the formal powdered tye wig, a style at variance with the preference of most of his fellow Americans. The high-collared blue silk frock coat, the embroidered silk vest, and black satin knee breeches are elegant and formal. The artist has picked out such details as the glittering diamond paste buckles on the knee breeches, the tight cuffs on the coat sleeves, which have to be unbuttoned so the embroidered ruffles can be seen, the billowing white cravat, and the touch of blue silk, a glimpse of undervest, on his chest.[3]   AR

1.   Elizabeth Mankin Kornhauser, *Ralph Earl: Artist-Entrepreneur* (Ann Arbor, Mich., 1989), 298–99.

2.   *The Marine Society of the City of New York* (New York, 1933); Malcolm H. Stern, *First American Jewish Families* (Ohio and Waltham, Mass., 1978), 139–40; George Cohen, *The Jews in the Making of America* (Boston, 1924), 156.

3.   Wearing two vests was the fashion in the 1790s; the colors usually contrasted, and the top vest was buttoned to reveal the edge (or sometimes the lapel) of the under one. According to Flavius Josephus (*Jewish Antiquities*, written c. 93–94), in the first century A.D. colors were assigned to the twelve sons of Jacob, azure being Judah's color. For the symbolic colors of Jacob's sons, see A. Rubens, *A History of Jewish Costume* (London, 1973), 16. Whether this sky-blue vest was chosen by the sitter or suggested by the artist to pay tribute to the tribe of Judah is anyone's guess.

49 Huldah Bradley, 1794

Oil on canvas

44 x 32 in. (111.8 x 81.3 cm.)

Signed and dated at lower left: "R. Earl Pinxt. 1794"

Technical note: the original frame, since replaced, was nailed directly onto the canvas, obscuring the artist's signature

Museum of Fine Arts, Boston

Ellen Kelleran Gardner Fund, 1940

50 Lucy Bradley, 1794

Oil on canvas

44 1/8 x 31 5/16 in. (112.1 x 79.5 cm.)

Signed and dated at lower left: "R. Earl / Pinxt 1794"

The Detroit Institute of Art, Detroit, Michigan

Founders Society Purchase, Dexter M. Ferry, Jr., Fund, 1940

Ralph Earl returned to Greenfield Hill in 1794, where he painted the two daughters of Samuel Bradley and Sarah Wakeman Bradley, whom he had painted on his first visit to the town in 1788.[1] Samuel Bradley (1733–1804) was a successful merchant, shipowner, and farmer; one visitor to his house said, "This gentleman is a farmer of opulence." His daughters, Huldah Bradley (1773–1842) and Lucy Bradley (1768–1823), received a handsome estate at his death.[2] Both remained unmarried and lived out their lives on the Bradley family homestead, which overlooked Long Island Sound. Huldah evidently leased a portion of the house to a nephew, William Bradley, Jr., where he operated a shoe shop and helped to care for Huldah in her old age. The sisters also continued to operate the family farm. At the time of her death, Huldah left an estate worth $5,262.42.[3]

The Bradley sisters are gracefully posed in identical gowns against a background that forms one continuous landscape, a panoramic view of the beaches of Long Island across the sound with a turbulent sky above. In spite of their similar attire, Earl manages faithfully to distinguish their features (Huldah is arguably prettier), and he ably evokes the beauty of this particular region. A traveler to the town in 1788, also struck by the view, noted: "Greenfield is pleasantly situated . . . we see the sand cliffs of Long Island, eighteen miles distant."[4] And in a poem *Greenfield Hill* (1794), Timothy Dwight, a native, said with words what Earl portrayed so well with paint: "Sweet-smiling village! loveliest of hills . . . [with] every charm, that rural nature yields."[5]

The portraits were intended to hang side by side; so they remained in the Bradley house well into the nineteenth century. *Lucy Bradley* was purchased from a family descendant, Louis E. Morehouse, by the Detroit Institute of Arts in 1940. *Huldah Bradley* was sold by the same descendant to the Museum of Fine Arts in Boston in the same year.[6]

Costume Notes   Sisters close in age were often dressed in similar clothing, a practice that continued into the present century. Here the Bradley sisters have chosen to be painted in gowns of pale pink silk tied around the waist with a white sash; they both wear buffons of starched white muslin with a spotted frill edged in silk. Around their wrists are white silk ribbons, a style introduced by such fashionable beauties at the English court as Georgiana, duchess of Devonshire, in the mid-1780s.[7] The sisters' hairstyles are also similar, loose curls with unraveling ringlets; Lucy's hair, however, does not seem to be curled as skillfully as her sister's, a detraction in an age when straight hair was anathema. By the mid-1790s, although the artificial-looking frizzed, powdered, and pomaded hairstyles were in decline and a more natural style was in vogue, curls or waves were still de rigueur, and since the hair was still worn long, considerable time and expertise were required in its arrangement. Apart from the facial differences, the sisters are distinguished by their accessories. Lucy holds a painted fan and Huldah a parasol or umbrella of dark green silk.   AR

1.   Elizabeth Mankin Kornhauser, *Ralph Earl: Artist-Entrepreneur* (Ann Arbor, Mich., 1989), 264–65. Earl also painted portraits of Walter Bradley (1788; private collection) and Mrs. Walter Bradley (Sarah Bradley) and their daughter Sally (1788; Louisiana State Museum), the son, daughter-in-law, and granddaughter of Samuel and Sarah.

2.   Samuel Davis, "Journal of a Tour to Connecticut – Autumn of 1789," in *Proceedings of the Massachusetts Historical Society* (Boston, 1869–70), 18. Samuel Bradley, Probate Inventory, Fairfield, 1804, Reel 300, Pkt. 1036, and his Will and Codicil, 1803, CSL, indicate that he divided his estate, worth $28,569, between his sons and daughters, leaving his sons twice as much as his daughters. His inventory included 308 acres worth $21,576 and such luxury items as a "Chaise and Harness," valued at $50.00. There is also mention of a slave: "Negro man named Coffee with his bed and bedding $120.00."

3.   Huldah Bradley, Probate Inventory, Will and Codicil, Fairfield, 1843, Reel 300, no. 993, CSL.

4.   Davis, "Journal of a Tour to Connecticut," 18.

5.   *Greenfield Hill*, in *The Major Poems of Timothy Dwight (1752–1817) with a Dissertation on the History, Eloquence, and Poetry of the Bible*, ed. William J. McTaggart and William K. Bottorff (Gainesville, Fla., 1969).

6.   Barbara Neville Parker, "Huldah Bradley by Ralph Earl," *Bulletin of the Museum of Fine Arts* 28 (August 1940), 53–55; Alan Burroughs, "Two American Portraits," *Detroit Institute of Arts Bulletin* 21, no. 1 (October 1941).

7.   See her portrait by John Downman (1787; Duke of Devonshire collection, Chatsworth).

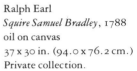

Ralph Earl
Squire Samuel Bradley, 1788
oil on canvas
37 x 30 in. (94.0 x 76.2 cm.)
Private collection.

Ralph Earl
Mrs. Samuel Bradley (Sarah Wakeman), 1788
oil on canvas
37 x 30 in. (94.0 x 76.2 cm.)
Private collection.

49

50

51 Jared Lane, 1796

Oil on canvas
48 x 36 in. (121.9 x 91.4 cm.)
Signed and dated at lower left: "R. Earl Pinx / 1796"
Kennedy Galleries, New York

52 Mrs. Jared Lane (Apphia Ruggles), 1796

Oil on canvas
48½ x 36 in. (123.2 x 91.4 cm.)
Signed and dated at lower left: "R. Earl Pinxt / 1796"
Private collection

Upon his return to New Milford in 1796, Earl painted the portraits of Jared and Apphia Lane, as well as a landscape of their recently completed house (cat. 53), one of three such landscapes he painted in Litchfield County that year.

Jared Lane (1745–1818) was the son of Robert Lane and Mary Thatcher Lane of Killingworth, Connecticut. He studied law with his uncle Partridge Thatcher of New Milford and in 1786 married Apphia Ruggles (1755–1818), daughter of Lazarus Ruggles (fig. 1.37) and Hannah Bostwick Ruggles (fig. 1.38), also of New Milford. In 1789 the couple moved from Sharon (they had been boarding with Apphia's sister and brother-in-law, Judson and Mabel Canfield; cat. 54) to New Milford, where they purchased fifty acres of land and a "dwelling house" from Apphia's father in the Still River Neck district of New Milford. Between 1791 and 1792, while boarding with the Ruggleses, the Lanes built either a new addition to the Ruggles house or a completely new house on the property. There they raised three children, and Jared operated a farm and established a nursery. Jared Lane introduced the Lombardy poplar as an ornamental shade tree; in the nineteenth century, it became the favored planting for most village main streets, including New Milford, where they "spread over the town in great profusion." He also functioned as a land agent, negotiating the sale of land in Vermont and Connecticut.[1]

Upon the completion of the house, Jared took advantage of Earl's presence in New Milford, commissioning portraits of himself, his wife, and a landscape view of the house and surrounding acreage. Jared's meticulous records of his various expenses are a rare resource for determining Earl's working methods and life-style. In a separate section of one account book, Jared Lane itemized the exact expenses involved in boarding Ralph Earl and his wife and paying for certain living expenses, as well as the cost of Earl's art materials and the price of each painting.[2] Because of the rarity

of such specific information, the entries are reproduced here in full.

As the ledger indicates, Jared Lane arranged to have his father-in-law board the artist and his wife while Earl painted the three commissioned works. Jared paid Lazarus Ruggles two pounds ten shillings for two weeks' board in June, during which time Earl painted Apphia's portrait, and an additional two pounds ten shillings for eighteen days in July, during which time Earl painted Jared's portrait and the landscape of the house, for a total of five pounds (approximately seventeen dollars). In addition, Jared noted charges for extra expenses, such as washing clothes and providing coffee. Of particular interest are the listings for "Spirits" and "Rum," which Earl required at work. While painting Apphia's portrait, he drank one gallon and two quarts of spirits and three pints of rum; while painting Jared's, one gallon of spirits.

The account books document the commonplace practice of boarding workmen and supplying them with alcoholic beverages while they carried out specialized tasks; for instance, when his new house was constructed, he provided board and alcohol for the plasterers, masons, and so forth.[3] At the same time, many of Earl's patrons abhorred this practice, including Benjamin Tallmadge, Moses Seymour, and David Buell, who were members of a temperance organization in nearby Litchfield. In 1789 they issued the following statement. "It is most sincerely to be regretted that from a mistaken idea that distilled spirits are necessary to laboring men, to counteract the influence of heat, and give relief from severe fatigue, that a most valuable class of citizens have been led to contract a habit of such dangerous tendency."[4] In certain respects, Earl's life-style as an itinerant artist in New England differed little from that of his fellow craftsmen.

In addition to paying for artists' materials (which are discussed in greater detail in chapter 3), Jared Lane paid Earl fifteen dollars for each portrait but no single amount for the landscape. Thus the total expenditure came to nearly twenty-four pounds, the equivalent of approximately eighty dollars. Earl was advertising prices of sixty dollars for full-length portraits and thirty dollars for "the smaller size" that year.[5] Arrangements for payment apparently varied greatly. In this case, Earl received a set sum for each portrait plus living expenses and artists' materials. In this instance, artists' materials were obtained locally, the varnish purchased at Elijah Boardman's shop. The local cabinetmaker, Jonathan Mygatt, made frames and prepared the canvases. The extensive inventory of personal effects taken at the time of Jared Lane's death does not list the two portraits or landscape.[6]

Earl's portraits of the Lanes are accomplished renditions, and the Lanes are suitably modest in appearance, reflecting their moderate means. Jared Lane is seated in a

Entries from Jared Lane's Account Book, 1796

May 23	2 Qts of Spirits for R. Earl while painting Mrs. Lane's Portrait	£	5.	0
	Prussian Blue 4^d & Spirits of Turpentine for Mrs. Lane's Portrait 2^d		0.	6
	3 oz of Stone Yellow 3^d & 1 oz of Vermillion 1 for Mrs. Lane's Portrait		1.	3
June 2	3 Pints of Rum for R. Earl while painting Mrs. Lane's Portrait		3.	9
June 4	Capt. Lazarus Ruggles By Boarding Mr. Ralph Earl while painting Mrs. Lane's Portrait 2 weeks [and] Boarding Mrs. Earl 2 weeks	2.10.	0	
	By Boarding Ralph Earl and his wife from July 10 to July 28; 18 days while he was taking a portrait and a landscape for J. Lane	2.10.	0	
June 11	Paid Ralph Earl for Painting Mrs. Lane's Portrait $15		4.10	
	Paid for Mr. & Mrs. Earl's Board while doing it		2.10	
June 14	Paid for Washing for Mr. & Mrs. Earl		2.	0
June 16	One Gal^n. of Spirits had June 10th for R. Earl while painting here		11.	6
	One pound of Coffee for Mr. & Mrs. Earl while he is painting here		1.	9
	Paid Jonathan Mygatt for making a Frame, straining on the Cloth and painting the same for Mrs. Lane's Portrait		4.	9
June 23	1 ½ yds. of Russia Sheeting for Jared Lane's Portrait		5.	3
July 15	½ oz of Prussian Blue 1/. Ivory Black and 1 lb of White Lead 1/. and ½ lb of Glue for J. L. Portrait	1.	3.	0
	Sugar of Lead and Spirits of Turpentine for J. Lane's Portrait	0.	9.	0
July 21	One Gal^n of Spirits for Mr. Earl while Painting J. Lane's Portrait		12.	0
Aug. 3	Paid Ralph Earl $15 for Painting J. Lane's Portrait	4.10.	0	
Sept. 19	Paid Elijah Boardman for Copal Varnish for 2 Portraits and one Landscape		3.	0
Sept. 30	Spirits of Turpentine to pay [back] some Borrowed to Varnish Portraits		1.	0

Source: Jared Lane, Account Book, private collection.
Note: Amounts are in pounds, shillings, and pence. Pounds are also symbolized by a slash (1/), pence by the letter *d*.

green-leather-covered side chair[7] and holding a magnifying mirror in his left hand and a letter inscribed "o Jn 24 / Jared Lane / New Milford / Connecticut" in his right. Earl includes a reference to Jared's nursery of poplar trees, the saplings seen through the window.

Apphia is shown seated in a Windsor side chair in a landscape setting; the composition is nearly identical to that of her sister's portrait, *Mrs. Judson Canfield* (cat. 54). Apphia wears a gold locket on a chain, loosely hung around her neck, and holds a fan in her lap. A view of the Housatonic River, which flowed by the Lane house, is seen in the middle ground, with distant hills beyond.

The portraits of Jared and Apphia Lane remained in the family and were on loan to the Metropolitan Museum

51

52

in 1945. The portrait of Apphia later entered a private collection, and the portrait of Jared has remained with the present owner.

Costume Notes   A portrait similar to Jared Lane's in sobriety of costume and indifference to fashion, is that of Thomas Shaw (fig. 1.34). The nonmatching coat and breeches of brown woollen cloth are probably of American manufacture. The cream-colored vest is open to midchest, the top edges falling to the shoulders. The unpretentious sitter has no compunction about being portrayed with a receding hairline.

Apphia Lane takes more interest in fashion than her husband. She wears a long-sleeved pink silk (possibly satin) dress, tied around the waist with a fringed sash; black silk wristbands remained popular. The most elaborate part of her costume is her cap of white gauze or muslin, with pendant lappets (long bands or streamers) looped up at the back.   AR

1.   Samuel Orcutt, *History of the Towns of New Milford and Bridgewater, Connecticut, 1703–1882* (Hartford, Conn., 1882), 300–302. Jared Lane, Account Books, private collection, indicate that he was selling his poplar trees. My thanks to John Wright for providing biographical information about his ancestor Jared Lane, as well as access to Jared Lane's original papers.
2.   Jared Lane, Account Book.
3.   For example, he lists the following in regard to the construction of his new house: "Dec. [1791] To Cash paid for 2 Qts. of Rum for the Plasterers" and in May "To cash pd for 1 Qt. Rum & Bottle for the Masons while toping out the chimney."
4.   Quoted in Alain C. White, *The History of the Town of Litchfield, Connecticut, 1720–1920* (Litchfield, 1920), 252.
5.   *Litchfield Weekly Monitor and Agricultural Register*, May 18, 1796.
6.   The omission of portraits from personal inventories is documented in Elizabeth Mankin Kornhauser and Christine Skeeles Schloss, "Painting and Other Pictorial Arts," in *The Great River: Art and Society of the Connecticut Valley, 1635–1820*, exhib. cat. (Hartford, Conn., 1985), 135.
7.   Jared Lane, Probate Inventory, New Milford, 1818, CSL, lists "1 green chair with cushion used by J. L."

53   Landscape of the Ruggles Homestead, 1796

Oil on canvas

38 x 52 in. (127.3 x 92.7 cm.)

Technical note: the canvas is in three pieces with a vertical and a short horizontal seam

Corporate Art Collection, Reader's Digest
Association, 1948

Jared Lane kept a detailed account book that documents the construction of a new house or wing on the property he had acquired in 1789 from his father-in-law, Lazarus Ruggles.[1] Lane's property in the Still River Neck section of New Milford, later called Lanesville, was located several miles south of the town center. According to the account book, John Couch contracted to build "the Northern part of the House" as well as a "Waggon House" beginning in January 1791, and work was completed at the end of 1792. There are various references in his records to the "new house" or the "northern" part of the house and the "old" or "southern" part of the house. It is unclear whether Lane simply built a large addition to the original Orange Warner farm or whether he built a new house nearby on the property.[2]

Earl created a picturesque setting for his landscape of the Lane house, conveying some of the pretensions of English country-house painting. The house is carefully rendered, including the Palladian features that relate it stylistically to both the Canfield house (cat. 54) and the Boardman house (cat. 58). A cupola crowns the top. The house is set back from the surrounding landscape, with the Housatonic River winding across the foreground. There are well-maintained fields, recently planted trees, and in front of the house, a white post fence running along the road. In the distance are gently rolling hills, typical of the region.

The landscape remained in the Ruggles-Lane house, which was inherited by Jared and Apphia Lane's three children. Their daughter, Maria Apphia, lived in the house with her husband, Dr. Amaziah Wright. The house, with the landscape, descended in the Wright family until 1948, when Kennedy Galleries of New York sold the landscape to a private collection.[3]

1.   Jared Lane, Account Book, "Record of Building Costs Materials, Labor, Interest, 1791–1817," private collection.
2.   The house that still stands on the property appears to be the original Orange Warner farmhouse, built around 1765. There is no evidence of a house resembling the one in Earl's landscape or the one Jared Lane documents the construction of; the latter included several mantelpieces and at least one chimney.
3.   Albert Reese, "A Newly Discovered Landscape by Ralph Earl," *Art in America* 36 (January 1948), 49–53.

53

54 Landscape View of the Canfield House, c. 1796

Oil on canvas
34 ⅝ x 72 ⅛ in. (88.0 x 183.2 cm.)
The Litchfield Historical Society, Litchfield, Connecticut

During a return visit to Litchfield County in 1796, Earl made his first trip to Sharon, where he painted the portraits of Judson Canfield and his wife, Mabel Ruggles Canfield, as well as a group portrait of their three children, Henry, Julia, and Eliza Canfield (Litchfield Historical Society). Probably in the same year, 1796, he painted a panoramic landscape of the outskirts of Sharon, including what, according to tradition, represents the Canfields' recently built house. The town is at the left, beyond the grouping of three large trees.

Judson Canfield (1759–1840) was the son of Col. Samuel Canfield and Elizabeth Judson Canfield of New Milford. After graduating from Yale College in 1782, Judson prepared for a career in law, taking over the law practice of his uncle, John Canfield of Sharon, upon his sudden death in 1787. The previous year Judson had married Mabel Ruggles (b. 1760), daughter of Lazarus Ruggles and Hannah Bostwick Ruggles of New Milford. Judson served as a member of the House of Representatives from 1791 to 1809.[1] While in Sharon, in addition to practicing law, Judson dealt extensively in real estate, buying and selling numerous tracts of land (thirteen tracts had houses on them).[2] In 1815 the Canfields invested large sums of money in Ohio Western Reserve lands and moved out west to establish the town of Canfield, Ohio. Evidently unhappy in this remote region, Mabel encouraged the family to move back east, to New York City, where they spent the remainder of their years.[3]

Because Judson Canfield was so active in buying and selling properties in Sharon, it is difficult to document the identity of the house Earl represents in the landscape. According to available sources, the Canfields resided in a house that they built in 1787 on property purchased from David Boland that same year. The property was located on the west side of Town Street, south of the meetinghouse, "with an old potash house standing thereon."[4] The house Earl depicts, however, is located outside the town center, on a toll road (a stone tollhouse or tavern is seen at the right). A figure stands in the doorway, and a sign inscribed with the letter "L" hangs from a post.

The house itself is situated in the middle ground, its construction reflecting the new Palladian style introduced by such local architects as William Sprats. Earl provides a view of two (of the possible four) formal entries, on the front and side of the house. A white fence and semicircular carriage drive are in front of the house, with a stone well to the left. Four formal entryways are characteristic of Connecticut houses built by William Sprats and Thomas Hayden. The Canfield house bears a strong stylistic resemblance to the Boardman house in New Milford (cat. 58), built by Sprats in 1793.

Earl rendered the lands surrounding the house in detail, though the ragged cliffs to the right do not appear to be typical of the rolling hills of this region, and the stone bridge and three geese on the river are most likely picturesque additions. Still, a river called the Oblong River ran near a toll road to the southwest of the town center, so there may, in fact, be some accuracy of detail.[5] Whether the house Earl depicts here was the Canfield homestead in 1796 remains a question.

Landscape of the Canfield House was given by Judson Canfield to his daughter, Eliza Canfield Tallmadge, who in turn left it to her daughter, the second Mary Floyd Tallmadge, wife of Edward Woodruff Seymour. She gave the painting to the Litchfield Historical Society in 1917.[6]

1. Charles F. Sedgwick, *History of the Town of Sharon* (Amenia, N.Y., 1898), 116; Franklin Bowditch Dexter, *Biographical Sketches of the Graduates of Yale College* (New York, 1907), 3:215–16.
2. My thanks to Jeanne Majdalany, Sharon Historical Society, for this information.
3. Judson Canfield purchased 171 acres in Canfield, Ohio, for five thousand dollars; my thanks to Mrs. Richard Crossen, historian, Canfield, Ohio.
4. Sharon Land Records, Town Hall, Sharon, 42:578, 43:102, 44:44–45; Leonard Twynham, "Colonial Sharon–'Fairest of Ten Thousand,'" in *Lure of the Litchfield Hills* 3 (September 1931), 19; Sedgwick, *History of Sharon*, 68–69, 116. My thanks to Elizabeth McClintock for gathering this information.
5. Map of Sharon, c. 1853, CSL.
6. My thanks to Lisa C. Kightlinger, Litchfield Historical Society, for this information.

Ralph Earl
Judge Judson Canfield, 1796
oil on canvas
48½ x 36 in. (123.2 x 91.4 cm.)
Collection of the Litchfield Historical Society, Litchfield, Conn.

Ralph Earl
Mrs. Judson Canfield (Mabel Ruggles), 1796
oil on canvas
48 x 36½ in. (123.2 x 91.4 cm.)
Collection of the Litchfield Historical Society, Litchfield, Conn.

54

55 Mrs. Elijah Boardman and Son, c. 1796

Oil on canvas

85 ¼ x 56 ¼ in. (214.0 x 142.9 cm.)

Technical note: the canvas is pieced with a vertical seam

The Henry E. Huntington Library and Art Gallery, San Marino, California

Virginia Steele Scott Collection, 1980

Ralph Earl returned to New Milford in 1796 and painted this portrait of Mary Anna Boardman on a scale as grand as that of his earlier portrait of her husband (cat. 29), painted seven years earlier. Mary Anna Whiting (1767–1848) was the daughter of Dr. William Whiting and Anna Mason Whiting of Great Barrington, Massachusetts. She married Elijah Boardman in September 1792, and the couple moved into a new mansion house when it was completed in 1793. Mary Anna and Elijah had six children, the first-born, William Whiting (1794–1871), appears here with his mother.[1]

In the portrait, Earl presents Mary Anna seated, holding her child. He includes his standard compositional elements: an elaborate carpet, red drapery, and a landscape view of the Housatonic River, which ran behind the Boardman house.[2] She is dressed in fashionable attire, suited to her role as the wife of New Milford's leading merchant.

Mary Anna Boardman left a memoir of her life that was edited and published by her son-in-law.[3] The portrait descended in the Boardman family until 1973, when it was acquired by Hirschl and Adler Galleries, New York. It was purchased by the Virginia Steele Scott Foundation for the Huntington Library in 1980.

Costume Notes   Shades of salmon and coral were very popular for dresses in the eighteenth century, and Mary Anna Boardman wears an elegant gown of coral-colored silk. A pleated muslin collar with an embroidered edge is wrapped around her bodice. At her waist is a sash of *chiné* silk, with a design of flowers on a white ground, bordered with dark green.[4] The floral touch echoes her headdress, which is composed of flowers and bunches of white silk ribbon.[5] The hair is elaborately curled all over the head, with long ringlets falling over the shoulders; when formally dressed (as in this portrait), many ladies would resort to false hair if their own was not sufficient.[6] A contrast to the frivolity of the headdress can be seen in the rather masculine felt riding, or outdoor, hat with its wide silk ribbon band and oval buckle. The child, dressed in his baby frock of white cotton, holds a silver and coral rattle and teething ring; coral, according to long-established tradition, was supposed to protect children from evil and bring them good luck.   AR

1.   Charlotte Goldthwaite, *Boardman Family Genealogy, 1525–1895* (Hartford, Conn., 1895), 334–35.
2.   Mary Anna Boardman, Probate Inventory, New Milford, 1850, Reel 1023, no. 294, gives a room-by-room inventory. The South Front Room contained "45 yds. carpet . . . $40."
3.   John F. Schroeder, ed., *Memoir of the Life and Character of Mrs. Mary Anna Boardman* (New Haven, Conn., 1849).
4.   Chiné was a textile design produced by dyeing the warp threads before weaving, which produced a slightly blurred effect; the eighteenth-century English term was clouded.
5.   Almost certainly the flowers in the headdress would be artificial, made of scraps of silk and linen. The manufacture of these decorations was a thriving specialist business in Boston.
6.   Until the end of the 1790s, when hair was often cut short *a l'antique,* the complicated hairstyles in fashion sometimes demanded the use of false hair. The *Times* of London in 1795 advertised "chignons of braids in 14 shades of brown . . . Brunswick fillets with curls . . . tetes, borders and every article in ornamental hair. Chignons changed, when not approved of, if not powdered." Quoted in C. W. Cunnington and P. Cunnington, *Handbook of English Costume in the Eighteenth Century*, rev. ed. (London, 1972), 386. The Cunningtons also quote Jane Austen as saying in 1799 that "flowers are very much worn." Ibid., 387.

57

56

56 Sherman Boardman, 1796

Oil on canvas

46 15/16 x 36 1/8 in. (119.3 x 91.6 cm.)

Signed and dated at lower left: "R. Earl Pinxt 1796"

The New Milford Historical Society, New Milford,
Connecticut

57 Mrs. Sherman Boardman (Sarah Bostwick), 1796

Oil on canvas

47 5/16 x 35 15/16 in. (120.1 x 91.3 cm.)

Signed and dated at lower left: "R. Earl Pinxt 1796"

The New Milford Historical Society, New Milford,
Connecticut

Earl had painted stylish portraits of the children of Sherman and Sarah Boardman during his first visit to New Milford in 1789. He returned to the town seven years later and painted far plainer images of the senior Boardmans, similar in their severity to the portraits of their relations Nathaniel and Tamar Taylor (cats. 31, 32).

Sherman Boardman (1728–1814) was the only son of the first minister of New Milford, the Rev. Daniel Boardman, an original settler of the town. Sherman inherited his father's lands and later acquired additional acreage for his sizable farm on the Housatonic River north of the town. He married Sarah Bostwick (1730–1818) of New Milford in 1755. Their house, built at the time of their marriage, still stands at Boardman's Bridge. A leading taxpayer, Sherman Boardman was active in various official posts, among them, representative to the General Assembly, deacon of the Congregational Church, and captain in the militia.[1]

In his portrait, Sherman is seated in Earl's stock red upholstered chair and is studying a map of Hungary, so inscribed. According to his family, Sherman was "celebrated for his attainments in geography," owning at least one book on the subject.[2]

Sarah Bostwick, the eldest daughter of Nathaniel Bostwick of New Milford, bore seven children, whom she helped educate. Having received a "better education than usual" for this period and having taught in the "common

schools" before her marriage, she was "competent to teach her children the first rudiments of knowledge" and to "contribute to their intellectual discipline."[3] Sarah's portrait is similar in composition to that of her husband, and her attire has as sober a style and color range. The landscape in her portrait appears to represent an orchard.

Both Boardman portraits remained in the family until they were given to the New Milford Historical Society in the 1940s.[4]

Costume Notes   Sherman Boardman wears an old-fashioned middle-class costume: black silk coat, vest, breeches, and stockings. The linen is plain. A silver buckle fastens the breeches at the knee. He seems to wear his own hair, which is naturally white; it is cut short at the sides and curls to the top of his coat collar at the back.

Sarah Boardman wears a black silk gown with elbow-length sleeves, which are edged with a white muslin frill. Her lower arms are covered with black mittens of fine cotton or silk gauze; the artist has shown the ties of fine silk or cotton that hold the mittens in place, which look like black threads where they reach the sleeve ruffle. Over her bosom Sarah wears a starched muslin kerchief, and over her shoulders a larger shawl of white spotted muslin. The white mobcap tied under her chin is trimmed with striped ribbon. Two touches of frivolity include the necklace of gold beads and the ivory fan painted with gold.   AR

1.   Charlotte Goldthwaite, *Boardman Family Genealogy, 1525–1895* (Hartford, Conn., 1895), 274–75; Samuel Orcutt, *History of the Towns of New Milford and Bridgewater, Connecticut, 1703–1882* (Hartford, Conn., 1882), 55–59.

2.   John F. Schroeder, ed., *Memoir of the Life and Character of Mrs. Mary Anna Boardman* (New Haven, Conn., 1849), 395. Sherman Boardman, Probate Inventory, New Milford, 1814, Reel 1023, Pkt. 296, CSL, lists one volume, "Moll's Geography."

3.   Quoted in Schroeder, ed., *Memoir of Mary Anna Boardman*, 397. For biographical information, see Goldthwaite, *Boardman Genealogy*, 274–75.

4.   The Boardman portraits are listed with a value of thirty dollars in Sherman Boardman's probate inventory.

58 Houses Fronting New Milford Green, c. 1796

Oil on canvas

48 x 54 ⅛ in. (121.9 x 137.5 cm.)

Technical note: the canvas is in three pieces, with a horizontal seam and with a vertical seam at the lower left

The Metropolitan Museum of Art, New York

Lent by Cornelia Boardman Service

Upon his return to New Milford in 1796, Earl painted a landscape view of Elijah Boardman's recently built house and shop and took a portrait of his wife, Mary Anna Whiting Boardman, and their son (cat. 55). In the landscape, Earl included, at the right, a view of the adjacent Bostwick or "Long house," in the southern half of which Elijah and his brother Daniel had first operated their dry-goods store. By the time this landscape was executed, Elijah had acquired the house and property.[1]

When he married Mary Anna Whiting in September 1792, the house was under construction; the couple did not move in until the end of the following year.[2] The Palladian-style house (which is still standing on Town Street) is attributed to William Sprats, who built a large number of houses in Litchfield County, many of them for Earl's sitters.[3] Of substantial size for the period, the house has an imposing front entry, its distinguishing feature. The pedimented pavilion projects beyond the main house and rests on four Ionic columns. The side entry is similar to the one on the Canfield house (cat. 54). An elaborate white fence, with urn-shaped finials on the posts, surrounds the house, protecting it from the road in the foreground. Next to the main house is a large driveway leading to Elijah's mercantile store. The neatly tended grounds with a gazebo on the side lawn run down to the Housatonic River behind the house. Earl includes the recently planted saplings that line Town Street and frames the landscape with two large trees in the upper corners. The pink and blue sky and hazy sunlight imbue the thriving village scene with an overall sense of well-being.

Landscape paintings of American regional scenery were extremely rare before the nineteenth century, and here Earl has accurately documented the architecture of the period, as well as conveyed the growing prosperity of this town. Elijah Boardman listed this landscape in his inventory of personal effects: "Mansion House Landscape . . . $5.00."[4]

1.   Land Records, Town Hall, New Milford, indicate that Daniel and Elijah Boardman purchased the southern half of the Bostwick house from Hannah Bostwick, widow of Daniel, and her son Samuel Bostwick, Jr., on December 20, 1784, for two hundred pounds. In April 1792 the brothers purchased the second, northern, half of the house.

2.   John F. Schroeder, ed., *Memoir of the Life and Character of Mrs. Mary Anna Boardman* (New Haven, Conn., 1849), 397.

3.   William L. Warren, "William Sprats, Master Joiner: Connecticut's Federalist Architect," *Connecticut Antiquarian* 9 (December 1957), 14–20.

4.   Elijah Boardman, Probate Inventory, New Milford, 1824, no. 288, CSL.

58

59 Mrs. Noah Smith and Her Children, 1798

Oil on canvas

64 x 85 ¾ in. (162.6 x 217.8 cm.)

Signed and dated at the lower left: "R. Earl Pinxt 1798"

Technical note: the canvas is in two pieces, with one
horizontal seam

The Metropolitan Museum of Art, New York

Gift of Edgar William and Bernice Chrysler Garbisch, 1964

Earl painted the most ambitious portrait of his career in
1798 in Bennington, Vermont, where he was commissioned to take a grand-scale group portrait of Chloe Smith
and her five children. He painted a separate portrait of her
husband. Although the Smiths were clearly prominent citizens of Vermont, one wonders what inspired the desire for
such elaborate pictorial images of themselves. Group portraits were rather rare in eighteenth-century America and
undoubtedly novel in Bennington.[1] Pamela Sedgwick, in
nearby Stockbridge, Massachusetts, had, however, considered a similar group portrait of herself and her children in
the previous year but felt the price for "full lengths" would
make the portrait too expensive (see cat. 59).

Noah Smith (1754–1838), originally a native of Suffield, Connecticut, graduated from Yale College in 1778 and
was acquainted with a number of Earl's Connecticut sitters.
He married Chloe Burrall (1757–1810), the daughter of
Col. Charles Burrall and Abigail Kellogg Burrall of Canaan,
Connecticut, in 1779; she was related to the Boardman
family of New Milford.[2] In the same year, Noah was admitted to the bar of the Superior Court of Vermont. He
delivered a speech in Bennington on the first anniversary of
the Battle of Bennington, in August 1778. Three years later,
the Smiths settled in Bennington, where Noah became a
prominent lawyer and was appointed state attorney.

The year Earl painted the Smiths' portraits Noah had
just been reelected a supreme court judge. He succeeded his
brother, Israel Smith, ousted because of his anti-Federalist
position. Noah also became the first grand master of the
Masonic Lodge in the state of Vermont. According to the
family history, his portrait hung in the Masonic Lodge in
Burlington in the nineteenth century. The Smiths spent
their final years in Milton, Vermont.[3]

In the full-length portrait, Noah Smith is shown in a
professional capacity; he is seated next to a table on which is
a large map of Bennington and underneath, a globe. In the
background are shelves of books, including Samuel Johnson's *Lives of the Poets* and Alexander Pope's translation of
the *Iliad*.

The Smiths had ten children, of whom five lived to

maturity. They are represented in the group portrait and
include (from left to right) Henry, Daniel, Noah, Jr.,
Eliza, and Celia, who is in her mother's lap. Their mother,
Chloe Smith, remains seated in a red upholstered side chair,
the picture of maternal affection, grasping the foot of her
youngest child, a gesture also seen in *Mrs. William Taylor
and Son Daniel* (cat. 34). Earl has varied the poses of the children and assigned each an attribute: Henry, standing, holds
a cane; Daniel is awkwardly posed on the sofa holding a map
of the world; Noah, Jr., stands on a footstool holding a hat
filled with grapes (a grape arbor is behind the figure); and
Eliza stands near her mother, holding posies. Earl includes
his standard props: red drapery behind the figure of Chloe
Smith, a patterned carpet, and a vista behind the figures of
the children.

Earl's *Mrs. Noah Smith and Her Children* inspired a simi-
lar, but naive, interpretation by his son Ralph E. W. Earl,
Family Portrait, which was painted in 1804 in the region of
Springfield, Massachusetts. Earl's son was likely with his

Ralph Earl
Noah Smith, 1798
oil on canvas
64 ¼ x 42 ¼ in. (163.2 x 107.3 cm.)
Goodman Fund, 1956.126. © 1990, The Art Institute of Chicago,
all rights reserved.

father in Bennington at this time, and the Smith portrait undoubtedly made an impression on the fledgling painter.

The senior Earl's portrait was purchased from the great-great-grandson of Celia Smith, Winthrop Barnes, by Col. Edgar William and Bernice Chrysler Garbisch, who gave it to the Metropolitan Museum of Art in 1964.[4] A copy of this portrait, probably nineteenth-century, is in the collection of the Art Institute of Chicago.

Costume Notes   Chloe Smith's costume is more comfortable than fashionable, although her high-waisted gown anticipates the neoclassical style of the turn of the century. Here it is worn for ease, either because of pregnancy or for post-childbirth comfort; it is a handsome brown silk, made all in one, a style known as a round gown, and fastened by a drawstring under the bust.[5] On her head is a mobcap of embroidered muslin, rather unflattering because it is pulled too far down on her forehead; similar muslin, with a small floral sprig, is made into dresses for the baby on her lap and the girl. A fringed silk shawl hangs over Chloe's chair.

The eldest boy, on the left, wears a brown coat (double-breasted and able to fasten both ways), a buff-colored vest and breeches, and English jockey-boots. This riding costume, worn with a bow-tied cravat, is a replica of adult dress, but the clothing of the two younger sons is the distinctive transitional style between the baby frock and grown-up wear. Both boys wear skeleton suits, a practi-

cal English invention popularized from the 1770s, which consisted of a pair of trousers buttoned into a matching jacket and worn with an open frilled collar. This costume was worn by boys from about three years of age up to seven or eight—sometimes as old as ten—after which they adopted adult dress. Both these boys in their skeleton suits—the trousers of which anticipate adult masculine costume of the early nineteenth century—also have shoestrings instead of buckles on their shoes; these were the forerunners of the shoelaces of the following century. Noah, Jr., holds Henry's riding hat; the fluffiness of the nap indicates a hat of demicastor, a mixture of beaver and rabbit fur.   AR

1.   Margaretta M. Lovell, "Reading Eighteenth-Century American Family Portraits: Social Images and Self-Images," *Winterthur Portfolio* 22 (Winter 1987), 243.
2.   Her brother William had married Esther Boardman (cat. 30) and was the classmate of Daniel Boardman (cat. 28) at Yale College.
3.   Franklin Bowditch Dexter, *Biographical Sketches of the Graduates of Yale College* (New York, 1907), 4:52–54; Walter Hill Crockett, *The Green Mountain State*, 5 vols. (New York, 1923).
4.   Stuart P. Feld, *Bulletin of the Metropolitan Museum of Art* 23 (April 1965), 300.
5.   A maternity dress, not dissimilar in style—that is, loose-fitting, pleated over the bust, and with a drawstring at the high waist—exists in the collection of Sturbridge Village, Sturbridge, Massachusetts. It is made of black silk (for mourning) and was worn by Betsey Rogers Barker (1765–1812) of Maine, who altered it last in 1795–1800. See Jane Nylander, "Textiles at Old Sturbridge Village," *Antiques* (September 1979), 603, in which the dress is illustrated.

Ralph E. W. Earl
Family Portrait, 1804
oil on canvas
46½ x 63½ in. (118.1 x 161.3 cm.)
National Gallery of Art, Washington, D.C. Gift of Edgar William and Bernice Chrysler Garbisch, 1953.

59

60 Captain Elijah Dewey, 1798

Oil on canvas
45 ½ x 35 ½ in. (115.6 x 90.2 cm.)
Signed and dated at lower left: "R. Earl pinxt 1798"
The Bennington Museum, Bennington, Vermont
Wadsworth Atheneum only

61 Mrs. Elijah Dewey (Mary Schenck), 1798

Oil on canvas
45 ½ x 35 ½ in. (115.6 x 90.2 cm.)
Signed and dated at lower left: "R. Earl pinxt / 1798"
The Bennington Museum, Bennington, Vermont
Wadsworth Atheneum only

Earl sought portrait commissions in Bennington, Vermont, in 1798, where he painted the local tavernkeeper and his wife. Elijah Dewey (1744–1818) was born in Westfield, Massachusetts, the son of the Rev. Jedediah Dewey and Mindwell Hayden Dewey. The family moved to Bennington in 1763, and the following year, Elijah is listed among the privates in the first militia company formed in Bennington.

During the Revolution, Elijah served as a captain of a local militia regiment, taking part in the Battle of Bennington in 1777. In October of the same year he witnessed Burgoyne's surrender at Saratoga. After the war, Dewey represented Bennington in the General Assembly intermittently from 1786 until 1813. He kept a tavern called the Dewey House (later the Walloomsac House), which still stands. In 1766 he married Eunice Brush (1747–88), with whom he had three daughters. Following his first wife's death, he married Mary Schenck (1756–1820) of Middlesex County, New Jersey.[1]

Earl painted portraits of the Deweys using his by-this-time-familiar compositional format. Elijah Dewey is seated in Earl's stock red upholstered side chair, red drapery behind him, leaning his right arm on a green-cloth-covered table. He holds a pamphlet in his left hand and gazes directly out at the viewer.

Following the aesthetic formula of his Connecticut portraits, Earl employed his skill as a landscape artist to enliven his portrait with a large and detailed window view of his sitter's tavern (now the Walloomsac Inn), an important town meeting place, but from a different perspective than in his *Landscape View of Old Bennington* (cat. 62). The substantial two-and-a-half-story structure with a gambrel roof is an accurate depiction of the building, which was constructed in 1783. Earl includes the distinctive white piazza on the front and side of the house; this element was not found in the Connecticut River Valley but rather can be traced to a Dutch tradition, in New York State.[2] Earl also includes a red rail fence, the Deweys' barn, and some livestock.

Mary Dewey's portrait complements her husband's, having such similar elements as red drapery, a red side chair, a green-cloth-covered table, and a window view. Earl includes a large tree in the landscape similar to the one seen to the left of the Dewey House in Elijah's portrait.

It is likely that Earl boarded at the tavern during his stay in Bennington. In addition to painting the Deweys' portraits, he executed an elaborate landscape view of the town of Bennington (cat. 62), which hung with the Deweys' portraits in matching mahogany veneer and gilt frames in the tavern.

The portrait of Elijah Dewey was purchased from the Dewey family for the Bennington Museum by subscription in 1913. The portrait of Mary Dewey and the landscape of Bennington descended to John and Laura (Van Der Spiegel) Merrill Penniman of Bennington and was acquired in 1981 by the Bennington Museum.[3]

Costume Notes   Elijah Dewey wears the formal costume of a prosperous middle-class man: a black silk coat, vest, knee breeches, and black silk stockings. The coat is extremely plain, with a high collar, wide lapels, and slit cuffs on the tight sleeves. By the late eighteenth century there were great improvements in tailoring; the elegance of masculine attire increasingly lay in high-quality (but not luxurious) fabrics that were so well cut that they did not require superfluous decorations or trimmings. The only vanity a man was allowed was clean, crisp white linen changed at least once a day. Another sign of the general new emphasis on personal cleanliness was the growing fashion for men to wear their own hair, cut short (as seen here), a style that was both practical and comfortable and that—more than any other sartorial manifestation—showed the wearer to be free of the aristocratic shackles of the Old World. Both in Europe and in the United States (but perhaps particularly the latter) it was increasingly difficult, by clothes alone, to distinguish between the gentleman, the merchant, the professional man, and so on.

Mary Dewey's black dress, starched muslin fichu, cap, and shawl are exactly what we would expect of a woman of her class with a moderate interest in fashion, content, as it were, to follow the latest fashions from a distance. Her cap, of white embroidered muslin with a frilled edge, is similar to those seen on many of Earl's middle-aged female sitters; they continued to be popular until the early nineteenth century. Muslin, either plain or figured, was the most fashionable fabric; it could be either English or Indian, the latter being coveted on both sides of the Atlantic.[4] Mary's scarf is a printed cotton, a fabric fashionable during the late eighteenth century for dresses and kerchiefs, which Abigail Adams called "bandanna handkerchiefs." These calicoes were imported into the United States from India and England, but in the 1770s, Americans themselves began to print cottons.[5] An unusual element in this portrait is the wedding ring; the custom of wearing a plain gold band was not firmly established until the nineteenth century, although rings can be seen in portraits from the mid-eighteenth century onward.   AR

1.   *The Life of George Dewey and the Dewey Family History*, 855–59, 870–72; *History of Bennington, Vermont*, 266–70. P. L. Schenk, *Memoir of Johannes Schenk*, 31–33, says that Mary Schenck married Henry Van Der Spiegel of Hunterdon County, New Jersey, around 1774; they had two children. Following his death in 1777, she married Daniel McEowen, an innkeeper in New York City, in 1784, and they had one son, Daniel.

2.   In the seventeenth and eighteenth centuries, a piazza was a long covered walk or loggia with a roof supported by columns. My thanks to Abbott Cummings, for identifying and commenting on this architectural detail.

3.   Research Files, Bennington Museum, Bennington, Vt.; my thanks to David Dangremond, for supplying information on the Dewey portraits. See also William Sawitzky and Susan Sawitzky Papers, "Ralph Earl," New-York Historical Society, New York.

4.   Abigail Adams, writing to her sister in April 1798, said that her everyday cap (worn indoors) was of "handsome muslin with a pleated border or a lace," and the following month she sent her sister muslin from Dacca (Bengal) that cost six dollars a yard to make up similar caps. See *New Letters of Abigail Adams, 1788–1801*, ed. S. Mitchell (Boston, 1947), 166, 173. Adams described these caps as "baby caps," since they were similar to those worn by infants.

5.   See Florence M. Montgomery, *Printed Textiles: English and American Cottons and Linens, 1700–1800* (New York, 1970). Another printed calico kerchief can be seen in Earl's portrait *Mrs. Moses Seymour and Son Epaphoditus* (1789; St. Louis Art Museum).

60

61

62

62 Landscape View of Old Bennington, 1798

Oil on canvas
36½ x 59¾ in. (92.7 x 151.8 cm.)
The Bennington Museum, Bennington, Vermont
Washington, D.C., and Hartford only

Ralph Earl painted *Landscape View of Old Bennington* for the local tavernkeeper Elijah Dewey and his wife, Mary Dewey, who hung it in the tavern along with their portraits. Earl's landscape is one of the earliest town views painted by an American artist and provides a fascinating look at a thriving town center in the late eighteenth century. Earl's painting provides a fairly accurate record of the houses and other buildings as they appeared at the time. Just as Earl's portraits serve to codify the social position of his sitters, so too does the landscape show the social structure of the townspeople and places of importance. In his landscape, Earl also pays homage to the recent history of Bennington.

Earl condensed the scene by foreshortening distances and slightly rearranging the positions of houses to provide an unobstructed view of each building. The topography is so precise that Earl may have used a visual aid, such as a camera obscura, to set the scene.[1] The town center lies in the middle ground, with meticulously cultivated and fenced fields in the foreground. Earl focuses attention on three major buildings: in the center is the impressive mansion house of Gov. Isaac Tichenor, accurately shown (with the possible exception of the hipped roof), including the formal gardens and an elaborate white fence in the front; directly behind the Tichenor house is the first (or possibly second) courthouse of Bennington County; and to the right, of equal prominence, is the Gen. David Robinson house, and at the left, the State Arms House, of brick. The site of the recent Battle of Bennington provides the backdrop for the central buildings, and the so-called North Mountains loom above the town. At the far right is the house of Elijah Dewey's parents, Jedediah and Mindwell Dewey; next to it, the house of Ethan Allen; and finally, the Dewey tavern.[2] Earl accurately depicts the town's red-roofed white houses, framed with white fences, and the red rail fences along the roads.

Of particular interest is the possibly unique self-portrait, seen at the lower left. The artist is seated under a tree with a pad of paper on his lap; he holds a pencil and is sketching a young boy, who poses in front of him. Although the inclusion of a self-portrait in a landscape followed a well-established convention, Earl shows himself—not sketching the landscape—but more appropriately employed in taking a portrait in a landscape setting.[3] The boy possibly represents Earl's own son Ralph E. W. Earl, who was frequently with his father in his final years; he would have been between ten and thirteen when this was painted. A second young boy, with a dog, is seated to the right of the artist.

This landscape descended in the Dewey family to John Merrill and Laura Van Der Spiegel Merrill Penniman, and was purchased by the Bennington Museum in 1981.[4]

Costume Notes   Earl wears the fashionable, informal, outdoor dress of the time, quite acceptable for an artist, including a dark blue coat with brass buttons and a red collar, a white neckcloth with a frill, buff breeches, black boots with brown tops, and a black cocked hat. He wears his own reddish hair tied at the back.   AR

1. The use of a camera obscura in landscape painting was fairly commonplace by the end of the eighteenth century. American artists known to have used this device include Benjamin West, Charles Willson Peale, and Ralph Earl's brother, James Earl, who lists a camera obscura in his will and inventory of 1792. See Helmut von Effra and Allen Staley, *The Paintings of Benjamin West* (New Haven, 1986), 435; Edgar P. Richardson, Brooke Hindle, and Lillian B. Miller, *Charles Willson Peale and His World*, exhib. cat. (New York, 1982), 90; Harold Spencer, *The American Earls: Ralph Earl, James Earl, R. E. W. Earl*, exhib. cat. (Storrs, Conn., 1972), 35.
2. My thanks to David Dangremond and Abbott Cummings for providing information on the buildings in Bennington. See Hamilton Child, *Gazetteer and Business Directory of Bennington County, Vt, for 1880–81* (Syracuse, N.Y., 1880), which contains excerpts from Hiram Harwood's list of old houses in Bennington. Harwood compiled this list around 1837.
3. Two other supposed self-portraits of Ralph Earl are known, including *Self Portrait* (St. Louis Art Museum), which may possibly be by Ralph Earl, but for which there is virtually no evidence suggesting that it is a self-portrait; see William Sawitzky, *Connecticut Portraits by Ralph Earl, 1751–1801*, exhib. cat. (New Haven, Conn., 1935), ill. 3, 12. A second profile sketch inscribed "Ralph Earl" is in the collection of the Hermitage, Hermitage, Tenn.; see Laurence B. Goodrich, *Ralph Earl: Recorder for an Era* (Oneonta, N.Y., 1967), ill. opp. contents.

   A few examples of conventional self-portraits in a landscape by American artists of the period are Michele Felice Corne, *Ezekiel Hersey Derby Farm* (c. 1800; private collection); John Trumbull, *Niagara Falls below the Great Cascade from the British Side* (1807–8; Wadsworth Atheneum), and John Rubens Smith, *Falls on the Sawkill* (c. 1820; Corcoran Gallery of Art).
4. Research Files, Bennington Museum, Bennington, Vt.

63 Reverend Ebenezer Porter, 1804

Ralph Eleazer Whiteside Earl (1785 or 1788–1838)
Oil on canvas
45 ½ x 36 in. (115.6 x 91.4 cm.)
Signed and dated on the reverse of the canvas: "R. Earl, Jr."
Private collection

64 Mrs. Ebenezer Porter (Lucy "Patty" Pierce Merwin), 1804

Oil on canvas
45 ¾ x 36⅜ in. (116.2 x 92.4 cm.)
Signed and dated on the reverse of the canvas: "Mrs. Patty Porter / R. Earl pinxit, 1804."
The Brooklyn Museum, New York
Gift of Colonel and Mrs. Edgar W. Garbisch, 1951

No record of birth exists for Ralph E. W. Earl, the son of Ralph Earl and his second wife, Ann Whiteside Earl, of Norwich, England. He was probably born in 1785, the year of his parents' arrival in America, or in 1788, after his father's release from debtors' prison.[1] The young Ralph may be the standing boy in *Landscape View of Old Bennington* (cat. 62), painted by his father in 1798. He received artistic instruction from his father; his first known signed portrait, executed under his father's guidance in 1800, represents Edward Gere (fig. 1.39) of Northampton, Massachusetts. After the elder Earl's death in 1801, Ralph continued to paint portraits in the style of his father in the upper Connecticut River Valley, as well as in Troy, New York, where his mother and sister, Mariann Earl, resided.

In 1804 Ralph painted the portraits of Ebenezer and Patty Porter. Born in Cornwall, Connecticut, the son of Thomas and Abigail Porter, Ebenezer Porter (1772–1834) graduated from Dartmouth College in 1792. In 1796, upon the death of the Rev. Noah Merwin, the Congregational minister of Washington, Connecticut, Ebenezer succeeded him. Shortly after assuming his duties as minister, he married his predecessor's eldest daughter, Lucy "Patty" Pierce Merwin. He became a respected minister in Connecticut and, in 1812, was appointed a professor at the Andover Theological Seminary, in Andover, Massachusetts, becoming its president in 1827.[2]

The Porters were painted by Ralph E. W. Earl in 1804, at which time Ebenezer had been forced to leave the pulpit, for "the severity of his labours, especially during the season of revival in 1804–1805, reduced his health so materially, that he was obliged to discontinue them altogether for nearly a year."[3] Thus it is not certain that the Porters were painted in Washington.

In these portraits, Ralph closely follows the model provided by his father, incorporating Earl's customary compositional elements, as well as his favored red and green palette. Presented at three-quarter length, Ebenezer Porter wears his ministerial robes and holds a book in his right hand, perhaps one containing his sermons, many of which were published.[4] Voluminous drapery provides a backdrop. Patty Porter, who is fashionably attired in a gray silk gown, is seated in a red side chair, which the artist has borrowed from his father's portraits. She is holding a piece of lace in her hand, with lace-making tools on the table. Two columns divide the interior space from the landscape background.

After completing a number of additional portraits, Ralph left for London in 1809, where he received encouragement from John Trumbull and Benjamin West. In 1810 he moved to Norwich, northeast of London, where he lived with his mother's father and brother and received patronage from John Money, his father's friend. He exhibited over forty paintings, mainly portraits, between 1810 and 1815, at which time he listed his address in Norwich at Judge's Old Lodgings, Charing Cross.[5] Ralph wrote of his good fortune to Trumbull, who was then in London. "I have taken the liberty to inform you and Mrs. Trumbull of my success on coming to Norwich knowing you to have much interest in my welfare – General Money whom you have heard me mention was my father's friend [and] has become my friend, and [I] have just finished a portrait of him to his satisfaction. . . . The General is a particular friend and correspondent of the Duke of Kent whom he is agoing to solicit the favour to let me paint his portrait for him."[6] Four years later, the artist traveled to Paris, where he spent nearly a year.

He returned to America in 1815, landing in Savannah, Georgia. Influenced by the history paintings of West and Trumbull, he planned to produce a painting of the Battle of New Orleans. On his travels through the South, to Alabama, Mississippi, Kentucky, and Tennessee, to take likenesses of the heroes of this battle, he first encountered Gen. Andrew Jackson, initiating a lifelong friendship.

Ralph settled in Nashville in 1817 and became the leading portrait painter in Tennessee. He painted numerous portraits of Jackson and married Jane Cafferty, the niece of General Jackson's wife, Rachel. In addition to his work as an artist, Earl joined with George Tunstall, a junior editor of the *Nashville Whig* in opening a "museum of Natural and Artificial curiosities," much like the museum founded by Charles Willson Peale in Philadelphia in 1784. Earl produced several of the "portraits of distinguished characters in Tennessee and elsewhere" that went on display there. As a result of his collecting activities for his museum, Earl was eventually appointed custodian of the Tennessee Antiquarian Society.

Andrew Jackson was elected president in 1828, and

64

63

in the same year his wife died. President Jackson wrote from the White House to his close friend Ralph E. W. Earl in 1829. "I find myself very lonesome, I wish you were here. . . . In your society I would find some solace for my grief." In June of that year, Ralph moved to the White House as "court painter." For the next eight years he painted portraits of Jackson and numerous visitors to the White House. When Jackson left his office to return to the Hermitage, Ralph E. W. Earl followed, living out his life in Tennessee.[7]

1.   Ralph Earl Prime, great-grandson of Ralph Earl, records 1788 as the birth date, in Prime to Thomas Hovey Gage, March 7, 1914, Gage Family Papers, Box 4, Folder 2, American Antiquarian Society, Worcester, Mass.
2.   "The Merwin Family Genealogy," MS, Connecticut Historical Society, 97; Franklin Bowditch Dexter, *Biographical Sketches of the Graduates of Yale College* (New York, 1907), 3:495–96; William B. Sprague, *Annals of the American Pulpit* (New York, 1857), 2:351–57; *DAB*, 15:89–90.
3.   Sprague, *Annals of the American Pulpit*, 2:352.
4.   Ibid., 2:356–57.
5.   Miklos Rajnai, *The Norwich Society of Artists, 1805–1833: A Dictionary of Contributors and Their Works* (Norwich, Eng., 1976), 47–48.
6.   Earl to Trumbull, February 18, 1810, Ralph E. W. Earl Papers (1810–38). On August 25, 1810, the *Norwich Mercury* observed the presence of Ralph E. W. Earl, "portrait painter . . . and the son of an artist who resided in Norwich some years since. His pictures are faithful likenesses, and he has had the happiness of being employed to portray very beautiful originals."
7.   Jackson to Earl, March 16, 1829, reproduced in Harold Spencer, *The American Earls: Ralph Earl, James Earl, R. E. W. Earl* (Storrs, Conn., 1972), 51; Spencer, *American Earls*, 48–59; Russell MacBeth, "Portraits by Ralph E. W. Earl," *Antiques* 100 (September 1971), 390–93; Elizabeth Mankin Kornhauser, *Ralph Earl: Artist-Entrepreneur* (Ann Arbor, Mich., 1989), 225–26.

65 Thomas Earle, 1800

Oil on canvas
37 ½ x 34 in. (95.3 x 86.4 cm.)
Signed and dated at lower left: "R. Earle Pinxt 1800"
National Gallery of Art, Washington, D.C.
Andrew W. Mellon Collection, 1947.17.42

Earl returned to his native town of Leicester for the first time a quarter of a century after his departure from his family in 1774. There he painted a portrait of his cousin Thomas Earle. Ralph Earl's father was still living in the town, as was his brother Clark, but there is no information concerning a possible reunion with his immediate family.

Thomas Earle (1737–1819) was the son of Robert Earle and Mary Newall Earle of Leicester. In 1761, Thomas married Hannah Southgate, also of Leicester. He spent his life in the Cherry Valley section of town, where he became a renowned gunsmith. According to the town historian, during the Revolution Thomas "manufactured a gun of exquisite workmanship for Colonel William Henshaw in 1773, and when Henshaw marched to Cambridge, in 1775, he took it into service. . . . Here it fell under the observation of General Washington, who admired it so much that he ordered one of the same pattern."[1]

The artist portrayed his cousin at the age of sixty-three, seated in the stock red upholstered armchair with his right hand resting on a map of East Asia. He is wearing spectacles, presumably to read the map to which he points. Earl frequently introduced maps of exotic locales into his portraits, but in this instance the significance remains unclear.

A detailed rendition of Thomas Earle's house and gun shop is seen in a window view. A river with a waterwheel runs nearby. For this portrait, the artist signed his last name with an "e" on the end like his cousin's.

The portrait descended in the Earle family to the subject's great-granddaughter, Harriet Chandler Schoepf, who sold the painting to a Mr. Coffin in 1917. It was purchased from MacBeth Galleries, New York, by the Worcester Art Museum in 1917 and subsequently deaccessioned to the Ehrlich Galleries in an exchange. Thomas B. Clarke purchased the portrait by 1928. The portrait was given to the National Gallery of Art, Washington, D.C., as part of the Andrew W. Mellon Collection in 1947.[2]

Costume Notes   Thomas Earle wears the black suit that by the late eighteenth century had become the uniform of the middle-class man. It is a tribute to the artist's ingenuity that he picks out small details to differentiate one masculine sitter from another—here, the fine fringed muslin shirt ruffle and the silver linked buttons (the ancestor of the cuff link) that fasten the shirt sleeves at the wrist.[3]   AR

1.   Emory Washburn, *Historical Sketches of the Town of Leicester, Massachusetts* (Boston, 1860), 61; quoted in Pliny Earle, *The Earle Family: Ralph Earle and His Descendants* (Worcester, Mass., 1888), 55–56.
2.   "Landscape and Portrait by Ralph Earl," *Bulletin of the Worcester Art Museum* 7 (January 1917), 7–10; Painting Files, Worcester Art Museum, Worcester, Mass., and the National Gallery of Art.
3.   See F. Russell-Smith, "Sleeve Buttons of the Seventeenth and Eighteenth Centuries," *Connoisseur* 139 (February 1957), 36–40. According to this article, the Yale University Art Gallery has a fine collection of gold sleeve buttons bearing the marks of American goldsmiths of the first half of the eighteenth century.

65

66

66   Looking East from Denny Hill, 1800

Oil on canvas

45 ¾ x 79 ⅜ in. (116.2 x 201.6 cm.)

Inscribed at lower left: "R. Earl Pinxt . 1800"

Technical note: the canvas is in two pieces, joined by a
    horizontal seam

Worcester Art Museum, Worcester, Massachusetts,

Museum purchase, 1916

Hartford only

At the very end of his life, Earl returned to Leicester, Massachusetts, where he painted a panoramic landscape of the
region in which he had been raised. The view was commissioned by an old acquaintance of the Earle family, Col.
Thomas Denny (1757–1814), who operated a hand and ma-
chine card manufactory in Leicester.[1] Denny had inherited
his family's house and farm, situated on top of a high hill in
the southeast corner of Leicester that had come to be known
as Denny Hill.

An acquaintance of Denny, Anna Henshaw, said Denny
had requested Earl to paint a landscape of the view seen
from his house because he had moved into a new house that
year and "wanted to take with him a picture of the view
he was so familiar with since childhood." Henshaw was
impressed with the accuracy of Earl's view and described
the finished landscape as "a most splendid panorama view
from Denny Hill, which embraces the surrounding country,
dotted with the white houses of the inhabitants and a dozen
or more churches. At the northwest is seen Leicester village
situated on a hill equal, if not superior in height, about two
miles traveling distance. . . . In the northeast in a valley are
Worcester and new Worcester villages. All around below are
hills and dales, woodlands, plots of grass, and arable fields,
delightfully diversified."[2] Later nineteenth-century sources
concur as to the accuracy of Earl's landscape, a painting
prized by the town inhabitants.[3]

Earl's view of his native town is the embodiment of the
pastoral ideal that figured prominently in English art and
literature of the eighteenth century, without a hint of the
savage wilderness that would become a subject of interest
for landscape painters in America in the nineteenth century.[4] Here Earl projects an image of a harmonious society
with unlimited possibilities, reflecting the aspirations of
the young nation. Farm workers till the soil at the left and
harvest hay in the well-kept and neatly fenced fields in the
foreground with the aid of an ox-drawn cart as cows graze
nearby. The Boston Post Road in the middle distance leads
the viewer's eye to the thriving villages of Worcester and
Leicester. Having carefully framed the scene with overly
large trees, the artist illuminates it with his customary pink
and blue sky.

The portrait descended in the Denny family, where it
hung in various houses until the 1890s, when it was placed
on loan at the Leicester Public Library. Mrs. Parkman T.
Denny sold the painting to a local art dealer, Mr. Coffin of
Worcester, in 1916. The Worcester Art Museum purchased
the painting in that year.[5]

1.   John L. Brooke, *The Heart of the Commonwealth: Society and Political
Culture in Worcester County, Massachusetts, 1713–1861* (Cambridge, Eng.,
1989), 305.

2.   Henshaw (1778–1854), handwritten MS, Worcester Art Museum,
Worcester, Mass. According to Thomas Hovey Gage, this description was
written in about 1800; see Painting Files, Worcester Art Museum.

3.   Emory Washburn, *Historical Sketches of the Town of Leicester, Massa-
chusetts* (Boston, 1860), 22; Christopher C. Denny, "Reminiscences of
Some Leicester Families," 1889, MS, copy in Painting Files, Worcester Art
Museum.

4.   Edward J. Nygren with Bruce Robertson et al., *Views and Visions:
American Landscape before 1830*, exhib. cat. (Washington, D.C., 1986),
21–37.

5.   Painting Files, Worcester Art Museum; "Landscape and Portrait by
Ralph Earl," *Bulletin of the Worcester Art Museum* 7 (January 1917), 7–10.

67 Reverend Eleazar Wheelock, 1793–96

Joseph Steward (1753–1822)

Oil on canvas

79 ⅛ x 69 ⅞ in. (201.6 x 177.5 cm.)

Hood Museum of Art, Dartmouth College, Hanover, New Hampshire

Commissioned by the Trustees of Dartmouth College

The impact of Earl's Connecticut portrait style on local artists is amply seen in the works of Joseph Steward, who was directly inspired by Earl's *Oliver Ellsworth and Abigail Wolcott Ellsworth* (cat. 41) when he attempted his first grand-scale portrait, *Reverend Eleazar Wheelock*.

Eleazar Wheelock (1711–79) graduated from Yale College in 1733 and became a prominent itinerant revivalist preacher in New England. His interest in the education of American Indians led him to open a private school for their instruction, and he later obtained a charter to establish Dartmouth College in 1770, in Hanover, New Hampshire. There he encountered Joseph Steward, who attended Dartmouth.

Steward was born in Upton, Massachusetts, and graduated from Dartmouth College in 1780. Trained for the ministry, Steward practiced for a time and, by 1788, served as the interim minister for the Rev. Samuel Moseley in Hampton, Connecticut. The following year he married Samuel Moseley's daughter, Sarah. When Steward's career as a minister was hindered, by poor health, he began to paint portraits.[1] Essentially self-taught, he relied on the example of such trained artists as Ralph Earl and John Trumbull, to whose works he was exposed in Connecticut.

Earl's extended presence in the Hartford area in 1791 and 1792 inspired many of Steward's best efforts. A year after Earl completed his monumental portrait of the Ellsworths, Steward accepted a commission from his alma mater to paint "a whole length portraiture of the late reverend Eleazar Wheelock DD founder and First President of this university to be deposited in one of the chambers of the college and Mr. Steward from regard to the university & memory of its founder having generously offered to do it at half his usual price for such portraitures viz for five guineas." It took Steward three years to complete the portrait of his former teacher, who had died fourteen years earlier while Steward was a student at Dartmouth. According to tradition, he based his portrait on a miniature of Wheelock. A contemporary recalled, "I saw that portrait painted at Hampton, Conn., when I was sitting for college with Parson Ludovicus Weld who sat for the lower half of the picture."[2]

The portrait was finally delivered to the college in 1796.

In the nearly life-size image, Steward reinterprets the compositional elements in Earl's portrait of the Ellsworths in a literal fashion that reveals his lack of academic training. Adopting Earl's bright palette of red and green and painting in broad linear strokes, Steward placed his subject in the center of the composition, offset by a window at the left and a large desk and bookcase to the right. Whereas Earl used red drapery as a conventional backdrop to enhance the importance of a subject, Steward painted an actual window curtain and tassels that do not relate to the figure of Wheelock. Eleazar Wheelock is seated in a red upholstered chair and, like Oliver Ellsworth, he holds a scroll; this represents the college charter. Finally, Steward includes a decorative, patterned floor.

Following Earl's example, Steward tended to be literal in his depictions of landscape features. In this instance, his view through the window is somewhat puzzling. Logically, the view should represent Dartmouth College as it appeared in the mid-1790s. When compared with an engraving of 1793, *A Front View of Dartmouth College, with Chapel and Hall* by J. Dunham and engraved by Samuel Hill, however, Steward's view appears to be an idealized image with fanciful elements that do not accurately represent the college buildings at this time.[3]

A more typical example of Steward's faithful landscape renditions is seen in his 1795 portrait of the wife and the daughter of Oliver Ellsworth's political associate Theodore Sedgwick (1746–1813) of Stockbridge, Massachusetts. In his portrait *Pamela Dwight Sedgwick and her daughter Catherine* (1795; private collection), Steward includes an accurate rendition of the Sedgwicks' house through the window, a view again inspired by Earl's earlier portrait of the Ellsworths.

In a series of letters from Pamela Sedgwick to her husband, who was in Philadelphia attending to the affairs of the new nation, the details of the portrait commission are related. Pamela informed her husband that Joseph Steward, "whose Character as a good Painter I have often heard, is now come into the County."[4] She indicated a desire to have all the children included with her in a portrait but thought "the children's ———— taken together with mine would make an odd appearance and full lengths would be very expensive. Mr. Steward's price for full lengths is from 10 to 12 guineas."[5] Instead, she sat with her youngest daughter, Catherine, but reflected, "I feel very sorry that a part should be taken without the whole." After the completion of the portrait, she wrote that "[my likeness] is said to be a very good one. I think its natural but handsomer than it should be."[6]

Steward's sitters may have felt that he captured a "very good" likeness, but not everyone who viewed his portraits appreciated their merits. More than a decade later, after meeting Steward and viewing his pictures in Hartford,

67

William Dunlap unkindly noted that "Steward painted wretched portraits. . . . What turned him from the cure of men's souls, to the caricaturing of their bodies, I never learned." [7] Dunlap may have been responding to the imitativeness of Steward's works, which rendered them somewhat lifeless.

1.   Thompson R. Harlow, "The Life and Trials of Joseph Steward," *Connecticut Historical Society Bulletin* 46 (October 1981); Harlow, "Joseph Steward and the Hartford Museum," *Connecticut Historical Society Bulletin* 18 (January–April 1953).

2.   Both quotations are in Harlow, "Life and Trials of Steward," 125.

3.   My thanks to Kenneth Cramer, archivist, Dartmouth College, for locating the engraving.

4.   Sedgwick to Sedgwick, 1794, quoted in Margaret C. S. Christman, *The First Federal Congress, 1789–1791* (Washington, D.C., 1989), 321. The portrait is illustrated in ibid., opp. 321.

5.   Sedgwick to Sedgwick, late December or January 1795, quoted in Colleen Cowles Heslip, *Between the Rivers: Itinerant Painters from the Connecticut to the Hudson* (Williamstown, Mass., 1990), 34.

6.   Sedgwick to Sedgwick, late December or January 1795, Sedgwick Papers, Massachusetts Historical Society, Boston.

7.   William Dunlap, *History of the Rise and Progress of the Arts of Design in the United States* (1834; reprint in 3 vols., New York, 1969), 2:151.

68

68 Jeremiah Halsey, c. 1796

Joseph Steward

Oil on canvas

43¾ x 38¾ in. (111.1 x 98.4 cm.)

The Connecticut Historical Society, Hartford

The year Steward painted this portrait of Jeremiah Halsey he also opened the Hartford Museum, which he patterned on the remarkable museum that Charles Willson Peale had opened in Philadelphia only a few years before. Both museums were intended to instruct as well as to entertain. Steward established his museum in two rooms on the third floor of the newly completed Hartford Statehouse.[1] There he exhibited portraits and depictions of historical subjects that he executed himself. In addition, he displayed curiosities of the natural world, as well as artifacts. In 1808, having outgrown the space in the statehouse, the museum was moved to a large room in a house on Main and Talcott streets. Steward operated the museum until his death in 1822.

Steward boasted in a 1798 advertisement for the museum he offered visitors "three hundred and fifty feet of paintings"; several feet comprised his portrait of Jeremiah Halsey. Born in Stonington, Connecticut, Halsey (1743–1829) was instrumental in raising money to complete the construction of the new Hartford Statehouse. In 1795, together with Andrew Ward, Halsey gave forty-eight thousand dollars to the state of Connecticut for this purpose. He received land on Lake Erie in exchange but lost money in the transaction. His contribution is commemorated in the portrait by the accurate view of the building through the window. Halsey is seated in one of the chairs he purchased for the statehouse from the local cabinetmaker Lemuel Adams. It is likely that Steward painted the portrait in his "Painting Room" in the statehouse, which he used as a studio beginning in 1796.[2]

Steward's portrait of Halsey demonstrates the obvious debt he owed to the works of Ralph Earl. Steward adopted Earl's palette of primary colors, as well as his standard compositional elements: the bookcase with inscribed titles on the spines of the books, a green-cloth-covered table, red curtains, and a window view of a specific regional scene.[3]

Because Steward exhibited a number of his own portraits in his museum, Earl's style (as interpreted by Steward) was dispersed to a wide audience.

1. On Peale's museum, see Charles Coleman Sellers, *Mr. Peale's Museum* (New York, 1980). For more on Steward's Hartford Museum, see Thompson R. Harlow, "Joseph Steward and the Hartford Museum," *Connecticut Historical Society Bulletin* 18 (January–April 1953); Elizabeth Mankin Kornhauser and Christine Skeeles Schloss, "Painting and Other Pictorial Arts," in *The Great River: Art and Society of the Connecticut Valley, 1635–1820,* exhib. cat. (Hartford, Conn., 1985), 139, 178.
2. Kornhauser and Schloss, "Painting and Other Pictorial Arts," 156–59. The statehouse was designed by the Boston architect Charles Bulfinch (1763–1844) and built by John Leffingwell (1755–1834), a master builder and contractor in Hartford. Ibid., 121–24.
3. The books are inscribed "Hazard's / State / Papers," "Lex Mericato," and "Hawkins / Pleas of / The Crown."

69   Comfort Starr Mygatt and His Daughter Lucy, 1799

John Brewster, Jr. (1766–1854)

Oil on canvas

54 x 39¼ in. (137.2 x 99.7 cm.)

Signed and dated at lower right: "March 1st 1799 / John
     Brewster, pinxt"

Technical note: the canvas is in two pieces, with a
     vertical seam

G. W. Samaha, Milan, Ohio (Photo courtesy Museum of
     Fine Arts, Boston)

70   Lucy Knapp Mygatt and Her Son George, 1799

Oil on canvas

54 x 40 in. (137.2 x 101.6 cm.)

Technical note: the canvas is in two pieces, with a
     vertical seam

Palmer Museum of Art, The Pennsylvania State University,
     University Park

Gift of Mrs. Nancy Adams McCord

John Brewster, Jr., has long been acknowledged to be one
of the finest early New England itinerant portrait painters.
During his early years, while painting in Connecticut in
the 1790s, he was the most gifted follower of the portrait
style made popular by Ralph Earl.[1] Brewster received his
first instruction in portrait painting from Joseph Steward
(cat. 67, 68), who was perhaps the most pronounced imitator of Earl's style. In addition, Brewster undoubtedly
studied Earl's Connecticut portraits directly, for he painted
in the same towns where Earl had found success. Brewster's grand-scale double portraits *Comfort Starr Mygatt and
His Daughter Lucy* and *Lucy Knapp Mygatt and Her Son George*
were painted in 1799 in Danbury, a town where Earl had
previously established his presence.

John Brewster, Jr. was born in Hampton, Connecticut,
the son of a highly respected physician, Dr. John Brewster,
and his wife, Mary Durkee Brewster. One of seven children,
John was born deaf. Fortunately, he was raised in a cultured
household that provided him with a far more enlightened
environment than was the norm in the eighteenth century
for a person with his disability. Within his family circle,
Brewster was shielded from the pervasive misconceptions
regarding hearing-impaired people that resulted in discrimi-
nation. By his early twenties, he could converse in a sign
language understood by the immediate family and friends,
read, and paint. The Cogswell family were close friends of
the Brewsters, and the Rev. James Cogswell (fig. 1.29),

who lived nearby in Scotland, expressed an interest in the
young boy, noting in his diary in 1790: "Dr. Brewster's son,
a Deaf & Dumb young man came in the evening, he is very
ingenious, has a genius for painting & & can write well
& converse by signs so that he can be understood in many
Things."[2]

Brewster received instruction in portrait painting from
Joseph Steward during Steward's stay in Hampton.[3] He
began painting portraits of family and friends in the early
1790s in a style that clearly demonstrates the impact of his
instructor. For example, for his portraits of James and Lucy
Eldredge of Brooklyn, Connecticut, Brewster created a simplified version of the compositional format made popular
by Earl and, later, Steward by placing his full-length figures in chairs next to a table and near an open window with
a view of a regional landscape beyond. The idiosyncratic
technique of the small white dots along the bottom of James
Eldredge's shoes, simulating a sewn sole, derives from the
example of Steward, as is evident in his *Reverend Eleazar
Wheelock* (cat. 67).

Brewster followed his brother Royal Brewster, a physician, to Buxton, Maine, in 1796. Taking advantage of his
brother's professional connections, Brewster became the
leading portrait painter in southern Maine in the early decades of the nineteenth century. In Maine, he abandoned the
full-length format favored in Connecticut, concentrating
on more fashionable bust-length or half-length figures. He
further simplified his compositions, ceasing to include the
furnishings and window views of regional scenery inspired
by the Connecticut works of Earl and others.

When the first permanent American school for deaf
people was founded in Hartford, largely through the efforts
of Dr. Mason Fitch Cogswell (cat. 40), whose daughter
Alice was hearing impaired, Brewster became one of seven
pupils registered in the first class. He returned to Maine
after three years at the school and continued his highly
successful career.

During the later 1790s, Brewster returned frequently
to Connecticut, where he painted portraits in the manner
of Earl and Steward, but he also demonstrated a distinctive manner of his own. Perhaps his finest efforts as an
artist are his portraits of the Mygatt family of Danbury.
Comfort Starr Mygatt (1763–1823) was a prosperous merchant and farmer who, with his wife, Lucy Knapp Mygatt
(1766–1804), was undoubtedly familiar with the portraits
Ralph Earl painted during his stay in Danbury in 1790
and may have been familiar with other Earl portraits in the
surrounding towns of Newtown, New Milford, and Litchfield.[4] Brewster was commissioned to paint portraits of the
Mygatts during his sojourn in the town from 1798 to 1799.
An account book kept by Comfort Mygatt indicates that
from November 24, 1798, to April 8, 1799, Brewster received various items of clothing from his store, including
a wool coat and "patent stockings," as well as such artists'

supplies as paintbrushes and cambric. The final "Cash for you to balance" in exchange for "Portrait Painting as to agreement" totaled sixteen pounds ten shillings.[5]

Brewster's portraits of the Mygatt family are exquisite in their simplicity. In a beautifully balanced composition, he places Comfort Mygatt and his daughter Lucy in an austere setting; their figures fill the canvas. Comfort is seated on a green Windsor side chair with a red leather seat and green fringe. The figures are placed against a plain gray background with a decorative, patterned floor. Their features are sharply defined and delicately molded. Brewster presents the five-year-old child in a flat, frontal pose, holding her father's hand in an endearing gesture.

Equally beautiful is the portrait of Lucy Mygatt, seated in a dainty black Windsor side chair and posed with folded arms, her left hand holding that of her two-year-old-son, William, who stands beside her. Above the child's head is a window view of the Mygatts' house and farm, with the surrounding fenced fields. Brewster depicts the window, without curtains or drapery, in a faithful rendition. As in the companion portrait, here the features of his sitters are rendered with great clarity and sensitivity. In spite of Lucy Mygatt's severe black gown, her face, as well as the face of her child, are sweetly portrayed. Brewster's inability to hear

John Brewster, Jr.
James Eldredge, 1795
oil on canvas
54 x 40½ in. (137.2 x 102.9 cm.)
The Connecticut Historical Society, Hartford.

John Brewster, Jr.
Mrs. James Eldredge (Lucy Gallup), 1795
oil on canvas
54 x 40½ in. (137.2 x 102.9 cm.)
The Connecticut Historical Society, Hartford.

undoubtedly heightened his perceptions, enabling him to portray his subjects with unusual honesty and strength.

Although Brewster borrows for his Connecticut portraits the scale and various compositional elements associated with Ralph Earl's works, he simplifies the compositions by reducing the elements to their essentials. In addition, rather than the bright palette of red and green favored by Earl and imitated by Steward, Brewster prefers a muted palette of earth tones and pale hues.

1. Biographical information on the artist was first presented in Nina Fletcher Little, "John Brewster, Jr., 1766–1854," *Connecticut Historical Society Bulletin* 25 (October 1960), 97–129, and Little, *American Folk Painters of Three Centuries* (New York, 1980), 18–26. More recently, Joyce Hill has presented new findings in "Miniatures by John Brewster, Jr.," *Clarion* (Spring–Summer 1983), 49–50.

Earl's influence on Brewster is discussed in Elizabeth Mankin Kornhauser and Christine Skeeles Schloss, "Painting and Other Pictorial Arts," in *The Great River: Art and Society of the Connecticut Valley, 1635–1820* (Hartford, Conn., 1985), 152–60; and Elizabeth Mankin Kornhauser, *Ralph Earl: Artist-Entrepreneur* (Ann Arbor, Mich., 1989), 157–59.

2. Rev. James Cogswell, Diary, December 13, 1790, CHS.

3. Ellen D. Larned, *History of Windham County, Connecticut*, 2 vols. (Worcester, Mass., 1874–90), states, "Under [Steward's] example and instruction a deaf and dumb son of Dr. Brewster acquired very creditable proficiency in his art and followed it through his life as a profession."

4. See Kornhauser, *Ralph Earl*, for a discussion of Earl's Danbury portraits, including *Jerusha Benedict* (1790; private collection) and *Thomas Tucker* and *Sara Tucker* (1790; private collection).

5. Comfort Starr Mygatt, Account Book, quoted in Hill, "Miniatures by John Brewster, Jr.," 49–50.

70

69

71

71 Deborah Richmond, c. 1797

Unknown artist

Oil on canvas

45¾ x 34¾ in. (116.2 x 88.3 cm.)

Inscribed on the back of the canvas (a new canvas lining —
the inscription probably reproduces one on the original
canvas): "D. Richmond Age 1797"

Abby Aldrich Rockefeller Folk Art Center, Williamsburg,
Virginia

The popularity of the portrait style that Earl introduced
in Connecticut in the late 1780s and practiced throughout the 1790s influenced, to varying degrees, a wide range
of local artists and their patrons. The portrait of Deborah
Richmond, most likely painted in Suffield, Connecticut, in
1797, demonstrates the impact of the works of Earl and his
imitators on lesser-trained artists.

Deborah Richmond, the daughter of Joshua Richmond
and Eliza Cushing Richmond, was born in Westport, Massachusetts, in 1772. Although she remained unmarried,
her sister, Elizabeth, married their cousin William Cushing
Gay in 1796, at which time she moved to his native Suffield.
William was the postmaster in Suffield, Connecticut, and in
1796 he inherited his father's, the Rev. Ebenezer Gay, Sr.,'s
house, called the Gay Manse. Deborah spent much of her
adult life living with her sister's family in Suffield,[1] as well as
with other family members. She died in Providence, Rhode
Island, in 1802.[2]

Her portrait has traditionally been associated with a
group of Suffield portraits first identified by Nina Fletcher
Little, including a portrait of Deborah's sister, *Elizabeth Gay
and Son William Cushing Gay, Jr.* (private collection), also
painted in 1797.[3] Although a lack of formal training is evident, the artist has created a delightful, two-dimensional
interpretation of the formal elements found in Earl's Connecticut portraits. He (or she) includes drapery behind
the figure, here a dark blue-green, decorative patterns on
the wall, painted and grained window moldings, and the
window view of a house framed by trees. The house has remained unidentified.[4] Deborah is sensitively portrayed, her
features delicately rendered. She wears a pale pink gown
with a rose attached to the bodice and holds a fan (which
descended with the portrait; Abby Aldrich Rockefeller Folk
Art Center collection).

The portrait of Deborah Richmond, like her sister's,
bears strong stylistic similarities to two documented portraits by the local engraver, painter, and counterfeiter
Richard Brunton (d. 1832), as we can see in his *Major Reuben
Humphreys* and *Mrs. Reuben Humphreys* (c. 1799; Connecticut Historical Society).[5] Because of the complexities of the
additional Suffield portraits, executed in the same decade,
which are also similar in appearance, further documentary
evidence is necessary for a firm attribution.

1. Land Records, Town Clerk's Office, Suffield, Conn., 8:266–67, 270,
273, indicate that William inherited his father's house in 1796 and deeded
it to his brother, Ebenezer, in August 1799. He moved into a new house in
1800; see William Gay to Ebenezer Gay, June 26, 1800, Kent Memorial
Library, Suffield.

Family correspondence in the Kent Memorial Library indicates that
Deborah spent a great deal of time with William and Elizabeth Gay in Suf-
field. One letter in particular, from William's sister, Lucy Gay, to Deborah
Richmond in November 1796, suggests that she spent time in the Gay
Manse between 1796 and 1799.

2. Biographical information on Deborah Richmond is contained in
Beatrix T. Rumford, ed., *American Folk Portraits* (Boston, 1981), 215; Eliza-
beth Mankin Kornhauser and Christine Skeeles Schloss, "Painting and
Other Pictorial Arts," in *The Great River: Art and Society of the Connecticut
Valley, 1635–1820*, exhib. cat. (Hartford, Conn., 1985), 162–63.

3. Nina Fletcher Little, "Little-Known Connecticut Artists, 1790–
1810," *Connecticut Historical Society Bulletin* 22 (October 1957), 101–4. See
Kornhauser and Schloss, "Painting and Other Pictorial Arts," 162–63, for
additional information on this group of portraits.

4. The house may represent a house in Suffield seen from the Gay Manse,
perhaps the mansion house of Ebenezer King, built in 1795 and located
one tenth of a mile away on South Street. See the Notebooks of Delphina
Clark, vol. H, High Street North, c. 1949, Kent Memorial Library.

5. See Kornhauser and Schloss, "Painting and Other Pictorial Arts,"
162–63, for this author's discussion of the similarities.

73

72

72   Ephraim Starr, 1802

Simon Fitch (1758–1835)
Oil on canvas
59 x 40 in. (149.8 x 101.4 cm.)
Wadsworth Atheneum, Hartford, Connecticut
The Ella Gallup Sumner and Mary Catlin Sumner
    Collection, 1961

73   Mrs. Ephraim Starr (Hannah Beach), 1802

Oil on canvas
58⅝ x 40¼ in. (148.2 x 102.2 cm.)
Wadsworth Atheneum, Hartford, Connecticut
The Ella Gallup Sumner and Mary Catlin Sumner
    Collection, 1961

Simon Fitch is noted for a small number of masterly portraits that were in part inspired by the works of Ralph Earl and his followers.[1] Fitch was a descendant of the Rev. James Fitch, the distinguished first settler of Norwich, Connecticut. Born in Norwich, Simon moved with his family to Lebanon, Connecticut, where he attended the school of Nathan Tisdale along with the artist John Trumbull.[2] There he married Wealthy Huntington in 1783. He was later a captain in the state militia. He remained for the most part in Lebanon until his death.

Simon Fitch was undoubtedly familiar with the family portraits painted by John Trumbull at his parents' home. In addition, Winthrop Chandler had painted members of his wife's family, the Huntingtons.[3] Although Fitch's brother-in-law, Dan Huntington, referred to him as a "portrait painter," there are only fifteen works assigned to Fitch, which date from 1795 to 1802. Because Fitch did not sign his portraits, firm attributions are based on contemporary sources.

His finest effort as an artist can be found in his latest known works, the portraits of Ephraim and Hannah Starr. These portraits are documented by early paper labels attached to the original stretcher bars, inscribed in pencil (possibly by the artist): "Portrait of Ephraim Starr / taken in the 57th year of his Age / by Simon Fitch in Feby 1802 –" and "Portrait of Hannah Starr / taken in the 56th Year of her Age / by Simon Fitch in Feby 1802."

Ephraim Starr (1745–1809) came from Middletown, Connecticut, a major port on the Connecticut River, where he came in contact with the Goshen, Connecticut, merchant Uri Hill. Ephraim worked as a clerk in Hill's Litchfield County store, and after his employer died of smallpox in

1766, he took over the business and married his widow, in 1769. Hannah Beach Starr (1745–1826) spent her entire life in Goshen and bore nine children.

Ephraim Starr was so successful as a merchant that he was able to retire by the age of forty-eight. His most profitable venture occurred at the close of the American Revolution, just before the evacuation of the British, when he purchased a wide variety of goods in New York City at a low price and sold this merchandise in his store in Goshen. In the portrait, Fitch shows his subject near a table on which is a large account book. Ephraim is writing on a piece of paper: "20 shares / New York / Bank" – words symbolic of his many investments. When he died, he left an estate worth over sixty-five thousand dollars.[4]

The Starr portraits display the conservative aesthetic associated with Connecticut portraiture in the eighteenth century, which is embodied in the works of such artists as Winthrop Chandler and to which Ralph Earl responded in his Connecticut portraits of the 1790s. Their scale and composition – the full-length figures seated in Windsor chairs next to tables and the decorative, patterned floors – relate these works to the compositions made popular by Earl.

Fitch adheres to a subdued palette on the thinly painted canvases and concentrates on the painstaking delineation of his subjects. The Starrs are, typically, shown in forthright depictions, devoid of flattery. Ephraim is seated in a green Windsor armchair, solid enough to hold his considerable bulk, of which he was evidently proud.[5] Fitch did not attempt to conceal the stress placed on the buttons of his stout subject's plain black vest.

Hannah, depicted with an equally stern visage, is staring boldly out at the viewer. She is dressed modestly in a voluminous green silk gown and a white cap with embroidered stars. She holds a closed fan and a moss rose. Like her husband, she leans on a country cherrywood table.

The Starr portraits descended in the family of the couple's fifth child, Abigail Starr Lyman. The Wadsworth Atheneum acquired the portraits from John Goodwin Lyman of Montreal in 1961.[6]

1.   The major work on Simon Fitch has been done by William L. Warren; see Warren, "Captain Simon Fitch of Lebanon," *Connecticut Historical Society Bulletin* 26 (October 1961); Warren, "The Starr Portraits by Simon Fitch of Lebanon," *Wadsworth Atheneum Bulletin* (Winter 1961), 7–17.
2.   Dan Huntington, *Memories, Counsels and Reflections by an Octogenary* (Cambridge, Mass., 1857), discussed in Warren, "Starr Portraits," 13.
3.   Nina Fletcher Little, "Winthrop Chandler," *Art in America* 35 (April 1947), special issue.
4.   Ephraim Starr, Probate Inventory, Goshen, 1809, Reel 706, no. 5453, CSL.
5.   Ephraim Starr's inventory lists "12 Elbow Windsors," "8 Common [Windsors]," and "6 fanned backed [Windsors]."
6.   Painting Files, Wadsworth Atheneum, Hartford, Conn.

74 Portrait of George Eliot and Family, c. 1796

Jonathan Budington (1779–1823)

Oil on canvas

44⅞ x 56¾ in. (114.0 x 144.1 cm.)

Signed and dated at lower left: "J. Budington Pinxt 79[?]"

Technical note: the canvas is in two sections, attached with a vertical seam

Yale University Art Gallery, New Haven, Connecticut

Gift of the descendants of Rev. Jared Eliot, B.A. 1706, and the relatives of Nellie P. Eliot, 1983.98

Hartford only

Ralph Earl's sustained presence in Fairfield County, Connecticut, where he painted portraits intermittently from 1788 until 1798, inspired the artistic career of the local artist Jonathan Budington. The son of Walter Budington and Ruth Couch Budington, Jonathan was born in the town of Fairfield. He married Sarah Peck in New Haven in 1820. Although his artistic career has yet to be fully explored, six portraits and one landscape ranging in date from 1792 to 1802 have been assigned to him.[1]

Portraits by Earl hung in houses throughout Fairfield County and were easily accessible to Budington. As early as 1789, a visitor to nearby Greenfield Hill noted: "Here are many family portraits, lately done by Earle [sic], who has painted many in this part of the country."[2] Young Jonathan Budington painted members of the same families that Earl painted, including the Burrs and the Hubbells. In 1802 he also painted copies of Earl's earlier *John Nichols* (1795; private collection) and *Mrs. John Nichols (Mary Hill)* (1795; private collection); the subjects lived in Easton, Connecticut.[3]

Budington's *Portrait of George Eliot and Family*, painted in Killington (now Clinton), Connecticut, around 1796, clearly demonstrates Earl's impact on this fledgling painter. George Eliot, Jr. (1767–1828), was described as "an extensive farmer, a man of means, a deacon in the Congregational Church, and prominent in public life. . . . He was a Jeffersonian Democrat."[4] He married Patience Lane, also of Killington, in 1790, and the couple had one child, Ely Augustus (1791–1870), who appears in their family portrait.

This is an ambitious composition executed on a large scale. Budington adopts Earl's favored palette and compositional elements, including the red upholstered round-backed side chairs, red drapery, shelves of individually titled books, and a green-cloth-covered table. He even went so far as to adopt Earl's distinctive manner of signing his portraits, using the expensive pigment red vermillion.

Budington, like Earl, imbues his portrait with personal details that provide an understanding of the social status and philosophical attitudes of his subjects. The prominent display of books in the portrait, a convention of Earl's Connecticut portraits, is an example. Ely Augustus holds open a book inscribed "THE child's DUTY to Parents"; the opening sentence reads: "Solomon sai[?] THEE." The importance of this message and its implications concerning the boy's education is reinforced by the gesture of Patience Eliot's left hand, which points to the book. In addition, George Eliot's political leanings as a Jeffersonian Democrat are made evident by the inclusion on the bookshelf of four volumes, two of which are titled "SMITH / WEALTH OF / NATIONS." Adam Smith's *An Inquiry into the Nature and Causes of the Wealth of Nations* (1776) explored the benefits of a liberal economic system that promoted the individual over the government. Finally, Patience Eliot shows off an elaborately embroidered drawstring bag, perhaps her own handiwork. Grouping the three figures close together conveys a sense of family unity, which is further demonstrated by their gestures of affection. The young son, Ely Augustus, stands between his parents with his right arm on his father's knee while his mother affectionately wraps her right arm around her son. Like his mentor Earl, Budington has provided far more in this family portrait than mere likenesses of his subjects. Rather, he has successfully conveyed a very personal testimony of the Eliots' middle-class status and unity as a family.

1. Paula B. Freedman has provided the most definitive information on this artist's life and works in her article "In the Presence of Strangers: Jonathan Budington's *Portrait of the George Eliot Family*," *Yale University Art Gallery Bulletin* 40 (Spring 1988), 22–30, 30n. See also Nina Fletcher Little, *Paintings by New England Provincial Artists, 1775–1800*, exhib. cat. (Boston, 1976), 98–99.

2. Samuel Davis, "Journal of a Tour to Connecticut – Autumn of 1789," in *Proceedings of the Massachusetts Historical Society* (Boston, 1869–70), 18.

3. See Little, *Paintings by New England Artists*, 98–99. Earl's portraits of members of these families, including the Burrs and Hubbells, are discussed in Elizabeth Mankin Kornhauser, *Ralph Earl: Artist-Entrepreneur* (Ann Arbor, Mich., 1989), 267–68, 292–93, 307–8.

4. *Commemorative Biographical Record of Middlesex County, Connecticut, Containing Biographical Sketches of Prominent and Representative Citizens, and of Many of the Early Settled Families, Illustrated* (Chicago, 1903), 887, quoted in Freedman, "In the Presence of Strangers," 25.

74

Select Bibliography

UNPUBLISHED MATERIAL

Adamson, Jeremy Elwell. "Frederic Edwin Church's 'Niagara': The Sublime as Transcendence." Ph.D. diss., University of Michigan, 1981.

Cogswell, Rev. James. Diary. MS, Connecticut Historical Society, Hartford.

Cogswell Family Papers. MS, Connecticut Historical Society, Hartford.

Cogswell Family Papers. MS, Sterling Memorial Library and Beinecke Rare Book and Manuscript Library, Yale University, New Haven, Conn.

Colton, George. Diary. MS, Connecticut Historical Society, Hartford.

Duane, James. Daybook F. Duane Papers. MS, New-York Historical Society, New York.

Earl, Ralph E. W. Papers. MS, American Antiquarian Society, Worcester, Mass.

Gage Family Papers. "Ralph Earl." MS, American Antiquarian Society, Worcester, Mass.

Hart, Charles Henry. Papers. "Ralph Earl." Microfilm, rolls 928–35, Archives of American Art, New York.

Kornhauser, Elizabeth Mankin. "Ralph Earl: Artist-Entrepreneur." 2 vols. Ph.D. diss., Boston University, 1988.

Lahvis, Sylvia. "Ralph Earl and the Eighteenth Century New England Landscape." Master's thesis, Oberlin College, 1971.

Lane, Jared. Account Books. 3 books. Private collection.

"Minutes of the Mayor's Court." 1785–87. County Clerk's Office, County Courthouse, New York.

Pelham, Henry. Letter. "Copley/Pelham Correspondence." Public Record Office, Archives, London.

Photograph Files. Frick Art Reference Library, New York.

Sawitzky, William, and Susan Sawitzky. Papers. MS, New-York Historical Society, New York.

Seymour, Moses. Account Book. MS, Litchfield Historical Society, Litchfield, Conn.

Shaw, Thomas. Ledgers. Nathaniel and Thomas Shaw Papers. MS, Sterling Memorial Library, Yale University, New Haven, Conn.

Strong, Nehemiah. Letters. Beinecke Rare Book and Manuscript Library, Yale University, New Haven, Conn.

Trumbull, Joseph. Letter. MS, Historic Deerfield, Deerfield, Mass.

PUBLISHED MATERIAL

Alberts, Robert C. Benjamin West: A Biography. Boston: Houghton Mifflin, 1978.

Allen, Whitney. "Ralph Earl: A Rediscovered American." Complete Collector 8 (November 1945), 20–24.

Ballard, Lockett Ford. "Paintings of Ralph Earl at the Litchfield Historical Society." Antiques 86 (November 1977), 959–63.

Barber, John W. History and Antiquities of New Haven, Connecticut. New Haven, 1831.

Bartlett, Ellen Strong. "Extracts from the Diary of Dr. Mason Fitch Cogswell." Connecticut Magazine 5 (January–December 1899), 532–37, 562–71.

Beardsley, William A. "An Old New Haven Engraver and His Work: Amos Doolittle." Papers of the New Haven Colony Historical Society 7 (1914), 132–50.

Bergengren, Charles. " 'Finished to the Utmost Nicety': Plain Portraits in America, 1760–1860." In John Michael Vlach and Simon Bronner, eds., Folk Art and Art Worlds. Ann Arbor, Mich.: UMI Press, 1986.

Burroughs, Alan. Limners and Likenesses: Three Centuries of American Painting. Cambridge: Harvard University Press, 1936.

Chase, Elizabeth A. "Ralph Earl's Portrait of Mrs. Moseley and Her Son Charles." Bulletin of the Associates in Fine Arts at Yale University 12 (February 1943), 1–3.

Cogswell, Frances Root. A Collection of Cogswell Family Letters and Diaries, 1772–1830. West Hartford, Conn.: American School for the Deaf, n.d.

Cooper, Helen, et al., ed. John Trumbull: The Hand and Spirit of a Painter. Exhib. cat. New Haven, Conn.: Yale University Press for the Yale University Art Gallery, 1982.

Copley, John Singleton, and Henry Pelham. Letters and Papers of John Singleton Copley and Henry Pelham, 1739–1776. Edited by Guernsey Jones, 1914. Reprint. New York: DaCapo Press, 1970.

Craven, Wayne. Colonial American Portraiture. Cambridge: Cambridge University Press, 1986.

Drepperd, Carl W. American Pioneer Art and Artists. Springfield, Mass.: Ekberg, 1942.

Dunlap, William. History of the Rise and Progress of the Arts of Design in the United States. 1834. Reprint in 3 vols. New York: Dover, 1969.

Earle, Pliny. The Earle Family: Ralph Earle and His Descendants. Worcester, Mass.: Press of Charles Hamilton, 1888.

———. Memoirs of Pliny Earle, M.D. Boston: Damrell and Upham, 1898.

Evans, Dorinda. Benjamin West and His American Students. Exhib. cat. Washington, D.C.: Smithsonian Institution Press for the National Portrait Gallery, 1980.

Failey, Dean F. Long Island Is My Nation. Exhib. cat. Setauket, N.Y.: Society for the Preservation of Long Island Antiquities, 1976.

Fawcett, Trevor. "Eighteenth-Century Art in Norwich." Walpole Society, 1976–1978, 46 (1978), 71–87.

French, Henry W. Art and Artists in Connecticut. Boston: Lee and Shepard; New York: Charles T. Dillingham, 1879.

Gage, Thomas Hovey. "Ralph Earl." Bulletin of the Worcester Art Museum 1 (July 1916), 6–10.

Gates, Charles O. Stephen Gates of Hingham and Lancaster, Massachusetts, and His Descendants. New York, 1898.

Gerdts, William H. "Additions to the Museum's Collections of American Paintings and Sculpture." Museum (Newark Museum) 13 (Winter–Spring 1961), 3–4.

———. "American Landscape Painting: Critical Judgments, 1730–1845." American Art Journal 17, no. 4 (1985), 2–33.

Goodrich, Laurence B. Ralph Earl: Recorder for an Era. Oneonta: State University of New York, 1967.

———. "Ralph Earl's Debt to Gainsborough and Other English Artists." Antiques 78 (November 1960), 464–65.

———. "Ralph Earl's First Royal Academy Entry." Antiques 75 (May 1959), 456–57.

———. "Ralph Earl's Portraits of Three Young English Ladies." Antiques 71 (November 1958), 418–19.

Gottesman, Rita Susswein. *The Arts and Crafts in New York, 1777–1799: Advertisements and News Items from the New York City Newspapers*. New York: New-York Historical Society, 1954.

Graves, Algernon. *The Royal Academy of Arts: A Complete Dictionary of Contributors and Their Work from Its Foundation in 1769 to 1904*. 8 vols. London: Henry Graves, 1895.

Green, Samuel M. *American Art: A Historical Survey*. New York: Ronald Press, 1966.

————. "Uncovering the Connecticut School." *Art News* 51 (January 1953), 38–41, 57–58.

Halsey, R. T. H. "Ralph Earl." *Metropolitan Museum of Art Bulletin* 1 (May 1906), 83–86.

Harris, Neil. *The Artist in American Society: The Formative Years, 1790–1860*. New York: Braziller, 1966.

Heslip, Colleen Cowles. *Between the Rivers: Itinerant Painters from the Connecticut to the Hudson* (Williamstown, Mass.: Sterling and Francine Clark Art Institute, 1990).

Isham, Gyles. "Correspondence." *Country Life* (May 1956), 934.

Kornhauser, Elizabeth Mankin. *Ralph Earl: Artist-Entrepreneur*. Ann Arbor, Mich.: University Microfilms, 1989.

————. "Ralph Earl as an Itinerant Artist: Pattern of Patronage." In Peter Benes, ed., *Itinerancy in New England and New York: Annual Proceedings of the Dublin Seminar for New England Folk Life, 1984*, 172–90. Boston: Boston University Press, 1986.

————. "Regional Landscape Views: A Distinctive Element in Connecticut River Valley Portraits, 1790–1810." *Antiques* 78 (November 1985), 1012–19.

Kornhauser, Elizabeth Mankin, and Christine Skeeles Schloss. "Painting and Other Pictorial Arts." In *The Great River: Art and Society of the Connecticut Valley, 1635–1820*. Exhib. cat. Hartford, Conn.: Wadsworth Atheneum, 1985.

Little, Nina Fletcher. *Paintings by New England Provincial Artists, 1775–1800*. Exhib. cat. Boston: Museum of Fine Arts, 1976.

————. "Recently Discovered Paintings by Winthrop Chandler." *Art in America* 36 (April 1948), 81–97.

————. "Winthrop Chandler." *Art in America* 35 (April 1947). Special issue.

MacBeth, Russell. "Portraits by Ralph E. W. Earl." *Antiques* 100 (September 1971), 390–93.

Marceau, Henri. "A Recently Discovered Portrait by Ralph Earl." *Gazette des Beaux-Arts* 23 (April 1943), 251–55.

Montgomery, Charles, and Patricia Kane. *American Art: Toward Independence*. Boston: New York Graphic Society, 1976.

Morgan, John Hill. "Ralph Earl and His Portrait of Truman Marsh." *Brooklyn Museum Quarterly* 4 (October 1921), 133–41.

"Ralph Earl." In *National Cyclopedia of American Biography*. New York: James T. White, 1901.

Nygren, Edward J., with Bruce Robertson et al. *Views and Visions: American Landscape before 1830*. Exhib. cat. Washington, D.C.: Corcoran Gallery of Art, 1986.

Orcutt, Samuel. *History of the Towns of New Milford and Bridgewater, Connecticut, 1703–1882*. Hartford, Conn.: Case, Lockwood and Brainard Company, 1882.

Parker, Barbara Neville. "Huldah Bradley by Ralph Earl." *Boston Museum of Fine Arts Bulletin* 28 (August 1940), 53–55.

Parks, Robert O. "Smith College Museum: Recent Accessions." *College Art Journal* 17 (Fall 1957), 73–75.

Penny, Nicholas, ed. *Reynolds*. New York: Harry N. Abrams, 1989.

Phillips, John Marshall. "Ralph Earl, Loyalist." *Art in America* 37 (October 1949), 187–89.

Pointon, Marcia. "Portrait-Painting as a Business Enterprise in London in the 1780s." *Art History* 7 (June 1984), 187–205.

Prown, Jules. *American Painting: From Its Beginning to the Armory Show*. New York: Rizzoli, 1980.

————. *John Singleton Copley*. 2 vols. Cambridge: Harvard University Press, 1966.

Quick, Michael. *American Portraiture in the Grand Manner*. Exhib. cat. Washington, D.C.: National Portrait Gallery, 1981.

Quimby, Ian M. G. "The Doolittle Engravings of the Battle of Lexington and Concord." *Winterthur Portfolio* 4 (1968), 83–108.

Rathbone, Perry T. "The Seymour Portraits by Ralph Earl." *Bulletin of the City Art Museum of St. Louis* 34 (Spring 1948), 22–27.

Reese, Albert. "A Newly Discovered Landscape by Ralph Earl." *Art in America* 36 (January 1948), 49–53.

Saunders, Richard H., and Ellen G. Miles. *American Colonial Portraits: 1700–1776*. Exhib. cat. Washington, D.C.: National Portrait Gallery, 1987.

Sawitzky, William. *Connecticut Portraits by Ralph Earl, 1751–1801*. Exhib. cat. New Haven, Conn.: Yale University Art Gallery, 1935.

————. *Ralph Earl, 1751–1801*. Exhib. cat. New York: Whitney Museum of American Art, 1945.

————. "Ralph Earl's Historical Painting: A View of the Town of Concord." *Antiques* 28 (September 1935), 97–100.

Sawitzky, William, and Susan Sawitzky. "Two Letters from Ralph Earl, with Notes on His English Period." *Worcester Art Museum Annual* 8 (1960), 8–41.

Schloss, Christine Skeeles. *The Beardsley Limner and Some of His Contemporaries*. Exhib. cat. Williamsburg, Va.: Colonial Williamsburg Foundation, 1972.

Sherman, Frederick. "The Angus Nickelson Family." *Art in America* 23 (October 1931), 154–58.

————. "An Early and a Late Portrait by Ralph Earl." *Art in America* 24 (April 1936), 86–91.

————. "James Earl: A Forgotten American Portrait Painter." *Art in America* 23 (October 1931), 143–58.

————. "Ralph Earl: Biographical and Critical Notes." *Art in America* 23 (May 1935), 57–68.

————. "Ralph Earl: An Eighteenth-Century Connecticut Portrait Painter." *Art in America* 22 (June 1934), 81–91.

————. "The So-called Ralph Earl Originals of Doolittle's Concord and Lexington Engravings." *Art in America* 24 (October 1936), 43–44.

A Sketch of the Origin and Progress of the Humane Society of the City of New-York. Together with the Act of Incorporation and By-laws, Inc. Pamphlet: New York Van Winkle and Wiley, 1814.

Spencer, Harold. *The American Earls: Ralph Earl, James Earl, R. E. W. Earl*. Exhib. cat. Storrs, Conn.: William Benton Museum of Art, 1972.

Stewart, Robert G. "James Earl: American Painter of Loyalists and His Career in England." *American Art Journal* 20, no. 4 (1988), 34–59.

Swan, Mabel M. "The Johnstons and Reas—Japanners." *Antiques* 47 (May 1943), 211–13.

Tallmadge, Benjamin. *Memoirs of Colonel Benjamin Tallmadge*. New York: Society of the Sons of the Revolution in the State of New York, 1905.

Trent, Robert F. "The Charter Oak Artifacts." Exhib. cat. *Connecticut Historical Society Bulletin* 49 (Summer 1984), 124–30.

Tuckerman, Lucy. "Landscapes and Portraits by Ralph Earl." *Bulletin of the Worcester Art Museum* 1 (January 1917), 7–10.

Washburn, Emory. *Historical Sketches of the Town of Leicester, Massachusetts*. Boston: John Wilson, 1860.

Washburn, Gordon. *Old and New England*. Exhib. cat. Providence: Rhode Island School of Design, 1945.

Wendell, William G. "Colonel Samuel Talcott and His Portrait by Ralph Earl." *Wadsworth Atheneum Bulletin* 5 (Winter 1963), 23–25.

Index

Page numbers in italics refer to illustrations. Paintings are by Earl unless otherwise specified.

Abigail Lyman Brackett and Child (Ralph E. W. Earl), 64
Adam Babcock (Copley), 10, 11, 104, *104*, 106, 108
Adam Babcock (Pelham), *11*, 104
Adams, John, president, 11–12, 74, 180
Adams, Samuel, 11, *12*
Admiral Richard Kempenfelt, 26, 28, 32, 118, *119*, 120, *120* (Kettle; Earlom)
Alsop, Mary, 53, 187, 188–89, *190*
Angus Nickelson and Family, 48, 75, *166–67*, 168–69
Ann Whiteside Earl, 30, *133*, 134
Architecture, 57–58, 60, 70–71, 72, 187, 208, 217
Augustus John, Lord Hervey (Gainsborough), 118, 120

Babcock, Abigail Smith, 10, 11, 104, *105*, 106, 108, 194
Babcock, Adam, 10–11, *11*, 104, *104*, 106, 108, 194
Barber, John W. (1798–1885), 14, 111
Baron von Steuben, 37, 86, 90, *137*, *138*, 138–39
Barrow, Thomas, 34, 35, 95nn95–96
Bathurst, Henry, second earl, 121, *123*
Battle of Lexington, The (Doolittle), 14, 111, *112*, *114* (advertisement)
Beechey, Sir William (1753–1839), 19, 168; painting by, *20*
Benjamin S. Judah, 55, 56, 86, 89, 90, *196*, 197
Bennington, Vermont, 61–62, 222, 224, 226–27, 228
Boardman, Daniel, 45, 47, 73–76, 152, *153*, 154, 157, 160, 161, 217
Boardman, Elijah, 45, 47, 58, 60, 73–

76, 83, 87–88, 90, 103, 152, 154, 155, 156, 157, 202, 213, 217
Boardman, Esther, 47, 74, 157, *158*
Boardman, Mary Anna Whiting, 58, 60, 152, 154, *212*, 213, 217
Boardman, Sarah Bostwick, 45, 60, 152, 154, 157, *214*, 216
Boardman, Sherman, 45, 60, 73, 74, 152, 154, 157, 161, *215*, 216
Boardman, William Whiting, 60, *212*, 213
Bradley, Huldah, 56, 198, *200*
Bradley, Lucy, 56, 198, *201*
Bradley, Samuel, 85, 198, *199*
Bradley, Sarah Wakeman, 85, 198, *199*
Brewster, John, Jr. (1766–1854), 66, 86, 91, 178, 242–43; paintings by, *243*
Brown, Mather (1761–1831), 22, 89, 90, 94n68
Budington, Jonathan (1779–1823), 67, 251; painting by, *252*
Buell, David, 60–61; 76, 97n122, 202

Callahan, John, 32, 95nn83–85
Callahan, Lucretia Greene, 32, 95nn84–85
Campbell, Samuel, 34, 95–96nn98–99
Canfield, Judson, 60, 202, 208, *209*
Canfield, Mabel Ruggles, 60, 202, 208, *209*
Canfield Children, 86
Captain Elijah Dewey, 61, 222–23, *224*
Captain John Pratt, 41, 186, 187, *192*
Carpenter, Mary Ann, 19, 89, 90, 115, *117*, 118
Carpenter, William, 19, 86, 90, 115, *116*, 118
Champion, Judah, 45, 46, 160
Chandler, Winthrop (1747–90), 6–8, 42, 56, 69, 70, 86, 95n97, 103–4, 154, 156, 250; paintings by, *9*, *57*, *102*
Clinton, George, 51, *51*
Cogswell, James, 39, 51, 97n126, 178, 242
Cogswell, James, Sr., 39, 51–52, *52*
Cogswell, Mason Fitch, 39–55 passim, 65, 83, 96n114, 142, 146, 152, 178, *179*, 180, 187, 192, 242
Colonel Benjamin Tallmadge and Son William Tallmadge, 49, 58, 172–73, *175*
Colonel George Onslow, 26, *27*, 28
Colonel Nathaniel Taylor, 161
Colonel Samuel Talcott, 51–52, 85, 86, 87 (reverse), 88, 89, 184, *185*
Colonel William Floyd, 55, 192, *193*
Colonel William Taylor, 47–48, 84 (detail), 127, 161, *163*, *164*
Comfort Starr Mygatt and His Daughter Lucy (Brewster), 66, 86, 242, *245*

Connecticut, society and culture in, 69–83. *See also* names of cities and counties
Connecticut River Valley, 7, 51–53, 55, 57, 58, 62, 67, 69–83
Connecticut School, 66, 99n184
Connecticut Wits, 43, 51, 178, 188
Copley, John Singleton (1738–1815), 2, 7, 8, 10–11, 13, 16, 18, 19, 22, 25, 30, 34, 42, 90, 103, 104, 106, 118, 121, 135, 154, 156, 188; paintings by, *12*, *22*, *104*, *105*, *123*

Daggett, Elizabeth Prescott, 11, 106, *107*, 108
Daggett, Henry, 11, 106, *106*, 108
Daniel Boardman, 45, 47, 73, 152, *153*
Davenport, Abraham, 43, 44, 97n126
David and Sarah Hubbell, 96n115
David Baldwin, 48, 49
Death of Major Pierson, The (Copley), 22
Death of the Earl of Chatham, The (Copley), 121
Deborah Richmond (unknown artist), 66–67, 246, *247*
Delanoy, Abraham, Jr. (1742–95), 16, 33, 69, 95n91
Denny, Thomas, 65, 236
Devotion, Ebenezer, judge, 8, 69, 83, 86, *102*, 103
Devotion, Ebenezer, clergyman, 8, 9, 103, 178
Devotion, Eunice Huntington, 86, *102*, 103
Devotion, Martha Lathrop, 9, 103, 178
Dewey, Elijah, 61, 222–23, *224*, 228
Dewey, Mary Schenck, 61, 222–23, *225*, 228
Dr. David Rogers, 43, 127, 142, *145*
Dr. Ebenezer Hunt, 62
Dr. Joseph Trumbull, 22, 127, 131, *132*
Dr. Lemuel Hopkins (Trumbull), 178
Dr. Mason Fitch Cogswell, 51, 178, *179*, 180
Dr. Seth Bird, 60
Don Josef de Jaudenes y Nebot (Stuart), 56
Doolittle, Amos (1754–1832), 14, 64–65, 111, 114, *114* (advertisement), *114* (portrait); engravings by, *112*–*13*
Drake, Marianne, 29, *128*, 130
Drake, Sophia, 29–30, *129*, 130
Duane, James, 34, 37, 138
Duane, Mary Livingston, 37, *38*
Dunlap, William (1766–1839), 1, 13, 14, 21, 56, 94n64, 95n84, 95n96, 239
Durand, John (active 1765–82), 8, 69; painting by, *8*
Dwight, Mary Woolsey, 13, 43, 194

Dwight, Timothy, 13, 21, 43, 55, 60, 81–83, *81*, 94n64, 194, 198
Dyer, Eliphalet, 12–13, *13*, 79, 146

Earl, Ann Whiteside, 30, 36, 60–61, 95n86, *133*, 134, 229
Earl, James, 2, 5, 6, 26
Earl, Mary Ann, 36, 61, 96n105, 134
Earl, Ralph (1751–1801): critical recognition of, 1–2, 26, 40, 66–67; death of, 1, 65; as Loyalist, 1, 6, 8, 14–15, 16, 34, 37, 111; early years of, 5–6, 92n1; early career in New Haven, 10–15; marriages of, 10, 30, 36, 60–61, 92–93n21, 95n86, 134; panorama of Niagara Falls, 14, 62–65, *64* (advertisement), 99nn172–79; English career of, 16–30, *17*, 90; New York career of, 30–39, *31*, 41, 87–88, 90, 96n109; Connecticut career of, *31*, 39–56, 69, 70, 71, 81, 86, 87–88; imprisonment of, 34–39, 95–96nn98–99; alcoholism of, 36, 60, 65; landscape paintings by, 45, 52–53, 56–60, 67, 206, 208, 228, *236*; final years of, 60–65; work in Vermont and Massachusetts, 60–65, 69; followers of, 66–67; working methods and materials, 85–91. *See also* titles of specific paintings
Earl, Ralph E. W. (1785 or 1788–1838), 2, 16, 36, 61, 62, 64, 96n105, 134, 219–20, 228, 229, 232; paintings by, *63*, *220*, *230–31*
Earl, Sarah Gates, 10, 32, 92–93n21, 95n86
Earle, Thomas, 65, 232, *233*
Earll, Clark, 5, 6, 10
Earll, Ralph, Sr., 5–6, 8
Eldredge, James, 242, *243*
Eldredge, Lucy Gallup, 242, *243*
Elijah Boardman, 45, 47, 58, 73, 83, 87–88, 103, 154, *155*, 156
Eliot, Ely Augustus, 251, *252*
Eliot, George, Jr. (1767–1828), 67, 251, *252*
Eliot, Patience Lane, 251, *252*
Eliphalet Dyer, 12–13, *13*
Elizabeth Gay and Son William Cushing Gay, Jr. (unknown artist), *247*
Ellsworth, Abigail Wolcott, 28, 52, 58, 66, 86, 88, 149, 180–81, *182–83*
Ellsworth, Oliver, *4* (detail), 28, 52, 58, 66, 86, 88–89, 146, 180–81, *182–83*
Engagement at the North Bridge in Concord, The (Doolittle), 14, *113*
Ephraim Starr (Fitch), 67, 249, *250*
Esther Boardman, 47, 157, *158*

Fairfield County, Conn., 43, 48, 56, 67, 70
Family Portrait (Ralph E. W. Earl), 219, *220*
Fitch, Simon (1785–1835), 67, 250; paintings by, *248–49*
Floyd, William, 55, 172, 192, *193*
Front View of Dartmouth College, with Chapel and Hall, A (Dunham), 237

Gainsborough, Thomas (d. 1788), 23, 25, 28, 56, 118, 120, 124; painting by, *23*
Gentleman with a Gun and Two Dogs, A, 28, *126*, 127
George Clinton (Trumbull), 51, *51*
George Eliot and Family (Budington), 67
Gere, Edward, 62, 63, 229

Halsey, Jeremiah, 66, *240*, 241
Hamilton, Elizabeth Schuyler, 37, 140, *141*
Hartford, Conn., 51–53, 57, 65, 66, 69, 70, 71, 73, 79, 99n17, 184, *185*
Hayden, Thomas (1745–1817), 58, 181, 208
Head of the Earl of Bathurst, Lord Chancellor (Copley), *123*
Henry, Edward L. (1841–1919), 192
Henry Daggett, 11, 106, *106*, 108
Homestead of General Timothy Ruggles (Chandler), 56, *57*
Honeywell, St. John (1763–98), 114
Houses Fronting New Milford Green, 60, 68 (detail), 76, 154, 217, *218*
Huldah Bradley, 56, 198, *200*
Huntington, Samuel, 6–7, 83, *83*, 103, 178
Hutchins, Hezekiah, 63, 64, 98n169
Hyndman, John, 25–26, *25*

Isaac Gere, 62
Isham, Sophia, 28–29, *29*, 150

Jacob Isaacs, 96n115
James Eldredge (Brewster), 242, *243*
James Tilley (Chandler), 104n8
Jared Lane, 59, 88, 89, 202–3, *204*, 206
Jemima Kingsley Gere, 62
Jennys, Richard (active 1766–1801), 58–59, 66, 90; paintings by, *59*
Jennys, William (1793–1807), 58–59, 66, 69, 90, 99n169; paintings by, *59*
Jeremiah Halsey (Steward), 66, *240*, 241
Jocelyn, Nathaniel (1796–1881), 109
Jocelyn, Simeon S. (1799–1879), 109
John Nichols, 251
John Trumbull (Trumbull), 178
Johnston, John (c. 1753–1818), 11, 32, 95n89

Johnston, Martha Spear, 11, 32, 135, *136*
Johnston, William (1732–72), 7, 8, 11, 69, 135; painting by, *7*
Judah, Benjamin, 55, 56, 86, 89, 90, 196, *197*
Judge Ebenezer Devotion (Chandler), 8, 86, 102, *103–4*, 154
Judge Elias Perkins, 98n143
Judge Judson Canfield, 209

Kempenfelt, Richard, 26, 28, 32, 118, *119*, 120, *120*
Kettle, Tilly (1740–86), 28, 118, 120; painting by, *120*

Lady Williams and Child, 24, 25
Landscape of the Ruggles Homestead, 59, 88, 206, *207*
Landscape View of Old Bennington, 61–62, 65, 222, 226–27, *228*, 229
Landscape View of the Canfield House, 60, 208, *210–11*
Lane, Apphia Ruggles, 59, 88, 202–3, *205*, 206
Lane, Jared, 59, 76, 85–86, 88, 89–90, 202–3, *204*, 206
Lazarus Ruggles (Richard and William Jennys), 59, *59*
Leicester, Mass., 5–6, 65, 92n16, *234–35*, 236
Litchfield, Conn., 43–45, 48–49, 51, 58, 60, 70, 71, 73, 76–77, 78, 99n17
London, England, 16–30 passim, 88, 90, 94n78, 118, 130–31, 229
Looking East from Denny Hill, 5, 65, *234–35*, 236
Lucy Bradley, 56, 198, *201*
Lucy Knapp Mygatt and Her Son George (Brewster), 66, 86, 243–43, *244*
Lyman, Medad, 10

Man in a Gray Coat (Copley), 135
Map of Connecticut (Doolittle), 71
Mariann Wolcott, 45, 150, *151*
Marianne Drake, 29, *128*, 130
Marinus Willett, 34, 51, 86, 90, 176, *177*
Martha Lathrop Devotion (Chandler), 9
Martha Tennent Rogers and Daughter, 43, 142–43, *144*
Mary Ann Carpenter, 19, 89, 90, 115, *117*, 118
Mary H. Buell, 60
Mary Ledyard (Mrs. Thomas Seymour, Jr.) (Johnston), 7, *7*
Master of Chancery Entering the House of Lords, A, 28, 121, *122*
Matilda Stoughton de Jaudenes y Nebot (Stuart), 56
Midshipman Augustus Brine (Copley), 118

Mr. John Hyndman, 25–26, *25*

Mrs. Abraham Beach, 96n115

Mrs. Adam Babcock (Copley), 10, 11, *104*, *105*, 106, 108

Mrs. Alexander Hamilton (Elizabeth Schuyler), 37, 140, *141*

Mrs. Benjamin Tallmadge and Son Henry Floyd and Daughter Maria Jones, 49

Mrs. Charles Jeffery Smith, 55, 194, *195*

Mrs. Ebenezer Devotion (Eunice Huntington) and Eunice Devotion (Chandler), 8, 86, *102*, *103*

Mrs. Ebenezer Porter (Lucy "Patty" Pierce Merwin) (Ralph E. W. Earl), 62, 229, *231*

Mrs. Elias Perkins (Lucretia Shaw Woodbridge), 98n143

Mrs. Elijah Boardman and Son, 58, 60, *212*, *213*, 217

Mrs. Elijah Dewey (Mary Schenck), 61, 222–23, *225*

Mrs. Ephraim Starr (Hannah Beach) (Fitch), 67, *248*, *250*

Mrs. Guy Richards (Elizabeth Harris), 85, 98n143

Mrs. Henry Daggett (Elizabeth Prescott), 11, 106, *107*, 108

Mrs. Humphrey Devereaux (Copley), 188

Mrs. James Duane, 37, *38*

Mrs. James Eldredge (Lucy Gallup) (Brewster), 242, *243*

Mrs. Jared Lane (Apphia Ruggles), 59, 88, 202–3, *205*, 206

Mrs. Jeremiah Lee (Copley), 154

Mrs. John Hyndman, 25–26, *26*

Mrs. John Johnston (Martha Spear), 11, 32, 135, *136*

Mrs. John Murray (Lucretia Chandler) (Copley), 103

Mrs. John Nichols (Mary Hill), 251

Mrs. John Watson, 49, 50, 51, 97n135

Mrs. Joseph Wright, 53, 188–89, *191*

Mrs. Judson Canfield (Mabel Ruggles), 203, 209

Mrs. Lazarus Ruggles (Hannah Bostwick) (Richard and William Jennys), 59, *59*

Mrs. Nathaniel Shaw (Temperance Harris), 98n143

Mrs. Nathaniel Taylor (Tamar Boardman), 47, 74, 161, *162*, 216

Mrs. Nicholas (Tamar Taylor) Masters, 161

Mrs. Noah Smith and Her Children, 61, 219–20, *221*

Mrs. Oliver Wolcott (Laura Collins), 45, *148*, *149*

Mrs. Reuben Humphreys (Brunton), 247

Mrs. Richard Alsop, 53, 188–89, *190*

Mrs. Samuel Bradley (Sarah Wakeman), 85, *199*

Mrs. Sherman Boardman (Sarah Bostwick), 60, *214*, 216

Mrs. Thomas Gage (Margaret Kemble) (Copley), 106

Mrs. Timothy (Mary Woolsey) Dwight, 13

Mrs. William Moseley and Her Son Charles, 53, 54, 150

Mrs. William Taylor and Son Daniel, 47, 48, 161, 163, *165*, 219

Money, John, 15, 16, *18*, 19, 26, 30, 40, 93n48, 94n49, 94n57, 115, 134, 229

Moseley, Charles, 53, *54*

Moseley, Laura Wolcott, 53, 54, 150

Moulthrop, Reuben (1763–1814), 106

Mumford, Henry, 18–19

Mygatt, Comfort Starr, 66, 86, 242–43, *245*

Mygatt, Lucy Knapp, 66, 86, 242–43, *244*

New Haven, Conn., 8, 10–15, 64, 69, 70, 71, 73, 76, 99n17

New London, Conn., 53, 55, 69, 70, 71, 99n17

New Milford, Conn., 43, 45, 47–48, 58–61, 70, 71, 73–76, 78, 152, *153*, 157, *158*, 206, 207, 217, *217*

New York, 30–39, *31*, *33*, 51, 55–57, 60, 62, 69, 86–88, 90

Niagara Falls, 14, 57, 62–65, 99nn172–79

Nicholas Shelton Masters, 161

Nickelson, Angus, 48, 75, *166–67*, 168–69

Noah Smith, 61, *219*

Norwich, England, 16, 18–19, 94nn52–54, 94nn59–60, 115, 134, 168, 229

Oliver Ellsworth and Abigail Wolcott Ellsworth, *4* (detail), 28, 52, 58, 66, 86, 88, 149, 180–81, *182–83*, 237

Oliver Wolcott, 45, 76, 146, *147*, 181

Onslow, George (1731–92), 26, 27, 28

Partridge, Robert, 19, *20*

Patrick Tracy (Trumbull), 118

Peale, Charles Willson (1741–1827), 16, 40, 47, 95n93, 138, 154, 229, 241; painting by, *83*

Pelham, Henry (1749–1806), 8, 10–11, 14, 16, 18, 69, 93n35, 104, 106, 111; painting by, *11*

Perilous Situation of Major Money and His Balloon at Sea, The (Murphy), 16, *18*, 19

Polly Wyllys Pomeroy (detail), 53, 55, 98n141

Pomeroy, Polly Wyllys, 53, 55, 98n141

Porter, Ebenezer, 62, 229, *230*

Porter, Lucy Pierce Merwin, 62, 229, *231*

Portrait of a Gentleman (Derby), 177

Portrait of Abraham Davenport, 43, *44*

Portrait of Ashahel Pomeroy, 88

Portrait of Edward Gere (Ralph E. W. Earl), 62, *63*, 229

Portrait of George Eliot and Family (Budington), 251, *252*

Portrait of Jeremiah Wadsworth and Son, Daniel Wadsworth (Trumbull), 52, *52*

Portrait of Silas Talbot, 32, *32*

Portrait of Thomas Barrow, 34, *35*

Portrait of Two Sisters, 22, *22*

Pratt, John, 41, *186*, 187

Pratt, Matthew (1734–1805), 16

Reclining Hunter, *ii–iii* (detail), 28, 124, *125*

Reinagle, Philip (1749–1833), 16, 19, 168; painting by, *18*

Reverend Abraham Jarvis (Durand), 8

Reverend Ebenezer Devotion (Chandler), 9, 69

Reverend Ebenezer Porter (Ralph E. W. Earl), 62, *229*, 230

Reverend Eleazar Wheelock (Steward), 66, 237, *238*, 239, 242

Reverend James Cogswell, The (Steward), 52

Reverend Judah Champion, The, 45, *46*, 160

Reverend Nathaniel Taylor, 47, 74, *159*, 160, 216

Reverend Nehemiah Strong, 13–14, 48, 88, 169, *170*, 171

Reverend Samuel Moseley (Steward), 160

Reverend Timothy Dwight, 13

Reynolds, Sir Joshua (1723–92), 25, 30, 34, 65, 88, 89, 90

Richmond, Deborah, 66–67, 246, *247*

Robert Boyd, 96n115

Robert Partridge, Mayor of Norwich (Beechey), *20*

Roger Sherman, *xiv* (detail), 11–12, 43, 74, 106, 109, *110*, 115

Rogers, David, 43, 142, *145*

Rogers, Martha Tennent, 43, 142–43, *144*

Romney, George (1734–1802), 25, 32

Royal Academy, London, 19, 21–22, 25, 30, 94n71, 94n73, 121

Ruggles, Hannah Bostwick, 59, *59*, 202, 208

Ruggles, Lazarus, 59, *59*, 202, 206, 208

Sally Buell, 61

Samuel Adams (Copley), 11, *12*

Samuel Huntington (Peale), 83

Sawitzky, William, 2, 111, 192

Sharon, Conn., 59, 60, 70, 208, 210–*11*

Shaw, Thomas, 53, 55, *55*, 206
Sherman, Roger, *xiv*, 11–12, 43, 74,
    75, 109, *110*, 115, 146
Sherman Boardman, 60, 73, 106, *215*
Sir Benjamin Truman (Gainsborough),
    23, *23*
Smith, Chloe, 61, 219–20, *221*
Smith, Elizabeth, 55, 194, *195*
Smith, Noah, 61, 219, *219*
Smith Booth, 85
Society for the Relief of Distressed
    Debtors, 35–36, 37, 39, 138, 177,
    178
Society of the Cincinnati, 37–38, 41,
    49, 78, 80, 135, 138, 177, 187
Sophia Drake, 29–30, *129*, 130
Sophia Isham, 28–29, *29*, 150
Southgate, William, 62
Sprats, William (1747–1810), 58, 60,
    208, 217
Squire Samuel Bradley, 85, *199*
Staircase Group (Peale), 47, 154
Starr, Ephraim, 67, *249*, 250
Starr, Hannah Beach, 67, *248*, 250
Steuben, Baron Friedrich Wilhelm von
    (1730–94), 37, 86, 90, *137*, *138*,
    138–39
Steward, Joseph (1753–1822), 52, 66,
    98n141, 160, 178, 237, 239, 241,
    242; paintings by, *52*, *238*, *240*
Stiles, Ezra, 48, 169, 171, 194

Strong, Nehemiah, 13–14, 48, 88, 169,
    170, 171
Stuart, Gilbert (1755–1828), 16, 22,
    40, 56, 88, 135; paintings by, *56*

Talbot, Silas, 32, *32*
Talcott, Samuel, 51–52, 85, 86, 87,
    88, 89, 184, *185*
Tallmadge, Benjamin, 49, 58, 160,
    172–73, *175*, 192, 202
Tallmadge, Mary Floyd, 49, 58, 172–
    73, *174*, 192
Taylor, Abigail Starr, 47, 48, 163,
    165
Taylor, Nathaniel, 45, 47, 74, 76,
    154, *159*, 160, 161, 163, 216
Taylor, Tamar Boardman, 47, 74, 160,
    161, *162*, 163, 216
Taylor, William (1764–1841), 47–48,
    74, 163, *164*
Taylor Children, The, 161
Thomas Earle, 65, *232*, *233*
Thomas Shaw, 55, *55*, 98n143, 206
*Three Youngest Daughters of King
    George III, The* (Copley), 22, *22*
Timothy Dwight (Trumbull), *81*
Trumbull, John (1756–1843), 6, 8, 10,
    22, 40, 51, 52, 57, 64, 65, 83, 118,
    178, 229, 250; paintings by, *51*, *81*
Trumbull, Joseph, 1, 21–22, 28, 30,
    32, 95n85, 131, *132*, 146

Vanderlyn, John, 64, 65, 99n172
View of the South Part of Lexington, A
    (Doolittle), 14, 111, *113*
View of the Town of Concord, A
    (Doolittle), 14, 111, *112*
*View on the West Mountain near
    Hartford* (Trumbull), 57

Wadsworth, Jeremiah, 51, 52, *52*
Waldo, Samuel (1783–1861), 192
Washington, George, 15, 35, 37, 40,
    51, 57, 79, 177, 187, 232
Watson, Bethia Tyler, 49, *50*, 51
West, Benjamin (1738–1820), 16, 21,
    22, 25, 26, 30, 34, 40, 48, 90, 131,
    135, 229
Wheelock, Eleazar, 66, 237, *238*, 239
Wicker, Jacob, 63, 64, 99n169
Willett, Marinus, 34, 51, 90, *176*, 177
William Carpenter, 19, 86, 90, 115,
    116, 118
Williard, Levi, 32, 34, 95–96nn97–98
Wolcott, Laura Collins, 45, 53, *148*,
    149, 150, 181
Wolcott, Mariann, 45, 150, *151*
Wolcott, Oliver, Sr., 44–45, 53, 76,
    146, *147*, 149, 150, 180, 181
Wright, Hannah Gilbert, 53, 188–89,
    191
Wright, Joseph (1756–93), 16, 36,
    96n107, 138–39, 177